The History of
Louisa Barnes Pratt

The Autobiography
of
A Mormon Missionary Widow and Pioneer

Volume 3
LIFE WRITINGS OF FRONTIER WOMEN

A Series Edited by
Maureen Ursenbach Beecher

Volume 1
Winter Quarters
The 1846–1848 Life Writings of
Mary Haskin Parker Richards
Edited by Maurine Carr Ward

Volume 2
Mormon Midwife
The 1846–1888 Diaries of
Patty Bartlett Sessions
Edited by Donna Toland Smart

The History of Louisa Barnes Pratt

Being the Autobiography
of
A Mormon Missionary Widow and Pioneer

*A New England Youth, At Nauvoo and Salt Lake City,
Mission to the Society Islands, Mormon Life in
California, Pioneering in Beaver, Utah*

Edited by

S. George Ellsworth

UTAH STATE UNIVERSITY PRESS
Logan, Utah
1998

Copyright © 1998 Utah State University Press
All rights reserved

Utah State University Press
Logan, Utah 84322-7800

Publication of this book was supported by a subvention from Richard Shipley

Typography by WolfPack
    Dust jacket design by Michelle Sellers

Library of Congress Cataloging-in-Publication Data

Pratt, Louisa Barnes, 1802–1880
    The history of Louisa Barnes Pratt: being the autobiography of a mormon missionary widow and pioneer / edited by S. George Ellsworth.
    p. cm. — (Life writings of frontier women; v. 3)
Includes bibliographical references and index.
ISBN 0-87421-252-9
    1. Pratt, Louisa Barnes, 1802–1880. 2. Mormons—United States—Biography. 3. Frontier and pioneer life. I. Ellsworth, S. George (Samuel George), 1916- II. Title. III. Series.
BX8695.p68 A3 1998
289.3'092—ddc21   98-25346
[B]   CIP

CONTENTS

ILLUSTRATIONS

FOREWORD

Maureen Ursenbach Beecher

By the most open definition, whatever a woman writes in the course of her life might be considered a life writing: a note, a letter, a recipe book, her personal phone directory, a diary or journal, her laundry list, a personal essay, an autobiography, memoir, or reminiscence. Each has its own way of reflecting her life experience, revealing her character to whoever might read the document thus created. And the overlap of one into the other increases the value of each as complement to the whole.

For the purposes of this present series, Life Writings of Frontier Women, three main categories are of concern: letters; diaries or journals; and autobiographies, or reminiscences, or memoirs. They bear distinctions of source and interpretation which must be understood if the text is to be accessed appropriately. Each form is true, in its own way, but contradictions and prevarications might well cast doubt on the writer's veracity unless the circumstances of its creation and reception be considered. Memory, immediacy, audience, intent, and the writer's sense of herself and her contemporaries all introduce some sort of distortion.

Letters have in the foreground the image of the recipient for whom they are created. The same event a woman would describe to any two separate readers would appear different in each case, not that both would not be factual, but that each recipient would be, in the writer's mind, aware of, interested in, and biased toward or against particulars of the event.

How a letter writer might describe the event to another person and how it might appear in her own diary entry would also vary. Diary entries are generally terse reminders to the reader of the larger picture—hints, suggestions, images written to remind the writer of what happened and how she regarded it. In her mind as she writes may well be other purposes for the exercise: to leave a record of her days for her posterity; to create a work of literary art; to justify her actions to an unknown reader; to purge herself of confused or emotionally laden feelings. Day by day, entry by entry, these and other agendas influence what the diarist writes, and how. Even so, the immediacy of the description enhances the event and draws the reader into the moment.

When at some given point in her life a woman decides to compile an autobiography, or memoir, or reminiscence—the boundaries of these genres are so fuzzy that there is little merit in trying to delineate differences—she takes on a new persona. She becomes the creator, in a sense, of her life. How she sees any given moment of the past is now determined not so much by what happened then as how she perceives in the distant view. What went before and what has intervened sets the event into a context which often alters its significance and the significance of its various aspects, so much as to make the later account seem at variance with the original. The longer view has, then, the advantage of scope and sequence, of distance and increased objectivity. The author-as-subject is also the author-as-object. The focus shifts with the point of view.

Only in the identification of the circumstances of the creation of the text can its meaning by captured. And even then there will be undercurrents and overtones to reach for, to ponder and guess at. Women's life writings become in the hands of distant readers as fascinating as the most carefully crafted mystery, with the added charm that the scenario is real life and the characters real people.

In the case of the memoir and diaries of Louisa Barnes Pratt, we have an overlap of genres which creates a richness in what might seem a straightforward text. Some of the remembered events in the memoir were composed fresh as their author sat in her cottage in Tahiti; some were recreated from diary accounts consulted as the diarist-turned-autobiographer reviewed them in her Beaver, Utah, home many years after the fact. The author-as-editor seems always to be looking over the shoulder of the writer, casting the events into the longer view, setting them in the context of the whole life so far. The complexity of the text is part of its fascination. The seasons of Louisa Pratt's life, her maturing womanhood, her circumstances, and their effect on her image of herself all affect her self description. For the historian combing the document for documentary evidence the complexity of the text makes more difficult the search; for the reader of a woman's text as a work of literary depth and insight, the same complexity is a mitzvah, a bonus. It becomes an integral part of the interplay of the writer's life-as-lived and her life-as-written.

The reader of this and the other texts in this series is invited to sit back, relax, and let the words flow. Consider the reading a conversation with a neighbor, an introduction to a new friend. Let her tell her life as she experienced it long ago and perceived it later. Go with her through the vagaries of her life, sympathetic to its foibles and idiosyncrasies. Walk the road together for a while and delight in your shared humanity.

ACKNOWLEDGMENTS

It was one thing for Louisa Barnes Pratt to produce her journals. It was another remarkable happening to have them preserved and made available. After Louisa, great credit goes to those who protected and preserved her journals, letters, poems, and essays. They were Ellen S. Pratt McGary, Ida Mae Wrathall, Ida Hunt Udall, Nettie Hunt Rencher, Lois Hunt West, and Pauline Udall Smith. Each of these drew from their treasured inheritances to contribute in making their family archives a living institution. The Addison Pratt Family Papers at the Merrill Library, Utah State University, are the repository of all source materials (besides the journals) relating to the family of Addison and Louisa Pratt.

Many secretaries watched as "Louisa" was worked on. Cindy Durtschi produced a fine typed copy of the entire collection, including the journals, and knew Louisa best and appreciated her. Professor Norman Jones and Carolyn Doyle and associates on the staff of the history department at Utah State University transferred the work to electronic files. I thank all who got into the act.

Yves R. Perrin of Papeete, Tahiti, and Salt Lake City helped the editor decide what to do with Louisa's writing of her understanding of Tahitian words and names. We decided to let them stand as she wrote them.

Maureen Ursenbach Beecher gave the editor the final necessary prod to give up the work to the publisher. F. Ross Peterson did a final edit of the manuscript before it was turned over.

Richard Shipley provided generous financial support to the publication of this book.

To Maria, of course, goes great credit for mastering family relations and related events, helping me much, and saving me from errors.

My debt to others is great, but faults in the work are exclusively mine.

Louisa Barnes Pratt in old age

INTRODUCTION

Of Mormon pioneer women known to me, there is not another that had quite the variety of experiences that Louisa Barnes Pratt had. A typical Mormon at first, she headed for Missouri after her conversion; built a cottage in Nauvoo after sending her husband on a mission to the other side of the earth, which left her without support and to rear four daughters; rode horseback across Iowa; lived in a cave at Winter Quarters, Nebraska, where she developed scurvy and lost her front teeth; and got her family to Utah in the 1848 Brigham Young Company. In this she is quite standard, except she did it all alone, without husband. Thereafter her experiences were unique. She answered a missionary call to join her husband in the Society Islands, hauled her wagon west from Salt Lake across the desert and the Sierra Nevada to San Francisco, and spent nineteen months on the small island of Tubuai teaching native women and children. Back in Gold Rush California, the family, penniless from years of mission service, recouped some losses by mining the miners. She lived through the experience of the Mormon colony at San Bernardino and the Mormon church's Big Move, under the threat of approaching federal troops, to the central valleys of Utah, and she spent the last twenty-two years of her life, without husband, in effect if not actually a widow, as a leader among the women of Beaver, Utah. She did it all without the help of any man: reared four daughters, provided for her family, and constantly demonstrated her faith and devotion, having built and left, at last, seven homes for the sake of the Latter-day Saints gospel. All this, and more, she narrates in her journal-memoir published here.

Creating the Text

In July 1850, as Louisa Barnes Pratt was leaving California to meet her husband on Tubuai, Society Islands, she commenced a diary, not her first such record, of her mission adventures. And no wonder, for her adventures, then and previously, were even more unusual for her time than they would be now. She would later revise her personal record as a memoir, drawing from memory to supplement and fill out the daily entries. In doing so, she recounted her life not only for her descendants but also in the hope of publication. A century later, that hope is here realized.

In keeping a diary of her mission and beginning when she took ship, she was imitating her husband, Addison Pratt, for he began his mission diary when, on 10 September 1843, he took ship from New Bedford.[1] When Louisa reached her husband on Tubuai, she learned that while he had recently been under house arrest, he had been writing a memoir of his early life. Similarly situated, Louisa again followed his example, and started work on her autobiography.

> Being now in my fiftieth year [she began] and having passed a life of deep experience in the changes and fortunes to which life's nature is always liable; and being in circumstances that afford me much leisure, I have resolved to make a record of the leading incidents of a career in a world where good and ill have been always contained.[2]

Reading over the "old letters which my mother and sisters sent me many years ago," and consulting her diary and journal, Louisa prodded her memory to create a comprehensive life story. Soon she would write, "I spent the entire day in Prayer House teaching the children and writing in my history." The exercise obviously pleased her: "I am surprised at the accuracy with which I call to mind the scenes in my early life. Almost every circumstance seems as vivid as the day it transpired."[3]

Over the next twenty years, Louisa completed the memoir of her youth and continued adding to and preserving her "notes, diary, and journal." In 1874 (she was seventy-two), she decided to compile these materials into one unified history of her life with the intent to publish it and the hope it would be widely read. She had tasted the pleasure of reading her words in print: extracts of her life on Tubuai and the Pratts' missionary labors there had appeared in the *Woman's Exponent*, a bimonthly tabloid newspaper edited in Salt Lake City by and for LDS women. She described her process of revision, undertaken during the winter of 1874–75:

> I commenced revising my lengthy journal of fifty years standing. [Since] there were abridgements and alterations to be made . . . the task must devolve wholly [*sic*] upon myself. Since then I have continued to write at intervals; having 9 quires of paper written fine on both sides to review, besides manuscripts of considerable amount.[4]

Ultimately Louisa produced a manuscript of eleven quires (signatures) of paper. She used the same stock of paper throughout, two kinds of ink, and wrote in her usually fine penmanship. Like many of her contemporaries who followed the same process, using their diaries as source for an autobiography, she abridged and altered the *Urtext* to create the unified flow of the memoir. It is an artful union of memoir and journal. Comparison of her two surviving journals ("A" and "B") and this later "history" verify that there were "abridgments and alterations," although the changes constituted more of a revised draft than a wholly new work.

The Story Told

Despite a very ordinary beginning, Louisa Barnes (pronounced Low-eye-za) led an extraordinary life. Born 10 November 1802 in Warwick County, Massachusetts, the fifth of ten children, Louisa lived with her extended family there and in Canada. On 3 April 1831 she married seaman Addison Pratt and set up farming on the shore of Lake Erie at Ripley, New York. Here in 1838 the Pratts were visited by Louisa's sister Caroline and her husband Jonathan Crosby, who introduced them to the new Church of Jesus Christ of Latter-day Saints, founded eight years earlier by Joseph Smith, the Mormon prophet. Their conversion was immediate, and their commitment lasting.

The two families followed their co-religionists, driven from Missouri where they had hoped to settle, to newly founded Nauvoo on the Illinois banks of the Mississippi River. From that place Addison was called on a proselyting mission to the Society Islands—Tahiti. Leaving Louisa and their four daughters to fend for themselves, he sailed halfway around the world, not to meet his family again for five years and four months, half a continent away. How Louisa and the children managed not only to support themselves but to move their household from Nauvoo to the Mormon refuge of Winter Quarters on the Missouri and then to settle in the valley of the Great Salt Lake is recounted in the following pages.

When the family reunited in Salt Lake City in 1848, Addison was given but a brief respite before he was called once again to take up his mission in Tahiti. This time Louisa followed, bringing their girls and her sister and brother-in-law Caroline and Jonathan Crosby and their son. Louisa's journal and memoir detail her teaching among the Tahitians: women and children, language and numbers, health and sanitation, cleanliness and handcrafts, ethics and morality, music and religion.

The life story of Louisa Barnes Pratt partakes of the spirit of nineteenth century America. Unusual as they were among easterners for their Mormon conversion, and for their travels to the South Pacific, the Pratts were part of the great westering movement of the century. Halfway across the continent when Addison left on his first mission, Louisa and her girls finished the trek alone, a venture not unique to pioneers. In the Old Fort in Salt Lake City, they set up housekeeping, continuing Louisa's teaching and the girls' schooling before following Addison to the Society Islands. The mission there was cut short because the French Protectorate government no longer permitted foreign missionaries to live and labor among the Tahitians.

The families reached San Francisco penniless and without tools or appropriate clothing but capitalized on the Gold Rush demand for labor. They settled in the newly established Mormon colony of San Bernardino, in southern California. The girls were now grown to maturity, the three oldest married.

Between husband and wife, however, tensions mounted as they took up the life of a Mormon family in a settled community. Addison, accustomed to preside in church matters, was largely ignored by already existing authorities in San Bernardino. He found time to hunt and fish, usually at the neglect of household matters. Noted Louisa: "O how have I involved myself, by taking upon me the support of my family and my husband [who] by being separated from us for seven years in fourteen has nearly lost all the ability he once had." Louisa could not relinquish leadership; Addison could not assume it. Two more times, in 1854 and 1856, he was called to return to the islands, but failed again to win out over French religious policy.

Meanwhile United States military threats against the Mormons in their headquarters city caused Brigham Young to call home the settlers remote from Utah. The San Bernardino Saints were to sell out and return. Or not. There was some freedom, it was said, to go or to stay. Debate followed. Addison and Louisa argued. To remain would be a sign of being "weak in the faith," or worse. Entrenched in her established pattern of obedience to ecclesiastical authority, Louisa would go at all costs. Addison equivocated. He had many reasons against residing in Utah. Disputes resurrected past disagreements and precipitated their separation. Addison stayed with daughter Frances and her husband Jones Dyer in California, and Louisa, accompanied by her daughters Ellen and husband William McGary, Lois and husband John Hunt, and Ann Louise and the adopted island boy Ephraim, returned to Utah.

The separation was not intended to be permanent, but the result was conclusive. Louisa, Ann Louise, and Ephraim settled in Beaver, in the center of the territory. Ellen and William lived sometimes nearby, sometimes in Ogden, north of Salt Lake City. Lois and John later returned to San Bernardino, stayed for five years, returned to Beaver, then went on to settle the town of Joseph, not far away, in southern Sevier County. They moved next to New Mexico, then settled finally in the Mormon outpost of

Snowflake, Arizona. Considering that her husband, a freighter, was gone for long periods, Frances pressured her father to stay with her in California. With her he lived, and there he died on 14 October 1872.

The most persistent question in the Addison Pratt family over the years has been the cause and occasion of their separation. In her life writings Louisa skims the surface of the problems, and little documentation on the matter is extant.

From all that does bear on the question, however, it is clear that the separation was rooted deep in their early life together; it brewed throughout the marriage. In the stress of the move occasioned by the Utah War in 1857–58 the final rift occurred.

The Pratt family was headquartered then in San Bernardino, where Addison felt unneeded and insignificant. His long periods of absence from home provoked talk both there and in Salt Lake City, where friends wondered why he eventually lived with Frances in San Francisco rather than with Louisa in San Bernardino. At the time of his going on his fourth mission, rumor had it that "Mr. Pratt did not intend returning to that country, that his intention was to spend his days on the islands." As Louisa bid him goodbye she confided to her diary "not knowing when the 'father' would return, or whether he would come at all."[5] He did return on 1 April 1857, just as his daughter, Ellen answered the query of her dear friend Ellen Clawson in Salt Lake City. He remained in the Bay area long enough to pay off debt incurred in connection with his last mission, his daughter explained, and because he "has an aversion to a cold climate, now he is getting in years, and has spent all his means for so many years, he dreads the thought of making another beginning in such a hard place."

Ellen then outlined the more probable causes of discord:

> [M]other has never seemed to feel at home since she left the Valley, and she thinks she shall never be satisfied till she gets back. She tries every way to encourage father about going there. Says she will uphold him to the last in any move he may see fit to make; but thinks he cannot go; he loves the Sea air, and wants to live where he can feel it; it makes him look so vigorous and youthful; he is scarcely like the same man. Mother has better courage to live in a hard place. She has had a deeper experience, and does not dread hardness so much. [H]er five years widowhood taught her great lessons of economy; and she has great zeal for this cause.[6]

Family tradition accepted the "geographic" explanation for the separation of the couple, as Louisa undoubtedly intended in her histories. Addison was expected, but "the time is not yet." Certainly there was reason for both father and Frances to remain in the pleasant coastal climate.

The lingering suspicion, disavowed by descendants, that he had become disaffected from the Latter-day Saints, seems more consistent with evidence now available. His and Louisa's relations to the church were nearly opposite: He spent but two years at church headquarters; she spent all *but* two years in a Mormon community. He was always away, she was always home. She had gone through the martyrdom and the expulsion from Nauvoo, sludging across Iowa, surviving Winter Quarters, and crossing the plains. All this had schooled her for the hard life of self-discipline, self-reliance, and obedience to counsel and for the support that came from being with the mass of gathered Saints. He, on the contrary, was far from that support. His work was not without discomfort, but through his various missions he became accustomed to leadership and to keeping his own counsel. He lived more by reason than by faith; she more by faith than by reason. Obedience to the dictates of faith came easily to her; to him independence of thought and action seemed more appropriate guides.

There were years of happy marriage, as happy as marriages need to be, but from the beginning their relations were strained. Each had been self-supporting, and habituated to certain patterns of life. From courtship days there persisted her intent to subdue him and bring him to her desires. She would effect "the destiny" conveyed in the dream she had after first meeting Addison: there came before her a "great wild fowl" which she enticed to come near her that she might "tame him." But when he settled on her lap and she attempted to smooth his feathers, he bit her, whereupon she "beat him with great severity until he appeared tame and perfectly harmless."[7]

The happiest and most prosperous years for the Pratts were spent at Ripley, New York, before they joined the Mormons; for two decades thereafter they were uprooted most of the time, enduring long periods of separation. Addison spent half his life in the church on mission; Louisa spent his absences feeding, clothing, and nurturing their four daughters, and crossing the continent with them. She was a single parent: provider, manager, father, and mother. Through a life closer to widowhood than to wifehood, she was teacher, comforter, doctor, and nurse to her own and to others. Louisa supported herself enough not to need Addison even when he was home. And when he was home, he was of little help. He failed to pick up the reins of leadership or assume the roles of provider, father, and husband, and she failed to relinquish them to him.

For his part, Addison bore his own burdens away from the family. At the outset of his mission he was instructed by Brigham to go and stay until he was released or replaced. He went, but there came no release, nor replacement, not even any correspondence, for three years. On 5 March 1846 he rejoiced: "This is the first letter from the Twelve [the Mormon Church Authorities]. I have received 2 previous letters from my wife, and these 3 are all the letters we have received from American in these 3 long years' absence from my family."[8] In Salt Lake City he reported his mission and obtained a company of replacements, but otherwise he received neither recognition nor calling. In San Bernardino, following his second mission, he had friends among the authorities, but also heard from dissenters criticism of the conduct of church business.[9] He was offended by the Saints' failure to observe the Word of Wisdom, the LDS Church health code which he had strictly enforced in the islands. And he objected to church courts which tried people on political issues, and "could not sanction for a moment anything like a rebellion against a 'republican government.'"

These differences, however, were minor compared with the turmoil induced in all Mormondom by the announcement of the practice of plural marriage. Prior to the public announcement in August 1852, secrecy and denial precluded discussion of the subject, but with the announcement church members had to take a position. On that subject Addison and Louisa differed emphatically. Louisa wrote, "Differences of opinion sometimes rose between us in regard to certain principles which had been revealed in his absence."[10] She would follow church leaders. Addison, denying the doctrine, refused to countenance the practice. He held firm to the teachings he had promoted in the islands which made chastity prerequisite to membership in the church. Family tradition has it that Louisa threatened Addison that if he did not comply, she would have herself sealed to the prophet Joseph Smith or Hyrum Smith. He didn't, and she did. Louisa had had years to acquire the attitude of compliance, gleaned mainly from her association with the plural wives of church leaders.

During the San Bernardino years frustrations and disappointments multiplied for Louisa. "Of domestic sorrows I forbear to mention. I carry them in my bosom, and bear my injuries in silence." Addison arrived in San Bernardino from his fourth mission on 1 April 1857, "looking very pale and fleshy, said he weighed 200 lbs.," recorded Louisa's sister Caroline. A week later the Pratts entertained the McIntyre family, together with Jonathan Crosby and Caroline. During the evening Dr. McIntyre took Jonathan outside privately and "informed Jonathan that he had been conversing with Brother Pratt" and found "to his great astonishment that he was not a true believer in the principles of our religion. That he actually denied the faith in some important points and spoke lightly of others. Said he was greatly disappointed in him . . . as he had been expecting to receive strength and encouragement from him, as he has been a traveling elder just returned from a mission. He did not wish to cultivate the society of such persons."[11]

Louisa's concerns mounted; she shared her concerns with Caroline, who wrote, on 13 September: "Sister [Louisa] and I took a walk around the lots. She told me some of her trials, with her husband, his hard speeches, and the disunion that existed between them. I felt sorry, to know their great unhappiness."[12]

The call to sell out their San Bernardino property and return to Utah as quickly and quietly as possible came to Jonathan on Monday, 2 November 1857. He was "to warn the brethren in his ward, that they might have timely notice." Louisa and Addison hedged and argued. They debated doctrine, the importance of following counsel, obedience to leaders, the Big Move, armed resistance to federal troops, and polygamy. Reconciliation seemed out of the question, but resolution was approaching the last week of December, when Pratt took his wagon to the shop to fix for the journey. "Said he was preparing it for his wife Louisa, but thought he should go another way."[13]

Addison and Louisa procrastinated while their children made ready and left. Caroline saw them off: Ellen and her husband William "both seemed very sad, could hardly smile," she wrote. "I tried to cheer them, but it seemed in vain. John and Lois set off first, and seemed in better spirits." Three days later she and Jonathan finished loading their wagon and set off. Louisa and others saw them off. Louisa "felt bad to see us come away and leave her," Caroline wrote.[14]

During November and December San Bernardino was emptied of Latter-day Saints. Lopsided trades had been made at great losses. Families retained only what wagons could hold. All the while Louisa and Addison debated and delayed the final decision. Louisa employed "entreaties" and "persuasions" in vain. Addison considered that he "made every humiliating and condescending proposition," that the case demanded. But "she only disdained" him and treated him with contempt." He made preparations to go to Utah but would not go without a reconciliation first. When he thought that impossible, they parted on the Mojave Desert. Addison looked after her and thought they had parted forever.[15]

In her memoirs Louisa presents the view that Addison was to stay, then go to San Francisco, get daughter Frances and her husband Jones and bring them to Utah the following year. In fact the separation was complete: Louisa returned to Utah and remained among the Mormons, while Addison remained in California with his daughter Frances.

It is understandable that Addison Pratt could feel angry with the church for breaking up the community and leading his wife and daughters away. He was bitter and hate-filled. He admitted saying things he ought not have, but he could have said more. Some Saints remained in San Bernardino or chose to move elsewhere, but the spirit of the times led to referring to any of those who remained as "apostate." Even though his only articulated objection to Mormon doctrine was over polygamy, Addison Pratt's name was included among those who stayed. Final judgment lies in other hands than ours.

But the story is not ended. Between the break-up in 1858 and Addison's death in 1872, family relations continued. The reader is encouraged to carefully examine the following developments in the pages of the journal-memoir.

Correspondence between Louisa, Frances, and Ellen in particular continued throughout Addison's life. Lois Pratt Hunt, another daughter, returned to California with her husband, John, and contacts developed, especially from July 1862 until the spring of 1863, when Louisa went to California on a visit to Lois and family. When she returned to Utah, Louisa managed to bring Addison back to Beaver with her. While in Utah, Addison Pratt visited friends and relatives, and left his mission diary in the LDS Church Historian's Office. He then returned to the family in Beaver and lived for over a year. A cold early winter set in in November 1864, and Frances's husband, Jones Dyer, came through Beaver enroute to California and induced Addison to accompany him. For the remainder of his life, Louisa and Addison corresponded. On his deathbed, Addison dictated a letter to "My dear Family." The letter is printed in *Journals of Addison Pratt*, 521–23, and when Addison died, Louisa wrote an "Obituary of a Mormon Elder" and got it published in the *Phrenological Journal* in March 1873. All of this indicates a continual family commitment which is both admirable and historically confusing. However, for most of the last fifteen years of Addison Pratt's life, he did not live with Louisa.

With the separation, Louisa, often a "missionary widow," was again without a husband. Still married, there was no man in her life, so she was again widowed "or worse." From 1858 to her death in 1880 she lived on in Beaver. She had a small house, large enough to entertain a few guests or to permit her to take a few pupils for classwork. Next door were the Crosbys, Caroline and Jonathan, and their son Alma. Between them, one imagines, were the necessary cow, sheep, pig, and chickens, a garden, and probably fruit trees. Like many another woman alone, Louisa could still barter, make and repair clothing, and sell books and subscriptions. In her own words:

More than half the years of my married life I have stood alone. Created the means to sustain myself and children: and although I had kind friends around me I had no one immediately interested to supply my daily wants. My cares often weighed heavily upon me, yet for the most part I have been cheerful.[16]

Her enforced self-sufficiency developed in Louisa a woman's rights philosophy: "I am not amenable to man neither will I suffer man to judge me," she wrote. She had succeeded without the aid of a man; she concluded that women have natural rights that should be recognized.

A woman for all the seasons of her varied life, Louisa possessed qualities of character appropriate to the roles she played. In youth she had developed a sense of independence, financial and other; she learned resourcefulness, self-reliance, and personal initiative. She had trained as a seamstress and became a school teacher. Her chosen path was hard; it is not surprising that the sorrow and depression she felt lie as an unintentional undercurrent through her life writings. "My domestic sorrows I forbear to mention," she wrote. "I carry them in my own bosom, and bear my injuries in silence."[17]

In Louisa's memoir and diaries is to be discovered a multi-layered narrative. She wrote herself as she perceived herself and as she intended to be perceived. She told the truth, as much of it as she could bear to reveal. It remains for the reader to mine Louisa's words for the unwritten, the implied, the unacknowledged realities of her life. For here was a woman of depth and feeling, of faith and obedience, of courage and persistence. There is much to be learned from her story.

Editorial Procedures

The complete extant diaries and memoirs of Louisa Barnes Pratt are here published for the first time. The handwritten text has been rendered according to rigid documentary editing standards, so the printed form may be trusted by readers and scholars alike as an accurate transmission of the originals.

The manuscript consists of eleven signatures, written on both sides of each page, the pages numbered from 1 to 550. The same stock is used throughout, each signature measuring 19.5 cm. by 31.7 cm. The front page of each signature shows signs of wear. The ink in the first part of the manuscript is light purple, and that in the latter part black. At the outset Louisa divided her memoir into short chapters, heading each with a Roman numeral, but she discontinued that practice after chapter 13.

The aim of the editor has been to reproduce Louisa Barnes Pratt's words in type exactly as she wrote them by hand. Word order, syntax, grammar, spelling, punctuation, and capitalization have been scrupulously retained. Even so, some editorial liberties seemed appropriate to the translation from text to printed page. Often the writing flows from page to page without consideration of paragraph form. The first line on each page is indented, often without consideration to thought or topic. Accordingly the editor has often divided the text into logical paragraphs and subdivided chapters into smaller sections according to the author's thought.

Punctuation marks are irregular in the original text. Though Pratt generally avoided using commas, apostrophes, and periods, a comma often appears between subject and predicate. She overused colons and semi-colons, occasionally stringing sentences together with semi-colons. These marks have been retained. Cross-outs have been retained throughout, but superscriptions have been brought to the line in the printed form. Any repeated word has been silently eliminated. A word or phrase inadvertently omitted is added in roman type and enclosed in brackets. Editorial explanations are likewise enclosed within brackets, but in italics. Louisa abhors dates and the use of personal names. Occasionally these have been supplied. Generally her spelling is correct—be it remembered she was a school teacher—but any misspellings have been retained. Capitalization, however, has proven difficult to render with certainty— Pratt's upper and lower case a, o, c, s, u, n, m, e, u, and r are very similar. Context has provided clues, and the editor has chosen accordingly. In every case where her preference might prove indicative of some idiocyncrasy of Louisa's personality, or of her circumstances—entries sometimes lose or gain a day when she is at sea—the error has been retained. Ellipses have been used to indicate missing words due to illegible, torn, or otherwise damaged portions of the manuscript.

Overall, the editorial policy has been guided by an attempt to present the author as she presented herself, with as much convenience as the printed page allows but as little interference as possible. That each reader might spend long sessions with the original notebooks might be preferable, but impractical. We trust this will prove a reliable and enjoyable second-best.

Abbreviations

The following abbreviations have been used throughout the work.

Names of persons:

AP	Addison Pratt
LBP	Louisa Barnes Pratt
EPMc	Ellen Pratt (Mrs. William) McGary
FPD	Frances Pratt (Mrs. Jones) Dyer
LPH	Lois Pratt (Mrs. John) Hunt
ALPW	Ann Louise Pratt (Mrs. Thomas) Willis
JC	Jonathan Crosby
CBC	Caroline Barnes (Mrs. Jonathan) Crosby
BFG	Benjamin F. Grouard
JSB	James S. Brown

Descriptive of manuscript materials:

A.	Autograph; in handwriting of author of piece.
Ms.	Manuscript.

S.   Signed with signature.
L. or Ltr. Letter.

Collected manuscripts:

APFP   Addison Pratt Family Papers, S. George Ellsworth
            Collection, Special Collections and Archives, Merrill
            Library, Utah State University, Logan, Utah.

Dramatis Personae

Louisa Barnes Pratt (whose autobiographical *History* is published here):
Born: 10 November 1802, Warwick, Franklin County, Massachusetts.
Married Addison Pratt, 3 April 1831.
Died: 8 September 1880, Beaver, Utah Territory.

Addison Pratt:
Born: 21 February 1802, Winchester, Cheshire County, New Hampshire.
Died: 14 October 1872, Anaheim, Orange County, California.

Their children:
Ellen:
Born: 6 February 1832, Ripley, New York.
Married (1) William H. McGary, 26/27 May 1856; separated May 1867.
    (2) John M. Coombs, 1 January 1873; divorced 26 June 1882.
    (3) William H. McGary, September 1882.
Died: 9 August 1895, Garden Grove, California.

Frances:
Born: 7 November 1834, Ripley, New York.
Married Jones Dyer, mid-November 1856.
Died: 25 November 1909, Anaheim, California.

Lois:
Born: 6 March 1837, Ripley, New York.
Married John Hunt, 4 July 1857, San Bernardino, California
Died: 9 March 1885, Snowflake, Arizona.

Louise (Ann Louise, often Ann Louisa, pronounced *Lu-eez*):
Born: 6 April 1840, Pleasant Garden, Indiana.
Married Thomas F. Willis, Beaver, Utah, June 1866.
Died: 1 April 1924?

Ephraim (adopted Polynesian boy):
Born: 20 September 1850, son of Benjamin F. Grouard and Nahina,
    Tubuai, French Polynesia.

Adopted by Louisa B. Pratt 8 March 1852. Left home, 1866.
As Frank Grouard: Indian captive, 1869–74; U.S. Army scout, 1874–91.
Died: 15 August 1905, St. Joseph, Missouri.

Caroline Barnes Crosby (Louisa's sister):
Born: 5 January 1807, Warwick, Massachusetts.
Married Jonathan Crosby, 25 October 1834.
Died: 16 February 1884, Beaver, Utah.

Jonathan Crosby (Caroline's husband):
Born: 20 July 1807, Wendell, Massachusetts.
Died: 12 June 1892, Beaver, Utah

Alma (Crosbys' son)
Born: 14 December 1836, Kirtland, Ohio.
Married: Mary Kelly, 21 May 1865.
Died: 14 November 1897, Beaver, Utah.

Author's Preface
Written at Tubuai, Society Islands, February 1852

My dear daughters,

Being now in my fiftieth year and having passed a life of deep experience in the changes and fortunes to which life's nature is always liable, and being in circumstances that afford me much leisure, I have resolved to make a record of the leading incidents of a career in a world where good and ill have been always contained. The reason which urges me most to this undertaking is I have been many years separated from my mother, whom I loved with a pure heartfelt devotion and her memory I this day revere no less than the spirit palpitating in my veins. Often when mourning that separation have I wished, O! how ardently, that she had bequeathed to me her own biography! With what enthusiasm should I, in my hours of solitude and sorrow, have poured over its pages, how eagerly drank in her sentiments which I ever considered faultless! I should have rejoiced and mourned with her alternately as she swam the stream of life smoothly, or buried beneath its stormy waves, she struggled for existance. All I have of her writings are a few letters addressed to me during an absence from home; these I esteem of great value.

And now, judging of the feelings of my daughters from my own for my parents, I am determined to leave for their satisfaction a portion of my history. I shall aim at nothing more than the simple relation of facts; and such circumstances as I have not the most vivid recollection of, I will not attempt to describe. I shall commence with my earliest remembrances, presuming that nothing that has ever befallen me, will be without interest to my children, and even their successors. And now my children, over whose welfare I have watched with the most sanguine hope, may you ever adhere to the principles of truth and love. Accept this as a tribute of my deep affection for you. Remember my weaknesses only to avoid them in yourselves, nor call that inperfection, which persons more wise than you may denominate wisdom. Treasure up in your hearts and practice in your lives the instructions I have given you. And be assured that not a sentence midst all my counsels has been uttered but with the purest desires for your happiness. Never talk of the faults of your parents, as it will serve to lesson the respect and reverence you should cherish for their admonitions. Cultivate your love and unvarying friendships for each other, and in a special manner for your own offspring, as also a spirit of tenderness and of patience. Avoid as much as possible all manifestation of irritable temper before the younger members of the household, as it will be a great disadvantage and increase your toil in the forming of their minds.

These remarks and sentiments may result in much good to you, when my tongue and pen are silent. Remember the unfavorable circumstances against which I labored in rearing you, and should your own be more propitious, be thankful and fail not to improve them. Remember the trust your mother reposed in her God. Be ye faithful in keeping His commandments; dominions, principalities, and powers, shall be thine! Farewell! and may you live to see much of the salvation of God, and the gathering of Israel, yea even the winding up scene: the coming of our Lord and Savior, and the redemption of Zion. These are the earnest desires of your ever faithful and affectionate mother—

Louisa B. Pratt

PART ONE

On Joining the Mormons

Youth to Arrival in Salt Lake Valley
September 1848

Addison Pratt

CHAPTER ONE

Youth

Memoirs, 1802 to September 1825

[Family]

I was born in the State of Mass. Franklin Co. town of Warwick. My parents, whose names [were] Willard and Dolly Barnes, were honest intelligent people. And though not from the wealthier ranks of society, they were in possession of a farm with many of the comforts and some of the luxuries of life. They were of honorable origin, my grandfather Barnes, whom I well remember, being distinguished for piety and wisdom. He was quite aged before the date of my recollections of him, and hard of hearing. Being asked whether he did not regret his deafness, he replied, O, no, it is a less affliction than the nonsense which forever assails the ear. He was applauded for patience and submission under severe trials, for his trust in God was unceasing. His name was Abraham, and the remark became current that he was as faithful in all things as that ancient worthy. The Scriptures and other moral writings he loved, and clove to with all his heart.

My grandmother was reputed to be amiable and affectionate, full of love and tenderness for all, and in an especial manner was she so for the children of her kindred whom she often amused with songs and stories of her childhood. Her sitting room was to all of the grandchildren a theatre, where tears and laughter ruled the hour.

My mother was the daughter of Capt. Joseph Stephens, of Petersham, Mass., who was the head of a large respectable family, my mother being the youngest of fifteen children. All that is possible for me to remember now, of him, is that he paid us visits on horseback, was very comical and amusing, and always boasting of his blood, or origin, was particularly fond of his relations, however distant. He lived to the age of ninety. His spouse also lived to a great age, and retained her mental faculties to the last unimpaired, in which respect she was more fortunate than he, as he became quite childish. I do not remember having ever seen her, but the report of her great wisdom was familiar to my ears. Ten of her children lived past middle age, all of whom married and were blessed with large families.

My mother has six brothers:—Lemuel, Stevens, Simon, Oliver, Gardner, Cyprian, and John; of all of whom I have heard her speak in terms of greatest affection. Her three only sisters, were named, Eunice, Damaris, and Polly. No women I always thought could appear so admirable in my sight. They have long since passed from earth, leaving a numerous posterity to perpetuate their names and memories. In the spirit land I hope to meet them again.

My father had two brothers and four sisters. Samuel, the eldest, was an exceedingly righteous man, and his children were trained to be like him, all of them being sweet singers. They seemed to have caught the gift from their mother whose hymns were ever resounding in their infant ears, and before weaned from the mothers arms they could lisp songs without losing the tune. Though poor, this family was contented and happy, were lovers of peace, and devoted to the cause of truth. My uncle Abraham was remarkably kind and sympathizing, but his habitual use of ardent spirits spread gloom over his household. His three daughters were fine amiable girls, who loved their parents, and mourned their unhappiness. My grandmother Barnes abode with this son, as he was the youngest, having the paternal estate. She shared the weight of sorrow, with the rest. As a contrast, her four daughters were intelligent and accomplished, blessed with talents and beauty, and great were the respect and admiration accorded them.

[Early Schooling]

My earliest recollections are of schooldays. The district schoolhouse was on my fathers land, so I was sent to it at quite an early age. But the first glimpse memory gives of my studies, I belonged to a large class that recited in the Understanding Reader, a very popular one in those days. I could then have been not more than four and a half years old, was very timid, fearing censure. Nothing grieved me more than reproof from my teacher. I remember being called up once by the mistress and placed on the dunce block, where I was kept till evening, and asked every few moments if I'd be a better child? My mortification left me no power of speech, though I longed for resolution to enable me to say "yes ma'am," which I did at last succeed in saying. No little prisoner ever enjoyed its liberation more. From my earliest childhood I was subject to deep sorrow through the smallest disappointments, and from incurring anyones displeasure. On the other hand I was given to great ecstacy of joy and delight—happy when praised, the reverse when blamed. I feel assured in my belief that children generally are not enough commended.

Going to a neighboring house on an errand, I had leave to stay half an hour, but told the lady two hours were permitted me. She was suspicious, and dispatched her little girl to inquire into the truth of my statements. I was called home and reprimanded severely, and felt the greatest contrition of heart, while mother painted my crime in its strongest colors, and rehearsed the threatenings of scripture "all liars shall have their part in the lake that burns with fire and brimstone." Do not recollect that she allowed me to think forgiveness was at all attainable. Her words had an immense effect on me, for it seemed I had committed that which was unpardonable. My age then did not exceed five years. I am not conscious of having told after this occurance, but one lie, which was not to my mother.

About this time I was to be sent some twelve miles from home, to live with an aunt, the sister of my father. She had two sons but not one daughter, so taking a fancy to me, she was anxious that I should become her adopted child, but my parents would not listen to such an overture. It was agreed upon only that I should attend school at her residence. Leaving home was a great trial though I had my aunt's children for company. So far from home I had not been before. I anticipated little pleasure on the trip, if I was to go on horseback, behind grandpa, who was deaf nearly. There was a consultation as to what I should take with me, whether all my toys and trinkets were to be packed up. I had six dolls, among other things with all their needful appendages. One of the pets, it was thought would suffice. I answered, that my content would be greater if all were let go. A hearty laugh then expressed consent to my wishes. Reaching our destination about dusk, my aunt showed her gratification by presenting me with some maple sugar. The house was large and the children were directed to acquaint me with its rooms and passages. Being left in my own apartment my heart heaved a heavy sigh, but after busying myself with making dollies comfortable, I fancied or hoped I should be happy. Bread and milk were served for supper, and though hungry, I could not eat, as I was thinking of being left alone in the morning, when grandpa would return home. I fell asleep, resolving to be up early in the coming day to see him start. Wearied from my ride, I slept soundly and too long to receive his goodbye. When I heard that he was already gone I burst into tears refusing all consolation. Auntie seated me on her lap, whispered about school, pony rides to church, and the playthings she was ready to buy for me. I concluded to give over my sorrow, was started to school, and received many compliments for my superior aptness for study. I was pronounced a great talker as well as one who loved mischiveous pranks; though all nature was never imputed to me. Many were the times I felt like resolving to keep my tongue perfectly still, but nature would assert itself, so that after my season of restraint, when left alone, I would soliquise to my hearts content. An old spelling book, about this time, falling into my hands, contained the story of Leonora, the prattler, who could not visit with her brothers and sisters because of her propensity to talk. This alarmed me so till I came to regard taciturnity as a most virtuous trait of character.

Once a month, my father would come to see me. He came on Saturday and returned Monday. The Sabbath then, was a most happy day for me, but on the following day I had tears aplenty to spare. Six months passed away, and my father disposing of his farm chose another country to settle in. My fears were great that I should be left behind; but, though my aunt plead strongly for me to be allowed to remain, I was overjoyed to hear her solicitations answered with a "no." I was called upon to make a lengthy visit to another of my aunts, whose name was Pomroy, and on meeting her daughter, who was about my age, I commenced as was my wont the practice of some of my tricky sports. Their house was commodious, and one of its large chambers we appropriated as a playhouse, and spent most of the time in aping the pursuits and manners of our schoolteacher.

[Move to Canada, July 1810]

It was esteemed one of the greatest undertakings in those days to quit ones native place. We were now starting on our journey to Lower Canada [230 miles]. Locks of hair were exchanged by parting friends, and tears unnumbered shed. We passed through the state of Vermont. Father had preceded us early in the spring and put in crops, but had not done any building. Still, the uncleared land he bought, for the country was new, possessed some accomodation for a family in the shape of a log house of one room, having a single door and window. The home we had left consisted of a goodly sized house, garden, and orchard. I remember my mother as she stepped on to the threshold of the hut we were to occupy, weeping very much at the thought no doubt of the contrast of our present and past prospects. Father was a very cheerful man, caring little about appearances. My sister, and brother were left at our former home, but we expected a reassembling of the family in the course of a year. Two of the children, a brother and sister, older than I, and three younger were with us. My father and brother worked on the land, my mother spun and wove, while I was intrusted with the charge of the younger children. My eldest sister was a great service because of her prudential and industrious habits in the long series of efforts required of us, in developing another farm.

The warm seasons were short and fleeting, the winter seemed more than to divide the length of the year. On the 29th of March following the year of our entrance into this hyperborean region, my mother gave birth to a daughter when the snow was six feet deep on the level and no fences visible over the whole face of the country. Roads were broken by throwing up on either hand immense banks of snow.

My mother was often sad and dispondent, bewailing the hard lot whose termination it was not easy for her to guess. My father though never lacked courage and he struggled on with patient constancy. He was a man who aspired after the christian character, was always reading something from the Bible, advising his children of its noble teachings. Though it appeared as much as he could do to meet other necessary expenses, I was kept at school most of the year. He was considered neighborly, kind, and faithful in friendships, quick in business, seasonable in his work, besides being given to much reading: and as his memory was of the most perfect kind, his conversation interested everybody, and instructed not a few with the maxums with which it was full. It is my painful duty not to leave unmentioned his taste for strong drink which he indulged himself in too much for his limited means and the comfort of my mother's heart. But to his honor be it said, he abandoned the practice when the first Temperance Society was organized amongst us, and spent the period of his life following in the greatest sobriety.

My Uncle, was prosperous in his labors, as he had grown sons to assist him. He had established himself in this part, before our arrival, and was advancing toward a state of wealthiness, while we were rising slowly if not imperceptibly from poverty's shadowy realm. Mother was proud and high spirited, fond of entertaining company, and sought to make a friend of every visitor. Industry and love of order were conspicuous in her household management. Her little log cabin was like a jewellers shop internally, so bright were her pewter basins and plates, and exquisite the arrangement of her cupboard, and other places of storage. The wooden buckets and keelers were made white with sand, and the floor of her domicile was scarcely less spotless. "A marvel of neatness," neighbors were accustomed to say on entering the door. Mother alone seemed sensible of our misfortune. For the children it was happy times, for we had enough to eat, drink, and wear, and could appear comely on the Sabbath. Wild berries were plentiful in the neighborhood, the gathering of which afforded a great pastime to us, and especially Dolly Sykes and myself, for she was my constant companion even if our dispositions were strangely unlike, hers being of a serious and prudent cast, mine almost the reverse, brisk and gay. The stories and songs of her mother were as much of an enticement to us, as our rambles in the woods. Love and murder were the things treated of in these tales and verses. Our affection for each other proved strong and enduring. She had an elder sister, whose prim and staid manners provoked our laughter, and criticism, for she was a religionist, which in those days possessed a meaning almost lost in these latter days of busy turmoil and strife.

At this time my age was about eight years. Though I ranked among the best readers and spellers, I could not write; which fault was owing more to the scarcity of material as copy books, ink etc, than to any lack of inclination on my part. I remember mother writing to a niece of hers about this period between whom and myself there existed quite an attachment. I requested permission to insert a few lines in the address; but no attention was paid to me. I began to expostulate with mother, when to satisfy me she said, "My dear you cannot write, I will send your love." This however was not sufficient, in my eyes. I obtained a scrap of paper and a worn out pen, and secluding myself from the rest, I began my note, printing letters from the spelling book. The pen appearing to me, after an attempt to use it, a very unfit instrument, I took up a darning needle which enabled me to persue my design without further stoppage. After all this trouble, my missive never saw the post for the reason that it contained some reflections upon my brothers which my blunt humor had suggested. I was indignant. But soon after my reward, as also theirs, who had slighted me, came by our relative making us a visit. She heard my complaint, and replied that my letter would have been fully as acceptable as any, that so ingenious a mind should be furnished with some kind of opportunity to progress. This lecture was not without its effects, for I soon wrote a legible hand.

My confidence in my mother was of the practical no less than the reverential kind. What she approved I never dreamt of questioning. Here is an illustration. The flight of a bee athwart the doorway, said Ma, announced a visitor. One day this wonderful insect buzzed about the open door. We happened to be short of butter, at the time, and the distance to market was great, so I was dispatched on the errand with orders not to tarry. I did make haste, told the lady of the dairy we expected company and that I must hurry. "And who is your company dear?", I was asked. I do not know, I replied, but a big bumble bee has been flying about the house all morning. She laughed, but I came near crying, as I was all the time serious.

The schoolhouse was about a mile from home. The road to it lead through the thick woods, and was marked only but cuts in the trees. Bears and other wild animals, jaunted the timber. So fond was I of school. that I suffered none of the terrors of the forest to interfere with my regular daily attendance, though the experience of one day was calculated to daunt the young heart. Returning home by this savage route one evening, together with a brother and a sister, we missed the way, and became lost in the dense shades of the forest. It was like "The blind leading the blind," for the efforts of all were equally unavailing. There was a prospect of the saying that "History repeats itself," being examplified in our case, as our fate seemed to be the same as the "lost babes of the woods". As luck would have it my little brother had a voice strong almost as the lion's, and our only safety seemed now to depend upon its use. The little fellow at my bidding, while his sight was dim with tears, yelled with all his might. And the echoes of this terrestrial thunder, reached our mother's ears, who was out in search of us. We were soon face to face with our parent, with our clothes and flesh torn in the conflict. Soon the woods were cleared away by the increasing toil of the husbandman. The berries of various sorts were undisturbed. Only as the task of gathering them was much lessened, it was made far less romantic. Maple sugar was a natural product of this country, so we never lacked for nice preserves.

At length, the school was held in the town, some two miles away; and we were obliged to traverse that distance every day if we wished to continue our education. In the winter season of course, home was our schoolroom where we conned lessons, under fathers eye. Some eight or more chidren when the weather was fair, gathered from the surrounding neighborhood, to start in company on this daily journey, in pursuit of knowledge. A bottle of milk (a coffee pot, or other vessel, was as commonly used) and a goodly allowance of food, supplied this little host with the strength needful for the days battle. There was a great quantity of strawberries, exposed to our sight, on a farm by the road. What a feast did they offer! and the temptation was too much for this band of youngsters, weary of their walk and their monotonous fare. The motion one day was "carried," without being "put" that we stop over into this paradisical spot, and partake of the forbidden fruit. The boys this time were no less bold than the softer sex for the guilt of the transgression was shared alike by all. But as the crowd rushed through the tall waving grass that hemmed about the object of our desires, we all seemed suddenly seized upon by the power of conscience, our footsteps faltered, and the little body of mauraders paused though but for an instant, and then pushed ahead, till we alighted in the midst of the patch of luxerey, but alas! the scene also of our woe: for a few moments had but passed, before we were supplicating the pardon of a man who stood over us with a large whipp. We received not a blow; but left the place with more of shame in our countenances than strawberries in our crops.

At school, the orthographical exercise absorbed the most of our time and attention, though it deserved the least. Websters Elementary spelling book one of my classmates knew by heart. I was able to keep next to her, for she stood always at the head of this class, except when she would display her affection for me by mispelling a word purposely to let me step into her place and wear the crown which did not belong to me.

I cannot forget a device which my younger brother employed to save him being sent regularly to school. The moment mother began preparing our dinners, he would complain of some ailment of body, generally the cholic, and his sonorous cries would alarm the whole house. But he was eventually cured either of his disease, or his wills, I will not say which. And true to his manly nature, he was disposed to shift on to me the burden of books and luncheon when we walked to school together; but this inequality of privelege did not approve itself to my understanding nor even to that of my mother's who brought her authority to bear in the matter.

My parents then belonged to the Church of England which prevailed in that country. The catechism of this Church was introduced into all of the schools, and though I had not been baptised, the task of answering questions, about my godfather, and godmother, was required of me. The printed lesson, furnished me with these answers irrespective of both understanding and conscience, which were I had to presume of little moment. The ten commandments I learned and the creed also. The latter taxing the memory, the former, the mind and heart. But I rehearsed them all equally well, for a piece of money was the reward for such excellence given by the great bishop Dr. Stewart whose visits to the schools were frequent. Being notified of his expectance, our lessons received a faithful review, and our clothes and habits a critical readjustment.

I was of a religious turn when young. At the age of seven, if left at home alone, on the Sabbath the time was passed not idly, but in the exercise of devotion, singing principally. My favorite hymn, which I sang with much unction began:

> Today with pleasure Christians meet,
> to pray and hear thy word
> And I would go with cheerful feet
> To learn thy will O Lord!

Though church, was generally at too great a distance, for me to attend, my mind was bent on the Scriptures so that I became familiar with every portion of them knowing the New Testament almost by heart.

The oddities of my behavior, gained for me a kind of celebrity. My pranks were ingenious as laughable. Being priveleged on Sunday to attend church, and having my wardrobe perfect all but a pair of shoes, I went to my chest after mother's instructions for me to go bare foot, and possessed myself of a pair of clean white stockings, and when within a few rods of the place of worship slipped them on. As I thought to be the only one of the family present that day at the services, I believed this freedom of action might be indulged without its being known at home. But my brother's eyes seconded by their telltale habits ruined the hope I had cherished on this occasion. A loud laugh was the only chastisement I received from my parents, and the many jocular allusions afterward made to this attempt of mine to introduce a new fashion, made me repent this one act, but did not cure me of my boldness.

My thoughts was allowed to be very quick and active, which gave me a presence of mind, remarked by many persons. I remember now, how soothing and encouraging was the influence of this praise upon me. One evening, being left in charge of the house, and the younger children, the room was seen to be in a blaze, near the chimney and close to the ceiling which put it almost out of my reach. I planned and executed, tied a heavy cloth to one end of the broom, dashed it in water, and against the fire, till a charred spot only remained to attest the danger we had been exposed to, and the courage that stayed its ravages. On the return of my parents, my decision, of course, was loudly applauded.

The actions of children are generally viewed too critically. We should expect less from them than we commonly do, though obedience may still be enforced, and with more success than when we prescribe for them the same rules which govern older persons. It is a shame, to be tormenting a child with the sharpest reproofs for mistakes in its behavior, which our own uneven and inconstant manners might be the occasion of. A misstep, a fault, an offense, should not be magnified into a crime, for then the judge it is that is the greater criminal.

The care of the smaller children was generally my duty: for which I proved myself competent by my love for them and unconquorable patience. They would fall frequently by losing their balance, as little ones are always apt to do, and my incessant watching could not prevent it. I was blamed and kept in constant fear, and as I was not gifted with omnipresence, and the law of gravitation would not relax in favor of the unknowing child, these summersaults were continually going on. My pity for the child and sorrow at being reproved filled my heart with a tumultuous grief, all the day through. But about this time, I acknowledge the guilt of a transaction in which I was the chief, or responsible actor.

When the old folks were at church one Sabbath, some boys came to visit my brothers. As I stood at the head of the house on this occasion, I felt it my business to devise means for the entertainment of our guests. And I do not doubt but I served my own pleasure, in trying to treat hospitably the young gents. A plaything, made of lead, and called a plummet was the rage among the boys of those days. So I took a pewter plate or two, and invited the boys to melt them on a shovel over the fire and employ the time in moulding them into the desired shape. They were not slow in joining me in this conspiracy against the sacredness of the Sabbath, and the interests of the family. Though the work was dispatched before the old folks came back, the whole proceeding was narrated to them by my brother, who of course feigned himself a spectator of the affair. My remorse in this instance seemed to double the punishment my mother administered.

My eldest sister Levina was kind and affectionate toward me, nor did I fail in my attachment for her which has seemed to increase with years. Though I have been long separated from my kindred, the sparks of affection seem to multiply by the lapse of time in some cases, and in others to sink into decay. She was a gay, cheerful creature, taking special delight in music and dancing, a very common passion indeed, but its charms were ennobling in their influence upon her. Our religion rather encouraged these innocent amusements, and the example of my sister prompted me to seek such diversions: but the guardian ship of our Elders tempered and restrained this desire for frolic.

I was always full of troubles, having my hourly mortifications, sure to say or do something that after a few moment's calm reflection became a source of regret. Though my spirits were buoyant and bright as a May Day morn, my heart ever felt the pricking of some thorn. I had been informed by my own observation that grown people were more censorious than they need be, and yet I was ever afraid of doing something that would induce people to apply to me the ugly epithets of unwise and careless. Fortune was kind once however, in providing me with a companion, a girl near my own age who was modest and retired, but never backward in correcting my false behavior. My only complaint against her was her silence when in company. Her conduct, however, I regarded with deep reverence, and she became my preceptor, without any effort or design on her part, in matters of deportment. In the school room, she appeared to less, and I to better advantage. My superior memory there enabled me to triumph over her quite often. I surpassed her in nearly every study. So that her innate wisdom, and my scholastic acquirements preserved for us the balance of worth and power.

Her image is distinctly interwoven with my first recollection of a ball I attended, when about ten years of age. Some young ladies of the neighborhood were the managing committee, my sister one of the number. She addressed mother a note, which was presented by the young master, who was to conduct me thither, dictating what I should wear, and who my partner was to be. My first sensations were those of fear and dread which it took some time for me to subdue. My destined partner received my mother's consent and then mine, if he would take my friend of whom I have just spoken, but if perchance she could not join us my engagement with him would be broken. He acceded very cheerfully to my proposition. A fine horse and sleigh awaited us at the door, buffalo robes and bells gave comfort to the body and exaltation to the spirits. My friend jumped into the sleigh with us, without being importuned in the least.

Our hearts beating responsive to the bells merry jingle, we glided along at a rapid rate. Our partner was very gallant, more so than skillful in his behavior, in resigning to us the whole seat, while he passed himself on the side of the sleigh which leaping as it were at a sideling place in the road, pitched him backwards into the snow. Our alarm was equal to his, though we caught the reins, both of us and cried out to the horse to stop! But the young man was still master of the situation, for he soon grasped the lines again, turning defeat into victory, by saying, "mind you'll frighten that beast and we'll have a runaway." Feeling that the disgrace was about equally distributed amongst us, we agreed to keep this adventure a secret; which resolution I believe we all faithfully adhered to for a proper length of time, and it served to perpetuate the bond of friendship between us.

Some time intervened before I attended another party, which was made as memorable as the first by a blunder of mine, which arose from my being a stranger to ballroom etiquete. I accepted the invitation of a young man, not my partner to the first dance. My friend called on me to explain the injury done him. I hesitated not understanding the nature of his complaint; my silence was allowed to answer for me. His pride was wounded. Some of my comrades I heard say, "she should have known better;" and my mother thought my age was a sufficient excuse for the error. My mortification was never so great.

My father continued still to labor in the improvement of his farm. My mother betrayed a sadness of spirit often which she could not help, when the recollection of the home and friends of her youth would rise in the mind.

[The War of 1812]

I was ten years old when, in 1812 the war between England and America broke out. My father, though a warm friend to the Constitution, living under the British Government was obliged to sustain its laws. Very few Canadians volunteered into the service, as the body of the settlers were Americans by birth and instinct; and were averse to fighting against the institutions of their beloved land. My father was pressed into the services, though his sympathies were not at the same time enlisted. His company was stationed to guard the line between Vermont and Canada. It was in the fall of the year, when he was called away; and when scant provision had been made for our winter's subsistance and comfort. We were excited, almost to the verge of insanity, at the thought not so much of his leaving us, as that he might never return. Mother did her best to soothe her children's fears, although in doing so she manifested an amiable insincerity, by requiring of us what she could not herself accomplish, for her sorrow she failed to diguise, even to our inexperienced sight. Two weeks had not more than elapsed, when the report reached us that the Company were all made prisoners.

From Burlington, Vt. a letter came to us giving an account of their disgrace, not their misfortune, for they were delivered as captives to the enemy by the treachery of their colonel who Arnold like, betrayed his country for gold. The missive told of suffering for want of sufficient clothes and food, it being winter, though he was made in a measure happy by finding himself among companions of his youth and school days, and even the officer of the post, where he was confined, was an old acquaintance, and their early friendship expressed itself on this occasion of apparent hostility.

My mother wept over the strange story, which interested while it appalled her, and the children were both pleased and alarmed. It was difficult to tell what fate was forshadowed by this note. He felt consoled, and yet tortured with anxiety and tears and smiles expressed the inward struggle of our feelings—fear and hope.

A period of two months had passed when one night the mother and her children encircled the hearth, and while the storm without raged in its wildest fury, wondered where and how situated was the absent one, in that hour of darkness, and the tempest. Our eyes were steadfastly bent upon those of our mother's, trying to decypher their expression, while she gazed toward the fire with an air of abstraction and melancholy, such as is forced upon one when reason and hope are at war within. At about 9:06 a knock at the door aroused us from our languid repinings for the hour was unusual, and the night hideous. We said "come in", without a suspicion having yet formed itself in our minds as to whether an angel, a demon, or simply a neighbor was about to appear in our midst. The door opened, and the person who entered wore the dress of a soldier, though so affected were his looks by both cold and adventure, that we remained for a moment in breathless suspense, till advancing toward the light the countenance of our father was revealed! to our curious and anxious scrutiny.

The embrace was followed by exclamations of joy and surprise and a chat that extended far into the night. We touched upon salient points of his experiences while away, by which we learned that his enemies or rather his friends, the Americans, though not in plain words, saying to him you can flee at any moment you choose, might as well have said so, for no watch or guard was kept over him: so in the dusk of the twilight he bid adieu to the frowning fortress which did connive at his escape. Under cover of the night, he would travel the distance of forty five miles; and under cover of the woods, he passed the hours of daylight. But when the line separating the beligerent nations was passed, he met with congratulatory welcomes from the inhabitants on his way, who assisted him on his route with a horse or other conveyance. He execrated the memory of the man who had betrayed his brethren; which taught him that treachery was the most dangerous of all foes. That bold act of perfidy, was punished, not by death, a mild recompense for such a deed, but by a dismissal from the service.

My father's greatest loss, on this occasion, was the injury done his health, by injudicious or rather necessary exposure: his physical strength seeming to wane from this time. The war raged around us in seeming concert with the blasts of the wintry season. The crops of the last year had not been abundant; and the price of provisions reached an enormous height which produced everywhere the opposite extremes of fortune, rapid exaltation, and precipitate distress. Six months swept by before we could hear of the fate of my father's comrades, who had obtained their release from imprisonment by an exchange of prisoners.

The day of the battle at Plattsburg [11 September 1814] was as solemn as a puritan Sunday to the people inhabiting its vicinity. The roar of musketry and cannon was borne by the winds over distant neighborhoods, and at my father's house was distinctly heard. Sighs and groans and prayerful ejaculations escaped almost involuntarily from the breasts of the people in their hamlets and their mansions.

I recollect the little faith we all had in the cause of our British friends. When George Provost marched an army into the states, the prophesies were of his defeat and he was beaten and routed.

[Family Reunited]

The war appearing to abate its fury, and a promise of peace being the hope of the hour, we eagerly discussed at home, the expediency of gathering into our little fold, the two absent ones of the flock, my brother and sister, whom we had left in New England. It was now the fifth year since the event of the separation during which time my sister, the older of the two, wrote us frequently and the burthen of her letters was the solicitation that she might be priveleged to come to where we were. About the end of January shortly after his return from the war, he did proceed on this journey with horses and sleigh to release from exile these young darlings of the household. Days and weeks passed, while we prayed for his safety and success. The news of peace between the two contending powers, just then was announced to the inhabitants, from the pulpit, press, and on the highway; and like a healing balm, to the distressed and wounded spirit, spread this grateful intelligence over the land.

At the appointed time my father reached home, bringing his treasures with him. The neighborhood was as much excited over this incident as a great metropolis would be by the visit of royalty. The newcomers were petted and reverenced too, by the family for a long time, were treated almost as guests seemingly ever after. Mother would never consent again to be parted from her children under any circumstances, except those ordained by nature's self.

[A New Cedar House: Growing Up]

The following season, we built us a house of cedar, on an eminence that overlooked a vast portion of the country around. The road of the time ran close by our homestead, but unfortunately for us, it being of a provincial character, was changed by government to another direction, which left us in a very isolated state. It was not all loss, however, this excommunication we were obliged to sustain, from the outer world; for habits of industry and sobriety were acquired by the children, under the teachings of our parents, when no other influence was brought to bear against their authority. Our reading was dictated by our mother, religious works being mostly recommended; fictitious writings generally denied. At the age of fourteen, "Charlotte Temple" fell into my hands. No work ever left so deep an impression on my mind and heart. I could repeat pages in some instances even whole chapters of it. Some of my friends who visited us perceiving the effect this novel had on my spirits, for it suggested phantoms of thought that compelled me to laughter and tears, expressed their surprise in a manner that almost took the form of a reprimand, at the indulgence shown us by our mother; who agreeing with the views of our guests, interdicted from that time all novel reading. I was taxed with the study of books, ill suited to my age and capacity; whose recondite terms obscured their sense to my undisciplined faculties; though many maxims were seized by the mind which gave to my thought a tincture of adult wisdom. Though of a naturally vivacious temperament, I became gloomily sedate by having my attention riveted upon the one subject, of the souls salvation.

At the age of fourteen, I was initiated into the Episcopal Church. I became desirous that my parents would settle for me the question now agitating my mind, whether anything wrong was implied in frequenting places of amusement. They appeared not disposed to favor our attending parties but I could not get them either to condem or approve.

In this period of my life, I was too deep a thinker (a virtue I'm afraid that has not grown with my years!) to be happy like others of my age. My scrutiny of every object was sure to disclose some deformity. I criticized myself severely; and never felt reconciled to my own weaknesses, whether pride of heart or love of approbation so inclined me, I was not able to pronounce. My mind was ever troubled with regret for past action. My errors of conduct were ceaseless and my shame as much so. Though I felt superior to these puerile delinquinces of conduct. I once engaged to accompany a young man to a party without first advising with my mother. He exposed us both to the attacks of slander by indulging too freely in the intoxicating cup. I avoided his company from that time; as well neglecting to seek my mother's councels on all such occasions.

My eldest sister, Lavinia, at the age of twenty three, married her first cousin Stevens Baker. The minister of course declared the union objectionable. But the match proved happy; and all became reconciled when a beautiful son was born. Here was something to interest me.[1]

[Living Away from Home]

Soon after this event, a cousin, sister to my sister's husband, married and moved to a populous village six miles from home. We had always been attached to each other, and now she pursuaded my mother to let me live with her: saying it would be an advantage to me: I would be introduced into fashionable company. I was to be with her as a companion. My mother consented but I was not willing to leave my school. I went, was treated with respect and kindness; was introduced to strangers the elite of the village, but their style did not please me. I was sadly homesick. Every entreaty was used to make me contented; tears and promises. But all in vain. I sighed for my mother's home, and my old familiar schoolroom. At length my mother sent my brother to take me home. I took a sad leave of my good friend and bid a cheerful good bye to "Slab City," as it was called.

I resumed my school studies but did not continue long till they were interupted by the marriage of another relative, who invited me to board with her and attend the government school, which was of a higher order. To this I readily assented. The man and his wife were in every instance extremely kind and indulgent. The gentleman's name was Samuel Maynard. He was one of those kind of men we read of, whose virtues we rarely expect to find in every day life. I was very happy in this family; and for six months went steadily to school. At length through an inadvertent act I was prostrated with inflammatory rheumatism. Nothing could exceed their kindness to me! A little girl by the name of Hannah Lie was my schoolmate, boarding at the same house. I had never been fond of her, although she was amiable; but when I came to be helpless, so faithful and attentive was she to me that a lasting friendship sprang up between us. As soon as I was able to ride I was taken home to my mother's and six months I was compelled to walk on crutches. My friends dispaired of my full recovery but seldom refered to it in my presence. My complaint confined me much to the house, which seemed tedious in the extreme. Occasionally did I wander away to a grove of trees, and seat myself to ponder over my affliction. When once seated it was exceedingly hard for me to rise; at such times a sense of my condition would fall with such might upon me, I would shed torents of tears: but when returned to the house would assume a cheerful appearance. Dear to me was life and liberty; and when my limbs refused to do their office I groaned in my spirit and was troubled. One year passed, and I began to recover.

When sufficiently able to walk without my crutches, I went nine miles from home to teach school. The inhabitants were scattered far and wide. I was required to divide my time among them; and when the walk was too long for me a horse and saddler were at my command. The habits of the people differed in some respects from those in my own neighborhood. I felt very lonely at time, but had great success with my school. I gained the entire approbation of my employers and was ever after counted a thorough juvenile teacher.

My mother had relatives living in Canada East on St. Francis River. There lived the niece my mother had raised, and to whom I addressed my first letter. My intimate friend, her brother, and myself contemplated a visit to that portion of the country by sleighing in the winter. The friends had heard of our intentions and were expecting us. The day was set to start, and every necessary preparation was made. The day appointed I was awakened before four in the morning: the news was announced to me that a sister older than myself had come from a little distance where she had been living and claimed the right to go instead of me. I felt the injustice of it most severely and did not contend earnestly, but submitted to the judgement of our parents. The cousins who were going with me were not so well pleased, neither were the relatives who were to receive us, for they had heard of the great friendship that existed between the two young girls from their childhood, and they had hoped to see us together. I shed many tears at the disappointment and my eldest brother kindly endeavored to console me; took me on horseback to ride, and promised me I should go with him to those relatives, but we never went.

Soon after this another project was on hand. My mother having a large family and several boys, was desirous that one of her daughters should learn to be a great seamstress. I was the one selected to go to a town in Vermont, and practice with an experience workman. The family with whom I had lived in such great harmony were located in that place and kept a publick house. They had influenced my parents to have me come to that town and engage in the business of making garments by rule. The person under whose tuition I was to remain a definite time was a young man, boarding in his father's family, and I felt quite happy. The father of the seamster had known my mother in her youth, and seemed disposed to treat me with great respect on her account, often expatiating about her beauty and amiable qualities, of which I felt flattered.

My instructor, though a fine disposition and good complexion, was not well formed! He was undersized with heavy shoulders, even to deformity. He was candid and sensible, wore an air of dignity; and was much respected. I treated him with politeness, never once dreaming of his entertaining any other sentiments towards me than what was due in my situation. I soon found I had misunderstood him; that from my first arrival he had serious intentions. The young man was wealthy, and my friends thought that such a union would secure to me a respectable home. These things were portrayed before me as inducements; but I frankly told my friends I could not marry the young man even for his weight in gold. I feared my refusal would lesson the attentions of the family toward me, but I discovered no change in them.

At the expiration of four months having acquired a tolerable knowledge of making men's clothing I proposed going home to my parents. Whereupon the young man suggested the idea of taking me home in a sleigh, as the snow was deep. Previous to my leaving, my mother and eldest brother returned from their visit to Massachusetts, called to see me. Mr Houghton, Sen., received my mother with great politeness and cordiality, but could scarcely believe she was the same person he had known in his childhood and youth. She responded to my request to leave, though my relatives urged her to use her influence to have me remain longer. In 1821 Feb. Mr. H. conducted me home to Dunham, LC [Lower Canada] where my parents lived. We parted in friendship, he inviting me to return, either for a transient or permanent stay, at any time I chose.

[Seamstress, Teacher, Proposals]

I was soon in credit with the people as a popular seamstress: being considered competent to make the finest broadcloth into garments. This made me very independent. I accumulated means very fast.

The following summer I was solicited to teach school in the district near where my eldest sister was married and located. For the first time in my life I was introduced to an English family: their customs at first appeared singular to me. As I became acquainted I contracted a high esteem for them. Their table manners were quite different from those in which I had been trained. I conformed in all things. If required to take a brandy sling to "stay my stomach," (as they called it) till tea was ready, I did so, eating a bit of cracker with it. If to sit an hour at dinner table, I manifested no uneasiness. They had a family of children, several in my school. I boarded with them. The eldest was a young man of twenty years, purely English; wore breeches and long stockings. The children were accustomed to have plays at evening in which I joined. The familiarity we were obliged to use in the plays I soon discovered was producing sentiments I did not wish to encourage. It was soon whispered among my friends that the young Englishman was "enamored with the teacher." The affair was disposed of in an amicable way, without any serious disappointment.

A schoolteacher in the same board made choice of me for his son; employed a lady friend to negotiate. She represented the young man in the highest terms, but it was a vague sound in my ear. I begged her to make an apology for me; which she did in as polite a manner as possible. It was my misfortune to meet the disapprobation of my friends if I allowed my mind to be attracted to any one; and as I was firmly resolved never to marry one of whom my parents did not approve I began to feel that a life of single blessedness was my destiny. I was independent. I could by teaching and sewing earn a respectable living for myself.

A new schoolhouse was erected in the vicinity of my father's residence. In that I had constant employment: for ten successive months, I was buried within the walls of that to me a prison. Spelling book and dictionary as indispensable as my clothing. Well as I had always loved a school, I became weary. The neighborhood was dull, too dull for one who loved excitement. About that time my eldest brother whom I had loved with all the ardor of a sister's affection left home and went to the far west. Unhappy circumstances attended his leaving, greatly increasing the grief of the family. From my eyes flowed torrents of tears. I became gloomy and discontented.[2]

CHAPTER TWO

Independent Young Woman

Memoirs, September 1825 to April 1831

[To Massachusetts]

About this time my uncle and aunt Baker contemplated a visit to Massachusetts, the place of my birth, where I had long desired to go. My mother having three daughters younger than myself at home, seemed willing I should go to visit her relatives, believing it would be an advantage to me in the way of improving my mind and manners. My uncle offered me a seat in his carriage, which I accepted. Well I immediately made the necessary preparations for the journey. My friends fully expected my return with my uncle; but that was far from my intentions; although I said but little about it. Our journey lay through a populous part of the country. It was autumn of the year 1825. All nature was in bloom and beauty! Although sad at the instance of leaving home, the prospect of a cheerful journey, a jolly old uncle for company, soon revived my spirits when out of sight of the old plantation. Our first visit was at Charleston, Vt. where we found relatives, who received us with great cordiality. It was a large village neatly constructed, and I had much pleasure in walking through it with my young lady cousins. We called at the state prison in Windsor, Vt. The sight of the convicts and their cells affected me very much. I had never seen anything of the kind before. I heard the gratings of the great wooden doors, they closed with a vengence that struck terror to my heart.

I felt pity for the poor prisoners: and I said to myself, "if I was their jailer I would let them all escape." The great majority in the workrooms were from eighteen to twenty five. We entered a long hall. On each side were looms. In the centre a man sat with a drawn sword in his hand. We passed up the aisle, no one turned his head to look at us, but kept steady at his work. At length my uncle discovered one whom he had seen in

Canada a short time before he left. He at that time told him he believed him to be a state prison character. He denied being a rogue, but soon after was sent to prison. How true it is, that the countenance betrays the character. I shed tears of sympathy as I left the prison, which were soon effaced by the sight of the beautiful villages we passed through.

We reached the superb little village of Brattleborough, Vt., about the middle of Sept. 1825. I was then 22 years old and though I had seen little of the world, I had a good knowledge of books, and had for the most kept good company, consequently I was not wholly unprepared to be entered into fashionable society.

I was delighted with everything that appeared gay and beautiful: The elegant buildings neatly finished and furnished, the flower gardens, shade trees, and front yards, adorned with shrubbery, far exceeded anything I had seen in the new country from which I hailed. At the beautiful mansion of Col. Chase we made our first visit in Brattleborough. We were received with great politeness and attention on account of family connexions. I thought of their poor relatives whom I knew in Canada.

I did not in the least feel envious at all the grandeur I saw, neither did it cause me to despise the humble manner in which I had been reared. I was a professor of religion, had been taught to view the hand of God in the various circumstances attending his people who assay to serve and obey his laws. After spending a few days with this interesting family, we pursued our journey to Guilford, where lived the family of my mother's brother; a widow with a son and two daughters. He had been a celebrated physician, had accumulated a large property, deceased, left his family in easy circumstances. A dissipated son was wasting the means, much to the grief of his mother and sisters. I remonstrated with him, when I had learned the facts. He would seem penitent at the time, reform at intervals, then return to his old habits. The young ladies were sensible inteligent girls. Great pains had been taken with their education; but the habits of their only brother, unmarried, cast a shadow over their young lives; and caused them to sympathize more deeply with their bereaved mother.

After spending a few days very much to the satisfaction of ourselves and relatives, we resumed our journey to Mass. 40 miles, which we performed in a day.

[Petersham, Massachusetts]

We drew up in Petersham at the dwelling of my mother's sister, also the aunts with whom I was travelling. She was quite aged, but seemed to have retained all the sprightliness and vivacity of youth, a trait said to be peculiar to the Stevens race. She appeared extremely happy to see us, and rejoiced over me as the daughter of her youngest sister.

So much did she look and speak like my mother, that I was quite overcome at the sight of her. She begged to know why I wept. I told her it was for joy that I had seen her face. I soon became warmly attached to her. Her husband had long been dead, and she lived with her son. She had a large pleasant room of her own, where she received her friends with such warm friendship and cheerful temper, she became proverbial for possessing a loving spirit. Never was I happier while I remained in the place than when visiting my dear "aunt Spooner," for that was her name. She was never weary of telling me stories of her youthful days, and of my mother, who was born after her marriage.

I had also another aunt in that town, nearly as old, and one uncle. That aunt had also been a widow several years. When I first went to her house she took me by the hand led me into a room away from the company when she gazed steadily into my face for several minutes in order to discern whether I bore any striking resemblance to the Stevens' race. Her blunt familiar remarks very much amused me. She was a tall well formed woman, black piercing eyes and black hair. There was a thoughtfulness and solemnity in her look, a dignified and lofty expression in her countenance.

She had wealth and all the comforts of life about her; and although naturally of a gay lively temperament, she wore the impress of sorrow. And truely did she have cause to mourn. Her eldest and youngest son were both confirmed drunkards. The eldest had been the pride of the family, had his portion from his father's estate, married a beautiful and amiable woman, but he squandered his property and brought his family to destitution. His wife like a patient angel bore her sufferings and made no complaint. The youngest son was educated at Providence, R.I. designed for a profession; but his parents' hopes were never realized. After his return from college he visited his relatives in Canada East. I was then a very young girl, but well do I remember the admiration he attracted. A more brilliant interesting man I never saw. We did not dream of the dissipated course he had been involved in, which was kept in check while he remained among his kindred. Years rolled away, ere I became acquainted in Mass. with his amiable wife, and she gave me a history of his downward course.

He went to the west, to retrieve his fallen fortunes, from whence word came to his kindred that he was sick, and in a state of destitution. Means and conveyance were sent to bring him home, but before the messenger reached the poor unfortunate, he was dead and buried! Great was the grief of his wife and mother! Thus faded in the prime of life, a youth who might have blessed the world, had it not been for that demon, alcohol!

My poor dear aunt trusted in the Lord, and was thankful for one temperate son, a bachelor of forty, who was kind and loving in her declining years. Likewise a daughter near that age, who remained unmarried at home with her mother having been in early life opposed in her choice, resolved to live a single life, though greatly sought after by many.

I had great enjoyment with my aunt and cousin, whose name was Sally Ward. I knew they loved me and I felt how much I contributed to their comfort by the gayety of my spirits. Bereaved as they were they needed a youthful merry heart to chase away the gloom that brooded over the grand old domicile.

I admired my lady cousin, for a lady she was, in the proper sense of the term, but it was difficult for me to come up to her standard of extreme neatness. She could scarcely endure to see a chair moved two inches out of its place and allowed to remain. I often avoided reproof by assuming a peak of humor to excite her mirth and make her forget my error. I had not been accustomed to jump in a moment if I saw a pocket handkerchief on the bureau, or a thread on the carpet.

Petersham was the town where my mother was born. It appeared to me that half the people were her relatives. My good old uncle had a large family, his name was Gardner Stevens. There was no end to my cousins. My uncle seemed proud to introduce me to his children. He had three sons, overseers in the factories at Lowel Mass., moral enterprizing young men. It was all the amusement I wanted to see my uncle and his two old sisters together, hear them sing songs and tell stories of their youthful days. I had solicitations from every portion of the town and country to visit my relations. It was high tide with me. I believe no place ever had more charms for my person than the town of Petersham, Worcester Co. had for "Louisa Barnes," for that was my name. I felt a sort of native pride that my mother was born and raised there.

I availed myself of an opportunity to make an improvement in my business as a seamstress, knowing it would be an advantage to me when I returned to my home in Canada. I was employed by a fashionable tailor who taught a more advanced method of cutting and making fine broad-cloth. The man though an excellent workman was not punctual: he would make promises he did not expect to fulfill, except by the earnest entreaties of his wife and employees. He at length left home, and his wife and I continued the business together.

We were patronized widely, won credit from every suit we made, especially were we applauded for our punctuality. If we promised work finished at a certain time we would ply the needles the whole night through rather than disappoint our customers.

[Athol, Massachusetts]

I was contented in my situation. But circumstances took place which caused my removal to the next village the town of Athol. I was pursuaded by a friend living there to set up business for myself, with a view to make more money. I had relatives living there. I accordingly removed, was very successful, employed a faithful young woman to work with me, and remained one year. The young lady was a most admirable girl endeared herself to me by . . . being true to my interest in all things. Her name was Sarah Buckman. The lady with whom we boarded was Mrs. Ball. She was our firm friend. Her eldest child was a son named Francis, three years old. He was a precocious child.

I took great pride in learning him to sing, an art which he possessed unusual talent. Many a dime did he earn by singing the songs I taught him, in publick places. The habit grew with him to manhood, as will be shown hereafter. I often visited my friends in Petersham, full intended to return there, and make it my home while I remained in the country. But fate had marked me for her victim, and I could not elude her grasp.

[Winchester, New Hampshire, Spring 1827]

I had a relative in N. Hampshire, town of Winchester; my father's niece. She was a well informed lady, who had travelled and acquired knowledge. She wrote me a pressing invitation to come and remain a while with her. She was a genteel milliner, kept house and carried on large business. I felt reluctant, but as I had left home to see the world, and learn what I esteemed worth learning, I concluded to go. I took up my residence with her, and we were very happy together.

She had very agreeable young ladies living with her whom she instructed in that branch of business. Winchester was a delightful village situated on the banks of the Ashuelot River, branch of the Conn. The scenery was grand indeed! I was often filled with inspiration as I walked beneath the shade of the umbrageous trees, on the banks of that beautiful stream of water. My cousin Miss Jennings seemed very fond of me. She was naturally of a cheerful temper, but the sorrows of her poor mother had cast a shadow over her spirit, which at intervals required great grace and exercise of faith in the final triumph of virtue over injustice to enable her to calm her troubled mind. Her father though fond of her was a tyrant in his family! He had by his cruelities blasted the peace of her mother, (my father's sister), and saddened the heart of her only sister, a young sensitive girl who grieved to see the unhallowed course of him, who by the laws of nature and custom she must call, Father.

The mother was one of those Godlike souls, of whom the world is not worthy. A rare jewel, a flower of intrinsic value, plucked by a rude hand and then trampled under foot! A being of so many graces combined that had she fallen into the hands of a worthy and virtuous man, he would have esteemed her a celestial star, sent to guide him through the darkened scenes of life! Happy was it for her, her only son was the exact reverse of his father. Her great humility, and reliance on a divine providence, "who shapes our ends," enabled her to lift up her head and rejoice in the midst of the most conflicting difficulties! Thanksgiving and praise were continually on her tongue! While I remained with my cousin she was married to a wealthy respectable merchant by the [name] of Henry Kingman. Thus were the desires of her heart granted unto her, as she was then able to provide for her beloved mother.

This marriage did not in the least interfere with the happy intercourse which we had previously enjoyed. The husband was good and kind, moral and temperate, but no professor of religion. Her father at the time of her marriage proposed making a wedding festival at his own house, where her mother was not an inmate. We all felt great reluctance in view of complying but such was my cousin's dread and fear of his displeasure that she consented. Her mother was invited and with the calmness of a summer morning she attended. There was an effort on his part to make a display and great demonstrations of joy were attempted, but we all felt that there [was] "a lion in the path." So sensibly does virtue shrink from mingling with vice.

Soon after this the unnatural husband made a deed of one of his farms to his son, binding him to take [care] of his mother and make her comfortable while she lived. All this she received as from the hand of God. My cousin's husband proved to be a faithful and indulgent companion and I was very happy with them. Strong ties of friendship grew between us which the lapse of years did not weaken.

In the spring of 1827 I commenced attending the Female Academy. Preceptor's name was Sereno Taylor, a "Freewill Baptist" preacher. Circumstances made it necessary for me to take boarding with a widow lady, by the name of Alexander. Her dwelling was most romantically situated. A large eight square roofed building at the far end of a beautiful grove of maple trees, it was a place of resort where merry throngs assembled, spread tables loaded with luxuries, to do honors to some grand occasion. Lovers of independence congregated there, as the rolling years brought around the Fourth of July. A walk in that grove by moonlight filled the soul with inspiring thoughts, both of nature and art!

Soon after I came to Winchester I visited Warwick, my native town, where I had been once before and made a short stay. At this time I formed more extensive acquaintance with my father's near relatives. I found another aunt by the name of Burnet, who had a beautiful family. My aunt to me seemed goodness incarnate! She often remarked that to have me with her was comparatively like being in the company of my father and mother both! In no other way could she have flattered me so much. I visited her eldest daughter who was married to a man by the name of Clapp, keeping house at Ervings Grant. For her and her companion I felt great admiration! They were persons of greater beauty and refinement than any couple I had ever met. Their union seemed complete.

I learned from their friends how indisolubly they were joined! They were merchandizing in a rough portion of the country among the rugged rocks and mountains of Franklin Co. Mass. but so much did I admire the happy couple, their dwelling place seemed a paradise to me. I pondered in my heart why they should be so extremely happy, when so many were bowed down with sorrow! I solved the problem in my own mind. They had lived pure lives before marriage, they loved God, and his holy laws, and truly loved each other. Their aim was to do good and to make others happy. What has a vicious life to do with happiness? It is incompatible; they cannot harmonize. While in my native town I made the acquaintance of the Rev. Mr. Smith, settled minister in the town where my Grandfather Barnes lived and died. He talked of the peculiar traits of his character, said he was the richest man he had ever known. I queried; I knew he was not rich in worldly goods; "he was rich" he remarked, "because his wants were all supplied; he sighed for nothing he did not possess."

The same clergyman composed the epitaph on my grandfather's tombstone. It reads thus, "In death's cold icy arms, Here lies the body of the virtuous Barnes. Death hurled his shaft, up through the starry road, And so Elijah went to God!" While visiting in Warwick I went to the old house where I was born, the house my father built before his marriage, and where my mother lived till she had borne eight children. In her bed-room I paused, and never can forget the sensations that passed through my mind! Though only six years and a half old, I had a vivid recollection of everything about the premises, which remained the same as when we left. I had been about sixteen years away. Little or no improvements had been made, the house was fast going to decay. I remembered the corner in the bedroom where my mother's bed stood from year to year, the cupboard where in sickness her nurse was sent to keep her medicine and food. I felt as if standing by my mother's tomb! I reviewed in my mind the trying scenes through which she had passed in going to a new country, and encountering the war of 1812 with all the attendant ills.

I withdrew silently, did not feel inclined to revisit the place. As I retired, I walked through the orchard and garden. Here thought I, "my infant days were spent; here I first learned to lisp my parents names; under the shade of these trees was I carried about in their arms; in the intervening years much of sorrow have they seen. The world is before me who knows the fate that may befall me!" Thus did I soliloquise and whenever after I had occasion to pass the place, I would sink into a deep reverie and become silent. The decay I everywhere witnessed, reminded me of the faded beauty and careworn features of those beings who in the bloom of life and vigor of youth, began in a family capacity on that spot. I wept, but they were not tears of anguish, but of sympathy for the absent ones.

I was often at the house where my grandparents lived forty years. Where my father was born, and his father died. I often sat in the room where my grandmother used to divert the children with stories and songs, all so vivid in my memory, and it seemed to me that her spirit was hovering over me, so sacred did everything in the room appear. After grandfather's death, she went to the town of Gill to live with her youngest son, Abram Barnes, where she died at an advanced age. All my grandparents lived to be several years over eighty. My father's eldest sister Polly Pomroy died with a cancer. She had two daughters who were like sisters to me. Mrs. Lesure who lived in Warwick was an estimable lady; had a kind companion, and a pleasant home. Many happy hours did I spend under her roof. She was a practical Christian.

At her house I became acquainted with an interesting and accomplished girl by the name of Caroline White, of Northfield, Mass. A strong friendship immediately sprang up between us. There seemed a mutual attraction at our first meeting. She was a lover of books, a popular teacher, and letter writer. Notwithstanding her high toned spirits and mirthfulness, she was a lover of the sublime truths of the gospel of Christ. I was soon made acquainted with her prospects for future life. She had a lover in the South Country, who wrote ardent letters; but he proved false; and she married an orthodox preacher by the name of Coal and moved to Amherst, Conn. I will now return to school from which I have wandered.

[The Henry Pratt Family]

I was very successful in my studies. Our Preceptor proved to be a first class teacher. A young lady by the name of Rebekah J. Pratt was my classmate; we occupied a seat together. She was a beautiful girl to look upon, and lovely in disposition. Music was her masterpiece, and chief delight.

Her father was by trade an organ builder, both parlor and church organs. In the dwelling house there was a Harpsichord, an organ always in the shop. It was a great place of resort for young people who loved music. I often visited the home of my classmate, where I was delightfully entertained with the sweet strains of the harpsichord. I was exceedingly interested with the family, soon immagined myself a favorite, an intimacy grew between Rebekah J. and myself. Our studies were in the same plane, with the exception of drawing in which she exceeded me. She was a thoughtful and serious turn of mind, invariably silent in company, and only with a few of her intimate friends would she appear sociable. Her attention was principally turned to music; in that she was known to excel. Although naturally inclined to silence and sadness, she seemed drawn towards me, on account of the gayety and cheerfulness of my temper.

She often entertained me with tales of her brother at sea, whom I had never seen. She told of his adventures, of his narrow escapes from death! He seemed to me a romantick being; such as I had read of; being bold and fearless amid dangers; who launching on life's ocean mane experience many miraculous escapes, and became renowned to posterity. I listened to every word with interest; and indulged a hope that I should sometime meet the brave young man! Which came to pass in process of time.

It so happened that while spending a few days in the family, the sailor brother having landed in Boston harbor, was impressed to visit his paternal home. I was introduced to him as a friend of his sister. His first appearance seemed rough and unpolished, but his countenance indicated a heart sincere, frank and ingenuous. There was novelty about him which attracted attention. He was mirthful in the extreme, fond of singing and telling wonders. He spent the winter of 28 at his father's residence.

He often mingled in the coteries, and amused the company with tales of his travels. To say that I admired his appearance would not be speaking truthfully, but there seemed some kind of an attraction, either from the charms of the sisters, the high respect I had for the family, or because fate would have it thus. We became in some degree attracted to each other. I had never before been acquainted with one who was engaged in a seafaring life. I was devoted to the religion of the day, which he, perhaps to please me treated with respect. He would accompany me to meetings for prayer and religious exercises, speak in honor of the cause. He left home in the spring, no promises on either side, and I knew not that I should ever see him again.

His sister Rebekah, often turned over the pages of her map in school to trace his course over the briny deep, while we were plodding through our studies. I sometimes involuntarily betrayed a sentiment of concern for the wanderers welfare though I little expected our acquaintance would ever be renewed. At no distant period his friends received a letter that his vessel had anchored in Boston Harbor. No mention was made of me, though he knew the intimacy between his sister and myself. I said nothing, but understood it to mean indifference. He went to Surinam, West Indies. When he returned to Boston he wrote a letter to me, saying nothing of his intention to come to Winchester. The following week he arrived in town by stage. I was greatly shocked when I heard of it for I feared it was on my account he had come. I seemed unwilling to be forgotten by him, yet did not wish to contract in intimacy doubting the propriety of encouraging the addresses of a stranger of whose private life I could know nothing. I was at that time boarding at the roundhouse at the upper end of the maple grove.

He made a short visit in town, and we sometimes walked by moonlight, under the shade of the beautiful trees. He went away, and we merely promised to write. I visited in Warwick, and my cousin Harriet Bass often talked to me of her uncle Lyman Barnes, my father's cousin. In early life he went to South America and married a wealthy creole, by whom he had two sons. They were brought early in life to Mass. to be educated. The elder boy had been an associate of my cousin Harriet, who described him to me as peculiarly interesting and accomplished. He had been one year at school in the city of London. He was at that time residing in Hartford, Connecticut. My cousin wrote him a letter for the purpose of introducing her cousin from Canada, whom she represented in a style peculiar to herself as being a singer of a high order, a poetess, and possessing qualities of mind which she believed were in accordance with his tastes. He soon returned a very interesting letter with a gross of compliments to the Canadian cousin; even naming the time when we might expect him to appear before us. The melodies must be selected, and preparations made to entertain him.

Accordingly at the appointed time he arrived. My expectations were more than realized. His countenance was sallow, and his features resembling the creole, with light brown hair and blue eyes. There was an air of familiarity at first, which placed everyone at ease in his presence; and which upon long acquaintance continued the same, never in the least degree relaxing into low humour, and undue freedom, invariably maintaining a dignity which characterises a person of refined sentiment and understanding. He was universally admired. It was proposed by our mutual friends that we together should visit our relatives in Petersham of whom he had heard, but had never seen. Accordingly a carriage was obtained and we had a pleasant trip of twenty miles.

My Southern cousin and myself were very welcome visitors at the dwellings of my two old aunts, of whom I have spoken so much. They were delighted to meet him, having been in their youthful days associated with his father. We spent a week most pleasantly and returned.

The first news we heard on reaching the town was that a stranger by the name of Pratt had come to town with his sister and was inquiring for "Miss Barnes," as I was then called. They had stopped at my boarding house, Mrs Rich my hostess kindly entertaining them. When we allighted at [the] house, the visitors had gone out. We waited their return in the parlor, talked of visits we had in contemplation. There was a shadow upon our spirits, a reserve bordering on silence, but not a word was exchanged of the stranger's arrival.

I felt that I was under no engagements either verbal or written; yet the publick inquiry proved at least that something was expected or required of me. My cousin appeared to feel that his presence would not be agreeable to the newly arrived; which occasioned regret on my part, as I had no opportunity to make an explanation. We parted, and I soon returned to my home in Winchester, and saw him no more. There was an interest awakened in our minds that I believe mutual; which by his great modesty was restrained when he found another presumed on a prior claim. We afterwards exchanged a few letters, friendly but formal. With me pleasant memories have ever remained of my southern cousin whose name was Sidney Smith Barnes.

While visiting with my friend Mrs. Rich, I became acquainted with a beautiful girl by the name of Emily Ball. We soon were very warm friends. She had a step mother, a bigoted Unitarian. Our religious principles were not in unison. I contended for the orthodox faith, the trinity in unity. She was very intolerant; and seemed suspicious of me without any cause, was inclined to censure, and speak ill of me to her daughter. She was rigid in every way; laying the greatest restrictions upon her stepdaughter who appeared to stand in great fear of her. She also took the liberty to speak against me to my friend Mrs. Rich, judging me to be too gay for a professor: expressing her doubts about the propriety of an intimacy between her stepdaughter and myself.

My pretended friend seemed to exult in having the opportunity to inform me what the censorious woman had said. It was presumed to be in friendship but it did not impress me in that way. I told her plainly she ought to have plead my cause to my enemy, and kept it hidden from me. I wrote a letter to the young lady my friend in the most affectionate terms, defending myself against the accusations of her mother. It was couched in words entirely calculated to excite sympathy and remorse for the injustice done me, on the part of the cruel mother. I did not utter one chastising word in a revengeful tone, but it had the desired effect.

The lady afterwards told my friend Mrs. B. that although the letter was every sense conciliatory she had never in her life felt so much reproved! Acknowledged that the perusal of it had caused her to weep the live long night. Said she would be willing to make restitution, but knew not in what manner she could. Never did I more sincerely love one not of my near kindred than I did Emily Ball. She seemed to me the essence of loveliness. I was fully sensible of her reciprocal tenderness towards me. She was grieved to the heart, for the injustice done me by her mother, and shed many tears.

In my letter to her I dwelt largely on the charity and virtue of my own dear mother! Like the image of a holy angel, did she seem to hover around me to console and comfort me when I was unjustly censured! To her, said I, will I return, and evermore devote the best affections of my heart! I had left her for the purpose of learning more of the world, and human nature, and I had learned it to my sorrow!

I went immediately to Winchester, told my cousin Mrs. Kingman my intention to return to my parents; she did not oppose me. I had then been four years from home, had spent the most of the time in the most agreeable intercourse with my relatives, never but the one time having been assailed by an enemy. My friends though sorry to part with me, as I with them, could not find it in their hearts to dissuade me from going to see my parents. I received many farewell letters, took an affectionate leave of my friends in Winchester. My cousin Mrs. Kingman and I wept much at parting, for we doubted whether we should ever meet again, and so has it proved, and she has long been gone to the world of spirits. Mr. Pratt accompanied me to Keene, N.H., where I took the stage. We parted with no promises on either side, but to write.

[Return Home to Dunham, Canada]

The two first nights I felt safe at the publick buildings where I lodged. In Rutland, Vt., I was very badly frightened. After retiring and bolting my door, I heard knockings on it, and though I knew they could not enter, I felt terribly excited and alarmed! The idea that I was in a Hotel, where there were disorderly persons, who would presume to disturb the quiet of a lone female. I at length summoned courage to cry out, "leave my door immediately! I will report this house for a hundred miles round and warn all honest people to shun it!" I heard no more noise at the door, but could hear low talking in an adjoining room. No slumber came to my eyes that night. I resolved to inform the Landlord, but left so early in the morning I had not time. I however wrote to him from my next stopping place, denouncing the character of his house and heaping anathemas on some of its inmates. The next night I was fortunate in securing a lodging in a room with an elderly lady and her husband. I arrived in St. Albans, Vt., stopt at a hotel, where on the sign I saw the name of S. Maynard. I entered and found my old friends, with whom I had been so happy in Canada.

I was cordially received, and I entertained them most cheerfully with my four years experience. I left the stage and took passage with a friend from Dunham. It was a short days ride, and I was soon at my sisters house. They not being apprised of my intention to return, at first did not know me. As soon as they recognized me, the house rang with exclamations of surprise and joy to see me alive and well! Great was the talk and little the sleep. Early on the morrow my sister and I started for my father's residence. As the carriage drove up my mother came to the door. She had changed and I wept aloud at the sight of her! My father looked more natural, and as he saluted me in his usual style, when meeting a friend unexpectedly, his words were "Bless my body," they sounded so familiar in my ears that I burst into laughter. All my tears vanished. The scene can only be immagined. My second sister Dolly Lockwood lived near; had just been confined with a young child. I could not wait to send my card, but rushed upon her suddenly. She being weak was quite overcome. Our Mother was there present with her six daughters. She remarked. "I am thankful to see you all together again, and you must never be unmindful of the source from whence this blessing springs as well as every other." No one knows the joy of meeting friends, but those who have been long separated. I soon began to inquire for my old companions, found that several had died and others were married. A new society had come on the stage of action, as agreeable in many respects as that existing when I left. My familiar friend and cousin D. Sikes remained unmarried, the same faithful girl happy to have our friendship renewed. Three sisters younger than myself were single, grown young women. Their names respectively, Caroline, Lois, and Catharine. By this time the twin children of our relative L. Stevens were of age.

The two young persons, a son and daughter, were unusually intellectual, great devotees to literature, though diverse from each other in disposition. The young man Dana L. engaged in the study of medicine. He seemed ambitious to make a display hence brought to his aid dictionaries, and extracts from distinguished authors. He aimed at oratory in its highest sense, and being witty and agreeable, managed to make his conversation interesting. As he became more enlightened, his flight was not so lofty. He acquired a thorough knowledge of the medical science, and was very successful in his practice. Lucy F. his twin sister was a humble devoted Christian. She was a model of amiability, was qualified for a teacher at an early age, was a great assistant in helping to raise a large family, all younger than herself. Though plain looking, she might be called beautiful. The beauties of her inner life shone in her intercourse with her friends. Between her and my sister Lois, grew a great intimacy. They were very religious and assimilated in social and domestic habits. It might be said of them truly, that meekness, gentleness and humility were all their own. Lucy was the greater student, my sister the more vivacious and attractive.

Mrs. S. often remarked to me, that were it not for her dutiful and affectionate daughter, she should feel herself in a state of banishment! Having emigrated to Canada against her inclination; loss of property had compelled them to seek a home in a new country; and great were the struggles they were called to endure. I have spoken of this family at length because the two young persons were my first acquaintance after my return to Canada, and conspicuous in my social circle. My friends were well pleased with the improvement I made in my business as a seamstress, and also with the knowledge I had gained from books. I was then qualified to control business for myself, and to instruct others. After the excitement of visiting was over I took a location in the centre of town.

I was very successful in accumulating means to make myself independent. It was soon discovered that I had a correspondent. That he was a young man, and had been to sea. All the friends seemed alarmed at the idea of my contracting an intimacy with one who had been a sailor! Their opinion was at once, he could not be a suitable person for me, though I assured them he had left that occupation on my account, and adopted another branch of business. But all I could say did not seem to satisfy them. He had been a roving man, what security had I that he would long abandon the habit? Hearing so much said of the character of sailors I became alarmed myself. My cousin Mrs. K. I knew had been opposed to it at the first, but seeing the change effected in him she became reconsiled.

He belonged to a highly respectable family. I knew his early training had been good, but how did I know what his habits or practices had been when far away from home. These reflections troubled my mind. I some-times wished our acquaintance had never commenced, then I thought how circumstances had combined to render it unavoidable. I was con-stantly gaining the confidence, affection and esteem of my friends, and I thought how hard it would be to part with them. Though full of life, health and spirits, I was often sad. My younger sisters soon became well acquainted with the young seaman in yankee land, by conversing with him in their dreams. Sometimes our letters were intercepted and delayed greatly beyond time. This caused extreme anxiety to both parties. I at length dreamed myself and the interpretation thereof was sure.

[A Prophetic Dream]

I saw in the air above me a great wild fowl soaring aloft. I reached forth my hands to entice him to come near me, that I might take hold of him and perhaps tame him. For a long time he kept out of my reach but at last lowered himself down and settled on my lap. As the wild bird alighted, I began smoothing his feathers with my hand, when he turned and bit me. I beat him with great severity until he appeared tame and perfectly harm-less. I felt pleased with my conquest, awoke and beheld it was a dream! Well did I understand the meaning of that night's vision, and I knew there was destiny entailed to me.

In the month of March 1830, the worst time for travelling in the whole year, after a separation of one year and a half, the person so much talked of made his appearance. It happened on a time when three young lady relatives had come to visit and stay overnight with us. We had gone out to spend the evening at a neighbor's: seven young girls; my three sisters, the three visitors, and myself. Suddenly there came a knock at the door, and a little boy entered. It was my sisters son who had come to conduct the gentleman to my father's house. He stole slyly up to me and says, "Miss lady. you must come home. Some one has come who wishes to see you." The whole troupe of girls were up in a moment and ready to start guessing the stranger's name at once. They made a rush to the door leaving me behind; reached home before me and were introduced to the stranger. Nothing could exceed the hilarity of the young ladies, when they were left to themselves in a room where the strange gentleman was disbanded of his hat and cloak. Every portion of them underwent examination, to see if indeed they answered the description given in the dreams. It was decided in the affirmative. My mother was greatly amused with the comical performances and the evening passed pleasantly. I might have been happier had I not been previously apprised of a contemplated settlement in the state of N. York. This led me to think too deeply of future prospects. It had ever been my lot when anticipating some new delight. I could see a cloudy atmosphere threatening. Such may be the testimony of thousands, for ought I know.

The cup of bliss for mortals not designed, But they may drink it in a State refined. A few things I had forgotten to mention relating to the family. Previous to this period my second and third brothers were married. Cyprian the elder of the two was a great Methodist, enthusiastic as I thought, though I had great confidence in his piety. He could not endure to hear a comic song or anything bordering on the ludicrous. His wife Sarah Chadsey was a good plain woman. She did not fully sympathize with him in his rigid discipline. My third brother, Lyman Franklin Barnes, married my early friend Dolly Sikes, bought a farm adjoining my father's and lived very happily. I felt how happy it would be for me to be settled near them all, but destiny pointed to some place far away! My friend D. S. previous to her marriage, had a severe sickness, for seven weeks reason was dethroned. She would often speak unkindly to her mother and sister. To me she was always affable, and yielding. I could soothe and quite her when no one else could. She was restored to health by means of cupping her head, and drawing the blood from the brain. While her delirium lasted it was terrible! For a long time after she would entreat us not to refer to that portion of her illness, when she had no control of her reason. She however fully recovered and was a healthy woman.

[Marriage to Addison Pratt, 3 April 1831]

I now return to the subject of my own marriage. I was a member of the Episcopal church. It was required that the "bands of matrimony" be published three sabbaths in succession in the church. There was a blunder made in the reading thereof much to the amusement of the mischievious young girls. Instead of reading Addison Pratt, Winchester, N.H., they left off the first name, connected the second with Win'r so the gentleman came out with a new name, by which he was arrested at the close of the services. It was however corrected the following Sunday. On the third day of April 1831 we were married.

The nuptial rites were celebrated at my father's house in presence of many of my relatives. The subject soon presented itself about moving away. The friends remonstrated, made us offers to induce us to remain. Mr. P.'s mind was fixed to go, and I did not feel at liberty to oppose it. He had travelled the world over, all places were alike to him, little did he realize how it would affect me to be among total strangers, not a single relative or acquaintance. The night previous to our departure I awoke at early dawn. I looked about the room, it seemed vacant, for my goods were all packed. I thought how lonely the family would feel when we were finally gone! I commenced weeping and continued till it seemed that my head was a fountain of waters! I went into my mother's room. She endeavored to console me.

She acknowledged that for two weeks the thoughts of my leaving had affected her health. But now she says, "Seeing it must be so, I give you up, trusting in the Lord to be your protector, also your husband, who I believe will be faithful to you." I thought how many times my mother had soothed me in trouble and soon I should be beyond the sound of her pleasant voice. "Sickness and sorrow may overtake me and there will be no loving sisters to come to my relief." My father entreated us to stay, poor old man, he feared he should never see me again. Oh, the ingratitude of children! Grieve the hearts of the parents, and plant thorns in their own pillows! My eldest sister Levina Baker came on horseback to bid us farewell. Many tears were shed, and promises were made to my mother that I should be permitted to return in two years. Dana Stevens and my brother Joseph Barnes went with us to St. Albans. We were kindly entertained by my good friends Maynard's and the following day launched forth on our journey.

CHAPTER THREE

The Years at Ripley, New York

Memoirs, April 1831 to June 1838

[Journey to Buffalo, New York]

We took passage on the Steamer *Phoenix*, across Lake Champlain. I had
never before been on a steamboat. The motion affected me some, but did
not prostrate me as it did the other lady passangers. I went into my berth,
and should have slept soundly had it not been for the wailings of the
women and children. From Plattsburg we embarked on a fine packet boat,
went down the northern canal to Troy. On board we found agreeable
company whose conversation diverted my mind, and at intervals I forgot
the sorrow I felt on leaving home. In Troy we found a family of Fields' I
had known in Winchester: this was an agreeable surprise. We pursued our
journey on the Erie Canal. Had pleasant company and landed safe in
Buffalo. We hired pleasant rooms, had them neatly furnished. While this
was being accomplished the time passed quite pleasantly. In a few days my
husband began to inquire for some lucrative business.

He engaged as mate on board a schooner, Capt. Scoville. The family
lived near and I was introduced to his wife. She was a kind lady and
showed me every attention. Our husbands sailed together; that formed a
bond of friendship between us. The city was delightful and together we
had many pleasant walks. But now commenced my loneliness. I would go
to a house of worship on the Sabbath, see all the style and fashions of the
day, gaze over the vast congregation, not a single familiar face! My husband at the same time I would think engaged in business as on any other
day laboring to waft the vessel that bore him away over the billowing waves
to its destined port. He would sometimes be absent two weeks occasionally
four, then came into harbor and spend a few days preparing for another
voyage, evenings take me to places of amusement, then a little ray of comfort would dawn on my heavy heart, and I could appear cheerful.

37

Mrs. Scoville and I knew the vessel on which our husbands sailed by the topsails and flying jib, as it was called. From my garret window with a spyglass we could discern it at an immense distance. For hours we would sit together at that window straining our eyes to catch the first glimpse of it, often being compelled to withdraw in disappointment. At other times it would heave insight three hours before it would come into port. We could then have time to make all the desired preparations. I had never before seen anything of a sailor's employment. I went on board the schooner to see what it was like. I became disgusted with it, could not consent that my husband should continue in that business for a livelihood. I now began to realize the effects our distinct habits of life would have upon us. I reflected on his limited experience in prosecuting business of a more domestic nature. These reflections made me very unhappy.

I had no one to converse with to give me encouragement. Mrs. Scoville was proud that her husband was capable of commanding and navigating a vessel. She would have me anticipate an honorable position for my companion, in a short future. I had no such ambition. She did not understand me. I was very homesick wished myself back with my dear ones at home! But as dark days are not all dark, so little blessings came to me one by one to keep my hopes alive. The family of whom we hired rooms had a lovely daughter, whose name was Thirza Harrison. She was my constant companion in the absence of my husband, when she could be spared from household duties and passed all her nights with me. She had a short time before this emigrated from England, left a lover behind, was often sad at the remembrance of one with whom she might have been happy could her parents have remained in their native country, or suffered her to choose her own destiny. In either case sorrow would have been the issue.

[Partnership with Horace Barnes]

I must record all the sunshine that dawned on me, amidst the clouds of gloom that obscured my sky. I had been in Buffalo but a few weeks, when from Chatauque Co., N.Y., I received a letter from my brother [Horace], whom I had not seen for eight years. That same brother of whom I have written, concerning his leaving home in Canada. He had heard of my residence in Buffalo and would soon be there to see me. This was joyful news indeed. The thoughts of meeting a beloved brother in a land of strangers, where not a soul lived I had ever known and loved, was almost joy unspeakable. A few days passed and behold he was in my presence. When the first excitement was over, so natural did he look and appear that I could not realize we had been separated so long. He remained one week with us; and the result was Mr. Pratt concluded to go home with him to that County and purchase land, then return and move me to the place. I was delighted with the idea.

My brother had resided there more than two years; had made many friends; they would be mine. I should have his society, could I be unhappy? Thus did I reason. Mr. Pratt with my brother made the purchase and returned. Now I must leave the Harrison family, my good Thirza, and Mrs. Scoville. But then I should rejoin my brother. Mr. Pratt would live ashore, and I should learn to know and love my brother's friends. I had a great desire to see the Niagara Falls: we were within eighteen miles. Steamers were running every day. We repaired to the landing (we had only that day to spare,) but behold, we were ten minutes too late! I never was more disappointed. From that circumstance I discovered what would be the bane of my life. My husband would always be behind time. The following day was appointed to embark for Chatauque. It happened as before, and we were too late. Mr. P. understood steamboat rules, I did not. A key was given me. I knew I must watch time for myself; and I was on the alert from that time onward.

The day was appointed for us to be in Chatauque to meet my brother. At early dawn I was on the mane. I had no intention of being left again. The wind was high and the boat loaded with lady passengers. I never witnessed a scene so distressing. Every lady was sick: several had young babes who were crying for attention, but were left in the berths unnoticed. The cabin maid had orders to admit no gentlemen into the ladies cabbin: it was impossible for her to wait on them all. The men without could hear groans of their wives and the cries of their infants, and could not render them any assistance. I had been previously instructed that on going on board I must take to my berth, and lie perfectly still in order to prevent being sick. Gladly would I have waited on the poor women, but I dared not stir. I now recollect my mistake, in recording the crossing Lake Champlain in the *Phoenix*. It only occupied a few moments. It was Lake Erie where the scene was so dreadful.

[Ripley, New York]

No poor creatures were ever gladder to see daylight appear! The steamer landed, and half dressed they crawled out on deck. Pale and immaciated we sought the fresh air. It had the effect to restore us, and we were soon able to go on shore. From Portland Harbor we took a coach to Westfield Village, a short distance. A private carriage awaited our arrival to take us to the town of Ripley. We allighted at the house of deacon Lomis, friends of my brother's, where we boarded till our own house was repaired. My brother was soon with us, and the two went to work on the farm they had bought in Co. At the expiration of five weeks I was moved into the house, found it a comfortable home. Now began my trials about housework. I had not for eight years done as much of that kind of labor as to wash and iron my own clothes.

This was in a country town where it was fashionable for good wives to do their own work, or at least, oversee it. My husband was conceited enough to immagine his knowlege superior to mine in reference to some particular branches of housekeeping, such as making soap and sausages. Some terrible blunders were made. I trusted to his judgement till I found by sad experience he knew less than I did. I then went to a good neighbor for advice. She counselled me to assume the responsibility in my own person, and not trust to my husband at all for, said she, "women should understand their own business." She offered me assistance in making light bread, and I soon became a model housekeeper. My labors multiplied. I found a farmer's wife had to work. It was great confinement. My brother's friends came to visit me, some of them were very agreeable and kind. Still their habits and manners differed from New England people.

My husband and brother assisted me in every way in their power. I took great pride in entertaining company, wanted everything done in the best style. Mr. Pratt had an hereditary propensity for hunting. The woods were full of wild game. This was very annoying to both my brother and myself. It was a practice I had abhorred, still I was fond of grey squirrels and wild fowls. I expostulated, reasoning on the value of time, but all to no effect. I saw clearly the effect the wild adventures of his youth had upon him. I was ambitious that my husband should obtain a good business character. I wished above all else that my brother should be satisfied with him in their partnership. We had lived on our farm about six months when our eldest daughter was born. This was a sore trial, that I had no mother or sister to come to me in my troubles. Dearer to me a thousand times than ever before, did my mother appear to be. I reflected with deep contrition on every instance wherein I had given her pain!

I now had new cares, and new pleasures. Notwithstanding all the tears I had shed during my pregnancy, my child was not inclined to cry often. She was considered by the neighbors a remarkable child. As my love for her increased, so did it grow stronger for my own dear mother. More than ever did I regret leaving her, knowing from this beginning how much I should need her sympathy in raising a family. I began to revolve in my mind the promise my husband had made my mother that in two years I should return, and visit her. When I mentioned the subject to him, he waved the conversation, as though he would prefer to talk of something else. My brother was a faithful friend, endeavored in various ways to lighten my burdens, and to make me contented. But there was a something underlying all my apparent comforts, my mind was ill at rest. Previous to my leaving home I had partially engaged my sister Lois to come to my place of residence, when I should write and inform her where I was located.

[Louisa's Sister Lois at Ripley, May 1832]

Accordingly I wrote a pressing invitation for her to come. Entreated my mother to give her consent. My brother also addressed her on the subject that if she would encourage our sister to come to us, we would do all in our power to make her stay agreeable, and help her to means when she wished to return. Our mother wrote an answer to our letter stating her objections. The distance was great, she was unaccustomed to travelling, she would have to go unattended, her children were being scattered. She says, "I must say with Jacob of old, Joseph is not, Simeon is not, and ye will take Benjamin away; all these things are against me!" She further remarked, "could I be assured she would go safely to your place, without accident, I could possibly consent. But should mischief befall her on the way, it would bring down my grey hairs with sorrow to the grave!"

After the perusal of this letter I felt that my hopes were blasted. I had wandered away from home, found my brother. I must not expect the family to follow me. I could not blame my poor mother. Father too and other relatives opposed. Time passed on, my babe was a solace and comfort, healthy and good natured. When I had no one in whose care I could leave her to go to a neighbors house, I would set her on the carpet, bid the dog lie down by her side, go on an errand, and perhaps be gone an hour, return and find her radiant with smiles, the dog still watching, both glad to see me. It happened one day in the month of May 1832 I was busy about my work my babe now four months old, was lying laughing in her cradle. We had named her Ellen Sophronia. I was at that moment pondering in my heart whether my hopes would ever revive about my sisters coming to be a light and a joy in my dwelling! I looked out at my door; and behold she came walking through the gate, as naturally as if she belonged there.

My joy was too great for utterance. I thought I was dreaming. She walked into the house, went to the cradle, and kissed the babe, before a word was spoken. I then exclaimed, "Lois, is it your own self?" Several times repeated with tears and sobs ere she answered, "yes, Louisa, it is myself, and I have come right from home." I asked, "are father and mother alive and well?" "They are, and all the rest of the family." I then ran up stairs where Mr. Pratt lay sick in bed, and announced the glad tidings! He rejoiced with me, and talked of the surprise it would be to our brother when he came in from his work, to find our sister had arrived. He came home at evening, and we spoke carelessly of a young lady who had arrived by stage and had called upon us. She walked into the room. We offered no introduction. He eyed her very closely, and exclaimed, "it is Lois!" He had not seen her for nine years.

The little girl he had left at home, had grown to womanhood, had travelled six hundred miles with no immediate escort, had found his residence, and no harm had befallen her! He seemed greatly to rejoice in behalf of our parents, who had tremblingly given their consent. I now felt blessed. I had a companion in the house, to go out and come in, to comfort and console me. One year passed away in comparative contentment and my sister appeared healthy and cheerful. She was a person of great piety, as free from guile as a mortal can be in this world of sin. She was small in stature, symetrical in proportions, brown hair and dark penetrating eyes. Her kindness and affability won the esteem of all who knew her. She loved Ellen, seemed always contented at home, never complained of loneliness. The two years (from my leaving home) had now rolled away, and I began to think of claiming the promise made my mother that I should return. Mr. Pratt did not incline to talk of it.

[Louisa's Visit to Home in Canada]

My sister was willing to stay and keep house for me, and after much consultation my husband acknowledged it his duty to assist me to means, and permit me to go. There were two ladies of my acquaintance in the place, going east to visit their friends, and I should have company a portion of the journey. After having taken an affectionate leave of my brother and sister and receiving their blessings (they both had firm trust in a divine providence) Mr. P. accompanied me to Portland Harbor. Saw me with the child safely on board the steamer, and we set sail for Buffalo. He appeared cheerful in parting with us, which was very gratifying to me. This time the weather was fine, there was very little sickness on board. Ellen was delighted with everything she saw, perfectly at home with strangers. We landed in Buffalo but my companions could not wait for me to search out my old friends. We took passage on board a canal boat, headed for Troy.

As soon as I could fully realize that I was on the way to my childhood's home where I should see my father, mother, three brothers, and three sisters, all my sadness fled. My heart was light, my spirits buoyant, and I looked forward with high hopes of happiness, with my kindred, and early companions of my youth. Strangers were polite and kind to me. My little girl attracted the notice of the passengers. She would sit for hours on deck with anyone who would take care of her, while I was employed in the cabbin. As we passed through the populous cities, the boat would halt, and passengers would walk out for pleasure. I was never detained on account of my child; some gentleman would invariably offer to carry her for me. In two weeks from the time I left home I was in White Hall.

On the route between the Junction and W.H. [White Hall], the canal had to undergo repairs. I hired a coachman to take me ten miles, to a village on the Hudson river. It was a most delightful town. I allighted at the house of a Quaker family, by the name of Williams. I found them the kindest most agreeable family I had ever met among strangers. They had two sons, and two daughters, all over twenty years, fine looking and well bred. It seemed like a paradise! Such neatness and order I never saw before. It was like a museum. Curiosities were desplayed in every portion of the dwelling. Their bedspreads astonished me. The mother took the child under her care and relieved me entirely. Had I been her own daughter she could not have been more interested and attentive. I remained with them two days.

When the boat came on its course, I went aboard and pursued my journey. In Whitehall I had a room at the hotel, in the third story of the building. I was not appraised of the precise time when the steamer would cross Lake Champlain, and being engaged with my child, I was a few moments too late. My disappointment was dreadful to be endured! I returned to the hotel, took my room and gave vent to my swollen heart in a torrent of tears!

My little girl seemed to understand that something wrong had taken place. She gazed upon me with imploring looks, as if she would ask in her silent way, "what is the matter?" She seemed unusually cautious about making me trouble. Twenty-four hours we kept our room, when the waiter true to his word, rang the bell in season for us to be ready. Only a few hours on board the *Phoenix*, and we were set on shore only twenty five miles from the home of my parents.

I took stage conveyance to St. Albans. Called at the publick house where my friends Maynards lived, when I left there; now occupied by another family whom I only knew by reputation. I soon made their acquaintance, learned the particulars of my cousin's death, and that her husband Mr. M. would be in from Dunham, the following day, when I should hear direct from home. Accordingly he came, brought his daughter, whom he consented to leave with her friends, and take me in his carriage to Dunham.

A short day's ride brought me to my father's door. It was ten o'clock in the evening. As we drove into the yard I saw through the window my mother sitting by the old fashioned fireside dressed for bed. My youngest sister hearing the carriage came to the door, listened a moment, went back and I heard her exclaim, "O, Louisa has come!" The house was all excitement: every live being was aroused. My father was awakened from his slumbers and told that his daughter had arrived from N. York. He replied with emphasis, "I don't believe a word of it!" He was convinced of the fact when the red headed girl was presented to him and introduced as his granddaughter. The child partook of the general joy, appeared as completely at home as though she had been there from her birth. Her grandpa immediately gave her a pet name, to which she readily learned to answer, appearing to appreciate the name of "Queen," which he was pleased to call her. The hours and days passed merrily, while receiving calls from surrounding friends.

The absent members of the family were soon apprised of my arrival and suddenly made their appearance. Any old associates lost no time in coming to welcome me, and warmly congratulated my parents on receiving me safely with an addition to the family. For several days the excitment continued, then we settled ourselves into more sober life. I would often walk over the old familiar grounds, see the footpaths I was accustomed to frequent in my childhood. A kind of enchantment came over me, I imagined myself in a fairy land. My mother would ask me at times, whether I realized all my expectations in coming home, and if indeed the pleasure equaled my anticipations. To which I always replied, "My most sanguine hopes are realized, mother. I am not in the smallest degree disappointed." "Oh," she says, "how thankful I am!" My child received so much attention, especially from her grandpapa, that she made rapid improvement. She amused him in his leisure hours, and he learned her to sing and dance. To visitors she was presented "the queen of N. York."

The summer passed pleasantly away. I had two sisters at home viz. Caroline, and Catharine. Two had married and located not far away. Two brothers married living near, [and] one, a young man at home. An own aunt and large family with whom I had been familiar from early childhood. I have frequently made the remark, that I believed I lived more real life during that period (four months), to which my visit was limited, than some persons of a less happy temperament do in a lifetime. As the time drew near for me to prepare for my return, I felt no reluctance. I thought of my pleasant home on the shores of Lake Erie, of my companion, brother, and sister; how anxiously they were awaiting the time. A sense of duty inspired me and gratitude to my kind Preserver, in whom I trusted to guard me safely back to gladden their hearts. The time was appointed for me to leave with my youngest brother who would accompany me to the steamboat landing. I went to take leave of my dear old aunt.

I bid the family one by one farewell; came to my aunt; she spoke in a most kindly tone, the wishes of her heart for me, commended me to the Giver of all good to guide me safely home. I kissed her and passed out into the street. I turned and looked towards the window, she was gazing after me with the saddest countenance I had ever seen her wear. It was an unearthly look. I knew she was thinking she would never see me again! My heart swelled within me, and tears bust from my eyes. In this condition I reached my mother's. She asked me why I wept so much. She said, "are you not willing to leave us and go to your home?" I answered yes, mother, but I grieve because something tells me I have seen my aunt Baker for the last time." She tried to console me as she wont to do in all my troubles. It was evening, and I had a few miles to go, to meet some friends who were to be my company on the steamer. My father objected to my starting in the evening, said it was not right. I tried to comfort him and explained the necessity. After a score of ceremonies we started, had scarcely drove out of sight when it commenced raining.

I was not prepared against the rain, so my brother drove back, to wait a little, and start again better protected. In order to excite a little mirth, I told them I had come back to finish my supper. At this we all laughed heartily. The clouds of gloom, and the rain cleared away, and we started the second time in good spirits. We reached the publick house in due time, and met the friends we expected. Early on the morrow we went to the landing. I bid my brother farewell; again went on board the *Phoenix*, to cross beautiful Lake Champlain. Now my steps were bending towards home. I resolved to be cheerful, for I felt I had been truly blessed. From Plattsburgh I took passage on a canal boat for Troy. As I went on board, I was agreeably surprised to find some of the same passengers who came out with me from Buffalo, on their return, as I was. We congratulated each other, and expressed ourselves highly gratified.

We glided pleasantly along. I felt disappointed in not being able to call on my new friends the Quaker family. This I could not do without being separated from my acquaintance on the boat. In a few days we went on shore in Buffalo. Sentiments of friendship were exchanged with my traveling companions. We had had a long journey together. We had walked about the cities of Atica and Rochester, had contemplated the wonders at Lockport; climbed up the five flights of stairs, and admired the works of art, while I exclaimed, "what is there, that the hands of men cannot do?" We parted; and I went on board the steamer bound for Portland harbor. I was now nearing home and as I tried to make Ellen understand who we were to meet, she would seem wild with joy and try to lisp the names. On a Saturday evening in Sept 1833, I was in Westfield Village, six miles from home. Sabbath morning I went in a coach to Ripley, called at a friends house by the name of Loomis. Here I met the good Mr. Harris, minister of the town. He saluted us with great cordiality, and admired the improvement the child had made.

[Return to Ripley]

I walked to the house of worship, in the porch met my brother, who expressed great pleasure on receiving us back again, free from all harm. We talked of Mr. Pratt's absence, (which I heard on entering the town) how he had been persuaded to accept a captain's berth on board a vessel, plying from Portland to Erie. I felt a cloud come over my spirits, but my brother assured me he would return when he heard of our arrival. His trips were never more than a week, the business commanded high wages, and vessels would soon be laid up for winter. I tried to feel cheerful, went home and saluted my sister. Ellen Sophronia appeared to know her aunt and everything about the house. She rushed through the rooms frantic with delight! She was most forward in talking, being now one year and eight months old. She made the most extreme efforts to tell her aunt where she had been, whom she had seen and the name Grandpapa had given her, she could speak plainly.

As the sun was setting that evening there was a wreck discovered. A vessel lying on her side. It was plainly seen from our door. There was great excitement in the neighborhood! I knew not but it might be the schooner my husband had under command. I trembled with fear! My brother with other men went out in a skiff to the wreck. Found men watching there, who informed them there was a woman in the cabbin, whom they expected was drowned as the vessel was half under water. I was relieved to learn it was not Mr. Pratt's vessel, but the fate of the poor female occupied our minds. The following day, the fifth after the wreck, the schooner was righted up, and behold the woman came floating out from the cabbin alive! Great was the consternation of the men! Her nephew the capt. of the craft caught her in his arms and fainted!

Her body was completely water soaked, but she had managed to keep her head above water. She told how miraculously she had been pre-served. There were crumbs of crackers, and tea, from the broken boxes floating about on the water; which she was enabled to grasp at intervals, and thus was she kept from starvation. Great was her faith in God! She did not fear to die, and was not in dispair in her perilous condition! Her husband received her as one from the dead. She lived two years, but was never strong as before.

Mr. P. having received information of our return, came home to visit us, spent a few days, but had engaged to run the vessel while the autumn weather continued favorable. My home now seemed more attrac-tive than it ever had before. Everything appeared new; my homesickness was gone. The singing of the birds sounded sweeter in my ears. The flow-ers were more lovely, the trees looked a brighter green, all because the sunshine of contentment had found its way to my heart. Oh, thought I, what a difference between happiness and misery!

Mr. Pratt expressed himself more than compensated for permitting us to leave him so long in witnessing the happy effect it had wrought upon me. My spirits were buoyant all the day long. It so happened when the letter was sent announcing my arrival home, Mr. Pratt with his vessel was anchored in Portland Harbor, six miles distant. It was evening. There was no conveyance at hand. He resolved to walk the long dreary road in the dark and set his eyes upon us before he slept. It was midnight, all were wrapt in profound slumber. A loud knock at the door awakened us; we quickly understood who was to be our guest, though we had not expected him for several days. The little girl in an instant recognized her father, partook of all the joy and excitement, and for several hours showed no signs of wanting sleep.

A few days passed and he was gone, he left us feeling hopeful for we knew the season for sailing would soon be over. My sister Lois at this time appeared healthy and strong. We had great delight in rehearsing over what each had experienced during the time of our separation.

We had pleasant friends, with whom we exchanged many agreeable visits. Lois was a favorite with all who knew her. Time passed swiftly till Mr. P. left his vessel in winter quarters, and come home. My brother taught school through the winter. My sister and I were expert needle women, we did our own work and some for others, but we always found time to read. We made it our business to read all the popular works in that portion of the country, such as history, moral, and religious books. We had no time to devote to novels.

[Lois's Illness]

Some time in the course of winter Lois began to show signs of ill health. It happened one day when Mr. P. and myself had been to a neighboring village and returned; my sister having prepared the evening repast. As we were about to take our seats at the table she withdrew to her room, and laid down upon her bed. It was such an unusual occurrence, we were all greatly surprised.

An elderly gentleman who was stopping with us and disposed to believe she had injured herself by lifting a heavy stick of wood. She affirmed it was not so; for though she brought in a large stick, it did not affect her in the least. She complained of no pain, but only a weakness. She continued in this state a few days, refusing to take medicine, or have a physician called. Her brother remonstrated, went and procured some strengthening bitters; which appeared to help her. She went from home a few weeks in which time I heard no complaint. In the spring she engaged to teach the District School. In the early part of Apr[il] she commenced, the weather was quite impossible. I felt troubled, and feared it might injure her. She seemed in a hurry, which was not her natural turn. Only one week passed and she came home with a terrible cough! She called it a cold, but to me there was an ominous sound in it. I sweat her with hemlock boughs and she so far recovered that she continued her school for four months. When she come home for a permanent stay, I discovered some hidden malady preying upon her system.

She had the greatest aversion to medical treatment! I must stand over her with earnest pleadings, with reasoning and entreaties, ere I could prevail on her to take anything prescribed by a physician. She had no faith in Allopathy; but simple remedies which she felt that nature demanded, she was willing to use.

In Nov. 1836, my second child was born. The winter following was a period of trial and anxious care to me. My burdens were increased, my sister not able to assist me. My heart was pained when I looked upon her wasted form; saw the color fading from her once blooming and rosy cheeks; saw dimness and languor in her eyes, which a few months before had sparkled with intelligence and animation. I dared not utter in her hearing what I feared! With an aching heart I wrote to our parents.

My husband was gone from home when my second daughter was born, did not return for two weeks. This, with the feeble state of health into which Lois had fallen, made me more than unreconciled. But our good brother, ever faithful to his trust, did all in his power to aid and comfort us. We had kind neighbors, and a kinder Providence, in which we trusted to order all the events of our mortal lives. Mr. P. soon returned to spend the winter with us which would have passed in comfort and contentment, but for the progress of that insidious disease, at times so deceiving but sure to hold the victim it has marked for its prey, mocking all efforts to arrest, or combat, and amidst the tears and prayers of beseeching friends, he lays a human form on his altar.

Towards last end of winter, I heard of "Latter Day Saints," in an adjoining town, who believed in healing the sick by faith, according to the ancient custom. In the honesty of my heart I went alone in my carriage, six miles, to search out the wonderful men, and entreat them to come to my house, that if possible my sister might be healed.

On my way I called on some good Presbyterians, told them my business. They commenced railing against these men, called them imposters, deceivers, and everything but good. I was pursuaded to relinquish my design and turn back without seeing them, to judge for myself. I never once reflected that there was no confidence to be placed in the opinion of unbelievers. Had I been wise I should not have stopt on the way and made my errand known. I returned to my home and informed my sister what the people said. She seemed disappointed. The strange men left the place, and we heard no more of them while she lived.

Early in the spring we took her to Westfield village, and placed her under treatment of a German Doctor. We had friends living there who were greatly interested in her recovery. Most deeply did they sympathize, and show every kindness in their power.

Likewise the Loomis family, who had discouraged me from applying to the men of God, to administer to the poor girl, in his name, were kind and solicitous for her comfort. Though intolerant in reference to doctrinal creeds, they were humane and benevolent.

Word at length came to us from our Smith friends where she was staying that she was failing. The sound fell on my ears like the tolling of a bell, to announce the exit of some poor mortal from the stage of life! Mr. P. and I started immediately with our two children to the scene of our anxious dread, to see if possible to have her brought home. During the ride I was wrapt in profound meditation. I revolved in my mind the circumstances that had induced my mother to grant unwilling permission for Lois to come to me; to comfort me, because I was lonely and discontented. Could I now send the sad intelligence of her true condition and paint the threatening clouds that were brooding over our atmosphere? To me it seemed a Herculean task!

I had not seen my sister for several weeks. As we drove up to the house she come out to meet us. I saw in a moment how much she had changed! There was a glare in her eyes, a hectic flush on her cheeks, a paleness on her skin which told how great ravages her disease had made! I took [her] by the hand [and] asked, "how do you feel Lois?" She replied, "I am no better. Louisa, will you write to father and mother, and have the letter mailed today?" I addressed a letter to my eldest sister, entreated her to come to our assistance. I knew she had means plenty, was brave and courageous. In a pathetic manner I described the alarming condition of our sister, and the uncertainty of her ever seeing her again if she did not come quickly. When I had finished, I read it to the dear girl, and we both wept sorely, knowing the sensations it would inspire when it should be read by the family at home.

That same evening we called in a new Physician. He blamed us for not applying to him at an early period of her disease. Said he, "three months ago I might have arrested the complaint, but now it is too late!" Although I did not believe him it grieved me severely! After all the sorrow I had felt, to be chastised for negligence was awful! The friends sympathized with us, and we adjudged the doctor as one speaking "unadvisedly with his lips." That night I laid on the bed with the sick girl, but there was no sleep for me. Her short breathing was so painful to hear! I asked her if she was pressed for breath. She replied "O, no, I breathe quite easily." I saw she was not conscious of her low condition.

I arose from the bed and went into the room where Mrs. Loomis slept. My bursting heart could not longer be controlled. She saw what was before me and pitied me. From her eyes tears fell fast, and I wept till it seemed that my head was a fountain of waters! Early the next morning we started for home, the weather not being favorable to remove the sick one, and the carriage not covered. I informed my brother of all that had transpired, and he set out immediately on foot; reached the place in the evening. He lingered long before he would enter the room, dreading to witness the change she had undergone! Which however could not have been so great to him as it was to me. He had been once to visit her, in the four weeks, she had been away. He hired an easy carriage to convey her home, and Miss Smith, her kind friend, was engaged to accompany them, and support the poor invalid in her arms.

The morning previous to their arrival I spent in the deepest agony! I expected them at an early hour and when the time had passed, all my fears were aroused, that perhaps she was not able to be moved. I watched the road, to catch the first glimpse of the coach. I prayed to the Lord, that I might never be under the painful necessity of writing to my mother that Lois had died away from my home. I even covenanted that if she might be permitted to return, I would endeavor by divine aid to be resigned to His will, if it were to remove her forever from my sight. I waited in excruciating suspense, a few moments, when lo, the carriage drove in sight. I shouted for joy and thanked the Lord. She was brought into the house very much exhausted. The windows and doors were widely opened, to fill the room with air. After a season of rest, she appeared comfortable. There was now another trial at hand for me. My husband had engaged to take charge of a vessel on Lake Erie, during the approaching summer.

The time had now arrived for him to leave home. What was to be done? Was there no alternative? He regretted his necessity to go from home; but he "owed money," could only raise it in that way. He took an affectionate leave of our sister, never expecting to see her more! I walked with him a short distance. We talked of the coming event. He counselled me to be prepared for the worst, to strengthen my heart by trusting in God, for said he, "it will be an ordeal you have never passed through, never having witnessed the decease of a near relative." I felt that in all my married life, I had not needed him to comfort me as I did then. I now had only my brother to whom I could turn for consolation. He was faithful and prayerful. Our sister was able every day to be up and dressed. When her friends called to see her, she would ask me if I could not "give her something to make her feel bright?" Oh, how I wished for power to revive her drooping spirits!

We sent to Fredonia for the renowned "Dr. White." He came fifteen miles to see her. He contradicted the statement of the boasting Physician. Said the consumption had been seated more than six months; that it was better she had not been aggravated with strong medicine; which could not have effected a cure. It was a great relief to me. He prescribed some harmless remedials for her cough, charged but little for coming, and I marked him an honest man. Some days she would so far revive, she would even talk of going home, remarking that it would only take nine days to go, "I am sure I can live nine days." I reminded her of her low state, and once I asked how she felt in regard to the change which we feared might take place. She replied "I think I am willing to go, but my mind is inactive. I cannot feel bright." Again she says, "I have not many ties to earth. Why should I cling to it?" I had a secret dread of speaking to her on the subject, which afterwards I regretted most sorely.

[Death of Lois, 12 April 1834]

As long as she was able to walk upstairs, she attended her secret devotions. Sometimes she would remain so long in the cold, it would give me great uneasiness. Ellen, the little girl, loved her very much. She would hang about the bed with the greatest expressions of sympathy, and when her aunt told her she was too weak to lift her, she would seem filled with pity and grief. Three days before her death she drew her chair up to the cradle, where my babe (four months old), was lying, took her in her arms, as natural as ever. I was astonished, for I had supposed her strength was nearly gone. Sabbath day the 12th Apr., many friends called to see her. She at length became weary, asked to let the people go, that she might rest. She says, "If I could rest, I should soon be better." I asked, "When Lois, will you be better?" She says "tonight." That night all but the watchers laid down, to have the place quiet. She changed suddenly. They called me to come quickly. I saw she was going, ran to the stairs to call my brother, but before he could reach the spot, she was gone!

The 11th April was her birthday, the 12th she died. 1834, 14th was the day of her burial. The cold was very severe. The wind blew almost a hurricane. It seemed to me the heavens and earth would come in contact with each other. Oh, how it heightened the gloom, and the solemnity of the occasion. Friends were kind and could drop tears of sympathy, but my brother and I were the only heart mourners. And when we thought of our numerous relatives afar off, not knowing that day the sorrowful scene we were passing through, the loneliness we felt is indescribable. When Ellen saw the coffin lowered in the narrow house, she appeared terribly excited. She was forced from the brink shrieking and crying to see her "poor aunt Lois." The good preacher endeavored to console us, choosing for his text these words, "Though I walk through the valley and shadow of death, I will fear no evil, for thou art with me, thy rod and thy staff they comfort me."

Many precious promises did he read from the holy book, and dwelt largely on the early piety and amiable qualities of the one we mourned, entreating us not to mourn as those without hope. We went to our desolate home. Ellen cried the whole night through. I called up the hired boy and girl, the latter read in the Bible; the boy rocked the child and tried to soothe her. She seemed to realize the some great misfortune had come to pass, and felt the influence of the spirit that oppressed us all. Oh, what is not human nature made to endure? So liable to pain and yet so exposed to it. Why could not our hearts been made of stone or steel? That the barbed arrows of this cruel world might not penetrate them to their inmost recesses! Well has the poet said, "The heart has many passages." But the middle aisle is sacred to home scenes and paternal intercommunion; the cord by which nature binds her children, our relentless foe can sever.

The week succeeding the solemn event was to me one of unrest, and deep sorrow, more than any other week of my whole life up to that time. Cold and stormy, no one came to comfort us but the good Mr. Harris, our preacher. He came and spent the night, said many things with a view to console us. I could not reason, the great loss was on my heart. She was too good to be taken in the bloom of her life when she might have been such a comfort to her friends. I thought of the pains which had been taken in her training and education. She was so amiable, so industrious, so devoted to truth, so cheerful, so free from guile. How could we have her hidden forever from our sight. The words of the Psalmist were continually on my tongue. "I am like an owl of the desert, or like a pelican of the wilderness, I watch and am as a sparrow alone upon the house top. I have eaten ashes for bread, and mingled my drink with weeping." Thus did I chatter while my parents were afar off, and my husband tossing to and fro on the billows of Lake Erie. There was, for some mysterious cause, silence between my brother and I in regard to the solemn event. We would sit a whole evening together and her name would not be spoken. Anguish had made us dumb. But Oh, there must be a letter written. That was my task, though my brother would help. Never in all the years I had lived, and never since that period had I such unwelcome labor to perform. I prayed for grace to assist me, and while scalding tears were in my eyes I begged my mother to forgive me for ever urging the departed one to leave her and come to me. My brother wrote the particulars of her burial and joined with me in asking pardon for our solicitations in tempting her from under their paternal care. Hopeful did we wait for an answer to arrive. At length, it came in our dear mother's handwriting. Full of grace and humility, calm resignation to the will of God, a free pardon for all we had said and done, balm for our wounds.

My youngest sister, Catharine by name, was then in a decline. She had cherished sanguine hopes that Lois would recover and return home. On hearing the sorrowful news, she writes to me these words. "No pen can paint the feelings of my heart, when I heard the death of Lois." She was a sweet writer, and notwithstanding the depth of her own grief, she could pour forth streams of consoling expressions to soothe my wounded spirit. She lived but two years after, and the same disease wrought upon her delicate form and her angelic spirit went to join her sister in the "Summer land." She was engaged to be married to a worthy young man, but earthly ties were all in vain.

Mr. P. made a short stay, was obliged to return to his business. While he remained, we conversed very little of anything but the sorrowful bereavement. When again left to pass my nights with only my two children in my room, I gave way to the severest melancholy. The Darkness of night was terrible. I thought a thousand worlds would not be too great a price, for perpetual sunshine. There were times when I could not pray. The heavens seemed brass over my head, and the earth underneath me like iron. This state of mind alarmed me. I, who claimed to be a follower of Him "who was a man of sorrows, acquainted with grief, and a mourner all his days." Why should I think it so strange that I was called to mourn. I doubted the strength of my faith, and feared for my soul's salvation. I wrote to my husband's father and mother in N. Hampshire, told them of my sufferings, entreated them to visit us. They replied in a most sympathizing tone, said they would come.

[Visit of Addison's Parents, Fall 1834]

Accordingly the September following, Father and Mother Pratt with their youngest son Horatio, a boy fourteen, came by stagecoach, spent several weeks with us. It was a great comfort to me to have their society in my loneliness. Mr. P. also left his vessel in care of another and came home to see his parents, did not return again during the autumn season. I told them of all the sorrows that had fallen to my lot. They were full of condolence and comforting words.

During their stay there was a protracted meeting which interfered with our enjoyment as Father Pratt did not approve the leading preacher's sentiments. He was a fiery zealot, intolerant to the highest degree, doomed all to everlasting perdition who did not subscribe to his creed. We all belonged to that Church and felt it our duty to attend the meetings. My second daughter was then eight months old. Mother Pratt became extremely attached to her. It was hard for her to leave us. We accompanied them twenty miles on their way home, bid them farewell, and I never saw them more!

Father Pratt soon after went to the state of Georgia, for the purpose of selling a large organ which he had constructed. His daughter Rebekah had gone there before to teach music in a seminary. While there he witnessed her marriage to a rich planter, by the name of Col. Bozeman. Great demonstrations were made. It was pronounced a happy union of hearts and hands. One year passed away. On the anniversary she was borne to her grave, leaving a most disconsolate husband, and an infant son two months old. Thus are the brightest hopes blasted. Thus ended the earthly career of my friend and schoolmate. Father P. returned to his home in N.H. with a fever, of which he never recovered.

[The Partnership Broken Up]

The ensuing winter my brother began to be discontented, became gloomy and showed signs of having been disappointed in love. He began to talk of having the property divided, the co-partnership dissolved. This was a new trouble to me. I feared he was laboring under some secret grief. He was nearing forty years, had never married. He felt his life a lonely one. He proposed division of the property; it was after some alter-cation, amicably settled; a division made, satisfactory to both parties. This event occured in the summer of 35.

[Enter the Mormons: Jonathan and Caroline Crosby]

The succeeding winter my sister Caroline came from Mass. whom I had not seen for four years. Her husband J. Crosby I had known during my residence in that state; many years had intervened when he knocked at my door, and inquired if himself and wife could lodge under our roof that night. He was answered in the affirmative, and told to come in. I had no recognition of him, but when he presented his wife, behold it was my sister. Great was our surprise and joy! We soon found they had a new religion. They had embraced the faith of the Latter Day Saints, and were on their way to Kirtland, O[hio].[1]

[The Latter-day Saints]

They tarried with us a month, gave us a Book of Mormon, and taught us concerning the great and marvelous work which had been brought to pass in this our day, by a revelation from heaven! They told us how an angel had appeared to a young man by the name of Joseph Smith in the State of N. York. All this was new and astonishing! We had heard a few items by letter, but nothing at all convincing to the understanding. My first impression was, "it is too good news to be true." We now had great subjects for conversation. The decease of our dear sister Lois, who had been more than a year gone, was brought fresh to our minds; and we min-gled our tears, and wept together. But the knowledge they had obtained concerning a future life, and the resurrection of the just was a comfort to me, although not full pursuaded of its entire truth. My husband seemed

decidedly opposed to their doctrines, though kind towards them as relatives. I could discern at once that the principles were not controvertible
from scripture.

I felt disposed to treat the subject with respect, reasoning that sensible people as I knew they were, having a perfect knowledge of the scriptures, would not be easily deceived. They pursued their journey to
Kirtland, and left us to consider the things they had told us, and ponder
them in our hearts. I would sometimes look in the "Book of Mormon,"
but could not find time to read it through, so immersed was I in worldly
cares. There were cows, calves, wool spinning to oversee and greater than
all, three children. The youngest named for my dear sister Lois Barnes
was born March 6th 1837. Oh, what a busy life was mine. With my daily
duties I found but little time to read, but I could think severely. I at length
wrote a letter to brother and sister Crosby, upbraiding them for not striv-
ing more throughly to exemplify the doctrines they had advanced.
Having boldly testified to their positive knowledge of the great things
they had told us, they should continue their labors until we were converted. This I wrote by the way of reproof for their neglect in writing, not
considering what the result might be.[2]

My neighbors often railed me about my Mormon relation. I would
on such occasions take up the scriptures and prove that it was no other
than the apostolic doctrine revived. Baptism for the remission of sins, laying on of hands for the gift of the Holy Ghost, healing the sick by faith,
casting out devils, speaking in tongues and prophesying. No one could
gainsay it, but still were inclined to . . . rail and ridicule. In the fall of 34
the Presbyterians held a protracted meeting, continuing the excitement
fourteen days. I attended regularly. The burden of the prayers were, "O
Lord, reveal the abundance of thy peace and truth." In the midst of the
enthusiasm, my brother-in-law arrived from Kirtland. We were sorry to
see him at that time as we were all on Mount Pisgah's top, and did not
wish to be interrupted while our wings were spread ready to soar away to
the celestial world, we knew not where!

Such was our enthusiasm, we had well nigh forgotten what we had
been taught about a new "dispensation of the fullness of times." In which
the Lord had set his hand to gather all things in one, even scattered Israel
from the four corners of the earth. We entreated him to say nothing of
his strange doctrines till our meeting was adjourned. Accordingly he went
with us several days to the house of worship, appeared a patient listener.
When it was adjourned sie ni die [sine die] the discussions commenced.
Our preacher was sent for and long debates ensued. We saw clearly that
he did not preach the fullness of the gospel. Where were the gifts and
blessings that were in the primitive church? Thus we reasoned, and he
could not answer us. He appeared very sad on account of the change that

was being wrought in us, or rather in myself, for Mr. P. all the while felt a spirit of opposition. My brother said very little, but seemed willing to investigate.

[The Pratts Join the Latter-day Saints, June 1838]

I commenced reading the Bible, by day and by night. I found the prophecies foretold that such a work would be brought to pass in the latter days. Our brother-in-law [Jonathan] went home [to Kirtland]. Himself and wife were expecting to start with a great camp for Jackson County, Missouri. My brother and I wished to go and see our sister [Caroline] before she left. Accordingly we went [to Kirtland] with our own carriage, left Mr. P. to keep the house, and take care of the children. We had a great visit, heard the testimonies of different persons who were renouned for truth and sobriety, who proclaimed to us in the name of the Lord, that an angel had revealed from the heavens the wonderful things which had been told us.[3] My companion in our absence had formed a resolution that if we found things even as they had been represented he would contend no more. We returned, told all we had seen and heard. Mr. P. then resolved to go and see for himself. He went, returned, and lo, had been baptized! [On 18 June 1838.]

It was then understood that our brother-in-law and sister should come to Ripley a distance of 100 miles and wait for us to prepare to accompany them to the "promised land." In a short time they were with us. My brother and I were baptized in the waters of Lake Erie, in the month of June 1838. It was then decided that brother Crosby and Horace Barnes, my brother, should take a journey on foot, to Mass. our native state, and to Canada East, where our parents lived, and preach the gospel to our kindred. They did go, and made known the strange things which had come to pass. My mother and youngest sister believed, but so great was the opposition, they were not baptized. I wrote letters to my kindred, and testified how the Lord had made known to me by the revelation of his spirit, that He was about to establish his great and last kingdom on the earth, never to be thrown down. I had called on Him in mighty prayer, and the light had burst forth upon my soul, like the sun bursting suddenly forth from behind a dark cloud!

CHAPTER FOUR

From Ripley, New York, to Nauvoo, Illinois

Memoirs, October 1838 to Fall 1841

[Selling Out at Ripley, October 1838]

From that time I had never a doubt. My soul was full of peace and joy. My brother made an agreement with our parents, a sister and brother, that when he had disposed of his property in Chatauque Co. N.Y. he would return to Canada, sell the Homestead, and assist in moving them with us to the centre stake of Zion in Jackson Co., Missouri. Thither did our warmest aspirations tend. The brethren returned; sold the farm and stock, and made preparations to start on the long journey, a thousand miles to travel in cold winter weather. My brother with his horse and carriage set out for Canada. The rest of us took up our journey for the "Far West". We parted with the full expectation that when we met again our father and mother, youngest brother and sister would all be with us. On the 25th of Nov. 1838, we bid farewell to our friends in Ripley.[1] Some were very kind, others were cool and reserved, greatly inclined to censure us, because we had embraced a new faith.

I can never forget the reflections which revolved in my mind as I passed through the town, and cast a lingering look towards the old house of worship, and the burial grounds where the remains of my dear sister lay interred. There were the little white stones I had caused to be placed to her memory, with this inscription: "Farewell dear sister, my sad heart still bleeds with anguish for thy loss, yet gladdens with the blessed hope of meeting thee again at the great resurrection morn."[2] I strained my eyes to catch the last glimpse, thinking of the great uncertainty that I should ever behold it again. To me, it seemed cruel to go and leave her grave alone. Not a relative to draw nigh and drop a tear on the sods that covered her. The weather was intensely cold. Although we were clothed in the best

57

possible manner to guard against the cold, we felt it most severely. Sometimes when we called to warm ourselves at a hotel, a second daughter [Frances] would be so benumbed with cold as to be almost speechless.[3]

[Pleasant Garden, Indiana, January 1839 to Fall 1841]

For five hundred miles mud was not seen on our wagon wheels, then came a January thaw. The most intolerable travelling that can be immagined. At this time we were detained in Indiana, Pleasant Garden. There we found a Mormon family. We felt quite at home with them. While waiting for the roads to become passable, intelligence came to us that we could not be permitted to enter the State of Missouri. The Saints were driven out enmass, by a ruthless mob; the State authorities taking no notice of it. Counsel was sent to all such as were en route for that state, to stop on their way, and seek an assylam; till such times as the church would, by the mercy of God, again be established. This was a terrible disappointment! I felt as I suppose our first parents did, when driven from Paradise. My anticipations had been raised to the highest strain, in view of going to the gathering place of the Saints; a spot of earth designated by the Lord.

There was now no alternative, we must be reconciled. We conversed about what the ancient saints were called to suffer, and the quiry arose, "why should we think to escape persecution, who have dared to believe the same gospel? even in prophets and apostles."

Mr. Pratt seemed much discouraged when he heard the Prophet was imprisoned. He soon decided to go to Vincennes, Ind. and purchase land; which he did, 260 acres at government price. Then indeed we were no better off for a home. It was covered with heavy timber; immense rock maple trees. He then concluded to purchase a hundred acres more with a small improvement, several log buildings. We moved on to it right in the thick woods. West of us lived a family of Kentuckians, a half mile away; east was a neighbor a mile and a half distant. This was a lonely situation. The national road ran twenty rods from the house. In the rainy seasons [the road] was almost impassable.

The village of Pleasant Garden was four miles distant, where my sister and family were located. Mr. Crosby was a cabinet maker; went into business with reasonable success.[4] The citizens seemed pleased with us, but apparently were afraid of our religion.

The church by this time had purchased a town on the Miss. called Commerce. They changed the name to Nauvoo. The Elders soon commenced to travel abroad to preach the gospel. Called on us in Indiana, urged us to go up to the church, which I greatly desired to do, but Mr. P. was much attached to the farm; often remarked that he would ask no better fortune than to finish his days there, were it not for the religion he had embraced. It was a situation wholly uncongenial to me. I had little or no society. I had sacrificed a pleasant home and agreeable companions, for the sake of going to live with the saints. I had been stopt on the way, and here I was alone in the woods. I often retired to the thick shades to weep, and brood over my sorrows. The winters were long and severe; we had unfinished rooms and smoky chimneys. The third winter our children were sick with conjestive fever.

The sickness of our children was a severe affliction for me, situated as I was so far from my sister and from neighbors. Our oldest daughter was very low, requiring attention through the night. Such was the intensity of the cold that ten minutes was as long as I could stand by her bed at one time without being in danger of freezing. I made it a subject of devout prayer that the severity of the atmosphere might be modified. When at last the blessing came, and the mild breezes began to blow, I walked abroad with a more thankful heart than had ever throbbed in my bosom before. So raging was the child's fever she did not feel the cold at all. Six weeks at one time passed and I saw not the face of a female friend. I afterwards told my neighbors I would witness against them in the judgement day for neglecting me in my afflictions. They acknowledged the justice of my complaints. Afterwards were very attentive.

For eighteen days the child's fever never abated. I called to mind my sorrows in the state of N. York, when my poor sister wasted away before my eyes, and how I prayed (O, how fervently,) that such an affliction might never again fall to my lot. I came now to claim the answer to my prayer, and entreated the Lord to spare my daughter's life! I laid hold on faith, and soon had cause to rejoice and praise God that my children were all in a state of convalesence, and soon recovered. In the spring of 1840 my fourth daughter was born, previous to the rage of the conjestive fever which carried away hundreds from the shores of time. About this time a Mormon Elder came that way, called on my brother-in-law to get his carriage wheel repaired. Mr. C. invited him to stop and preach. The people assembled, and a deep interest was manifested. The second or third day when he would have pursued his journey, going to the shop for his wagon wheel, behold it had been taken away, whither he knew not. This put an end to his going on his journey, so he continued preaching, till a great excitement was created.

The region of country came out to hear the new preacher, whose name was Almon Babbit. He was reputed a profound reasoner; and judging from the attention paid to his preaching, we were hoping half the population would be baptized. Six persons only had applied, a small branch organized, when Elder B. expressed his intention to pursue his journey. We expostulated, reasoning from appearances that many more would be added to the church. He replied "no, there will be no more additions at this time." He further added, "I inquired of the Lord concerning my labors here, and he showed me in a dream, six persons who would embrace the gospel." He left us and went on his way, and after a few months two more were added. They were baptized by Orson Hyde in the adjoining county. Meetings were held regularly in Pleasant Garden, and sometimes at our residence on "Croys Creek," as the place was called. We felt joyful in meeting together, a little band, twelve in number. We were strong in the Lord, and testified boldly to our friendly neighbors, that the priesthood and gifts of the gospel were again restored to men on earth.

We had great pleasure in entertaining the travelling elders. Lonely as our condition was we felt it a high privilege to have the servants of God coming right from the body of the Church, call upon us, sing psalms, and pray, tell us of the faith and zeal among the saints, filling our hearts with praise and thanksgiving. I began to be very desirous to go to the church. Mr. Pratt, hoping to make me more contented to remain there until he could sell our farm for its full value, sold a piece of land and bought a house and lot in Pleasant Garden, that I might live near my sister. Also a carriage, having a gentle animal I could drive myself. I could drive to the farm when Mr. P. was there at his work, at the close of the week give him a ride home. Those who did not know the inward workings of my mind, complimented my pleasant surroundings.

[On to Nauvoo, Fall 1841]

In vain did I strive to be contented. My heart was set on going to the church. I prayed earnestly that the Lord would open the way. After much deliberation Mr. P. concluded to rent the farm, and also the village property and take up the line of march for Nauvoo. Long and severe was the struggle. We had two teams and young cattle to drive, there was no company going, no one to help. The time appointed to start arrived, still no one engaged to assist. I prayed with all the fervor of my soul. Just as I was about to give up in dispair Elder Gurley rode up to the door on horseback, returning from a mission east, bound for Nauvoo. The first words I said to him were, "Brother Gurley, we are all ready to start for Illinois, but there is no one found to go with us. Will you wait, and help us on the journey?" "Yes," he replied, "I am the very man to assist you, cheer up your hearts, all is right, I have come in good time." I felt that a load of a thousand pounds was removed from my shoulders, and as much more from my heart.

I soon found brother G. knew what it was to move. He commenced at once to pack the goods, a business he seemed perfectly familiar with.

We had a gentle animal (which I could drive myself,) and a Barouche [a four-wheeled carriage], with two spring seats convenient for myself and my four children. Mr. Pratt had a yoke of Durham cattle, equal to two yoke of common oxen, which he drove, and carried an immense load of goods. Elder Gurley drove the cows and young stock. I never felt in finer spirits, although I left my sister behind, for I knew she would soon join us. We had a prosperous journey of 270 miles. Many pleasant calls I had on the way. Being able to drive much faster than the ox team could travel, I could gain time to make calls, which I did, at the most respectable look- ing places, where we were often treated with the greatest hospitality, fruit generously given us to take on our way.

There was a circumstance transpired while I lived in Pleasant Garden, Ind., which I had forgotten to mention among the reminiscenses of that place. I will now refer to it. One beautiful summer morning, the sun was shining with unusual splendor, not a cloud to obscure the hori- zon was observed by myself. I proposed to my sister that we would take a carriage ride to the next village, ten miles distant. We could drive the horse ourselves. The weather being very warm we dressed in white muslin. Besides myself and sister, my four little girls were appareled for the ride. We drove on merrily, a few miles, when we discovered a small cloud arising. We quickened our speed thinking to make the place ere a storm would overtake us. Loud thunders roared. The storm was well nigh upon us. I drove up to a house, thinking to allight and go in, but to our astonishment the horse refused to stop. He persisted in going ahead.

Accordingly we drove on a half mile further, halted at a gate. The people came out to help us in. The horse made no resistance, seemed very willing to be tied. We were throughly drenched. The storm was terri- ble. When the hurricane subsided we started for home. Trees had fallen in every direction. Precisely on that spot where the horse had shown such a determined will, there lay an immense tree, turned up from the roots. Had the horse been left there he would have been killed, and the car- riage broken to atoms. We pondered upon the event as we rode along having to pursue a Zig-zag course to avoid the trees which had fallen across the road. We concluded after thinking deeply upon the ways of Providence, that it was a premonition of the horse, that he might escape death, and save the carriage to take us to the promised land.

But to return to our journey. We had very little money to pay our expenses. Elder Gurley gave me two dollars, which a woman stole from my satchel while left in her care a few moments. I said, "She shall see the time when she will need money and cannot obtain it."

My husband reproved me for stopping at such a filthy looking place, hoped I would learn a lesson from it, and remember, said he, "that the appearance of such miserable poverty is a token of dishonesty." We sold

articles we had to spare to get feed for our teams. Soon we were overtaken by a company of Saints from the State of N. York going to Nauvoo.
Glad and thankful were we to see them for though entire strangers their
interests were blended with ours, which made us friends at once. It was
agreed that I should travel on with them (as they all had horse teams,) as
far as Springfield Illinois, where I was to wait till the ox team came up
with the goods. Elder Gurley went on with the stock, I with the carriage
and the children, in the company.

We arrived in Springfield in a day's drive, forty miles, where we
found brethren who showed us every kindness in their power. Sister H.
Bishop waited on me as she would an own sister. I never met a more
benevolent woman. She went out with me to visit the members of the
church in that branch and I felt that I had communion with saints in very
deed. The company passed on, leaving a boy with us to help us on the
remaining journey. Mr. Pratt soon came up, and we pursued our way, with
the blessings of the kind hearted brethren showered upon our heads. We
were obliged to camp out one night, and my babe was sick. Our tent
would not shed rain. That night a terrible thunder storm arose. In a short
time our bedding was drenched through. A long and tedious night was
that to me. I was in great fear about my sick child. The morning came
with no signs of fair weather. We journeyed on with wet bedding till we
came to the house of a Good Samaritan. The kind hostess made a large
fire and dried our bedding and all our wet clothes, assisted in nursing the
sick child, and refused pay.

I made her a present of maple sugar, with which she was much
pleased, and in my heart I prayed the Lord to bless her. In Beardstown we
found an old acquaintance, a young woman we had known in the State of
N. York. She was married and settled in the place. She received us with
great cordiality, caused a good supper to be set before us, which we faint
and weary heartily enjoyed. With buoyant spirits, I travelled on till we
began to near the place of destination. It was Saturday. I revolved in my
mind the pleasure I should have driving into the city that night, and the
following day attending divine worship, with the saints, seeing the
prophet Joseph, and hearing from his lips the words of eternal life. How
sadly was I disappointed. We fell in company with a German who lived
five miles out of Nauvoo, in the dead woods. He conversed with Mr. P.,
encouraged him to stop in his settlement, being a better place to keep
stock. He was at once pursuaded, and to my utter astonishment required
me to turn off the main road, with the horse I was driving, and follow his
team to the German's residence.

I made my objections all in vain. With a heavy heart I turned the
carriage out of the good road, into a rough uneven one, and followed the
loaded wagon. A mile brought us to a small log house in the midst of

heavy timber. Instead of opening a gate we had to climb a high fence to enter the dooryard. I was dumb with disappointment. I kept silence even from good words. There were nine children in the family, the parents, or rather seven of us, making eighteen in all, to lodge in one room. I laid my beds on the floor with the others, pondering in secret what I would do on the coming day. I felt a strong will, not easily to be shaken. Early did I arise carried my beds to the wagon, and made preparations to continue my journey; intending to make the town in time for meeting.

This same family had made their exit from Missouri in the time of the great persecution of the saints, thought themselves happy in finding that sequestered spot away from the confusion and strife. I had often wished I could have gone to the centre Stake of Zion, even to have shared the fate of those who went, but when I listened to their tales of horror, it made my blood almost chill in my veins, and I felt to thank the Lord that events were ordered so as to prevent our going there. But to return to the manner in which I succeeded in getting to Nauvoo that day. While the men went out to gather the stock and yoke the oxen, I packed the wagon. When that was done I walked with the children to find their father and the cattle. We came up to the men talking very diliberately together. [They] had suffered the stock to stray off into the thick timbers, where it would be difficult to find them. I retired a little way off, sat down upon a rock, and gave vent to my full heart in a shower of tears. I felt my spirit rise up in rebellion against such irregular management. In a few moments I recovered my resolution, and rushed in to the dense forest to assist in searching for the cattle. To my great joy they were soon found and we were soon started on our way. We reached Nauvoo while the people were convened in a grove for publick worship.[5] I called at Pres't B. Young's whom I had seen in Indiana. Sister Y. though a stranger, spoke kind and encouraging words to me, and I felt my burdens lightening. We drove up to the grove just as the meeting closed; and those who had known us and shared our hospitality in Indiana, came to the carriage, and accosted us in the most cordial manner, invited us to their homes, congratulating us on our arrival in the City of the Saints.[6]

CHAPTER FIVE

Nauvoo, Missionary Widow

Memoirs, Fall 1841 to Spring 1846

[Arrival at Nauvoo, Fall 1841]

We put up with an acquaintance living near the grove, staid a few days, then hired a house for five dollars per month. In the best room was twenty bushels of corn which could not be removed for several days. I kept my goods packed, did the best I could with little room. It mattered not to me so long as I had accomplished my desires, and was safely moored in the City of Nauvoo. Our cows soon went dry and we had little to eat. We had no money to buy meat or butter. Two articles of food we had plenty, flour and maple sugar. I was constantly hungry for lack of variety. Mr. Pratt went into the country to gather corn on shares. I resolved to have something more to eat.

One day a woman came to my house with pork lard and butter. I decided at once on a trade. I had a large churn, she would buy it and give me a good price. I had more flour than we should need for several months, obtained from the sale of a cow. Fifty pounds of flour and my churn would purchase quite a quantity of lard, butter and pork. I should then be independent, able to entertain my friends. I made the purchase. I then resolved on having mince pies. I sold a set of german silver teaspoons for a bushel of apples, traded for beef in another way, and the grand result was I had it in my power to make a feast and invite my neighbors, who had lived poorly as I had, and for a greater length of time.

When fairly installed in my new home my next motive was to find who I had for neighbors. I called at the nearest house, and commenced inquiries. I soon found that the lady and my self had in childhood days been schoolmates in Lower Canada. Great was our suprise and joy! Though fifteen years had intervened, we both had a vivid remembrance of pleasant scenes enjoyed together in that far off country from which we strayed, and the gospel had again brought us together. Mr. P. soon returned from the country with corn, and having learned of my ability to supply my own wants, seemed much amused, and gratified. He had all the while felt disheartened about living in the City, but as soon as he commenced work on the Temple, and receiving reasonable wages, having the company of faithful brethren, who were zealous in the cause, his hopes revived, and all his doubts and fears vanished like the morning dew. Never did I feel happier than when my husband was employed on that beautiful super structure, for $1.00 per day and board himself.[1] We could live comfortably and hear the Prophet preach every Sabbath day. My heart rejoiced all the day long.

We bought a house and a lot of Lyman Wight. The soil was exceedingly fertile. It was cheering to watch the growth of vegetation on that soil. The husbandman labored not in vain. One year and a half passed pleasantly away. Our spiritual enjoyment was inspiring in a high degree.

[Addison's Mission Call to the Pacific Islands, May 1843]

In 43 Mr. Pratt was called to go on a mission to the South Pacific Islands, ordained and blessed under the hands of Joseph Smith the prophet, together with Noah Rogers [, Benjamin F. Grouard,] and Knowlton Hanks, companions in his ministry.[2] I had greatly desired that he might be sent to our kindred in the eastern states, but never had such a thought entered my mind that he would be sent to a foreign land. My four children to be schooled and clothed, and no money would be left with me. In those days nearly everything was trade; making it more difficult for a mother to be left to provide for herself and children. My heart felt weak at the first, but I determined to trust in the Lord and stand bravely up before the ills of life, and rejoice that my husband was counted worthy to preach the gospel.

The parting scene came [on 1 June 1843]. The two eldest daughters wept very sorely. We walked with him to the steamboat landing. He carried the youngest child in his arms. It was told us he would be absent three years. Little did we imagine such momentous changes could take place as we realized before the expiration of two years. When it was first announced to me that his mission was the South Pacifick Ocean, and for an absence of three years, a weeping spirit came upon me which lasted for three days. I then became calm and set about preparing his wardrobe for the event. He was often in a thoughtful serious mood. It was unfortunate at the last as he stept on to the steamboat the children saw him take his handkerchief from his eyes. They knew he was wiping away his tears. It was too much for them. They commenced weeping. The second daughter was inconsolable, the more we tried to soothe her, the more piteous were her complaints. She was sure her father would never return.

[Life in Nauvoo]

Time wore away our sorrows and we commenced the active duties of life. I was left in a poor house and very small. Mr. P. had purchased timber for a small frame building, it remained for me to get it put up and covered. I had property in the state of Indiana. I determined to try my credit with a stranger who had never seen me, to obtain lumber to build my house. I went to a man by the name of Ellison who owned a steam mill, and related to him the circumstances of the case. I wanted the lumber on credit, my prop. was 270 miles away; it was in good hands and was sure to come. Said I, "'tis true I am a stranger, but you need not doubt a woman, as a general thing they are more punctual than men, but if you require security I will refer you to two responsible men." He assured me he had no reluctance in giving me the lumber on my own reliability.

The first day of June 1843, was the day of his departure. The friends staid with us till night, went home and left us alone. Sadness took possession of our minds. It was not long till loud thunders began to roar. A terrible storm was at hand. A family living across the street had a leaky house, frail and uncertain. Soon they all come over for safety through the storm, thankful we were to see them come in. They talked comforting to us, sang hymns and the brother prayed with us, and staid till the storm was over.

By degrees we became reconciled to the separation. The first accident that happened after the departure of the elders, was: Frances the second daughter went across the way where they were laying a floor a deep cellar beneath. She fell through and struck on the bottom, on the hard ground. She was taken up almost lifeless, and brought home. The first thought I had was, "the devil thinks he has power now the head is gone." I immediately resorted to cold water, bathed her, and sent for the elders. They administered to her, and she soon recovered. Next the eldest daughter was taken with a fever. We did not call a physician, but called on the Lord in faith, believing in annointing with oil and laying on of hands. She was soon well, and we went forward cheerfully in the duties of life. I commenced building a house. Disappointments crossed my path at almost every turn, which only made me the more determined. Soon after the frame was raised some brethren came from Indiana and brought me two yoke of oxen, a wagon, a two years old colt, and a cow. The latter I sold for a stove. The colt I broke to ride while I was building my house. He soon became gentle as a pet lamb, would follow me about like a house dog. I rode him nearly every day.

I had much business to perform in carrying my building forward. Men were continually disappointing me in doing the work. Then I must ride away to hire others. Father Cutler (Committee on the Temple) was accustomed to remark, "If all the sisters were enterprizing like Sister Pratt we should not see so many ragged men about the streets." In the midst of my business my children all were taken with the measles. Their father had not then left the coast of America. I wrote to him the intelligence that all our children were sick. That was the last he heard from us for three years. Their sickness was very severe. I watched alone with them by night and day. The youngest child three years old mourned for her father, complained that he "preached too long," even before he had reached the scene of his labors. My prayers were incessant for the recovery of my sick children. The fourth day I saw favorable symptoms, and very soon they were strong and well. My house was commenced in Sept. The 15th of Nov. I moved into it, after having it neatly finished. I had a rich carpet which I brought from the state of N. York, one of my own make of which I was proud.[3] My business as a seamstress ennabled me to procure many articles of furniture, with which to adorn my rooms. After the house was finished I sold my horse to the miller, who had trusted me for lumber, received payment in breadstuff and groceries which made me very comfortable. Notwithstanding my success I was subject to severe fits of melancholy. I felt a loneliness indescribable! But as St. Paul said, "though case down I was not in dispair." My belief in the gospel was a secret joy.

The ensueing fall there came a letter from brother Noah Rogers to his wife announcing the death of Knowlton Hanks, Mr. Pratt's missionary companion. The same letter refered to one written by Mr. P. to his family, which had not been received. Every mail was watched, and with breathless anxiety I would wait for the return of the runner to the P.O. One morning I went to the room where my second daughter slept. She says "mother there are two letters at the Office for you, and the commencement of one is My dear Family." I concluded it was a dream, however sent immediately, and found it even so. Great was our joy to receive the letter, although we mourned sorely over the sad news, that the noble young man had gone and was buried in the sea! Mr. Pratt endeavoring to console us by relating his happy state of mind in his latest hours, and the visions that were given him, one, he related as follows.

"I dreamed I went to the spirits in prison: it was an immense space; multitudes of people which no man could number; they looked like real life. I asked, "can these be spirits? I was assured they were. I looked east and west; at length I saw a stand, some one had been preaching, the people were dispersing from around it. I saw no children there. I looked to see if there were any persons I knew. I saw none. I learned they were to assemble in the afternoon, then I should see those I knew." Again he dreamed. "I heard the last trump sound; saw the multitudes which John saw that no man could number, small and great, standing before God; I saw no young children there." The method of burial relieved our minds in regard to the sharks devouring the dead bodies thrown into the sea. Mr. P. thus remarks. "the weight of sand attached to the corpse will carry it below all ravenous fish; the density of salt at that depth will preserve the body from putrefaction; and there it remain pure and entire, till the morning of the resurrection, and then he will come forth!" We felt comforted.[4]

I paid the miller who trusted me for the lumber promptly, as I agreed, thus securing his confidence so that I could go to him and get credited for any thing he kept for sale, which often relieved my necessities. When I had done using the animal I broke to ride, I sold the same to him, receiving in different payments necessaries for my family. In a certain time when my supplies were exhausted, I went to Mr. Ellison to solicit means. He was very obliging; let me have groceries, and a due bill for lumber, which I sold for money on my way home. The children had been the greater part of the day with very little to eat. It was near dusk when I returned. They were hovering over a low fire when they heard footsteps approaching. They ran to meet me with joy, exclaiming, "oh Mother where have you staid so long? we are cold and hungry!"

I showed them what I had brought, the gold piece with which I could buy a barrel of flour. We could borrow some for our suppers, which we did, made a cheerful fire, set the table with comparative luxuries and with thankful hearts acknowledged the goodness of God. Another instance of sudden joy I will relate. We had lived on in the usual way till the barrel of flour was spent. I had debts standing out at a distance. I began to be in want of flour, meat, and wood. The children were inquiring, "what shall we do, mother?" I replied, "complain to the Lord." I began to revolve in my mind what the nature of my complaint would be? Should I tell the Lord that those who owed me were unfaithful, would not pay me promptly for my labor? Just as I was on the point of commencing my prayer, "Chandler Rogers" drove to my door with a heavy load of wood. A brother came from Carthage, with a hundred weight of flour, and twenty-five pounds of pork. I withheld my prayer.

We had not time to utter our complaint to the Lord till deliverance came. Frances the second daughter in her accustomed manner exclaimed: "why mother, what a lucky woman you are!" I would here ask, who knows how to appreciate the blessings of life but those who are sometimes straitened? Let pinching hunger come how sweet is a morsel of the coarsest bread! Thus was my life made up of a mixture of joys and sorrows. Notwithstanding the appearances I kept up I sometimes felt very helpless and inadequate to the burden that was laid upon me. I felt like an orphan child, and thought every one ought to pity me. On the other hand, some who were indebted to me seemed to think I ought to pity them, and forgive them their indebtedness. In the spring of 44, I took up a school in my own house. I was attended with great difficulty and confusion; being a crowded school in a small room. But it brought me in a little; though the people were very poor and unable to pay.

There were continual hostilities in Nauvoo from either one source or another. Brother Joseph Smith went with his wife to Dixon, an adjoining County to visit his wife's relative. Officers from Missouri were lying in wait to kidnap and take him across the river, for which they were to receive a reward. They started with him, called at a publick house for the night. When he made signs to the landlord that he was a free mason, he was immediately taken out of their custody. The two men were arrested for assault and battery, brought to Nauvoo in chains. There was great excitement, when it was reported that the prophet was returning, bringing his enemies as prisoners. The people ran in the streets to meet him, the prisoners were greatly alarmed, for fear that violence would be done to them. They were assured that no harm should be done them.

Lawyer Dixon attended Mr. Smith on his way home, addressed a crowded assembly in his behalf, while the two prisoners were sitting by his side on the stand. After the exercises, . . . exciting in the extreme, Mr. Smith invited or rather conveyed the prisoners to his house, took off their shackles, seated them at his table, with his wife and mother, treated them as friends instead of enemies. He gave them their liberty. They went to Carthage, and cursed their bad luck in not getting their prey across the river and receiving their booty. So little did unmerited kindness humble their proud hearts. The mob still continued threatening, and soon it became necessary for the safety of the city to keep a standing army. The brethren came in from the country to render assistance in case the mob should make an attack on the town.

[The Martyrdom and Aftermath, June 1844]

It was eventually announced that the government of the state had taken up arms against the Citizens of Nauvoo: they had supposed they had only a ruthless mob to contend with. They then knew they had no foe to fight, when their arms were demanded, gave them up without resistance. Joseph Smith was then demanded, summoned to Carthage to be tried for treason. The governor pledged the faith of the state that he should have a fair and impartial trial. He at first seemed unwilling to go; but being urged by some who had more confidence in the governor's promise, he consented. He was heard to say as he rode on the way, "I am going like a lamb to the slaughter, henceforth it will be said of me, he was murdered in cold blood." There was great anxiety among the Saints when they knew he had gone to Carthage. On the morning preceding the murder the Governor rode into Nauvoo with troops, made a speech to the people in which he railled them in a sarcastic manner for carrying arms.

While the governor was speaking the report of guns was heard from Carthage. He was in bold terms affirming that Gen. Smith's going to Carthage according to demand had saved the City from being harmed and the women and children from being put to the sword, and perishing by it. The moment the guns were heard he dismissed the assembly abruptly, jumped on his horse and rode away, as if fearing the people would divine the import and he would be in danger in spite of his troops. He continued his journey, not even stopping in Carthage to witness the bloody deed committed, not halting till he had gone twenty-five miles beyond the place. The brethren went with great speed to the spot, anticipating the tragedy. The citizens were greatly terrified supposing the exasperated Mormons would burn their town, but so intense was their sorrow, revenge found no place in their hearts. Dumb with anguish even to profound silence, they laid the dead bodies of the two noble martyrs in their wagon, all in their bloody clothes and drove solemnly towards the city where thousands were watching in breathless sorrow for their return.

Such consternation was never known, since the rocks were rent and the sun darkened, when Christ the Lamb was slain! I had previously had a presentment that some terrible calamity was at hand, but did not believe the men would be slain! Had the sun and moon both fallen from their orbits, and left the world in total darkness, it would not have betokened a more irretrievable despolation. I thought the church was ruined forever. I rushed into my garden, when the news was confirmed, and poured out my soul in such bitterness as I had never felt before. The inconceivable cruelty of our enemies! Oh, could they know what they had done. Would not their hard hearts relent! What now remained horrible for them to do!

This was the 28th [27th] of June 1844. At dusk a report came that a thousand dollars reward was offered for the head of the prophet, and the mob was at Warsaw coming across the river! The [Nauvoo] Legion was called out in the night. Such a tramping of horses was never heard before. The bass drum beat with astonishing loudness. Every blow seemed to strike on my heart, and did really inflict pain, so dreadful was my fear. It was a still night, and the moon was at the full. No season was ever more sublime. A night of death, it was, and everything conspired to make it awfully solemn. The noise of war was suddenly heard, the voices of the officers were heard calling the men together and coming in the distance made it fall on the heart like a funeral knell. The women were assembled in groups, weeping and praying. Some wishing terrible punishment on the murderers, others acknowledging the hand of God in the awful event.

I could feel no anger or resentment. I felt the deepest humility before God. I thought continually of his words, "Be still and know that I am God." My children clung to me with great fear. They heard talk of hiding them in case the mob should come in. The question arose, where could we hide them. A deep cellar was suggested, a trap door, and carpet overspread. They shuddered at the thought of being concealed in such a place. We concluded to take our chances together, and trust in the Lord. I went to bed, but not to sleep. I could hear the men on parade. My whole system was in agitation. I arose in the morning with great prostration. I walked my room to and fro, and talked to the Christian world. "Ah." said I, "you have accomplished your desires at last! Your influence has murdered the prophet! Like the Jews of old you gave your voice against him. From the first, you declared him an impostor."

I continued my soliloquy upbraiding the sectarian churches. I had belonged to them, and well did I remember how they exclaimed against a man they had never seen; and condemned his doctrines, having never heard them only by idle report. I concluded by saying, "as your fathers did so do ye." I awakened the children, told them to dress and we would go and see the poor dead men. It was the day appointed, and to appearance all the world was there. The Saints had assembled from the settlements abroad through the country. The coffins' places were in a long hall, in the Mansion House, a door at each end. The multitude were required to pass through, looking at the corpses as they passed which occupied the time from early sunrise, till dusky evening. The features of Joseph S. looked natural, those of Hyrum were terribly mar'd and disfigured. My second daughter [Frances] trembled exceedingly at sight of him. I regretted having brought her there to witness the spectacle. The elder one grieved as we all did, but betrayed less excitement. The bodies were conveyed, whither we knew not.

My feelings continued so intensly agitated that the third day I was nearly blind; could not bear the light from the windows. Father Henderson, a good old man, came to comfort me. He reasoned a long time; said, it was an event in the economy of Heaven, that it would be overruled for the advancement of the cause of Christ, and further his belief was, that they would not sleep long, ere their resurrection would take place. The latter, though I did not fully endorse, awakened in me a feeling of inspiration, an animated hope that Gods great work would roll on, in spite of men and devils. I began gradually to be more resigned, and to contemplate future prospects, in regard to the progress of the church.

When the solemn event took place, the Twelve apostles were nearly all absent. They soon returned and we were all anxiety to know what they would say. Pres't Brigham Young spake words which pierced my heart like a dagger.[5] Said had I been here Joseph should not have gone to Carthage.

The bare idea that any one, or many had been in fault was terrible to me. I do not believe he intended it for reproof. It was all so ordered. Had "Joseph" given the command every man woman and child would have stood in his defense; even to the loss of their own lives. Afterwards brother Willard Richards rehearsed what transpired at Carthage Jail.[6] Said everything to console the people. That it was to accomplish a purpose in the Almighty disposer of events: refered to many remarks of the prophet Joseph during his confinement, showing that he was aware of his approaching disolution, of the hymns they sang in prison, and how calm he was. All this served to comfort us; every consoling word, was like water to a thirsty soul.

From that hour I watched for words of comfort, and drank them in, as I would an antidote to relieve pain. The enemies stood afar off and wondered, seemed waiting to see if the saints would seek revenge the wrongs done them. When they found it was not their design, they again began their aggressions. In the meantime the work on the Temple rolled on with astonishing rapidity. Means came in from every quarter. Everyone seemed inspired with renewed vigor and determination to have the Lord's house completed, and their blessings received before being compelled to leave the place, which was soon anticipated after the tragedy. No measures were taken on the part of government to bring the murderers to punishment.[7]

There was no lack of evidence in regard to the perpetrators of the bloody deed. I was intimately acquainted with one Miss Graham, a truthful amiable girl who was living with an aunt of hers in Warsaw at the time. She testified in Carthage Court, that the mobbers ate supper at the Hotel where she lived that night on their return from the scene of action, that she heard certain individuals calling them by name boast of their conquest, killing prisoners in jail. One says, "it was my rifle that did the deed." Another, "it was mine," etc. And thus they exulted in the committal of as blackhearted a crime as ever stained the annals of history. Was the testimony heeded by the judges of Illinois? It was not. The stain is on that state, and will remain till the great judge of all comes in power to avenge the blood of the innocent. Then Governor Ford will have a fearful account to give!

"It must needs be that offenses came, but woe to them by whom they come!" We all struggled hard to bear our great bereavement, and not suffer our lips to curse our enemies. Our hands and hearts were employed to hasten the completion of the Temple. The sisters even resolved to pay fifty cents each towards buying the nails and glass. By strict economy I obtained the amount. I started in good faith to go to the Temple office to bestow my offering. Suddenly as I was wending my way, a temptation came over me. I paused. I turned over in my mind, how many things I needed for family use, and that money would relieve my present necessities. In an instant more I resisted. Said I, "if I have no more than a crust of bread each day for a week, I will pay this money into the treasury."

I went forward with hasty steps, paid over the money and returned feeling a secret satisfaction. The next morning as I was sitting near my front door, a brother passed along and threw a silver dollar on my carpet. I sprang to my feet to see who it was. Saw James Harman a southern brother passing. At sight of me he said "I am going across the river to be gone several days. Something may prevent my return; keep that in remembrance of me." This he said in a mirthful mood, but I felt seriously grateful. I went to the store and purchased the articles I very much needed. I thought how soon the money I had given, was returned double to me. Bishop Miller was exceedingly kind to me, not only to render aid in time of need, but to speak comforting words. It was a cause of grief to me when I heard he had become disaffected, and had withdrawn from the church.

[My Situation]

As my children grew older I felt the greater need of their father. It was hard to provide their living, keep them at school, discipline their minds take a course to keep them cheerful, and secure their obedience. Oh! what a task for a poor mother left without means! To keep my spirits from sinking under a weight of care. I was obliged to keep cheerful company. This led to criticisms from some of my neighbors, not well versed in the science of human nature. I conversed with them, endeavored to explain to them the nature of my situation—left alone as I was with four children, how liable I was to become despondent, that I needed every encouragement, their friendship and approbation, to enable me to endure—all which they were ready to acknowledge, and to assure me of the unvarying friendship which ever after was confirmed by acts of kindness.

One good friend I would not forget to mention, Mrs. Delany Parker, my neighbor in Nauvoo. When she heard persons whom she knew did not understand me, censuring me for slightly differing from them in tastes and habits, she reproved them sharply, warned them not to harm a hair of my head! For said she, "I heard brother Addison Pratt prophesy, that those who showed kindness to his family should be blessed, and those who dared to injure them the Lord should render unto them according to their deserts."

Another circumstance transpired in which I saw the mercy of God manifested toward me in a peculiar manner. My brother-in-law J. Crosby went on a mission to the states, returned with the small pox. I took my four children and went to see him, not knowing the character of his disease. My two youngest children had not been vaccinated.

I went to his bedside. He told me I had better go out, as there was reason to fear his disease was contagious. The news spread rapidly that we had been exposed to small pox. The neighbors were all alarmed, dared not come to my house. In nine days from the time my third daughter [Lois] began to have a fever. I sent for the elders, to administer. They were afraid to come. I then declared in the name of the Lord, that the terrible disease should not come under my roof. "The devil," said I, "shall not have power thus to afflict me!" I then laid hands on my child, and rebuked the fever. Eleven little pimples came out, which never filled. In a few days the fever was gone. I showed the child to one acquainted with that disease. He said it was an attack, that I had conquered it by faith. I thanked the Lord; while I realized what a determined will may accomplish with a firm trust in God.

I had myself been innoculated 17 years before. I did not fear in the least that I should take it. My brother-in-law expressed a desire that I would come and see him, as I was not afraid. I knew my neighbors would fear for me, so I dressed myself in disguise and went. My sister met me at the door and gave me a cordial. He was sitting in a chair clad in clothes dipped in oil. One solid scab covered him, not a natural look remaining. I thought of poor old Job, that it must have been the same disease, I believe that was the origin of the loathsome contagion. My sister took care of him through the whole and escaped unhurt, even as I did. To God we gave the glory.

I desire to make honorable mention of those who were my benefactors. Capt. O. M. Allen of the Nauvoo Legion kindly invited me to call on him whenever I needed assistance, which I did in several instances, and received immediate attention.

Brother Samuel Parish, a Canadian, often relieved me of a heavy burden. It was his custom to call in when he saw my woodpile growing low, in cold weather, and inquire where I expected to get my next wood. Assuring me that if I was not certain of being supplied in time, his team and boy would be at my service, and I must have no uneasiness. Faithful was he in every time of need, and always refused pay. At length there came a time when I had it in my power to remunerate him, and I did so, with a thankful heart. Other men there were who made promises to Mr. Pratt, previous to his leaving home who never fulfilled one iota of their promises; but were hard in their dealings with me, even refusing to pay their honest dues. No doubt they have died poor.

The son of my Canadian friend, Samuel Parish, was a boy fourteen, most obliging and generous. He was often called upon to chop wood at my door. Never did I know him frown, even if called after a hard day's work. Neither would he like some boys chop a scanty pile and run away, but would invariably leave more than I had reason to expect. Fifteen years after a separation, caused by the expulsion of the church from Nauvoo, I went to the dwelling of Joel Parish, which was a large stone building; found him with a fine looking wife and child, prosperous and happy. I told him I always knew he would be blessed, because he was a faithful boy, willing to help those who needed his assistance.

But I have digressed, and must return to the work on the Temple. Notwithstanding the threats of the mob, the work steadily progressed. The working men slept within the wall, with their rifles at their heads at night.

[Last Days at Nauvoo]

The mobbers had sworn that the top stone should not be laid. When the time came the people were privately notified, to be on the ground at sunrise. With glad and anxious hearts, we all hurried to the spot. The top of the building was covered with men, while multitudes surrounded the walls below. Pres't Brigham Young laid the top stone, and then began the loud hosanahs! Seven times to the top note of our voices, the men swinging their hats, did we all shout Hosanah to the Son of David! Blessed be the Lord our God. The whole heavens rang with sounds of joy. A band of mobbers [was] standing a few rods from the crowd, watching to take Brigham Young, when he came from the building. In this they did not succeed, for he walked in the centre of more than a hundred men. It was impossible for them to approach him.

Before the completion of the Temple, the mob again commenced their depredations upon the Saints living in the adjacent towns. In the summer of 1845 I went to Bear Creek a distance of twenty miles from Nauvoo. I was spending a few days with my much esteemed friends, Erastus and Ruhamah Derby. While there the mob burned the buildings of the people in Lima. The alarm was given and men went from Bear Creek to disperse the maurauders. Mrs. D. was greatly alarmed, could not compose herself to sleep after her husband left. There was no other dwelling within a half mile. She determined to sit up and watch while I went to bed and slept soundly. The men had left each of us a gun, which we were authorized to use if we should be molested; but neither of us knew enough to handle firearms, so we lent our guns to those who would go to the rescue of the invaded.

The succeeding night Sister D. was sleepy; I told her to retire, and I would watch. She seemed almost afraid to trust me, but I prevailed on her to take rest. When I found she was fast asleep, I crept to a couch and laid down. She awoke before morning, as if some spirit impressed her that I was not watching. Several days passed in suspense, and no news came. At length Mr. D. came home; said the Mormon's houses were burned, and the mob dispersed. The people were in tents and wagons, sick persons in the damp and dew; having been taken by the mobbers from their beds, and laid on the ground, exposed to the night air. They however, lived, and fled to Nauvoo, where they were hospitably received, and rooms provided for them to live in.

In the autumn of 1845 the Saints entered into a treaty to leave Nauvoo the ensueing spring. No pen can paint the anguish of my heart when I heard the news. It fell on my ear like the funeral knell of all departed joys. What could I do, thought I, with my little means, and my helpless family in launching out into the howling wilderness. I had no male relative to take charge of my affairs. My brother-in-law and family were not prepared to go at the time, were struggling hard to make preparations. I was almost in despair, when I reflected on the burden I had to bear, and my companion on the opposite side of the globe! An indescribable melancholy came over me at times, when I thought of my devotion to that beautiful City! My mind wandered back to the poor Jews, when they were compelled to leave the beloved city! Oh! how sorrowful I was! but the watchword was "go!" Like the pilgrim, "take your stuff and travel on."

I had yet some property remaining in Indiana. A house and lot in the village of Pleasant Garden. I sent by letter and sold, gave a bond for a deed, which I wrote out myself, according to my best judgement. A yoke of cattle and wagon were sent me, which would ennable me to launch forth on the fearful, and more than dreaded journey! To others it did not appear forbidding, women who had husband and sons, prospects of the journey seemed romantic. We were going away from our enemies. Little did we think how soon they would follow us.

Late in the fall I took a young lady boarder by the name of Catharine Philips. She had come from Pittsburgh with a widowed mother. She was a delicate girl, not able to do hard work, had no means to pay her expenses. She could help me some; was affable, orderly and exceedingly neat and clean in habits. It was a real comfort to have a companion in my house who would keep every article in its proper place. When the church left Nauvoo she went back to Pittsburgh to join her mother, who went before her. We parted with regrets, and although she has since returned to the church, I have never met her. The Temple was completed ere she left Nauvoo, and she received blessings therein, which greatly rejoiced her heart, lonely and desolate as she felt.

After very great suspense, I was called to the Temple, to receive my blessings,[8] where I encountered a grievous disappointment! Not in the character of the blessings, but in not being permitted to remain through the day, as I had anticipated. The house being crowded, the overseer requested us to withdraw, and make room for others. I remonstrated, but all in vain. I retired with a heavy heart. Afterwards I had frequent opportunities of attending the different exercises in the House and felt that all was made right. It was a glorious sight to go through the stately edifice, and examine the varied apartments; the architecture of which we all believed was dictated by the wisdom of God.

CHAPTER SIX

In the Exodus from Nauvoo to Salt Lake Valley

Memoirs, Spring 1846 to September 1848

[Exodus from Nauvoo, Spring 1846]

At length the time came that we must leave our beloved Temple, Our City, and our homes. I forbear to dwell upon the solemn dread which took possession of my mind. Almon Babbit called to see me. I asked him if he could divine the reason why those who had sent my husband to the ends of the earth did not call to inquire, whether I could prepare myself for such a perilous journey, or if I wished to go or stay? His reply was, "Sister Pratt, they expect you to be smart enough to go yourself without help, and even to assist others." The remark awakened in me, a spirit of self reliance. I replied, "Well, I will show them what I can do."

Early in the spring of 1846 men came up from Indiana bringing to me the remaining avails of our farm. There were cattle, and a new wagon, well covered. It did indeed look like encouragement to undertake the journey. An order came on Almon Babbit, Committee of Church Sales, for fifty dollars, to be paid me. I saw the way opening, still I did not wish to go. My heart drew me towards my childhood's home, where my parents still lived. I asked counsel of Orson Hyde. He said, "If the spirit directs you to go to visit your kindred, go and it shall be well with you, and be overruled for the best." I was on the point of selling my team and wagon for money to go. In the mean time the authorities (first Presidency), and a portion of the Church had started, were camped on the west side the Miss. River, suffering with cold, and deep mud. As I did not feel quite clear in my mind, I wrote to Pres't Young, told him my intention to go back to my kindred. He did not write an answer, but sent by a brother who was present when my letter was read. His reply was, "Tell sister Pratt to come on. The ox team salvation is the safest way." He says, "brother

78

Pratt will meet us in the wilderness where we locate, will be sorely disappointed if his family is not with us."

Upon this I nerved up my heart and put all my energies to the test, to get ready, determined to follow the church, come life or death! Men came in from the country to buy furniture and purchase other property. I had a good lot well fenced, a house which had cost at the least $300, three hund. All I was offered was eighteen dollars. I refused; would choose to make a full sacrifice. The first thing I sold was my stove, which cost sixteen dollars. All I was offered was 50 lbs of flour, and two blankets, in amount $7.00 I accepted, though in one hour I repented my bargain.

The buyer was an insolent fellow, said so many insulting things about the people who were forced to sell their property for the merest trifle; tantalizing and abusing them for being subject to the wills of brutal men, and himself one of the same kind. The weather soon became very cold, and never did I need anything more than I did the stove. I was obliged to sit by my kitchen fireplace, a poor miserable hearth, and my heart accorded with the surroundings. It was gone, and I must dispose of all my furniture as quickly as possible! which I did for less than a quarter its real value. My wagon was packed, ready to start, when a man came from the country. Said he would buy my house and Lot and give me a yoke of oxen. I snatched my pen and paper, sprang into my wagon, made out a quit claim deed, according to my own judgement, without any guide. Just as I finished it, brother Joseph L. Haywood came up. I read the deed to him, asked if he thought it would do. He replied, "if you had consulted a dozen law books you could not have made it more to the purpose."

He then inquired if I kept a day book. I replied in the affirmative, "well," said he, "write it down, that your posterity after you may know what a smart mother they had." As we finished the conversation, the old gentleman's son came up and interfered with the trade, claimed the cattle, and the bargain fell through. I swept out my pleasant house, which I had built by my own economy, closed the doors, and bid farewell to it! I had sold one yoke of cattle for forty five dollars, fifty Mr. Haywood paid me, which fitted us up for provision and clothing. I had two yoke of oxen, two cows and a good new wagon. I was comparatively rich, and by this time began to be in fine spirits. Several of my neighbors who were not ready to start escorted me to the river, and sincerely wished me good fortune.

As I was passing down the streets of Nauvoo, I cast a lingering look at the beautiful Temple. I felt inclined to say as the poor Jews said of Jerusalem. "When I forget thee Oh, Nauvoo, let my right hand forget her cunning. If I prefer not thee above my chief joy!" I began by this time to feel comparatively happy. I am another woman compared with her who groped about the house two days ago. I believe that was the worst day of all my life. My grief was of a peculiar nature. I did not feel willing to disclose the whole cause to anyone. The load not being ready to cross that night I went to Sister Hiram Kimball's and slept there. I had called at the P.O. as I came down, and found a letter from Mr. Pratt, on the far distant Isles of the South Sea.[1] This gave us all great joy, for many months had passed away and not a word had we heard from him. I carried my letter where I went to spend the night, and they all rejoiced with me.

The letter contained good news. The kind man wrote he was sending money to his family, by one Capt. Hall, who belonged in Boston. He had agreed to forward it to the church. Moreover it informed us that my husband had received two letters from me which had been written two years, the first he had heard from his family in that length of time. He says he will never leave us so long again, that if he returns and is ever sent back he shall insist on taking his family.

As I failed in getting the cow as I had expected on the west side of the river, I went back to Nauvoo to obtain one from the tithing office. I went direct to brother Haywood's as he was the man who had charge of business. I was agreeable surprized in finding a pleasant company assembled to celebrate the 5th anniversary of their marriage. I was on the point of making apologies for intruding. Brother Haywood placed me a chair at his right hand, at the same time repeating the passage of scripture which runs thus. "Sit thou on my right hand until I make thine enemies thy footstool." I felt honored, and free to partake of their bounties which were large. I spent the night, obtained a good cow to take back. A man going over the river kindly offered to drive her, and everything conduced to banish gloominess from my mind and make me reconciled to undertake the ambiguous journey.

I reached my home which was on wheels; found the children all cheerful. Brother B. [Busby] informed me that the company had been waiting sometime for him, and were disposed to start on and leave me; but he told them he would not move till I was ready to go. May 31st, pitched our tents between Farmington and Bonaparte. At the latter place we bought flour best quality, $1.25 per hundred. Bought Ellen a shawl $2.50.

[Across Iowa, Summer 1846]

Across the Des Moine River the boat was drawn by pullies. I was in great fear that the ropes would break. We got safely over, and my driver called to see his mother, whom he had not seen for some little time, having been with his father in Nauvoo. She was opposed to his going on with me, unless the family were ready and could join our company. A scene ensued. I plead with his mother, told her I thought it would be unjust to detain him there and leave me without a teamster, when his father had given his full consent for him to go with me. Tears were shed by both parties, till at length my pursuasions prevailed, and we moved on with the company, which was then small. That night camped where there were forty wagons. It looked cheerful after travelling all day over a desolate country, and intolerable roads to salute a large company of our brethren.

It became necessary to have my wagon overhauled, goods repacked. For that purpose everything was taken out and put in the tent. It being late in the afternoon, there was not time to replace them before the dusk of evening. No signs of rain till we were all locked in the arms of morpheus. Then suddenly the loud thunders began to roar! Fierce lightenings flashed! I knew my tent would not shed rain, and I dreaded the consequences of a hard shower more than I ever did in my life. I prayed most fervently that the storm might pass over and do us no harm! Suddenly the clouds began to disperse, the thunder rumbling in the distance. I looked abroad and saw the clear sky. I felt a glow of gratitude I shall long remember.

I found great pleasure in riding horseback. By that means I could render some assistance in driving the stock. There was in the company a comical fellow by the name of Ephraim Hanks. He had charge of the loose cattle, was a dashing rider, gave me lessons in that art, till I became very expert. He assumed the name of title of Captain, gave to me that of Comodore. I was quite proud of my title, arose early in the morning mounted my horse to help gather up the stock. It was air and exercise, besides amusement, which kept my spirits brisk. We camped on a creek which I shall name Musketoe Creek, for the want of a more suitable name, and that could not be, for the insects are worse than the locusts of Egypt. Our friends who were behind overtook us at this place and the camp was organized. The brethren met by themselves, organized and chose a president without the aid or counsel of the women. This evening, the sisters propose to organize themselves into a distinct body, to prove to the men that we are competent to govern ourselves. If they set the example of separate interests, we must help carry it out.

June 6th we started early, thought to accomplish a good day's drive. The loose cattle were very unruly and hindered us. We have in our company a young man whom the girls have named "Green Horn." He blundered into a mud hole and broke his axle tree. So here the whole crowd must be hindered to wait for repairs. My eldest daughter said to him, "had your head been right side up, you might have saved us all this delay." He submitted to the jokes very patiently as the loss was general. My two cows are very docile, and willing to be driven, but we have one in the herd our Capt. says is not a Mormon! She has nothing of a gathering spirit, seems determined to go back, and he says "if she was mine, I would never take her to Zion." While waiting to repair the broken wagon one of my cows had a young calf. This was an amusement to the children, as for a few days he would have to [be] carried along in the wagon. A beautiful creature he is! White as snow, with a few red spots.

While the company was staying encamped, I took a horseback ride to visit a camp of Saints two miles ahead, found them to be a company from Laharpe Illinois. They invited me to eat and drink with them when they learned who I was, and treated me with true politeness. On my return I found a good kersey [light weight woolen] blanket in the road. When I reached camp and gave a history of my adventures, I was highly complimented. Thus something in the line of social enjoyment was continually transpiring to cheer our hearts amidst all the trials. My horse came back on the gallop, which occasioned some merriment, as he was very dull going out.

7th day [of June]. Nearly ready to start again. Phineas Young passed our Camp this morning, in from C. Bluffs, on his way to Winter Quarters.

Last evening the ladies met to organize. Mrs. Isaac Chase was called to the chair! She was also appointed President by a unanimous vote. Mrs. L.B. Pratt Counsellor and scribe. Several resolutions were adopted. 1st Resolved, that when the brethren call on us to attend prayers, get engaged in conversation and forget what they called us for, that the sisters retire to some convenient place, pray by themselves and go about their business. 2nd if the men wish to hold control over women let them be on the alert. We believe in equal rights. "Meeting adjourned sin ni die. [sine die]" We have to let our "Calf baby" ride in the front of the wagon, but he is so very handsome, and so gentle, he is no annoyance.

8th day. Yesterday we travelled over the most intolerable roads! It was a query in my mind, how the first company going as they did early in the spring ever forced their way through so much mud! I was led to exclaim, what is there in all the world the Mormons will not attempt to do?

We were compelled to create our own amusements. When we camped near a level spot of earth where water had been standing and dried away, the young men would propose a dance. The older ones feeling the absolute need of diversion, would accede, as it would cost nothing and would most likely cheer and enliven us on our wearisome journey. In the midst of our amusements we did not forget our prayers. We have large campfires around which we all gather, sing songs, both spiritual and comic, all very appropriate.

9th day. Last evening Brother Markham camped with us on his way back to Nauvoo, to bring on a load of provisions. He informed us the "Twelve" had gone on to Council Bluffs. We have very little hopes of overtaking them. I begin now to admire the country, such a beautiful rolling pararie!

10th day: Last night we camped on the bank of a creek about a hundred miles from Nauvoo. The last house we shall see for the present, and that not a house, though a hut, where the inmates keep ardent spirits and bacon. The spelling on their sign is "flower" for flour, "baken" for bacon. We laughed at their lore. Have just struggled through a three mile mud hole and have arrived again at a Mormon City, of tents and wagons, white with black spots emblematical of the lives we live in this world of change. We work hard to live and we earn our enjoyments by the sweat of the brow. What a pity, that any poor man should be without land to till, when there is so much lying vacant, so beautiful, good and productive! Sister Eldridge and myself have had a long ride on horseback, taking a view of the country and admiring it.

Sometimes I feel cheerful. Again it comes suddenly to my mind how far I am going from home, parents, and every relative I have in the world! But the Lord has called us, and appointed us a place where we can live in peace, and be free from the dread of our cruel persecutors!

12th day. Yesterday for the first time my wagon had to be dug out of the mud. One wheel ran off a bridge. It made racking work, broke my table which was tied on behind. This morning our company broke up: three started back to Bonaparte after flour, left their families encamped to wait their return. The rest pursued their journey as usual, are now 55 miles from the main camp. Last evening there was great sport in our camp. The young man we call Capt. dressed in woman's attire, danced to amuse us. Several in the crowd did not know who it was, thought it was some strange lady who had come in from another company.

June 15th: We have at last arrived at Mount Pisgah. Look around to find myself a location. Poor people! here they are in the sun without houses. I pity them! May the Lord reward for all their sacrifices. I have just returned from a long walk have been taking a survey of the place entire. On the Bluffs is a beautiful grove of oak trees. Beneath the towering branches we can pitch our tents and be sheltered from the sun's scorching rays. Several little cabbins begin to make their appearance. The P.O. is laughable. A little log pen 10 by 8 covered with bark.

18th day: I have at length got my habitation moved up into the mount; my tent pitched under the shade of three oak trees. The children are delighted. A pleasant family by the name of Hallet are very near. The man is gone with the Pioneers, and the poor woman is sick.

23rd day. The wind is blowing a heavy gale: it seems as though the very heavens would come down to earth! The tent is pinned down, or it would be carried away. The elements are in great commotion, and my mind is dark and dismal! I think, "what if we have to wander forty years in the wilderness, as the children of Israel did!"

25th. We have just experienced one of the severest storms of thunder and rain, I ever knew. We are all drenched out. So here we are wading in mud over shoes, trying to get our breakfast. We moved our beds into Mrs. Hallet's tent the succeeding night where [we] slept quite dry.

4th day July. Went to a wedding party; had music and dancing; a thunder storm to wind up the celebration.

5th day. Elder Little arrived from New Hampshire: he came to my wagon early in the morning, informed me he had brought the money my husband had sent me from the Islands. This was good news, as I had been waiting for it, to pursue my journey.

8th day. Sister H. Silver and myself went across Grand river to visit Mrs. Bullock. We invited Brs. Benson and Little to accompany us. We had a fine agreeable visit, came home by moonlight. The ensueing morning I invited to breakfast Messrs B. Young, W. Richards, E. T. Benson, J. C. Little. H. Silver was with me, and we rehearsed the incidents relating to our visit the preceeding day, which occasioned some mirthfullness, and made the time pass pleasantly away. Soon after we had an evening party in the open air. The said gentlemen took an affectionate leave of us all and went on to the Bluffs. A little before their departure, recruiting officers came there, to enlist men for the Mexican War.[2] 500 men were demanded; quite a number were taken from that place. The young man who had driven my team to that point, remained there as his parents had arrived. I had engaged another by the name of William Sterritt, a kind and faithful young man. I was in great fear that he would be called to go as a soldier to the war. I made a request of brother Heber C. Kimball that his name might not be written on the list. He promised me it should not.

"Father Huntington" and C. C. Rich were the Presidency there, two as good men as ever took upon themselves the name of Latter Day Saints. When I was imposed upon, they interposed, and caused restitution to be made. When I heard the news of Father Huntington's removal from this sphere I said, "a righteous man has gone to receive his reward for all his noble deeds, his integrity and faithfulness."

16th. Last evening called on Sisters Markham, E. R. Snow, and Dana. They all seem resigned to the times and circumstances. I wish I could. I pray earnestly for submission. Now preparing to leave Mount Pisgah. People all around me are taking chills and fever.

July 29th. A sorry time it is. Many are sick. Sister Hallet is very low. I have for some time had charge of her babe seven months old. Last night I had a serious exercise with her, was up and down alternately. She refused all consolation. At length my bedstead (one I had made myself) broke down. I then made my bed on the ground. There was a bottle of bitters standing near. I thought perhaps a few drops might lull the child to sleep. She struggled much under the operation. I then gave a dose of cream. I thought if the poor child could speak she would tell me I would kill her with kindness. I felt sorrowful on leaving the sick woman and the babe, as the other members of the family were also in the same condition, not able to help each other.

Aug 1st. Left Mount Pisgah with an agitated mind, sorrow for the afflicted ones and regret that any one should wish to wrong me, and have to be compelled to act justly.

3d day. Camped by a beautiful stream, where we found a spring of clear cold water. O, how delicious! The first cold water I have tasted since my arrival in Mt. Pisgah. At that place the water was fearful! It oozed through marshy ground where it was supposed buffaloes had been mired, and buried. We met brother Hallet on the way returning from the Bluffs, informed him of the sickness of his family; entreated him to make all possible haste to get home! He seemed much affected with the news, assured us he should lose no time, neither did he, but was soon taken sick, and the first news we heard he was gone! Likewise a little girl twelve years old, and the babe! oh! the sickness was terrible! The next place was an Indian Village. They flocked around us with corn and cucumbers; it looked delicious in our sight. We purchased of them, paid them in sea bread.

9th day Sabbath. Camped on the broad pararie, near bro Felshaw and Wooley. Not a tree to shelter us from the scorching sun. It seemed that we must dissolve with the heat! Our cattle left us and we were obliged to remain through the day. The next day found the cattle, went on a few miles. The young men were sick, not able to drive teams or cows.

11th day. For the first time my cows were missing. I found them, lying down in the bushes after going over a great portion of the range. Camped on "Musketoe Creek," nearly eaten alive with insects. The creek is miry, cattle drink with great difficulty. This country never could have been designed for human beings, the water is so poor! Here and there we find a little spring.

10th day. We are through with another musketoe night, were just on the moment of starting when J. Fox's horse took to his heels and away he went. How long we shall be detained is uncertain. I intended to have described a bridge we crossed a little west of Indian Village. Not much to the credit of the many teams which have passed over, or rather their owners. It is very long, made of large logs, very uneven, one side being two feet higher than the other. It took one team a quarter of an hour to cross over. In the midst of all the perplexities, my health continues good, and that of my children, who seem to enjoy the journey. My oxen and cows do not incline to stray at all; they really appear to understand that they have a duty to perform. I have much to be thankful for.

A long time has elapsed since I have written in my journal. A crowd of cares caused by extreme sickness in my family, has prevented me.

When I last wrote I was on the road between Mt. Pisgah and Council Bluffs. We traveled in company with brs. Truman and Fox.

I have mentioned the death of brother Hallet, and two children. I now hear that his wife has followed him; likewise a sister Gould, member of the same family (who were my pleasant neighbors beneath the oak trees,) both gone to their long home! Brother Sterritt was faithful and good to us. We got along smoothly till some began to be taken sick. Brother Fox was first attacked with intermittent fever. At the Bluffs his sister and niece were both laid on beds: the latter died with only a week's illness, a girl 15 yrs. I was also seized with the same disease, brought on by washing in the hot sun without a shelter. Others besides were taken; and we were all admitted into a Sister Henderson's house, a kind lady she was! We were in the woods, low on the bank of the river, we could feel no air stiring. We had no cool water, the warm river water was sickening. I offered to pay five dollars to any one who would go to a certain cold spring and bring me a jug of water. They said it was too far to bring it, it would get warm on the way. I believed cold water would cure me. I believe it now. When I had partially recovered, we started to go to the main camp. 18 miles west side the Missouri.

There were so many teams ahead of us we had to wait nearly the whole day for our turn. I was extremely weak! There was great confusion on the boat, the cattle were frightened. I was terrified, and it caused my fever to return. There was a dreadful hill to climb as we drove off the boat, deep mud, and at the top thick woods. It was dark, and we dared not drive on. Had no place to pitch the tent. So there we must remain till morning, musketoes beyond endurance. I, with a raging fever, the four children with me on the bed. The ferry man's wife lived at the top of the hill, in a little cabbin.

[At Winter Quarters, Fall 1846 to Summer 1848]

At twelve o'clock that night the good woman hearing groans of distress, came with a light to my wagon. Had a light shone down from heaven it could not have rejoiced me more! She instructed the elder daughters to remove things from the front end of the wagon, set them outside on the mud, make themselves a bed separate from mine, that their "mother might have some chance to rest." They did as she directed, and I was more comfortable. Besides, she brought me a cup of warm coffee, and something to eat, which greatly revived me; and ennabled me the better to fight musketoes. The driver was out herding the cattle; came to us early in the morning. No poor mortals were ever happier to see daylight appear! We told him our adventures during the night, and we all pronounced blessings on the Good Samaritan. That day we drove on, camped at night by some cold springs. Now, thought I, will be a good chance for me to get all the cold water I can drink! I resolved to make up for the past sacrifices.

The children were told to bring a large coffee pot full, and place at the head of my bed, in the tent. I felt that a great luxury was to be enjoyed. I drank lavishly through the night. The following day [I] was conveyed to camp half dead with cholera morbus! The sisters thronged about my wagon, all anxious to do something to relieve me. One proposed brandy and loaf sugar. I told her if she would bring it in a glass tumbler, with a silver teaspoon, I would take it, but would not drink it from a "tin cup!" She laughed heartily, and made haste to bring the medicine according to directions. It had the desired effect, and I was better. But that was not to be the end of my sufferings. The shaking ague fastened deathless fangs upon me, from which there was no escape! I must bow my head and submit to my fate.

I shook till it appeared to me my very bones were pulverized! I wept, and I prayed. I besought the Lord to have mercy on me. The sisters were moved with sympathy. They assembled at my tent, prayed, annointed me with oil, and laid their hands upon me. Although I was not wholly restored, I was comforted, and enabled to bear more patiently my distress. I had money to hire a good nurse. A faithful one she was. She was always cheerful, even merry, which was better than medicine. Sometimes myself and three children would all be shaking at once. The nurse would go from one to another to administer relief in every possible way; held the watch to let us know how the time passed. We knew the moment when the agitation would cease, and our systems became tranquil. Then the fever would succeed, which would last nearly as long, but less painful to endure.

I at length got my chills broken, was relieved for a short time; but a cold rain storm and exposure, caused a relapse. I was in my wagon, my children all sick in the tent, except the youngest daughter six years old who escaped it all; and was able to wait upon the others, which she did to the admiration of all who knew how faithful and brave she was. A cold dreary winter was before us. I hired a man to build me a sod cave. He took the turf from the earth, laid it up, covered it with willow brush and sods. Built a chimney of the same. I hung up a blanket for a door, had three lights of glass to emit light. I built a fire, drew up my rocking chair before it, and that moment felt as rich as some persons (who have never suffered for want of a house) would to be moved into a costly building. Thus we learn to prize enjoyments by sacrifices.

I paid a five dollar gold piece for building my sod house, 10 x 12. An old ox with a lopt horn, had the habit of hooking everything that came in his road; greatly did he annoy me, by throwing down my chimney. It had several times to be rebuilt. Sometimes just as I was preparing a meal, and almost famishing for refreshment, down would fall my chimney. I knew not which to condemn the brute or his owner. I tried to refrain from cursing either. My mind was wholly occupied about my diet. I had so far recovered that I desired nothing on earth so much as to satiate my appetite with some luxury. There were no vegetables in the camp, for this reason nearly all were afflicted with scurvy, a terrible disease! I pined for vegetables till I could feel my flesh waste away from off my bones! I would have given a yoke of oxen for a cheese, had one been brought to my door.

About the middle of winter I began to recover my health. I could walk a half mile. I went forth from my cave in the earth, gazed abroad on the face of nature, and breathed a new atmosphere! I went to the store of Messrs. Whitney and Woolley to get articles I had sent money to St. Louis for, by them. They had lost the bill and would not let me have the goods. Returning after dark I fell on the frozen ground and sprained my knee. I had to be helped home and was thrown on my bed for two weeks, only being removed to have my bed made. My limb swelled to an astonishing size! Continued swollen during the winter. The pain I endured I will not attempt to describe. For several weeks I went about on crutches. At length my chimney entirely failed, and I moved into what is called a "dugout," five feet under ground. It was a very damp unhealthy situation. There I had the scurvy.

A long cold rain storm brought more severely again the chills and fever. These with scurvy made me helpless indeed! The air in my cellar was too confined. I resolved never again to complain of a cold house and fresh air. I had willows laid upon the ground, then a thick carpet spread double, straw bed, and lastly feathers. I could feel dampness through them all. On examination I found my carpet and straw bed were quite wet. I left the place and determined to sleep in it no more. I went into my wagon, a heavy rain came on, I was forced to keep closely covered which caused me to sweat profusely for three days. This broke my chills, and I began to recover. Oh! how sweet is sympathy to a poor afflicted soul! While living in the "den" under ground, Brother Anson Pratt, (P.P.s brother) came to see me. When he saw the condition I was in with my four young children on my heart and hands, he sat down and wept a long time.

His tears seemed to comfort me. He says, "I will go and see if a room cannot be found for you." There was none to be had. In the midst of our sufferings there was something always to cheer us. The most of the Twelve had gone with the first Presidency to explore a Country beyond the Rocky Mountains. The leading men who remained did every thing in their power to keep life and spirit among the people. Picnic parties were encouraged; the poor brought out to eat and drink; the best the place offered was set before us. We listened to the strains of cheerful music, met and conversed with old friends whom we had known in days brighter and happier than those. Our hearts were made to rejoice in anticipation of a time to come when we should greet each other in a goodly land, away from our cruel oppressors.

I now determined to add one more to my many efforts to buy me a dwelling above ground. Some were beginning to go to the mountains with their families. I found a cabbin to be sold for five dollars. I made the bargain and moved in to it. I thought in that I could keep dry in a rain storm; but I was mistaken. The first thunder shower I caught a barrel of water in my fire place. I went about making repairs. I hired a floor laid of split logs hewed, which cost six dollars. So there I dwelt in a eleven dollar house. I had a six lighted window, felt quite exulted! I had cause to look up. I was well. My daughters also were by this in good health. The eldest [Ellen] could teach a juvenile school, assist me in providing for the family. The second daughter [Frances] was unusually smart to do outdoor work. She could make garden, take care of the cows in winter. Sometimes when charity was cold she chopt the wood, with a little help from the kind neighbors.

Many of my friends sickened and died in that place, when I was not able to leave my room, could not go to their bedside to administer comfort to them in the last trying hours, not even to bid them farewell. Neither could I go to see their remains carried to their final resting place where it was thought I would shortly have to be conveyed. The Lord had more work and suffering in store for me, and I lived, with all my children, to be a witness of his faithfulness to those who trust in him. I had a bowery built in front of my house where I could seat twenty-five pupils, which my daughter and I taught with pleasure and profit. In speaking of the faithfulness of God towards those who trust in him, I now recall an instance I would not forbear to mention, which took place while I was destitute, and unable to labor.

On a time when I was out of means to buy food, I went to Col. Rockwood with a request that he would buy a feather bed of me, which I offered for $12.00. He was preparing to go to the mountains with the pioneers, had not the means to spare. I remarked to Sister R. that I had nothing in my house to eat. She replied, "You do not seem troubled, what do you expect to do?" I answered, "Oh, no, I do not feel troubled. I know deliverance will come, in some unexpected way, and when I see you again I will inform how it came." I walked home, and on my way called at brother J. Busby's. [I] said nothing of my circumstances. He began inquiring about an old fashioned iron crane I had brought from the State of N. York. Said he, "if you will sell it, I will give you two bushels of corn meal, and take one to your place this evening." I then mentioned what I had said to Mrs. Rockwood.

Thus in many instances have I been relieved, when apparently there was no prospect before me of help from any quarter. Many there were who would divide their last morsel with one in want, but humbling it is to an independent mind to ask of those who have nothing to spare. I make a record of these things, that my children and others who may read these memoirs may be admonished to trust in the one, who is all powerful to save! Almighty to deliver! At times the weight of cares I have upon me, the anxiety for the proper training of my daughters, seems insupportable. I nerve up my heart, and determine to live till my husband returns, that I may have one more day of rejoicing in my toilsome and weary life!

After I had been deprived the privilege of attending publick worship for eight months on account of ill health, I at length was permitted to go. It seemed to me the heavens were smiling upon me. In the afternoon I attended a prayer meeting. The sisters laid their hands upon my head and blessed me in a strange language. It was a song; a prophetic song! Mrs. E. B. Whitney was interpreter. She sang in our tongue. That I should have health, and go to the vallies of the mountains, and there meet my companion and be joyful! I was then fully expecting him to come to that place, before I could with my family undertake such a journey. I still desired to hold on to that belief, but was admonished by those who heard the prophesy, to accept the contrary and strive to be reconciled. I felt the undertaking to be impossible! I saw no way whereby I could obtain means to fit my children out with what would be indispensable.

[Across the Great Plains, 1848]

President Young said I must go, that I must do what I could, and he would assist me. When I had decided to go, and asked strength and courage of the Lord, means came flowing into my hands. Things I had thought of no value, that I should throw away, were sold for a fair price, to those who were not of our faith, or who were not prepared to go at that time. The President ordered my wagon made ready, a thousand pounds of flour was allotted me, a yoke of oxen in addition to what I owned, a man hired to drive my team. Fifty dollars worth of store goods was appropriated to clothe myself and children, this with what I obtained by my own economy made me very comfortable. I began to feel myself quite an important personage! It was hard for me to wave the dread of (as I felt,) a never ending journey!

I gave my eleven dollar house to a neighbor who moved it across the river, to Canesville, I started on the dreaded journey with a saddened heart, affecting to be cheerful as far as possible! My good teamster was not permitted to continue with us, having been sent back to Iowa to bring on families left behind. The one hired was a stranger. The question whether he would be companionable, or agreeable, could not be a consideration, however important, it might be to us so immediately concerned. We were organized in President Young's fifty wagons, with Captains of tens, a head commander over all. Six hundred wagons in the whole company, travelling three abreast. As we made our own road, we could easily make a wide one. We camped at Elkhorn River more than two weeks, waiting for others to join us. We were thirty miles from our starting point. While we lay encamped a sister by the name of Taylor died with the measles.

It was a sorrowful affair! She left a husband and four children to bewail her loss. To make a lone grave by the way side at the beginning of our journey caused our hearts to flow out with sympathy for the poor young girls, left to pursue the wearisome route over the deserts without a mother. The company were generally healthy, even those who started on beds were soon able to enjoy the amusements accessible to all, such as climbing mountains and picking wild fruit. The gloom on my mind wore gradually away. When I had been three weeks on the way there was not a more mirthful woman in the whole company. The grandeur of nature filled me with grateful aspirations. The beautiful camping grounds, which were so clean, that one was led to conclude no human foot had ever trodden there. So green was the grass, so delightful the wild flowers, so umbrageous the grounds on the banks of the rivers!

The president counselled us to rest from traveling on the Sabbath day. He said, "write it in your day book when you travel on Sunday, then notice your success through the week, and you will find more time lost through accidents than you had gained by traveling on the day appointed for rest." We were convinced of the truth of his remarks, were willing to rest from our labors and assemble ourselves together for publick worship. Sometimes the whole camp of six hundred wagons [would] be within visiting distance. Then indeed it was like a city of tents and wagons. The cheerful campfires blazing at night, far away from the civilized world, reminded us that our trust must be in the Lord. He who clothes the lillies of the vallies, and notices even the little sparrows, would assuredly watch over us.

When we came to the Buffalo Country we were full of wonder and admiration. Nothing could be more exciting than to see them in large droves or herds, marching as orderly as a company of soldiers. Nothing seemed to daunt them. If they were headed towards our traveling companies, we would make a wide passage for them to cross our path, and they would march along so majestically with their great bush heads, turning neither to the right or left, not seeming to notice us at all, while we would stare at them with breathless anxiety, thinking how easily they might crush our wagons, and do us great injury were they to become furious. The men would not fire upon them when they were near us, but follow them to their haunts, capture one, kill, and haul it to camp with two yoke of oxen. The meat would keep sweet without salt, till perfectly dried.

Nothing I had ever seen amused so much as watching the buffaloes. As well as I loved the meat, when I saw the men pursueing one intending to kill him, I always wished in my heart he might elude them and escape with his life. I have seen them wade into the deep water almost over their backs. Knowing the men could not follow them prompted by instinct they were impelled to strategy like human beings. I felt it a crime to destroy the life of such knowing animal. The Platte River country was beautiful. The women in small companies were often seen walking on its banks by moonlight, bathing in its waters, our hearts at the same time glowing with wonder and admiration at the beauty and sublimity of nature, alone in a great wilderness, far from the haunts of civilization, none but an occasional red man wandering along in search of game to gaze on the beautiful scenery and pluck the wild fruit.

On Sweetwater we camped for two weeks or more to recruit our teams, but it proved fatal to many. There being alkali in pools about on the range, the cattle drank it and several of them died. While we remained there teams were sent by the pioneers from Salt Lake to meet our company and help us on our journey. This gave us new courage. My daughters wore out their shoes, and I made them mocasins of buckskins. We had many rambles on the steep hills where we could overlook the surrounding country. The men talked of the great future when the "Iron Horse" would be wending his way over the silent vallies and through the Rocky Mountains; and thus pave the way for teeming multitudes to locate on the beautiful praries! We traveled hundreds of miles without seeing a single tree.

When at length we came to a lone cedar tree we stopt our teams, alighted, and many of the company walked quite a distance for the pleasure of standing a few moments under its branches. Looking up we saw something lodged among the thick boughs, apparently for concealment. The boys tore it down. Wrapt in a thick buckskin, or rawhide was an Indian papoose. There was a horn of powder and I think a knife. The men caused it to be replaced. A strange idea of burial have the poor savages.

Independence Rock was another novelty. The size was immensly large and rather difficult of ascent. A thousand names were inscribed on the rock, which proved we were not the first adventurers. Freemont had been there, also the pioneers to Salt Lake Valley. We left our names with the rest, and as we descended, in a crevice of the rock was water dripping down into a spring.

With much exertion we crowded through a narrow passage, and got to the spring, and drank our fill of the sweetest coldest waters, I have seldom tasted. O, how delicious to the taste in a hot day! After being for months obliged to drink river water (and sometimes from sloughs) to come to a cold spring to quench our raging thirst was a luxury we could appreciate. Although we had been compelled to leave Nauvoo we did not feel like outcasts. We realized that our Heavenly Father had made a beautiful world, and desired that his children should enjoy it, and if our enemies would not allow us to remain neighbors to them because of our being peculiar in our religious views, we found by launching out into the wilderness, how much romance and beauty there was in nature, where she dwelt alone!

We found there was room for all. It is wisely ordered that those who are not congenial to each other can separate, and live, not as enemies. As we drew nearer the place of destination our hopes began to brighten. Rumors from the camps already landed in Salt Lake Valley came out to meet us with cheering news. A little Scotchman told us that soldiers from the Mexican war were on their way home, coming in the north route from California. That intelligence had reached the pioneers that Elder Addison Pratt was in their company. He says to my daughters, "I shall hasten my return, and go out to meet the battalion boys, shall see your father before you will, shall have the pleasure of informing him that his family are in the company and will soon be in the valley." Our hearts began to swell with joy in view of the prospects that were before us.

Aug 19th day. Still travelling through Canyons, deep mudholes, willow brush, big rocks, steep hills, objects that seem almost insurmountable. Still nothing impedes our progress! Slowly we move along, gaining a little every day. We find an opening every night for camping, clean and pleasant. I feel now as if I could go another thousand miles. Frances our second daughter makes her fire the first of anyone in the morning. It is her greatest pride to have people come to her to borrow fire, and praise her for being the lark of the company. Going through the willows a slat was torn off the chicken coop and the only surviving hen was lost out. We did not miss her till we camped at night. When the children found she was gone they could scarcely be restrained from going back on foot to recover the lost treasure. "Such an extraordinary hen, that knew the wagon where she belonged and laid all her eggs in it, and had travelled a thousand miles!"

20th. This morning arose with cheerful spirits, anticipating the arrival of our Camp in the desired haven. We begin to think of green corn, cucumbers, how delicious they will be to the poor fasting pilgrims! We have ascended an eminence, where with a spyglass we can see the great Salt Lake in the valley of which the Saints are located, our hearts leap for joy!

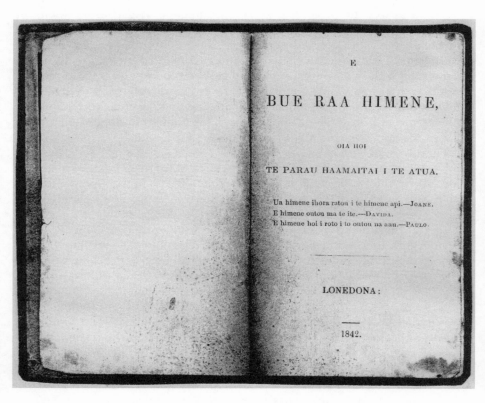

E

BUE RAA HIMENE,

OIA HOI

TE PARAU HAAMAITAI I TE ATUA.

Ua himene ihora ratou i te himene api.—JOANE.
E himene outou ma te ite.—DAVIDA.
E himene hoi i roto i to outou na aau.—PAULO.

LONEDONA:

1842.

Tahitian translation of the Book of Mormon

PART TWO

On a Mormon Mission to Tahiti

Salt Lake Valley
September 1848 to April 1850

The Mission to the Society Islands
April 1850 to July 1852

Benjamin Grouard

Benjamin Grouard and one of his families

CHAPTER SEVEN

In Salt Lake Valley

Memoirs, September 1848 to April 1850

[While some exiled Saints scattered into the frontier population, three movements emerged to help unify the Mormon people and get them to their destined Zion: (1) the Pioneer Company led by Brigham Young; (2) the passengers on the ship Brooklyn, *led by Samuel Brannan; and (3) the Mormon Battalion led by U.S. Army officers and Mormon soldiers.*

The Pioneer Company was the most important and consisted of companies which traveled westward from Nauvoo across Iowa to Winter Quarters, arriving in the valley of the Great Salt Lake July 1847. Simultaneous with the exodus from Nauvoo was the passage of some 230 Saints from the eastern branches of the church aboard the ship Brooklyn, *which sailed from New York around the Horn, arriving in San Francisco 29 July 1846. Many* Brooklyn *Saints remained in California. Others made their way to Salt Lake Valley. At the Iowa camping grounds the third group splintered off: The Mormon Battalion enrolled at Fort Leavenworth and marched along the Santa Fe Trail westward to San Diego where it mustered out of service. Some soldiers headed for the Great Salt Lake or Winter Quarters to meet their families. Others headed for the gold fields of northern California.*

President Young's Pioneer Company set the pattern for thousands of westering Saints who travelled from staging stations in Iowa across the Great Plains to the Salt Lake Valley. Brigham Young returned to Winter Quarters in 1848 and led the companies which included Louisa and her daughters. They arrived in Salt Lake on 20 September 1848. Eight days later, 28 September, Addison Pratt, the missionary, arrived from California. The Crosbys were in Willard Richards's company and arrived 12 October 1848.]

21st day [September 1848]. Yesterday P.M. we drove our teams into the centre of town, (so called) camped on the green near the Fort, built of adobies covered with dirt. Many old friends came out to greet us, and gave us a hearty shake of the hands. They had preceded us to the promised land and glad were we to see their faces once more![1]

22d day. Mrs. Addison Averet invited us to dine with her, we had a splendid dinner of vegetables. I had also green corn for my supper the first night. In the afternoon Sister Rogers came to see us, whose husband had shown us great kindness in times of distress in Winter Quarters. We had never seen her, but we felt the highest respect for the wife of him who had pitied us in our affliction. She invited us to share what conveniences she had in the way of house room; which we accepted, and found her an amiable lady. She had a good garden, and was very liberal in giving us all the vegetables we could use.

There was a large bowery built where publick services were held three times on the Sabbath day. Again we heard the voice of the Presidency and the Twelve sounding in our ears in a land we could call our own. My heart was more than glad. I was expecting my husband every day. I had heard that my sister and family were in a company crossing the plains, I knew they would soon be in. I felt that in the midst of trials, the Lord had remembered mercy.

The third day after our arrival Sister Rogers was delivered of a child. She was able on the second day to sit up and play the accordian.

[Reunion of Louisa and Addison, the Crosbys]

On Wednesday, 27th, horseback men began to come in from the camp of returning Soldiers. They informed us Mr Pratt would arrive the following day. Brother Parley P. proposed getting a carriage and taking us out to meet him. The children were greatly elated at the idea of seeing their father whom they had not seen for five years and nearly a half. Ann Louisa the youngest, said to the children with whom she played, "They tell me I have a father but I do not know him, is it not strange to have a father and not know him?" Thursday came, the day was bright. I went into my wagon to dress myself for the ride when the children came running to announce their father's arrival! He had just come off a long journey, looked rough and sunburnt. None but the eldest daughter recognized him, the others did not seem pleased with his appearance.

So much did we seem like strangers we scarcely knew what to say to each other. Ellen turned a little pale. The youngest put her hand behind her, would not reach it forth to receive her father's. He then presented her with all the toys, books, and curiosities he had brought her, then asked, "will you now have me for your father?" The answer was quickly given in the affirmative and they became very good friends.

The scene evidently affected him, as the feelings between him and his children were coincident. It was sad to realize what a change the lapse of years brings! Changing forms and features in the domestick circle, even to cause estrangement in long separation, which should as much as possible be avoided. Nothing short of the interest and advancement of the Kingdom of God could justify so lengthy a separation.[2]

Sabbath came, our daughters dressed themselves to accompany their father to the place of worship. A thousand eyes were upon us. So long had we been accustomed to receiving sympathy from those who saluted us, "I wish you much joy" (as hundreds clasped our hands) had a strange meaning. I would thank them but did not feel excited. To see the husband and father so long absent again with his family was a pleasant sight to all who had felt a deep interest for us in our great loneliness. For the soldiers who had just returned from a long campaign a feast was made, to which the "father" and his family were invited. It consisted principally of the fruits of the earth, produced in a land we could call our own, by the labor of the energetic pioneers. "The Father" took his seat on the stand, where he could see his daughters, grown up in his absence, join in the dance. It was a novel sight to him.

We soon purchased a house in the Fort of George B. Wallace, very comfortable. A young man by the name of John Eager who came from California with Mr. P. boarded with us. We had cheerful company every day in the house. What a change for us. We appreciated it and felt quite happy. Our evenings were spent in lively conversation, listening to the experience of the "missionary," interesting tales of the Islanders, which we never tired of hearing.

When three weeks had passed away, Dr. Richards arrived with a company from the east; in which was my sister and her family. We had a house to receive them in. The amount of conversation was unparalleled. My brother-in-law had remained in Nauvoo through a mob war, had lived two years in Iowa, while I lived in Winter Quarters. Our experiences had been varied, and much of a thrilling and startling nature. It was not strange that the rehearsals were incessant.

As often as I reiterated the trying scenes I had passed through in the five years, his spirit would seem to change, as I dwelt on the benevolence of some and the neglect and unkindness of others. Towards the first he would shed tears of gratitude, in view of the latter he would appear stern and irrascible. I was soon admonished to be cautious in my manner of relating incidents. I would not dare mention the name of one who had done us an injury, or had closed his ears to our complaints in time of trouble.

. . . The winter evenings passed pleasantly away. My sister lived near me. My third daughter [Lois] lived with her, as she had no daughter of her own, and but one son [Alma].

Provission was very scarce, but for the most part we had plenty of the necessaries and some of the luxuries, brought from a foreign country, so that we were ennabled to invite our friends to visit us. I had learned not to feel alarmed when our supplies grew small, and no prospect of replenishment. I was accustomed to remark, "One need not fear, the Lord will provide." It was a great encouragement to my husband to see me hopeful and trusting.

Differences of opinion sometimes arose between us in regard to certain principles which had been revealed in his absence.[3] He seemed to have forgotten that the law of progression governed us. Things perfectly familiar to me were new and strange to him. This occasioned impressions in his mind that errors had crept into the church. And though he would often acknowledge that I had acted wisely in my long widowhood, and merited praise for my faithfulness, still he sometimes annoyed me with petty jealousies, so detrimental to domestic happiness.

During the winter Mr. Pratt taught an evening school, to instruct those who desired to learn the Tahitian language. Our children were all sent to a daily school, made comfortable for shoes and clothes, we all realized the blessing of having a father to provide for them. Spring returned. Mr. P. engaged in farming.[4]

[A Second Mission Contemplated]

The subject began to be agitated of his being called to return to the Islands, with his family and several elders with a view to enlarge the mission. (Many were anxious to go with us.) It was deemed necessary to wait till after harvest in order to procure supplies to serve us on the journey to the pacific coast. Six families were appointed to go with us, we were all in fine spirits. Business was arranged to this effect, land disposed of, goods and articles we did not wish to carry bargained away. We saw no obstacles in the way of our going at the appointed time, when lo, all taken by surprize, the whole gentile world came rushing to the gold mines!

California, was the emigrants watchword! Every thing imaginable [was] being brought into the Mormon Forts for sale; at almost as low rates as goods could be bought in N. York City. Their teams were jaded, wagons broken down. Now, they wanted fresh animals, and pack saddles. It was a fine chance for trade. We could hear of great destruction of property and strife on the route to California. It was deemed advisable for the missionaries to defer their contemplated adventure till the excitement was over. Thus were we held in suspense most painful to endure! For myself I had no fears of trouble on the way, my trust was in the Lord. Our friends seemed fearful and solicitious. President Young would not counsel Mr. Pratt to take his family, would only consent that he should take them on his own responsibility, if he had faith and courage. I felt it was all the liberty he need ask.

The council at length proposed that Mr. P. should go with his wife and leave the children. The idea to him was preposterous! He could not consent to it for a moment. The children were frantically opposed! Frances the second affirmed with great emphasis, "You cannot leave me I will run behind the wagon and cry all the way to California!" The idea was soon abandoned. There now appeared something left for us to decide, which we could not do. We resolved to go and lay our case before the President and ask him to decide for us. It resulted in counsel for the family to be left again, the "elder" to go by himself. I remarked to Sister Young, in a humorous tone, "If I am left again I shall choose another man." She replied, did not believe I would, I had been faithful so long. Says, "you are not in earnest." "I am more than half so," I answered. She sympathized, said what she could to comfort me. I felt aggrieved and weighed down with sorrow.

We went to our home and informed the children of the decision. They commenced weeping, and continued in tears nearly the whole time for three days! The second girl wept incessantly. She had overheard what her father had said about leaving us and "going out free." She did not like the sound. She came to me with the very serious air, saying, "Mother, I have concluded to stay and let you go rather then you and father should part." I refrained from smiling at her sincerity; I saw the struggle she was enduring. I told her I believed all would be overruled for our best good. We would trust in the Lord, however trying it might be. The following day was solemn. We were all in tears. The scenes of other years came before me, when I had my family to provide for and little or no means. My heart shrank from the repetition of past trials.

While in this disturbed state of mind the Twenty Fourth July drew near. A great celebration was on hand. Preparations must be elaborately made for a great feast. With my saddened heart how was I to perform my task? The day was anticipated as one of great joy, being the day on which the pioneers landed in Salt Lake Valley. I had my part to act. Could I affect to be cheerful when my fate was not decided, and I was held in cruel suspense? My heart trembled like a leaf in autumn, ready to fall to the ground! The day preceding the celebration brother John Brown and wife came to see us, and spend the night. I assumed a cheerful appearance, as they were friends for whom I had a high respect. I arose early in the morning ate a slight breakfast, and before seven o'clock we were on the way to the bowery.

I had pain in my head, and was otherwise indisposed. All was life and animation. How is it possible thought I, that one can be sad in such a place as this. The processions all in uniform, was an admiring sight. The music was exhilirating in the highest degree. The tables were spread with the choicest varieties of things produced from the richest soil, and by our own hands labor. I was seated at the table, which extended through the entire bowery. The sight was grand! Not a mouthful could I eat. I rushed out of the crowd, went in to a tent and laid down. So oppressive was the heat I could not remain there. I went back to my seat and determined to rest there to the end of the exercises. The speeches and toasts were exciting. I was forced to smile, even to outbursts, and to my surprize I found myself a partaker in the meriment.

I made a mighty effort to banish every thing else from my mind, except the pleasant scenes before me. I began to be interested in what I heard, and ere the close, I was quite free from pain. No sooner had I reached my own home than I set my table, made coffee, had a variety of every thing good, and ate a hearty meal. I seemed to enjoy the food as a sort of revenge for not being able to eat any thing at the feast. I began trying to be reconciled to have my husband go and leave us again. Exciting stories were told about robberies on the route. I had no fears. Frances would often say, "Pa will not be so safe to go alone. The robbers would be more likely to plunder a lone man, and take his team from him, than they would if he had his family. They would pity a poor woman and children!" Poor child, said I, you know but little about robbers. A few days passed in suffering suspense, and word came to us from elder C. C. Rich to call at his house.

We went fully expecting a communication of some importance. The moment I was seated I fixed my eyes intently upon his, and was ready to listen with intense interest! He at length remarked thus, "I have been talking with President Young and it is now decided that brother Pratt shall remain at home until next spring." Joy too great for utterance sprang up in my heart. I thought what glad tidings it would be to our four daughters. I wished to be the bearer of the news, but there was a listener, who ran before us and informed; and ere we reached home they had been to nearly every house in the Fort to tell the news. The friends rejoiced with them and when we entered the house they were sitting cozily around the fire talking it over; their countenances beaming with delight. Mixture of joy and sorrow, is life!

[Addison Recruited for the Jefferson Hunt Party]

Congratulations from the friends were repeated over and over. Plans were laid for the winter. Three weeks had passed away and no vision had crossed our minds that another trial was at hand. A company of emigrants came in bound for California, the south route. They had engaged Capt. Hunt to pilot them through an unexplored region. It happened one morning while I was preparing breakfast that Capt. H. called at the gate and requested Mr. P. to wait on him a few moments. In an instant I

suspected what was in contemplation. It ran through my veins like electricity. I said to myself, "he is soliciting company for the expedition." And
so it proved. C. C. Rich and A. Pratt were chosen to help or accompany
Capt. Hunt in piloting the emigrant train through the Southern route to
the Pacific. Again our hopes were prostrated. It seemed cruel in the
extreme, but not a word was to be said.[5]

It was for the gospel we were called to make sacrifices, we must have,
like, "Moses," respect for the recompense and reward. We were in no situation to be left. No house built on our city lot, wood at a great distance. I
ground down the rebellion of my heart, determined to let it break rather
than murmur at my fate. I expressed my entire willingness to have my
husband go. In some parting lines I wrote, "Now I am fully reconciled to
say adieu." My daughter says, "O, Mother it sounds too willing; do change
it a little!" Accordingly I did, writing, "I must try to be resigned." I felt
great anxiety about the children. They were now at an age to need a
father's counsel; were often inclined to disobedience, and though not
decidedly stubborn it required much reasoning and expostulation to
guard them against the influences of giddy companions!

The 4th of Oct was the day appointed for him to start. All was bustle
and confusion, a very little time allotted for preparation. I happened to
say something in the tone of complaint, my companion having already
more on his mind than he knew how to bear, gave me short answer, and
appeared exceedingly irritated! I felt for a moment that heaven and earth
were combined against me. I indulged in a profusion of tears, struggled
to suppress them, resolved to cherish no unkindness in my heart towards
him. He gave us the parting hand, and at the instant I felt quite comforted. By the generous aid of some brethren from California he left us
means to sustain us through the winter. He had been gone a half hour or
more, when a sister Thomas, an intimate friend of his, called to bid him
farewell. She wept sorely, when she found she had come too late. I knew
he had to call at Brother C. Rich's. Thinking he might be detained there
I proposed going in pursuit of him.

We did so, found him on the street. Sister T. with kind words gave
him a parting blessing, which he returned, they made their adieus, and
we walked about with him till he was ready to leave town. We parted at the
corner near Orson Spencer's residence. The children were with me, and
we made our way back to our lonely dwelling. Brother James Brown
though appointed on the mission was not ready to start with the company, but would follow on. He walked home with us, seemed much
affected in view of our bereavment. He bade us a kind good night, and we
were again alone. I struck a light in the house, but so vacant did it seem
we all sat down outside. The light was burning in the empty room; truly it
was like the night of death.

Brother Johnathan Holmes lived in a room adjoining, the kindest people in the world. I urged the children to go with me to sit awhile with them, but no, they would indulge their grief in silence. I left them weeping, and went in for a few moments relief. They were full of sympathy, and kind expressions, assuring me of their unvarying friendship, which ever after proved firm and unshaken. When the evening was far spent we went into our desolate house. Soon the children feeling exhausted sank into profound slumber. Then it was I gave vent to the feelings of my heart in a torrent of complaints. I wept, I groaned, I prayed, exclaiming "will my sufferings never come to an end?" I felt free to indulge my grief because there was no eye or ear to witness it. I retired to my bed, but not to sleep. Nature's sweet restorer would not come to me. I arose in the morning pale and languid. My sister Crosby spent the day with me. She entreated me to be comforted, to acknowledge the hand of God in whatever fell to my lot.

[Rendezvous at Cottonwood]

Towards evening, to our great surprize the young man H. Blackwell who had started with Mr. Pratt returned. Said they were detained at Cottonwood on account of a lame ox. They had sent him back to get another. I asked, "why did Mr. P. not come himself?" He replied, "He did not wish to have the parting scene repeated." I sat down immediately and wrote him a letter. Truthfully I remarked, "Had you returned yesterday it would have given me greater joy than your presence did after a five years absence!" No sooner had the letter gone, than I resolved to go myself, thinking he might be detained there several days. I mentioned my intention to Brother Holmes. He fully approved of it, and said I should have his horse to ride.

The distance was ten miles and although I had been there I did not know the way. I made ready early and rode out into the street. Brother Horace Eldridge saw me and inquired, "where are you going?" "To Cottonwood, but I do not know the way." I told for why, and he kindly offered to go with me. He was on his horse, and we rode on briskly together. We talked much of the unexpected departure, and of the uncertainty of our overtaking the company. My heart vibrated with hope and fear. As we drew near John Brown's I saw the covered wagon and knew it. Mr. P. was in the yard yoking the cattle to move on. He seemed greatly surprized to see me. We went into the house and very soon our eldest daughter arrived from Provo, where she had been with others on a visiting tour.

As soon as she alighted from the carriage we discovered she had received an injury. Her head was bandaged, and one eye was bruised and swollen. Her father raised the bandage to examine her eye, was moved to tears at the thought of the narrow escape she must have made. We all dined together at Brother Brown's. The company then started on to go a few miles and camp. Mr. Eldridge returned home. J. Brown offered to go with me, and we rode with Mr. Pratt to his camping ground and staid over night. Early in the morning we bade him farewell, himself and companions invoking the blessing of God upon us. They started on their dangerous journey through a trackless wilderness and we hastened back in time to breakfast with Bishop Crosby's. I began by this time to feel quite cheerful, the burden on my heart was lighter.

[Winter of 1849–50]

Brother J. Brown escorted me back to my home in the Fort where the friends greeted me with smiles, feeling assured at the first sight the excursion had done me good. My recruited spirits reflected on the children, and we felt more like ourselves again. We turned over our blessings, counted and found they were many. We had $65.00 in money, grain to last us through the winter, besides two fat cattle. Conference commenced that day, I attended the next. I looked over the congregation, noticed there were several missing; and though I felt lonely, it was not a feeling of dispair. A brother came to board with us and furnished our wood. He was help and company. About the middle of winter he became uneasy, wanted to go where he could make money. We felt sorry to have him leave us, entreated him to stay.

He told us he had engaged his brother to get wood for us; he failed to do it, and we were left without in cold stormy weather. Then it was Brother Jonathan Holmes showed his friendship for us in an act of kindness few men would have performed under the circumstances. He was a shoemaker, accustomed to keep indoors in cold weather. He took his team, went eight miles to get a load of wood for us. I felt grateful indeed, and never can I forget it. The people commenced to make feasts, to invite their relatives and friends; and a few would remember a poor lone woman like me, whose husband was on the opposite side the globe, preaching the gospel. Generally those were invited who were able to return the act of civility, contrary to the injunction in scripture. "When thou makest a feast, call in the poor, the halt," &c.

On several occasions I was very much grieved, being forgotten and neglected at festival associations by those on whom I had a claim for friendship and attention. I would at such times endeavor all in my power to find an apology for them, rather than believe it intentional, cruel as their forgetfulness might appear. I could not endure that the ardor of my attachment should be cooled towards them. Ah! how much grace do we need in our hearts to enable us to respect the injunction of the Apostle!

"Mind not high things but condescend to men of low estate." I often asked, "why should the reverses of fortune, occasioned solely by obedience to the gospel subject one to indifference on the part of others living under the same law, who happen to be more fortunate. Independent of my own experience personally, I have observed it in many instances. I was never without sympathy, a balm for incurable wounds!

When the winter was over, the man who had left us in cold weather, returned having been in great difficulties with Indians and deep snows, enduring great fatigue, and making nothing. By this time we had become accustomed to struggling on alone, as we had done in former years, and it was not to be expected that any man would involve himself with the care of another man's family without a suitable remuneration. In my loneliness my old friend Joel Parish did not forget me. He sent his son sixteen miles with a load of wood. Likewise Brother Thomas Tomkins sent the same distance to my relief. At one time when I had solicited wood from the bishop of my Ward and was refused, on the ground that there were others more needy than I was, I wrote a note to Bishop Addison Averett, of another Ward, informing him of the circumstances. He came immediately with a carriage load already cut for the fire. Thus did I learn the difference in the dispositions of men.

[A Visit from Sister Mary Ann Young]

On a certain day in the month of March Sister Marian Young called at my house to inquire how I was feeling, and whether I had any request to make of President Young. So distracted were my thoughts I knew not how to answer her. She asked, "have you a desire to go to your husband?" I dared not say I had, so great was the dread of such an immense journey. I could not choose between the performance of it without my companion on the way, and another five years widowhood! I told her Brother Tomkins had offered to take us to California in case the Church decided to send us to the Islands. As soon as she heard that I saw she favored my going, and I regretted telling her. I trembled alternately, sometimes fearing I might be sent, and again that I might not. Could I have received an affectionate letter from my husband encouraging me to come it would have tranquilized my mind.

I found my spirit growing rebellious; imagined my trials greater than any other woman's ever was. I imagined my companion was glad to go from home because I could not always manage to please him. From the indulgence of that unhappy spirit I suffered more than from all the privation and poverty I had passed through. I laid my cause before the Lord, and plead with Him to let the day dawn, and the day star arise in my heart. I besought the sisters who pitied me to pray; which they did with fervor, and assurance that all would be overuled for my good. Conference drew on; I knew my fate would be decided. A thousand miles travel over an unsettled country, 500 miles voyage at sea, to labor among a people distinct from my own.

I saw there was but two ways, stand alone and assume great self reliance, be father and mother both to my children, create means to sustain them, live crowded up in a Fort, a complete mudhole in wet weather. If I was sent to the Islands, my daughters, the elder ones now nearly at a marriageable age, must be taken from their associates, to a foreign land. For myself I would not decide, but earnestly sought to know the mind and will of the Lord. In conversations with Dr. Willard Richards, I remarked to him, that were I an elder I would never consent to stay so long from my family, that I would go deliver my message as speedily as possible, and return to fulfill my domestic obligations. He smiled, and though he did not in words concur, I knew he felt the justice of my sentiments. I was between two great fires; which ever way I turned I would encounter the flames. I wrestled in prayer, my friends prayed for me, and all their prophesies were that I would go to the Islands of the seas, to join my companion. There I should be blessed in teaching children of nature whose minds were dark, to know and love truth.

[Louisa, Daughters, and Crosbys Called to the Mission]

1850, 6th of April. I attended Conference. I listened to the first discourses, they were comforting. At length the appointments were given out. Brother T. Tomkins was appointed to go to the Islands and take Addison Pratt's family! I heard no more. An indiscribable sensation pervaded my whole system! Several persons were appointed to go with us, in whose society I could not foresee much pleasure. At intermission I went to President Young's. I talked with Sister Y. and urged the promise I once had, that if I went my sister should go with me. She promised to use her influence, and the succeeding day my brother-in-law was appointed on the mission. I had thought if that was done my mind would be relieved.

I found I was mistaken. I now felt to blame myself for my solicitations. She had a pleasant home, and was comfortable. Her home must be sold to make the necessary preparations. She was tranquil and unmoved. A short time was allotted us to make ready. I was extremely weak. My good friends, Holmes, stood by me in every time of trial. My daughters had all they could do to pay farewell visits and receive calls. Sister H. kindly offered her assistance to do every thing that seemed burdensome to me, thus proving herself a friend in time of need. Sister Daniel Russell spent days with me, aiding by her agreeable conversation to strengthen and encourage me. I disposed of various little articles which it was impracticable to take with me, which gave me great pain to part with. Some of these were curiosities my husband brought from the Islands, dear to me beyond description. The circumstances attending the disposal of them occasioned me a reproof the most cutting of any I ever received in my life.

I betrayed a childish spirit owing to the great weakness of my mind at that time. The person did not understand my situation, it was not in my power to maintain that dignity and self control that the friend had expected of me. My friend Sister Holmes deeply sympathized, and felt that I was unjustly reproved. I told my grief to Sister John Taylor; she tried to soothe me, and heal my wound, but Oh, my heart was sore! The dear woman had discerned my anguish and entreated me to confide my secret to her. I loved her from that hour.

The hearts of many seemed open to assist me. I saw a rising interest in my welfare. Homes were offered my eldest daughters if they would remain with the church and let their mother go, but all the generous offers were unheeded by them. The novelty of the journey, and the prospect of meeting their father prevailed over every other consideration. I was very successful in obtaining supplies for the tour by land, in San Francisco we were assured we should find liberal hearted Brethren who would fit us out for the sea voyage.

[Farewells, Blessings]

May 7th [1850]. Left the old Fort. We sold our 'Dobe room for $25.00. Started at 5 o'clock, after a day spent in bustle and excitement, buying, selling, parting with friends, giving and receiving gifts. With great reluctance I bade them farewell. True friends have they been to me, tried and proven. I thought in the morning it would be impossible to get my goods packed to start, [so] they were tumbled in without order, and when the last article was deposited I felt a thousand pounds weight roll from my heart and shoulders. Sister Glover had presented me with some tea in a glass jar, it was set loose in a trunk not locked. The trunk [was] placed on a large chest in front of the wagon. All unconcerned, we let the wagon start. Down went the trunk. Everything fell on the ground, the jar broke, and behold, all my tea was spilt in the sand. I did not think it worth a moment's thoughts, compared with the great things in contemplation.

We made a call at President Young's, found supper ready. We partook of their hospitality, and Brother Y. blessed me. He said I was called, set apart, and ordained, to go to the Islands of the sea, to aid my husband in teaching the people. That I should be honored by those with whom I travelled, that all my wants should be supplied. That no evil should befall me on the journey, that I should lack nothing. I should have power to rebuke the destroyer from my house, that he should not have power to remove any of my family, that I should do a good work, and return in peace, many other things. All which he sealed upon my head in the name of the Lord.

I thanked them for all their loving kindness, bade them farewell, and we drove to the Warm Springs, and stopt with Brother William Hendricks. Some of the friends came with us there, and spent the evening. We were kindly entertained, and the following day a company of young people travelled fourteen miles with us. We called and spent the night with those who had been our benefactors in troublous times. The good old people, Joel Parish and wife, loaded us with blessings, shed tears at the remembrance of our past sufferings, and prayed earnestly that we might be protected on our long journey till we should reach in safety the desired haven. Brother J. Holmes had just then moved into that settlement. He came to me and said, "Have I in every thing done as you wished me to do, and can you carry a good report to Brother Pratt of my faithfulness?" I assured him he had done all and more than I could have presumed to ask, and I prayed that blessings might follow him all his days, and I knew brother Pratt would say amen!

CHAPTER EIGHT

Mission Begun, Salt Lake City to Sacramento

Memoirs, 7 May 1850 to July 1850

[Mission Begun, Salt Lake City to Sacramento]

After exchanging tears and adieus, six wagons started on, 24 persons in all, expecting to overtake a small company at Bear River.[1] We found the Weber very high, the water running over the middle of the bridge. We got safely over, called at Brown's Fort, where dinner was prepared for us, by a good sister, whose name is Abigail Abbot, a neighbor in Nauvoo. She made me a present of a good cheese. Her daughters accompanied us on horseback several miles. We came to Ogden river, had a almost perpendicular hill to come down. The men let the wagons down by the help of ropes. Had a severe time in crossing the water. After we crossed the bridge the wagons mired; the men were in the water up to their waists, more than an hour.

Mr. Tompkins was wroth because some who got over first did not come back to help others. He had cause to be angry. After we were out of the water it began to rain severely. We travelled three miles and camped at Brother Chase's to wait for fair weather. We heard the Weber bridge washed away the night after we crossed over. Who can say we did not cross in the right time. We came to Bear River, found President Clark's company waiting for us. With great exertion we got the cattle over. Camped on the bank.

13th day we crossed Malad Creek, one of the most intolerable places my eyes ever beheld! Cattle and men up to their backs in mud for twenty rods, and more. What a world is this, thought I. Men will travel over it however impossible it may be! We got out of the mud at last, camped at two o'clock. I have a great aversion to camping before night. I cannot feel well when a good day's drive has not been accomplished.

110

In the afternoon the company was organized. Passed resolutions to keep the Sabbath day. Likewise to have morning and evening prayers. H. Clark President, W. Huntington, Counsel. We have music in the camp, two violins and a flute, besides there are many singing birds in this country, which delight me very much. Now 24 miles from Bear River, a place of hills and dales. Sister C. C. and I walked out among the hills. As we were returning two bullets whistled by our heads. We started with fear! We came to camp found Hanks and Moses had been firing guns for sport, not knowing anyone had gone out. They were admonished to be more cautious. The evening was spent in singing hymns, and spiritual songs. How comforting to hear prayers in this lonely spot of earth! What an idle life to travel with ox teams. And yet no other would do so well on such roads. I gaze around me, see the wagons all corraled, cattle lying down at night. Scenes of other days come vividly to mind. What wandering pilgrims we have been!

18 day. Travelled 20 miles camped at three o'clock. I walked alone; climbed upon a huge pile of rocks. From their heights I had a full view of the surrounding country. I called to mind the lapse of ages those cragged rocks had remained there. They were covered with moss of various colors. I examined every part of them with intense interest. I gazed towards the valley where I had left the saints, an ardent desire sprang up in my heart that I might live to return to them.

[City of Rocks]

23d. On account of the Cazyer river being too high to be forded we had to go round the mountain, came to camp at 4 o'clock, called the place City of rocks. We all went out on an exploring excursion, returned fatigued, but much amused. The beautiful white rock resembling marble made us wish they were in some location where they could be made available.

21st. We have been traveling over mountains all day the most delightful scenery my eyes ever beheld. Ridges of hills of all sizes and shapes variagated with shrubbery, mostly cedar. The hills resemble the orchards of New England. What a prospect for a painter! I found stones I called connelion, white clay, of which the boys made pipes, was found in quantities. A snow storm overtook us, we could not start till one o'clock. Mr. Tomkins found a sheet iron stove; gave it to me. I found it very useful.

30th day. Started very early. Travelled a short distance, come to a stream of water called Martin's Fork. We found written on a board, "Too deep to ford, remove your loading, prepare a wagon bed for a boat." We did so and all got safely over with hard labor. Very deep mire on both sides. The brethren were all merry, making a scene of amusement of it.

31st. Crossed one of the tributaries of St. Mary's. Made a bridge of willows, drew the wagons over by hand. When the last wagon was over the men commenced hallooing to the top of their voices. The next crossing was effected by doubling teams.

1st day of June. Crossed Martin's Fork. Water being high we took everything from the bottom of our wagons and piled them on our bedsteads, by that means we got safely through. The same day one of the Indian boys belonging to the company put a can of powder into my stove. Not for mischief, but coming in from hunting, the stove being tied on the outside, he thought to remove it as soon as we came to camp. Boy like, he forgot it. I built my fire put my kettle on. Once I removed the kettle and leaning over stirred the fire. My cow was grazing a little way off, an impression came to me, as if some one had whispered "walk out where your cow is, and look at her." I did so, and while I was standing there I heard a report like a canon fired. I returned immediately, found my stove blown over the top of a covered wagon! It was crushed, as with a sledge hammer.

My kettle was set upon the ground badly bruised. The boy was severely reprimanded, and I had serious reflections the remainder of the day. The fact of my being warned to walk away from the spot an instant before the explosion, caused me to realize that a protecting arm was held over me, and that my guardian angel must have been very near me for which I felt thankful. Some there were who felt as I did, were serious over the affair, the more giddy portion were disposed to ridicule the effect it had upon me, and in their foolhardihood would laugh at the idea, of being solemn at the instance of so marvelous an escape.

June 1st. This day seven years since my companion started on his mission to the Pacific Islands. A day of days was that to me! Had I known on that day what seven years experience would bring to me it seems to me, one glympse of it would have struck me out of existance in an instant. It was wisely hidden from me. Sorrows mountains high have rolled over me, and yet I have withstood all the storms of adversity, am still alive and on my way to the Islands of the seas, to teach the poor, dark people the gospel that has cost me so much.

2d day. Awnings are spread in front of our wagons where we are to hold publick worship. Elder J. Busby made some spirited remarks. All the speakers acknowledged we had been signally blessed on our journey. The brethren decide on a frolic, to help them over the impassable gulphs, rocks, and dust, almost to suffocation. I told the Captain if he should send me ahead to explore I should return with an evil report and declare it impassable to go that way. St. Mary's River flows in grandeur here. Dust we must have while we travel near it.

[Along St. Mary's (Humboldt) River]

12th day. Horn sounded at 4 o'clock. Camp started before breakfast, travelled a short distance. Stopt for the day to enjoy a good rain which we have long wished for.

14th day. A beautiful road all day. Found a splendid camping ground, large shrubbery on the banks of the river, good wood. Emigrants overtook us from Ohio out of provisions. The company invited them to breakfast. Sold them breadstuff.

15th day. Made a blunder, travelled ten miles in a wrong direction, a level road, but deep sand, came upon Capt. Smith's company. Camped to spend the Sabbath. Emigrants attended our meeting at 8 o'clock. Brother Clark preached the gospel sermon very much to the purpose. Elder Busby bore testimony with great warmth, and readings of expression. After meeting two strangers called upon us, said they were from Nauvoo. The very sound of the name thrills through my nerves, recollection of the past rushes to my mind. Emigrants from all parts are thronging the way to the mines; little or no provisions; poor worn out animals.

17th. A country of desolation have we passed today. 25 miles without feed or water. Barren sandy plains. Camped on a slough fed by Mary's River. Our wagons stand on a ridge of rising ground, our fires blazing high below. The reflection on our white houses on wheels presents a romantic sight. The moon shines with unusual brilliancy. The scenery in the evening is delightful.

19th day. Started on the desert. Filled everything with water. The country presents an exceedingly singular appearance, perfectly level: has every sign of having been the bed of a mighty river. The ground has a yellowish cast, without a particle of vegetation. Under the lee of the mountains there is the appearance of water, very deceiving to the traveller. As we approach, it recedes from our view, [and] we are reminded of what we have read and heard of an oasis, so alluring to the poor thirsty men and teams.

[Salmon Trout River]

We are at length safely over the desert, travelled till two o'clock, rested the cattle till daylight. Started on again through deep sand. I walked from sundown till eight o'clock. I went into my wagon slept awhile, then walked again, all of us, till we came to Salmon Trout River. Ten o'clock we saw the water. The poor cattle could scarcely be kept from rushing into the river with the wagons. The men gave them water in buckets, all they dared to let them drink.

Badir the Socialist has made trouble in the camp by coming without supplies. Mr. Mills the phrenologist who hired his passage with him, is now destitute; likewise a family he engaged to take through. Although the two men above mentioned are not of our faith, the brethren will not see them want for food.

Just over another 20 miles desert, without feed or water, camped on the bank of the river, a most delightful place. The trees are large and standing in close proximity [with] heavy foliage. Here the young men (about nine in the evening) blackened themselves and had an Indian war dance. The old Socialist being far in the rear, the artificial Indians started back with a view to frighten him, were defeated in their plan, returned disappointed, went down the river with a view to use water as a means of turning back to white men. Spent one whole day in settling difficulties. Got them all settled, retired to a grove and made a swing. Had a large rope suspended from a high tree. The moon arose about nine, in all its beauty. I have never witnessed grander scenery. The towering trees, the murmuring waters, the clear blue sky bespangled with stars, the grand queen of night, all combined to make the scene strikingly lovely.

Better than all, we had agreeable company. The following day travelled through deep sand not so rough as common. The mountains on one side covered with large pine trees growing quite to the summit, from which flow out several beautiful streams of swift running water. Thick shrubbery growing luxuriantly on either bank, the broad prairie adorned with green grass, resembling the meadows of New England. The whole scenery is exquisitely beautiful. We have not seen on the whole journey so rich a growth of grass. Farewell to the deserts. We have prophesied a settlement here in future. 100 miles from the mines.

28th. Started early and came to the mammoth pine trees. I stood beneath the shade of one tree, which would make lumber enough to build two common houses. To see such astonishing trees growing out of sand and gravel not a particle of soil, filled every beholder with wonder and admiration. We passed today beautiful streams of water flowing down from the mountains, cold as ice, and clear as crystal. We have overtaken Mr. E. Hanks' company who left S.L. Valley three weeks before us. They have travelled on the Sabbath, we have not, and have gained on them.

29th. This morning men were sent ahead to explore the road over the mountains. Met travellers coming from the other side, who reported the road passable. They concluded to relinquish the excursion and to stop here several days. The heat, though excessive, is rendered more endurable by the cool breezes from the mountains. Emigrants are coming to our camp half starved. We are compelled to feed them, cannot resist their entreaties.[2] Elder Moses delivered a lecture on the doctrines of our church, to which the strangers listened with apparent interest.

[Ascending the Sierra Nevada]

Now at the base of the mountains of rocks, covered with immense trees. What supports the roots I cannot imagine, not the least appearance of soil. Seven miles we traveled through the canyon a road too intolerable to think of. No person looking at the opening would suppose for a moment that wagons could pass without being broken in ten thousand pieces. But we came over safely, not a thing broken. In crossing a bridge where the water was running very swiftly one of the cows fell off and floated down the river as fast as the current could carry her. The men ran with a Larryette, hauled her out badly bruised.

July 5th. Now over the first mountains. To describe the road in justice would be impossible. Snow, rocks and much perpendicular heights, declinities deep and dangerous, yet we got safely over, with only a few trifling accidents.

I rode up the mountain on horse back. With great exertion I clung to the horse. I rode down in the wagon which fatigued me more than walking would. Is it possible that men can love gold to that degree that they will climb these mountains to obtain it? Oh, I pity the poor cattle! How faithfully they serve men, who are often unkind to them.

6th day. Now on the top of the second mountain, travelled over snow in some places thirty feet deep. The wind is blowing a heavy gale, cold as Greenland. The cows are left behind, a sad mistake.

7th day. Rumbling down the mountains all day. I had to lie in bed sick. Was not able to sit up. I hope I may never pass another such day.

8th day. One of the horses gone. Oh, the crowds that throng this highway going in search of gold, crowding about our wagons to be fed. We must feed them either for pay or without. They must have starved to death had we not been here with provisions and we only brought what we thought would serve us through. I wonder our stores are not exhausted.

[Tragedy Springs]

Today passed "tragedy springs" where three men on their way to S. Lake were murdered by Indians for their horses and clothes.[3] They were found and buried by their comrades, who in a few days overtook them. A bag of gold was found on the neck of one, which the Indians in their fright had not discovered. It was taken to the man's family and great lamentation was made over him who had toiled to gather the gold. Their graves are near a spring of clear water, and carved on the trunk of a large tree is the account of their sad fate. Many travelers there pause to gaze upon the spot, read the inscription, and sigh over the sorrowful end of their fellow men. The spring thus derived its name, Tragedy.

9th. This morning the men started in pursuit of the lost horse. They soon got on track of Indians. They took the squaws prisoners in hopes the Indians would bring back the horse. They were ensconced in the brush. The white men dared not venture in. The two Spanish boys well armed rushed down. One old Indian pitched battle with them. They shot at him but not to kill. He ran screaming. The squaws cried bitterly. Four guns were heard at camp. The white men returned. The boys were left behind, horse not found. Then we felt sure the poor boys were killed. Some said no they are not killed, have we not prayed that all our lives might be preserved. After a length of time the boys returned alive to the great joy of the whole company. They were good Spanish boys.

10th day. Roads unaccountable! Up and down like the affairs of life. Met traders with flour and groceries for the poor emigrants. The men went out in search of gold, found enough to buy some wine and brandy, to rejoice over the event of getting safely over the last mountain. We shouted glory halleluiah! Some of the crowd thought as did the father of the prodigal son "It was meet that we should make merry and rejoice." They wanted a jubilee.

[Into the Gold Country]

18th day. The horn sounded for preaching. The people assembled, prayed and sang hymns. In the midst of the exercises, Mr. Gilbert (outside the camp) commenced whipping his boy unmercifully. The meeting was interupted. One of the brethren commanded him to desist, which he resented. They called him to an account. A few there were who sought to justify him. The women soon after engaged in a lengthy discussion on the government of children, not however, till the meeting closed. We all "got the case." Now we are fairly in the gold country. A land of desolation, a barren desert. The poor diggers look forlorn. Behold, two men I saw from the State of Illinois. From the immediate vicinity of my brother, whom I have not seen for many years. They knew him and could inform me of his welfare.

I have been truly homesick today. May the Lord speed us on to our place of destination. Oh, what a dismal country! no feed no green thing growing, nothing here but gold.

16th. Camped in an oak grove near Brown's a fictitious name for Porter Rockwell. Found a spring of clear cold water.

17th. Today arrived Mrs. Amasa Lyman, C. C. Rich whom we all were most happy to meet. They brought me a letter from my husband dated April 14th. The same day he set sail at San Francisco for the Islands. The heat is almost insupportable! Several old friends who came to this country before us today called to see us. Men are reckless in this country.

There is great want of female influence. Filth and confusion throughout the whole country. Sister C. C. and I visited Browns and Stewards. They treated us kindly, made us presents. They make money by selling liquors and provisions to emigrants. To be obliged to see drunkenness and hear profane swearing, to earn a livelihood, and that without cessation, how can they endure it!

Preaching today by Bros. Rich and Lyman. To see their faces and hear their voices proclaiming the truth so far from home, is comforting to the soul.

23d Camped six miles from Sacramento. The publick buildings are made of cloth. Br. Crosby sold his oxen and wagon for $225.00.

24th. One year ago today we attended the great celebration in S. L. Valley. Oh, we hope they will remember us today and drink us a toast. We are camped on the north Fork of the Sacramento River. Water clear and soft. The brethren who went back to the mountains after ice and snow for S. F. market have just returned, tired, themselves and teams worn out. The price has fallen from one dollar, to five cents per lb.

[Sacramento]

25th. Came down to the Great City, that has made such a raise in the world. A great city it is, for the age of it, but so filthy it is dangerous for people to stop there.

CHAPTER NINE

From San Francisco to Tubuai

Journal A, Part 1, 26 July 1850 to January 1851

[Sacramento to San Francisco]

July 26th [1850] Pitched our tents on the bank of the river where we unloaded our waggons, and the man who had purchased them took them away. I saw my old waggon go, which for four years had been a sleeping room for the children: it was the last piece of property that remained of all the labor of our youth. I received thirty dollars for it.

The heat was intolerable, not a tree to shade us from the scorching sun; such excessive heat I am certain I never felt before; we were cooking over a hot fire, preparing food to go on board the bark, *Alden*, Capt. Alden, on which we had spoken our passage to San Francisco. Soon after we unloaded our goods, several gentlemen called on us with bottles of beer, wine, lemonade and mince pies to treat us; and to congratulate us on our safe arrival in the new country; they were very polite, and we were greatly obliged to them; being weary and overcome with heat, we needed refreshments.

Brs Lyman and Rich called and made us a visit in the tent. We took one walk into town, bought a few goods; the streets were full of old clothes and rubbish thrown out of the stores. Mr. Hues from St. Lewis called on us, the husband of Mary Parker, whom we had not seen from the time of our leaving Nauvoo; he informed us that his motherinlaw died at his house in St. Lewis of the cholera and that he had sent his wife with two children to Nauvoo that they might escape it. Several of our company called to bid us farewell, whom we felt sorry to part with.

The third day we went on to the Bark. J. Pendleton and M. Leonard came off to see us; the former looked very sad at parting with our daughters as to all appearance he had great attachment for them; the latter expressed concern about our taking passage on the Bark said we should

118

be a long time going to Francisco and the musketoes would trouble us; he wished he could see us safe on board a good Steamer, and I felt the same. The Bark was large and convenient but the hands had been sick a long time and every thing about the ship was dirty, exceedingly so. In vain they tried to get underway, the wind was against us; the first day by beating hard we made about a mile and a half, tied up to a tree at night; the bushes were thick on the bank and the musketoes were like sands on the shore for multitude.

One gentleman came in to our cabbin and contended about the berths; his wife being there he thought it his privilege to sleep there of course; we told him it was a new idea to us that gentlemen must lodge in the Ladies cabbin; he appeared resolute and determined to have his choice in the berths; we all retired and were in hopes to have a good nights rest; the musketoes soon commenced their ravages upon us, and he was the one to leave the cabbin and flee out for quarters on deck, and never adventured himself there again. We were all obliged soon to leave the cabbin, but we had no place of resort, for they were equally as bad on deck.

I wrapt myself in a thick blanket sat in my chair and tried to sleep, in spite of all my efforts to cover myelf they would find their way to my flesh, and being about two thirds larger than common insects of that class they inflicted pain like that produced by the sting of a bee; my feet and ankles became swolin and inflamed as did every part of my body where they bit me; day after day passed, and not one hour's sleep in a night did I have until I was so exhausted and worn out that I was not able to sit up; and yet could not lie down having every moment to fight as for my life; I prayed earnestly to be delivered; the children complained most bitterly we were all troubled and knew not what to do. The Capt. sent repeatedly to Sacramento to get a Steamer to tow the Bark down, obtained several promises which were not fulfilled. At length a little Steamer about half the size of the Bark came and after getting up steam for a long time attempted to pull us along; we rejoiced and thought we should soon be away from the musketoes; but all our hopes were vain; she could not stir us at all, gave up and roared away back to town.

After suffering a whole week being bruised and mangled by those cruel insects, Br. T. concluded to go to town and engage a steamer to call and take us off; he made a partial engagement but did not finish the bargain, promising to return if he concluded to accept that man's offer, he left him to make further inquiry; he found another boat; the Captain agreed to tow the Bark down but was not ready to sail; the former Capt. with whom he had partially agreed, came on, called for the passengers aboard the Bark, said Mr. Tomkins had agreed with him to call and take 20 passengers; we asked why he did not come on the boat himself, he replied he was left by accident. He made us believe what he told as well did the Capt, and he advised us to go. We made all possible speed to take our things off. Seventeen passeng[ers] left, the rest remained on the Bark, among them were my brotherinlaw and sister, he refused to leave believing the Capt meant to deceive us. Away we went on the steamer; Sister Tomkins declared her belief in what the Capt had told, that her husband had agreed with him to take us off. We rejoiced greatly that we were leaving the musketoes behind and were in hope that the loss of blood would be regained when we gained the residences of our friends in Francisco. We looked about the boat found it very comfortable. We put on clean clothes and took seats in the Cabbin.

Presently a gentleman came in, introduced conversation, asked where we had come from, where we were bound and several other questions. As soon as we mentioned Salt Lake he asked if we were Mormons? I told him frankly we were; he then wished to know something about our belief. I wanted to inform him in a short and comprehensive manner; instead of beginning with the bible, I asked him if he had heard of Joseph Smith? or I remarked that I supposed he had; he said yes, and asked if we really believed him to be a prophet. I told him we knew him to be a prophet, and that he had commenced a new dispensation on the earth, in which all things spoken by the prophets of old were to be fulfilled, that the gifts and blessings which existed in the church anciently were restored to our church, that knowledge and faith were prevalent, that the sick were healed by that faith, devils cast out, and promises obtained; that the gathering of Israel was fast taking place, and thus did I rehearse our belief like a lesson I had learned by heart, telling him in plain terms it was verily true; he appeared astonished that I should speak with so much confidence, said he could not believe it. I replied his disbelieving it could not make it untrue; he appeared disturbed and left the cabbin. I had with me one of Orson Pratt's pamphlets concerning the origin of this work. I laid it on the table covered it with a bible lying there, that some one might find it when I was gone, and perhaps the same gentleman, as he belongs to the boat.

We chose our stateroom went to bed the berths were clean, and now thought I sleep will be sweet tonight. I had not closed my eyes till I discovered that I was in a nest of bedbugs. I removed my bed to the floor and even there I could not keep clear of them; so the night passed away and the morning found us in the harbor.

[In San Francisco, 11 August to 15 September 1850]

We found our friends in the city who received us cordially, and bid us welcome to their houses. After four days came brother Tomkins; was not at all in a good humor, highly offended that we had left the Bark in his absence; Said he was there in four hours after we left with a steam boat to tow the vessel into the bay where she would be able to make her way along. His wife's feelings were hurt and he finally made an apology and it was settled.

I visited several of the *Brooklin* families found them very kind and liberal, they made me presents and treated me well.[1] With Sister William Morey I felt myself at home. Sister Corwin invited me to her house which was at Mr. Samuel Brannan's, a most splendid situation: the house was like a king's palace; I remarked to Mrs. B. that such a house would do me but little good in that place, but if I had it in the church at Salt Lake I should enjoy it. Br. William Lewis who was keeping a publick house at a place called Mission Deloras three miles from town came after us with a carriage and invited us to spend some time at his house. We accordingly accepted his invitation and were cordially entertained. The old mission was built in the year independence was delcared; it resembles some old ancient abbeys, and that is what it is, built by the Catholics and used for a nunnery formerly; it is of immense size but very low, long dark alleys, which strike the mind with horror. Some parts of it were fitted up in good style or at least confortable to relieve travellers; there were several very agreeable gentlemen boarders there. We spent near two weeks with the family; our elder daughters having been acquainted with Mrs. Lewis in the valley, were pleased to renew their acquaintance. With Br Quartus Sparks family who lived near I spent several days very agreeably; it is indeed very interesting to find brothers and sisters in strangers; they made us presents and showed themselves very friendly.

I cannot say I was pleased with the place; the city is built in a bed of sands and the wind blows a gale every afternoon; so there is always a cloud of dust which makes it disagreeable going out. A large fleet of ships were in the harbor, they looked to me like a funeral procession; all was bustle and, confusion; the streets narrow and dirty; there had been a great burning a little before we arrived there, but repairs were soon made; it is one of the greatest commercial cities in the world.

Br. William Carrington and wife were kind, received us into their house and boarded us for two weeks; his wife though not a member of our church, is a remarkably friendly and good disposed woman perfectly neat and industrious. She [is] one of those domesticated females who are so tenacious of order and good management they make a home so comfortable that one cannot help being pleased with them and contented in their dwellings.

Ten days after Mr. Tomkins came, the Bark landed with the remainder of the passengers; places were provided for us all and all the attention paid us we could ask for. The Bark had been baffling about in the bay for two weeks and those of us who left it were not sorry; except we thought it a pity to pay so much money to one who had deceived us. Br T. though a good man in many respects, is subject to little flurries of temper and impatiences; he felt it was draining very strong on his means to procure a passage for so many, and so it was, and whenever I heard of his making any complaint it was bitterness to me.

There is something so humiliating in the idea of being dependent that although he was called and duly authorized by the Church to go with us, and I knew we were both engaged in the same common cause, yet so much did I regret that I had not means of my own to go on an errand for the Lord at my own expense, that at times it made me quite unhappy. What I do for the cause of Christ I desire to do wholly at my own expense; and I pray for the means, that I may show my liberality and my willingness to do those things necessary to be done. And if any one gives, or lends to me in time of need, and thereby inspires my confidence, I pray that they may never in any way allude to it, in my hearing, as it will be sure to give me pain, and cause the favor to lose half its value. I can feel an obligation, it is not needful to tell me. Sister T. never but once refered to what she had done for us and then it was in a passion and I forgave her. She was good and kind, and her faith in this cause was strong.

[Voyage from San Francisco to Tubuai, Society Islands]

After a tarry of five weeks in Francisco our passage was engaged to Tubuai on board the Brig Jane A. Hersey Capt. Salmon. We set sail the 15th of Sept. [1850] in fulfillment of a dream Ellen had dreamed two years before being the precise time shown in the dream. We found the Captain a polite well bred man; likewise Capt. Hull who belonged on Tahiti and had come out in the vessel; both very gentlemanly and agreable. Mr. Poole a small owner in the Brig had his wife with him, a sprightly young woman of 17. She was company for our daughters; of english descent, proud and haughty but very interesting in conversation. There were several very clever young men sailors who seemed desirous of showing us every little kindness in their power; likewise the steward was a well bred negro from Boston; he was obliging and endeavored to make us comfortable. Our cabbin was large built on purpose for us between decks; there were in all twenty two passengers of the Mormon fraternity.

I had never supposed I should be sick on the water, on the contrary I was the first one taken. I took to my cabbin and my berth, determining to remain there till completely recovered, but I soon found I could not endure the close air in the cabbin. I was obliged to keep on deck all in my power; and altho it sometimes seemed like raising the dead to get out of my berth and dress myself yet when I found my life depended on it I made great exertion for no dread could be so great as that of being buried in the sea. Many a time when I felt that I could close my eyes and in a few moments drop out of existence a thought would suddenly cross my mind Ah, you will have to be buried in the sea if you die here! in an instant I would arouse myself, and make a desperate effort to go on deck; and it happened well for me that my eldest daughter was sick but a few days. She was able to take care of me, which she did faithfully. Day after day I laid on the hard deck with only a few blankets under me thinking of my weak body and my disheartened mind.

I complained in my heart of my fate which seemed to be that of always traveling about the world without my companion; some days I was able to read and having some interesting magazines with me I often found things suited to my condition, from which I drew instruction; hour after hour I would listen to the roar of the foaming billowing waves, and lift a silent prayer to him who has power to control the raging elements that he would preserve us from a watery grave, and carry us in safety to our place of destination.

When the cry of porpass or skipjack was heard I would call for some one to lift me up, and holding on to the side of the vessel, I would indulge my admiration till I almost forgot my weakness and pain. I constantly wished for something to excite as I found it a great means of throwing off a sense of my bad feelings, but oh, Sea sickness how horrible! it is continually dying, and yet you live! it is not to be told but only to be felt. The company were nearly all sick at times no one felt like praying or admistering to the sick, and for that cause I felt darkness; I longed to hear prayer, and to have hands laid on me; once I mentioned it but was told it was not best, there were so many unbelievers about us, but the apology did not satisfy me. I thought the devil might take his own course and I would take mine, and that was not to be afraid of him; I thought often of the words of the psalmist. "I kept silence even from good words, but it was pain and grief to me."

There were some jealous persons among us who wanted to get something to tell from one to another; a principle so detestable that he who calls himself a Saint should spurn it as he would a venomous serpent; that such a spirit was among us only showing itself in a small degree, was a grief to me, for I felt I had all I could bear without it.

For the first time in my life I took food as a medicine; forcing it down as I would a nauseous draught that was given to save my life; two or three times a flying fish was found on deck, which was cooked for me and was sweet to my taste; the only thing that I relished the whole voyage.

I should have often engaged in conversations, in vindication of my principles but by some of the breatheren it was not deemed wisdom to speak much upon them, for fear of creating prejudice; I therefore held my peace many times when I felt it would be a comfort to me to talk. I wished to be submissive to counsel. The weather was fine the most of the voyage; a

few days head wind was all the difficulty we met with; and had it been possible to have shaken off my seasickness I could have passed the time very
pleasantly. We spoke an american whale ship on the passage, from that we
got some green bannanas; they were the first I had ever seen, and tho'
very hard and unfit to eat I snatched them as if determined to make them
relish whether they would or not, the steward told me to wrap them in a
woolen cloth and lay them aside for a few days; which I did, and found
quite an improvement. On the whale ship they were trying out oil, we
could smell it plain tho' quite a distance from us. The Capt. came on our
ship and brought a little girl about six years old a very pretty child; his wife
was sailing with him; she had a pair of twin boys born at sea, they were at
that time near six months old; their father held them up for us to look at,
and though we could not seem them plain, we praised them and
remarked they were fine boys to be born on the boisterous ocean.

Five days before we reached Tubuai we saw the Pamutus at a distance an Island at sea is a gratifying sight; it breaks the monotony and
excites hope, and ere long we shall enjoy land again! We looked through
the spy glass and saw cocoanut trees, but were not near enough to discern
buildings. Hope then began to spring up in my heart that the voiage
would soon be over; two days before we landed I had a fainting turn the
severest I had ever had in my life: I called on the Elders to admisters to
me, they did so, and from that hour my darkness fled, and I was relieved
in body and mind.

As we drew near the Island, the children began to talk of meeting
their father; it never once occured to them that they should not meet him
the first moment when we landed. Frances, the second daughter had
often been sad on the way; frequently would retire to some secluded
place to indulge in silent reveries; when the Ship hove in sight of Tubuai
which was on the 19 Oct She was constantly on deck looking over the rail-
way towards the desired haven, her countenance brightened up with joy
no traces of subsequent sadness remaining; the hours seemed long, the
wind was contrary for a whole day we lay off and on; often looking
through the Spy glass endeavouring to descry some object to confirm our
hopes that all would be well with us when we landed nothing could we see
resembling human life: the great cocoanut trees towered their majestic
heads far above the horizon and their long leaves were waving in the
breezes; but the living beings were enshrouded in the thick foliage of the
shrubbery which grows every where over the Island. Ellen was certain her
father would come on board the brig as soon as it landed, as for myself
the thought of getting off the water and leaving my seasickness behind
was my highest ambition. What I should find or whom concerned me
very little. I wanted fried chickens and fish and something I could eat, a
good soft bed to sleep on; ah, thought I how thankful I shall be!

[Family on Tubuai, Pratt detained by French at Tahiti]

The 21st day in the afternoon the pilot come off to us. I looked at him from head to feet as a representative of the people with whom I must reside he had a rather huge appearance tho' I thought him good looking. I spoke to the Capt. to ask him if Paraita [Pratt] was on the Island. he answered he was not; in a moment Ellen's face was like marble. She sat down with folded hands and closed lips. I was prepared for the disappointment for I had pondered it in my heart and said to myself that such a thing would be like the rest of my luck or fortune. The idea was he was a prisoner on Tahiti the pilot said he was kept there by the governors orders: it did not alarm me; so seared was my heart with what I had suffered on the vessel I was sure all would be right when I was righted again. The man went off and the Capt sent word to have Mr. Grouard come on board, during the interval the daughters walked thoughtfully about deck.

At length brothers Grouard and Alexander came off to the Brig; they could scarcely believe their own eyes that such a company of American brethren had come to their Island. Br. Grouard had been seven years shut out as it were from the world; he had acquired an air of dignity and sobriety very nearly similating him with a Catholic monk; his eyes were sunken apparently with sorrow and his whole appearance was grave and majestick. I had seen him in the vigor of youth and thought him a gay lively man, now his look was full of wisdom and years. he however appeared happy to see us and very respectfully invited us to go on shore.

We were conducted over the coral reef with great care; the Island at a little distance presented a pleasing appearance, the beach being skirted with ito [*aito*], and boorou [*purau*] trees, together with bananna and cocoanuts, and a variety of shrubbery of the most living green; it being then the 21st of Oct. a season in which we expect to see the leaves turn yellow and fall off; not to see the least sympton of such decay, conveyed a pleasing sensation to the mind. The buildings tho far from being elegant, had an appearance of romance; little white cottages in the woods, shining through the green trees away from the hustle of the busy world, far, far away over the mighty ocean! to find the remnants of Israel enjoying tho' in a rude state an incessant Spring; this idea was exhilirating to one tired of the sea as I was. The buildings are built low but very long; plastered with lime made from the coral rock inside and out; there cannot be a purer white. I thought of eating the good fruit and weak as I was I walked with a light step.

A multitude of people were assembled on the beach as soon as we stept on the land they saluted us with ia, ora, na oe [greeting; peace to you], calling us each by a Tahiti name as we were introduced by Mr.

Grouard the Missionary. I first inquired for Paraita's old friend namely Nabota and Terii; the head governor took me by the hand and said "vau aratai oe [*vau araitai ai*, I will lead you]"; he would lead me; he had a piece of blue drilling bound about his loins coming a little below the knees, then a short blue jacket which did not meet the "para" by four inches; a place between showing the naked skin. We led the way, and the whole company followed. I could hear them laughing behind me but did not look back. I was trying hard to talk with my guide, but little could I understand of his language.

We soon reached the place where our friends resided. Telii had been sick with the measles, and was in bed when she heard the news that "no Paraita fetii [belonging to the Pratt family]" had come, she immediately laid aside the sickness and commenced cooking; in the same dwelling we found brother Gruard's native wife; sitting in the window with a loose dress on and a young babe in her arms. She appeared very diffident and inclined to hide herself. She would stay outside the house and occasionally peep in at the windows. All the people on the Island were in a short time assembled, and we were introduced to them and received the accustomed salutation ia ora na oe, peace be with you, ia ora na tou haere mbi te Tubuai nei" that is peace be with you in coming to Tubuai.

Supper was then served up, a large table was brought to the house, pigs baked under ground fish fried, bread made of pea [*pia*, arrowroot] a variety of the fruits of the Island all cooked in the native ovens. We ate and rejoiced. I saw a little man standing outside who I thought resembled an american; I accosted him, saying, I suppose you call yourself a white man among the people here? he replied that he was an american and the first man Parita baptized on the Island. I then recollected hearing him spoken of as being a faithful man.

The evening drew on, and the people came in to sing; the house was crowded, there was long grass spread for a floor on which the people all seated themselves; the musick was delightful; their voices are loud and clear and no singers can excel them in keeping time. Queen Rapah [?] came with the rest, and urged her to be seated in a chair, but she refused, prefering to be on a level with the others. The moon was then at the full, and the house was surrounded with large shade trees covered with bright yellow flowers; I looked upon the humble people seated on the ground singing the praises of God. I gazed upon the scenery which surrounded the dwelling, the pale rays of the moon shining through the trees in a thousand shapes, the tall cocoanuts were growing in front of the house, their branches high up in the air, the great itoes above all, which seen by the queen of night throwing her rays so gently over them, while the immagination made warm with the reality of the distance we had come and the suffering it had cost us to gain an admittance here, the object of our coming, all conspired to fill the mind with ideas great with meaning and I felt that God was in it all.

Br Gruard endeavoured to encourage us by telling us often that when the *Messenger* returned from Tahiti he was certain Br P would be on it. Sometimes a thought would cross my mind "he is the same as a prisoner", the next would be it is for the Gospel; and that reconciled me.

We spent the first day or two in gazing at everything strange and new, in looking at the people, and trying to speak their language; feasting on the fruit, and so forth.

The Second morning the *Messenger* hove in sight. Br. Gruard came in with the news, while I was yet in bed; he said to me, take courage Sister Pratt I believe Br P is on the vessel; but it did not prove so; a letter came saying the governor would not consent to have him come at that present; it was a disappointment, but we submitted to it patiently.

The church here had commenced to build a ship. Soon the elders who came out with us engaged with them, except Br Dunn who went to Tahiti on the same ship we came in. One week was spent in conversation. Br. Gruard had been preaching among the Islands seven years, and had seen no one direct from the Church, his mind was excited at seeing so many, he had many questions to ask. Our native friends repaired the house and fenced a lot for us; we planted a garden; it began to be November when we planted corn and beans; we had only to dig up the ground with a spade, it was very loamy and mellow; vegetation grew finely; the man who fenced the lot planted out 80 bananna trees; beneath all these were the vegetables and flowers planted. Soon we had a fine garden to look upon.

The second week we went to Mahu on a visit; here was where Mr. P. landed when he first came to this Island, and where he took up his abode; the family was still living there with whom he resided; they appeared friendly; their daughter a little girl about 13 was the wedded wife of Br. Alexander. She looked like a child, and appeared like one. The old Fare bure ra, stood near the beach, a tall ito in front of each door. I went into the house where six years before my husband had been want to pray. I went up into the pulpit as the sun was setting, and on my knees I gave thanks to my father in heaven who had preserved our lives in crossing the great waters! The second day I returned on horseback. The children complained some of being lonely, often expressed a wish that their father was here to take them about the Island, and show them the curious places he had told them of. I tried to be resigned, and endeavored to amuse myelf with learning the native sisters to knit, it helped to pass off the time tho' it seemed long at the best.

Christmas came, Sister Crosby myself and our children made a little feast, invited Br and Sister McMertry to eat with us; the rest of the white brethren were all at Mahu; we had string beans and cucumbers; for New

Years we had green corn; the weather was very warm.[2] It seemed strange
to us who had been raised in a cold country, where at that season it was
common to see 6 feet of snow.

The people seemed very anxious to teach us their language nearly
all our evenings were spent in reading and translating the Scriptures it
was a source of great amusement to us to be learning a new language or
at least new to us. There were so many mistakes made to excite merriment and a little ridicule, it answered well for diversion; the house for the
two first months was nearly always thronged at night with the people talking reading and singing; many of the people had never seen european
females before; our eldest daughter played the accordian which was great
amusement for them, it was diverting to us to exhibit our little curiosities,
to witness their admiration and pleasure in examining them, they think
no country can be like America to contain so many wonderful things;
they seem to have an idea of their inferiority and are willing to learn any
thing that does not require too close application.

I brought with me the likeness of brother Joseph Smith and Hirum
which I hung up against the wall in the sleeping room; all the people on
the Island came to look at it; there was a brother here from Ana, one of
the pamutu's, one evening when we were all seated about the table reading, he left the room and went in to look at the picture; he kneeled
before it in order that the painting might come in range with his eyes, (as
it was hanging low). For a quarter of an hour he looked steadfastly upon
it, I believe without turning his eyes; I did not suppose it was an act of
worship but he wished undoubtedly to imprint the lineaments of the features upon his mind. I could not help admiring his devotion. I knew his
faith in the Gospel was strong and he felt a solemn pleasure in surveying
the features of the murdered prophet and patriarch.

The natives generally have a great share of reverence they have great
faith in the ordinances of the Gospel such as baptism and the laying on
hands for recovering the sick to health. I brought with me a bottle of consecrated oil which was blessed by brother Brigham Young and other of
the authorities, previous to my leaving Salt Lake. The females had great
faith in the oil, when I told them from whence I had brought it, and by
whom it had been blessed. They would frequently bring their young children to me when they were sick to have me annoint them, give them oil
inwardly, and lay my hands upon them in the name of the Lord; if I told
them they would soon be better, they seemed to have no doubt about it,
and so it was to them according to their faith. They take great pleasure
apparently in reading the Scripture and in prayer; they are very punctual
to observe family devotion, early risers, often before the dawn of morning,
they rise, the first thing done is to call the family together and fall on their
knees in prayer; they then ring the bell and go to the house of worship, to

read the bible; if their teacher is present they require him to explain what they read, if it is not decidedly plain to their understanding. They have very little reading except the bible, some few small pamphlets containing Catechisms, books to learn the use of figures &c. They make many feasts; instead of eating in large companies they divide out the food and carry it about among the friends of which their teachers get a large supply.

[Grouard's Birthday Feast]

January 4th 1851 Elder Gruard made a great feast to celebrate his birth day; it being the 33d anniversary: it was held at his dwelling house, a very long building; about one hundred people were invited. The food was purely native, with the exception of 50 mince pies, which were made for the special purpose, and they were nothing less than splendid. The guests did not assemble until the table and food was all arranged in order; a large quantity of leaves were spread upon the ground extending from one end of the room to the other, on which were placed the dishes in form; the food standing in the centre as is usual; a young cocoanut was laid at each plate; that fruit bearing upon a light yellow, contrasted beautifully with the dark green leaves; as I walked into the house and beheld the great quantity of food, which I knew was of a most delicious kind, all arranged in such native neatness; I looked upon it with great admiration. I thought I had never seen any thing to equal it. The guests were then seated around the low table and enjoyed themselves I have no doubt better than many in high life do, with all their extravagancies and superfluities. We complimented the Lord of the feast upon the good quantities of every dish; and after a little season spent in lively conversation having feasted ourselves to the full, we returned home.

Elder Gruard remarked, that in thirty three years from that day, he designed making another feast at which time if living he should have attained his sixty sixth year. We all replied that it was hopeful (tho' doubtful) that we should be able to attend, and that the feast might equal if not surpass the present one in excellence.

Mr. Gruard is a gentleman somewhat distinguished for beauty and graceful appearance: not many of his years show so evident marks of beauty as he does at the present, tho' by being excluded too much from Society, he has acquired too much gravity and sedateness; though well informed and accomplished he is often rather abrupt; he combines the orator the philosopher the preacher of truth and righteousness, with the Sailor and native of the Islands; varying in his appearance to suit the circumstances; [*Memoir:* He feels himself to have been victim of misfortune from his early life; he is . . . still a firm believer in the fullness of the everlasting Gospel, as revealed through the Prophet Joseph Smith, and through it hopes to be

redeemed.] he has had two native wives by whom he has had three children, one daughter and two sons: the mother of the daughter being dead I
proposed to Elder Gruard on my first coming to the Islands to place the little girl in Ellen's charge. She is an unusual sprightly child and has made a
rapid improvement: being at this time able to speak tolerable english and
to read small spellings; now only four years old; she had never learned one
word of english from her father.

Mr. Whittaker an inteligent englishman was living here with his
Tahitian wife a very good disposed woman: resembling himself in appearance about as much as a sheep resembles a bear. He has since removed
with her to Tahiti where he is zealously engaged in preaching the fullness
of the Gospel. He is an excellent man, full of faith and good works. I have
no doubt that there are thousands of men less accomplished and less amiable than he is who have married women of refinement and sensibility;
he appears satisfied with his coloured wife, says she is very useful to him,
how unequally paired are many in this world.

Thus the time passed on and the children were every day wishing
for their father to come; it seemed cruel to them that after performing a
journey of five thousand miles they were not permitted to meet him, for
whose sake alone they had endured the hardships of so long a journey.

[Pratt's Arrival at Tubuai, January 1851]

Towards the last of January Capt Johnson's vessel from Tahiti was
descried at a distance the pilot went off to it and returned with the joyful
inteligence that "Parita" was on board! The children were so elated they
were afraid to believe it, fearing it might possibly be a mistake. It was soon
confirmed, and straight way we all repaired to the beach; where the help
of Tamatoa's spy glass we were enabled to discern him walking the deck,
he had grown exceedingly fleshy and to the children he looked like a
man of renown, and such he is. He was soon on shore with his luggage, of
which a part consisted of a large bag full of Tahitian oranges much larger
and sweeter than those growing on Tubuai. It was a great day with us all;
and the tales of one year and a half's separation were not soon told. Br
Busby had left the day before for Tahiti, which we all very much regretted; it seemed providential that I did not go. I had several times almost
concluded to take passage on board the ship with Mr B. but the morning
he sailed, I had an impression it was not best; had I gone, I should have
missed my husband on the way, and been left three months on Tahiti
without any chance to return.

CHAPTER TEN

The Island Tubuai
A Missionary Family I
Journal A, Part 2, January to 18 September 1851

A few days were spent in conversation, when the work on the vessel was renewed. Mr P engaged in making the sails. Nearly all his time was spent at Mahu except the sabbaths; but now that we knew where he was and what he was doing, we felt quite reconciled to do without him.

[The Busbys and Tompkins]

There was much talk about the propriety of Mr Busby's leaving. He had been sent here to preach the gospel but finding great difficulty in acquiring the language, and his health being somewhat impaired, he resolved on leaving the mission; he is a man who has for years been subject to what is called the hypochondria; at which times he appears to lose his faith in almost every thing: when not under that influence he is counted a great comic of hilarity and jokes, full of zeal for the cause of truth, affectionate and warm hearted to his friends, some natural talent, with a neglected education: he is poorly calculated to brook the ills of life; having an ambition very much above his abilities, he claims more compassion than he receives; as do all melancholly persons; because they are so few who feel for sorrows they themselves are not subjected to.

March the 1st every day finds me at the old Fare bur raa [meeting house; house of prayer] teaching the natives, and my own children, studying Tahiti, writing, &c. Mrs Tomkins and her two little daughters I have instructed from the first week of our landing here. Sister T is an excellent woman; frank generous ambitious, light hearted and full of mirth, a good natural understanding but entirely without education; a great desire to learn, but a memory so treacherous that it is in vain for her to endeavour to attain to any considerable share of knowledge; what a misfortune to be neglected in childhood! many parents do not consider it as they should. Mr T tho a little better educated being able to read some, is however inferior to her in judgment: he has many good traits of character of which he appears to be very sensible; exceedingly conceited he assumes an air of importance; willing to confer favors he wishes those who share his liberality to feel and acknowledge their obligations to him; and being very much given to satire, it is difficult for one always to maintain that respect for him which he requires and being exceedingly variable in his disposition he is at one time ready to oblige, while at another he would be decidedly opposed to it, under the same circumstances. his conversation is often very oppressive, as his jokes are principally founded on facts, and sarcasm comes in for a large share where there is the least occasion for it: his expressions often wounded my feelings, because I had placed confidence in him and expected more perfection in him than I had reason to; and there is where I have received a thousand wounds when a little cautiousness in giving persons power over me might have prevented it; but it takes a person's whole life to learn human nature, and at last he must be comparatively ignorant. The less we have to do with the world, the more peace we have; and a secluded situation with a competency, a few choice friends to partake of our joys and sorrows, better fits a person to enjoy this life, than to move in the bustle of the busy world, to mount the hill of fame, or to shine and dazzle in Courts. But every one for his calling, some are called to hassle with the world; to contend with the raging elements of passion, to war with the evil propensities of man's nature, and to sow the seeds of truth and virtue in soil where there is little fruit to be expected; but such ideas have been so often developed it is unnecessary to repeat them, and I will pursue my journal.

Time passes on, and we have little to complain of, but flies and musketoes. flies, especially, are very annoying here in the winter; which is June July and August. no other insects are at all troublesome. no venomous reptiles except one called the Santapied; the sting of that is about like that of the bee. I have never seen one stung by them, tho I often find them about the house. The weather is very warm, but it is not oppressive: the pure air from the sea is at all times refreshing. The climate on Tubuai is really very healthy.

[The Launching of the *Ravaai*, Missionary Ship]

About the third week in May we were all invited over to see the *Raivai* [*Ravaai*, the fisherman] launched; the Sabbath previous [we] sailed around in the new boat Br Whittaker had just completed.[1] we set sail about sundown did not make the opposite side till late in the evening; the moon shone very bright and we experienced no inconvenience by being out in the night. When we landed we saw a good fire burning which looked very cheerful shining through the trees. the friends came to meet us on the reef and carried us in their arms to the dry land; there were ten females old and young in the boat. The people had been a long time learning tunes to sing, and making preparations to have a great dance at the launching. the vessel had to be drawn a considerable distance by hand which required all the strength of the Island; the part not belonging to our church refused to assist unless the king would grant permission for them to have a dance; it was granted, and great pains was taken to procure ornaments; they were busily engaged for a long time in making native cloth, and painting it with brilliant colors; it was very gay; it was cut in pieces about two yards in length a hole in the centre to put the head through, and when thrown carelessly over a snowy white dress had the appearance of taste. Early on monday morning we assembled ourselves to see the parade and witness the maneuvers. Officers were chosen to conduct the movements. A messenger was sent before them to announce their approach; there were two large companies each company occupying his own space of ground in the dance; they had no musick except what they made by singing, and so clear and loud were their voices, one would almost immagine himself listening to an italian band. Their dancing was in form and order, and great exactness in time was observed. To describe the different exercises, the unheard of gestures, and the scene throughout, would require a painters art; it differed entirely from anything I had every seen before.

There was a vast amount of food prepared and laid in a pile; a number of hogs roasted whole, all the different fruits of the Island prepared in various ways for eating; a clean spot of ground was selected, and spread over with cocoanut leaves, on which the food was laid: men were then appointed to divide it out to the respective families, and a portion to the foreigners according to their numbers.

When the first exercise of dancing was over they commenced pulling upon the vessel; ropes were attached to it on each side, of which all the people men and women and children laid hold; they were obliged to take advantage of the low tides or stand in water up to their waists. many severe efforts were made before the vessel was started at all; loud and incoherent ejaculations of a te, a! te, a! were heard. the wives of the missionaries were spectators. they were not for a long time invited to take hold of the ropes; at length an old man fastened on an additional rope and called for the "vahine papa's [foreign women]" I went forward and laid hold; it happened that instant to move for the first time; loud acclamations resounded almost deafening about the strength of the foreign women; it soon went to the edge of the water; from whence it was moved but a short distance each day, for four days. The dancing still continued;

and the feasting untill all the food was consumed; the labor was then suspended till more could be cooked; and we returned home before the vessel went off into deep water.

[About the first] of May she was brought round on the west side [of]
the Island. Great rejoicing was manifest when the ship was seen under sail.
Preparations were then made for a voyage to Tahiti, and the pamuto's
[Paumotus]; and the tenth day they sailed. Br Gruard was appointed Capt;
Alexander first mate. Elder Pratt and our eldest daughter E [Ellen] took
passage on board the *Ravai* (fisherman) It was anchored a mile and a half
from town we all walked up and went on board sailed down till we came
opposite the town; the boat was sent to bring us on shore where we stood
and saw the new ship move off under full sail. The women on the beach
whose sons had gone were lamenting in a most piteous tone wringing
their hands and tearing their hair; it is a custom the people have here
when their friends die or go to sea. we had not thought of weeping at seeing our friends leave till we heard their cries.

The elders all left the Island except A [Alvarus] Hanks; he was left
to look after the women, as sort of shield and protecter; we all expected
to be very lonesome but on the contrary we enjoyed ourselves remarkably
well. The natives nearly all left the village and went back towards the
mountains to dig pea, that is arrowroot. So the village was very still and
quiet. I spent much time in reading and writing. I read Mr. Williams' missionary enterprizes among the Islands,[2] I was highly pleased with it I had
no idea of the immense numbers of Islands that have been brought to a
knowledge of the scriptures and have abandoned idolatry the labors of
the british missionaries have certainly been great and have been attended
with great success; they have prepared the way for the true gospel, and
they do indeed deserve great credit for what they have done; they have
been zealous to promulgate what light they were in possession of, and
they could not be blamed for not teaching what they did not know. I am
often pained at hearing them found fault with. I often ask why is it that
human beings are so inclined to find fault with each other, when all are
so imperfect? that they are what they are answers the question.

[Mountain Climbing Excursion]

June the 7th. we took an all day walk; we clim[b]ed the highest peaks of
the mountains and surveyed the surrounding scenery; the atmosphere
was a little heavy so that we could not see clearly at so great a distance as
we otherwise could; but we made many little discoveries which interested
us; found many little plants and shrubs entirely new; the brake which is
common in America, we found grown to large trees some thirty feet high
with branches more than ten feet long the trunk of a pithy substance

about four or five inches in diameter, perfectly straight; affording a beautiful shade for the goats which we found feeding on the mountains. The beautiful little grotto's and arbours seemed alluring, almost sufficient to tempt one to seclude himself and live alone with nature; there he might stay and sleep in the bowers, no cold winter to oppress him, cool breezes to fan him in summer; when hungry he could go down to the foot of the mountains where grows a plenty of good food and fruits, which is free for all; where thought I could another such place be found where man could live alone without labor and suffer so little?

After having fatigued ourselves till we had hardly strength to walk, we commenced our return; we plunged down the steep precipices through the thickets where before entering it appeared impossible to make our way through: but we found goat paths through the dense brush and shrubbery which facilitated our way down. I however became so completely overdone that I was obliged to sit down upon the ground and slide down the last mountain. Mr Hanks left us and hurried home to prepare supper. Sister C and I sent the children ahead with a sufficient apparatus to make a cup of tea which consisted of a coffee pot and two saucers: we had prepared ourselves with some refreshments before setting out on the excursion. They struck up a fire on the bank of the first stream and when we overtook them the tea was made.

I sometimes thought I should be obliged to sit down and send for help. but little faithful Ann Louise encouraged me by suffering me to use her for a staff; and at last I reached the foot of the mountain in safety; and we all sat down to rest ourselves and drink a cup of tea. we did not reach home till after dusk. So lame was I for a whole week I could scarcely walk; but I could now say I had seen and walked on the top of the highest mountains on Tubuai, and I thought it was worth the pains.

[Native Foods]

It was amusement for us to see the natives make their pea [*pia*, arrowroot]; it grows in the ground like irish potatoes; the method of grating it is a novel thing; they tie a hard stout cord around a block of wood, on which they pulverize the root; then through a cloth fastened on to a frame they strain it off, rinse it a number of times, settle it, drain off the water and it is done; no whiteness can exceed it; they then spread it on native cloth in a close yard made for the purpose, and dry it in the sun. It is most delicate food when prepared with the water of the young cocoanut and a little of the cream: with eggs and the flour of the arrowroot, puddings of the choicest kind can be made. All the while the labor of pea was going on, the dancers kept up their exercises; it is their custom to make amusement of almost all kinds of labor; thus filling up their time with play, like children.

There is one kind of labor however of which they do not make play, that is the cultivation of tarrow; it is very laborious. Swampy ground is used for the raising of that vegetable. ditches are dug on all sides of the parcel of ground appropriated to the purpose, that the water may be let on or drawn off as may be required. the tarrow grows in water which is constantly kept running; as often as it is taken up for the use the tops are replaced and so the patch is kept good for successive years. Many years ago when there were many more inhabitants large portions of the Island were appropriated to that purpose. now it is all grown over with grass, and from the mountains it has the appearance of a garden overgrown; the ditches at that distance resembling paths between the beds, and surrounded by so many large fruit trees, it looks like some cultivated spot on which great labor has been bestowed, but it has lain in that same condition for many years.

[Return of the *Ravaai* from Her Maiden Voyage]

The *Ravaai* (fisherman) is the name of the new ship recently built here; it is a staunch vessel of about eighty tons burthen built of tamanu [large timber tree] wood a species of mahogany equal to it and more enduring; it is almost as hard as iron. It has a convenient cabbin containing twelve berths. She made the passage to the pamutos and returned in six weeks, the precise time proposed for her to return. We did not expect her so soon, for we thought people never came at the set time; however, on the evening of the same day we walked on the beach, as if we would expect to see her coming in. Frances remarked thus, "O if I could see the *Ravaai* heave in sight I would dance for joy!" but no, she said in another moment, "I would rather they would not come till we are better prepared. I wish to clean the house and make some little arrangements." At that instant the cry was heard, pahi a hoi [a boat is here]! it resounded from one to another, who all cried the same as loud as they could scream; it was dusky and we could not clearly discern it; but we ran in the direction of some clouds which we thought was the ship, till we were convinced of our mistake, and then we ran back again; it laid off and on through the night and came to anchor early in the morning. Two hours before day found us all up cooking our breakfast, and preparing to receive our friends.

It was the 21st of June about seven in the morning our friends came on shore Br Brown came with them from Tahiti. They all looked healthy and were in high spirits. Ellen was pleased with her voyage. She had excited much curiosity among those who had never seen a white woman before. She carried with her a musical instrument with which she diverted many who had never seen such a thing in their lives; they made her several nice presents, and two females had proposed to make friends with her, one on Tahiti and the other on Ravaivi [Raivavai] the custom is advantageous to foreigners who come here; one who calls himself your friend will feed you while he has a morsel for himself: and if he owns any thing you want, it is at your service.

Br Brown spent one week with us and we had a fine visit; he is a clever young man, bids fair to make a good Tahitian scholar.[3] While the ship was lying here we had lively evenings. Br Gruard left his wife at Auu ra [Anaa?]; he seemed in better spirits than I ever saw him; he seemed free to act himself whereas when his wife is present he appears under restraint; so much is she inclined to jealousy, that she makes herself unhappy as well as her husband.

The 4th of July we prepared to go to the motu Islands [low island] lying a little east of this; but the weather became squally and we concluded to give it up. It was brother Brown's birthday; we felt anxious to have some little extra's performed, but the rain prevented. So we went over to brother Gruard's and were all weighed. I weighed 109 pounds as much lacking one pound as I did when young. The next day being the 5th the ship sailed; taking all the Bullocks from the Island. Our boy went for a pleasure trip. Mr Hanks went to join the elders at the paumotu group. The ship being gone and all settled, we renewed the schools; for a while the boys seemed very anxious to get a knowledge of figures. but it soon became an old story with them; several learned very well, but they do not like strict discipline, neither close application. This is the sixth week since the vessel left the 2d time; we still continue the school both for ourselves and the natives.

24 July Spent the day in the old Fare bure ra [meeting house] teaching school it never once occurred to our minds that the day was passing away unheeded; we had intended in some way to celebrate it, but the ship left on the 4th and the most of the white men being gone away on her there were not enough of us to make it any object to get up a feast or party.

[A Horseback Ride to Mahu]

The 25th Mr P and myself went on horseback, to Mahu; had a beautiful ride; I was charmed with the scenery, the tall Ito trees [*aito*, a tree] over-shadowing the beach present a most splendid appearance; some of the branches extending for more than 50 feet, forming a complete shade over the beach; it was low water, and the beach was covered with a variety of shells. I felt delighted with the ride. We reached the town about 4 oclock in the evening many of the people were out fishing, did not come in till quite dusk, by which time I was quite hungry; they appeared pleased to see us and gave us a good supper, and I do not remember ever having enjoyed a meal better. That night there was a severe gale of wind on the sea; the waves roared like thunder; and we were alarmed for the safety of the ship, which we knew was lying at Matauru. We spent the evening in telling interesting stories about America; the native bretheren and sisters were greatly amused with my stories about Buffaloes, which I managed to make them understand though my talk was rather broken; they praised me, said I had done well to learn what I had.

We spent the Sabbath went three times to the house of worship I understood but little of the preaching but was quite charmed with the singing. Rui a toru the brother where we staid is a great man for the scriptures he is very desirous to have light and knowledge; he is indeed a wise man for a native or a tauturu oe [assistant] as he calls himself. Monday 26th we came home it was high tide; in some places the water was very deep on the beach; a view of the sea was grand; far off near the reef the waters were a clear bright color, of blue and green intermingled; the reflection of the sun upon it gave it a spangled appearance, as if ten thousand diamonds were shining there. Ah, thought I, your beauty displays itself to the eye, but your threat'ning voice warns us that death is concealed beneath your billows; we reached home and found there had been a severe gale of wind, the ship of whose safety we were apprehensive had been driven on to the rocks; and many were engaged in trying to get it off; the trees near the house were stripped of their verdure, the ground covered with leaves and foliage; some of the bananna trees were blown down; the vessel was saved and soon put in repair.

It was the Brig *Ann*, Capt Harrington belonging to Tahiti: he brought a quantity of damaged goods, of which I purchased a hundred and twenty four yards, in exchange for a dress pattern I brought from California a small sum of money; besides the making of five pairs of pantaloons; likewise I bought ten pounds of sugar. I found when I came to make up my cloth, that I lost but very little; some of it being only slightly mildewed, but the strength not injured.

[Reflections, Meditations]

We are placed here with no salary and forbidden by government to ask any thing of the natives but the Lord provides for us in a way we little expect before hand. The natives give us food and that is all they have to give; and often that is only vegetables; as they are not always supplied with fish for themselves: fortunately the missionary is a gunner: when we lack meat he goes to the woods for wild hens, and to the tarrow patches for ducks; and thus supplies his family with meat: so the poor elders of the last days struggle through life sustain themselves and preach the gospel: no livings to grow rich upon like the Rectors in England; but with their own hands they labor for their own support; and teach the people; looking for a reward in future, even a crown of glory with the ancient Saints, who endured hardness as good soldiers.

Three little girls we have in charge, to whom we are teaching the english language; it is really an agreeable task: to see their powers of mind developed, and their aptness to learn, reconciles me to labor with this people; being convinced that they are capable of being highly improved. When they are first taken from among their friends, they are exceedingly wild; they have no idea of modest deportment; to race and run like the wild animals is all they know; very soon however they become domesticated; they will sit at the table and receive food on their plates, handle a knife and fork; and behave quite becoming; they have sweet melodious voices for singing, are very fond of musik; our three eldest daughters have each one in charge; to instruct in habbits of industry and learn them to talk and read.[4] The grown persons seem to take great delight in reading; they read the scriptures faithfully: the old man who provides a great portion of our food, and sleeps in the cook house, often is heard reading his bible at a late hour of the night.

17 of August being the Sabbath, after noon we had a discourse in our own language. Elder P spoke upon the first principles of the gospel for the benefit of our children, and two white men came to hear who do not belong to the church, we were all edified and comforted and I felt that the truth, is always good to hear.

In the evening I went down to Sister Crosby's for some reason I could hardly tell why a lonely feeling came over me. I went home, the evening was far spent; a native brother and sister came in to be instructed from the bible; while their teacher was thus employed I thought I would seek a lonely and silent retreat and spend an hour in prayer and meditation. I retired to the far end of the garden; I had pain in my heart, a word of reproof had fallen on my ear, it heightened my sadness. I hurried to seek a secluded spot; the footpath led underneath large trees, the stars were looking out in all their brightness; the bright blue sky shone in tranquil beauty; the moon was gone, and the twilight shades seemed passing lovely; the wind was low, all was still, save the loud roar of the old oceans waves; they murmured in the distance; the air was mild and balmy; I sat me down, the place seemed sacred; I gazed up into the sky and thought of the bright world where our Saviour dwells; I sighed and prayed. I thought of the dear sisters in the valley of the mountains, and longed to commune with them. I thought of, and loved those most who like me have had sorrows; so clings the heart to objects assimilated with it. Two or three hours passed away and I was not aware that I had been out so long. I occasionally looked to the window to see if the light still continued there; a calm came over me, it was sweet and silent; it seemed to me that holy beings were around me; it seemed a foretaste of happier days; I had been thinking of blighted joys, of days when I looked upon the world as full of charms, of the change that came over my brightest prospects, and how my sun of hope went down in early life; then I thought how the bright star of the gospel had arisen in my hemisphere, with what enthusiasm I had followed it, what dangers I had encountered and what deliverance I had found; how my life had been preserved, and how many dear friends I had in the church who I believed sincerely loved me. A holy calm came over me, such as I seldom feel; I looked towards the window, I saw the light extinguished, I hurried to the house fearing a reproof, for staying out so long; which I met, but being slight I bore it, and did not suffer it to distub my peace. I retired to rest and slept soundly. So ended the 17th night of August.

[Missionary Works]

22nd day   Arrived the ship *Ravaai* from Tahiti. We were all greatly rejoiced to see it safe back; as we had had fears respecting her safety their had been several severe gales of wind. Our friends Haamatua and family all came; they brought their children and presented them to us. Said here are your children; we commit them to your care; do with them as you think propper. they are really good good children, and I look upon them as my own, and already I feel an affection for them. O what a work is there to be done here! how much these children need benefactors to raise them; like the wild animals in the woods they run at large; and if they were tamed and cultivated they would be gentle and amiable like our own children. I can say I love them for the sake of pity, and compassion, and because I see they are human beings like ourselves; they have the same kind of sympathies the same affections; those who know the truth love it and devote their hearts to it.

23d day   I am going to Mahu on horseback to spend the Sabbath with my Companion.

25th day   yesterday being the Sabbath we had four publick exercises, three in native one in english on the first principles for the benefit of our children. It seems always new and good to hear the doctrines of the church set forth. The evening was spent at Br Crosby's in singing hymns; our new children are beautiful singers. While we were all seated around the room I looked about and could not help thinking how pleasant it was for us to be together and enjoy each other's society in this remote corner of the earth. I mean those of the same nation: when we are separated we feel lonely. when we meet we feel a double pleasure for having been parted. To day our school has been quite enlarged; but the dancing party came in sight and hearing, and disturbed us much, with their wild musick, we all heartily wish they could be prevailed on to give it up.

26th day. This morning had flour for breakfast, a luxury we seldom have. J Layton brought a barrel from Tahiti, invited us to partake with him; he is a generous fellow, well calculated to provide for a family; but he has a native wife who knows nothing about houskeeping; so he must be father and mother both, to his children. The natives are fond of flour; when Haamatua vahine, saw the flour brought in, she said in the native tongue, "it is for you and me" I told her it was and that I would divide it when cooked.

27th day. Yesterday caught a severe cold; the first I have had since I came to this Island; a sudden change in the weather has occasioned it. I had a bad night, slept but little; feel very unwell today; my spirits are drooping and despondent; a thunderstorm awoke me in the night, and for several hours I lay thinking of the storms of life, some of which had fallen on me; and more heavily than even my most familiar friends have been aware of; but hope soothing consoling gladdening hope sometimes bursts into my often languishing mind and tells me there is a brighter day to come; a day ushered in by the gospel which I so gladly hailed when I heard the sound; "this hope supported me when I bade my native land farewell."

29th day Yesterday the whole family went to the other village and left me alone in possession of the house. I was pleased with the idea of staying alone, my house is thronged so much, and more especially since our friends came from Tahiti. I thought it would be so still and quiet to be left a few days; one day and night has passed and I have not been one hour alone; in this old Fare bure, ra, I can sometimes retire to myself and be out of sight, and this is all the place I have unless I go in to the woods, or to my yard in the evening. I often ask the question Shall I ever have a house with a private room in it? where I can retire for communion with God and with my own soul? I look forward to the time, and would even dare to hope. This morning our good friend Haamatua came from Mahu to bring me some food; so thoughtful he was about me because I was left alone; but it was unneccessary, for I had plenty.

[Conversations with Grouard]

Br Gruard spent the evening with me and we had great conversation, he is generally interesting; it is evident he is not very happy in his companion, but he makes the best he can of it, and tries to think it all right; how unfortunate for one to be looking in vain for happiness to the source where he desires most to find it!

31d Yesterday was Sabbath and we had a very thin meeting in consequence of so many having gone to the other town. We had however three services, a few words each time; I was quite alone at home, except brother Gruard called in the morning and took breakfast with me; he feels discontented and longs to go to the church. I wish indeed he could go; he has lived here among the Islands secluded from the world so many years that the idea of going to Salt Lake appears to him like going to heaven; but here he is tied up, a vessel on his hands and a native wife, in debt and a little income; he feels that he has been an unfortunate man and indeed his early associations have made him so; he has now his third wife and yet he feels that domestic happiness has not yet fallen to his lot; and he sighs for it in secret; whether there are grounds for hope I know not; it seems hard that for a little mistep in youth one must drink sorrow the remainder of their days; but it is even so, as we sow, so we must reap. I hope deliverance will come to all like him eventually, whose souls are in bondage. The laws of nature must be obeyed or misery will ensue; if an unwise step is taken even if no one but self is wronged, yet the result of that false step will be unhappiness, in a greater or less degree according to the nature of the act or deed done; it is not that any one wishes a little error punished, or that God is offended, but simply the natural result of mismanagement, bringing its own train of evil consequences, which cannot be avoided. How good it is to be guided by wisdom and guarded by truth; how many a precious youth might be snatched from the whirlpool of bitter regret, would the hand of experience lay hold on them and lead them back before they have advanced too far on the fatal ground.

[Missionary Life]

Sept 2d Mr P went to the mountains yesterday and killed a goat; we are all very fond of the meat, but the natives are very squeamy about eating it; we can hardly prevail on them to taste it, except those who consider themselves belonging to our family; they seem to think they must love whatever we do. O that I had means to provide for the children I have taken under my charge; house room that I could keep them under my immediate direction. I could keep them from running with other children in the streets, by whom they will be sure to be contiminated. Our house is small, I can only accommodate a few at the table, and I have only lodgings for six besides my own. I am pleased with the improvement they are making: it is really amuseing to hear them try to talk english.

Last evening we spent a portion of the time in singing, as we generally do our evenings. A young woman has lately come from Tahiti with Br Layton, whom he has taken in charge to watch over. She is really a splendid singer after the native style. She is quite young, but young as she is, she has lived a long time in sin; being instructed by her mother to commit sin to get money; thus are these poor children abused. She is very pretty, and looks innocent. I feel sorry when I look upon her inteligent countenance, and hear her pleasant voice, that she must be sacrificed to so base a purpose; there is something ensnaring in her very looks; had I no daughters of my own, I would take her and teach her to love virtue and practice it; but as it is it would not do; her conversation would stain the purity of their minds.

3d day The weather is fine and the air delightful. I spend the most of my time at the Fare burera from the window I see the children running and racing like so many wild animals. Many pretty looking inteligent countenances I see among them; growing up with no more cultivation than the pigs have: once in a day we call them to school to read, they are so wild and restless it is very unpleasant to keep them long in; some of the more steady ones we keep sometimes a half day. I should indeed be thankful to see something done for them; it seems hard to see human nature abused and neglected like the brute creation. I now call to mind the poor red men in our own country, suffering in cold weather; here they are exempt from that, they do not realize suffering here, but by growing up in ignorance they bring curses on themselves, which are entailed to their posterity.

4th day. A great many people are now sick with colds; something like the quinzy prevails; they want me to nurse them and I have nothing to do it with; they have nothing fit for sick people; they ask to have their teas sweetened, though they know I have no means of buying sugar; but they seem to think missionaries can have whatever they want: they call on me for medicine, and I feel aggravated to tell them I have none; it is really important that persons sent to reside among them should be provided with little necessaries, and especially with simple medicines to nurse the sick; it increases their confidence in us when by any means we are enabled to do them good: they are poor helpless creatures in many respects. When the wind blows from a certain quarter here, it afflicts the people; they have colds and headaches. it does not however affect us so much, we are better guarded by the manner in which we clothe ourselves: they ought to have their buildings constructed with conveniences for making fire in them.

5th day I feel unwell this morning from eating too many dried banannas, they are too clogging to eat on going to bed. we have nothing here to eat between our meals, unless we take a piece of cold tarrow, and unless one is very hungry it is not an object: Oh, what do those who live in luxury know of the privations of the missionaries, who carry the gospel to the heathen? they can live in ease, eat and drink what they please; they have their good in this life.

6th day Sabbath. Held three services, Paraita the third, broke bread, procured from the ship *Ravaai*; generally bread and fruit is used, and cocoanut water instead of wine. In the afternoon arrived the Rurutu vessel with several passengers from Raivai vai, they brought word that the house for the missionary is finished; so I suppose we shall soon be going there; the people are very sick there, and undoubtedly need our aid: but the dread of going at this time, is that a vessel belonging to the King is getting ready to follow us, to carry a company of what is called tu hauries [*ori*,the dance; Arioi Society, privileged libertines?] that is, a gang of dancers; they have never heard the true gospel, and it seems an unfavorable time to carry it. This gospel will be new to them, and this dancing tolerated by the french government I suppose will be new also, as I understand it has never been practised on Raivaivai. I earnestly pray that something may prevent them from going, but the Lord will order all things right.

7th This morning eleven persons were baptized; some were sick baptized for the recovery of health others for the remission of sins a large company collected and we sang a hymn at the water's side. This afternoon called at the Fare bure ra three females from Rurutu very neatly clad, and appeared quite inteligent. I asked them in the Tahitian if they had heard of "Paraita." they replied "e tuutu tahito ne [?] Rurutu." That is "he is of old report on Rurutu." I asked them if they would like to hear about the Mormon church? they answered e, but as I could not speak Tahita very well, I asked them to call at the house and Paraita would tell them about it. The people of that Island are of good report; the English missionaries have done well for them, in teaching them habits of industry and cleanliness.

8th last evening the people came to sing and continued till very late. they were learning new tunes; I listened to them with pleasure for a long time. I at last became weary and went out walked in the door yard and listened to them; no people can excel them in keeping time but they wear out a tune in learning it; whenever a new tune is introduced, it must be sung over and over a hundred times if it takes so long to learn it; all in one evening; not willing to postpone it till another time. This morning I went out to meet the Rurutu friends: they wished to learn tunes of us; I sang one hymn ten or 15 times in succession, by which time they sang it well.

The two little girls, we have taken lately, sing delightfully; it is equally as pleasant as having an instrument of musick in the house; they sing with energy as if they felt the thrilling effect of their musick in their own hearts. I look upon them with admiration when I see them thus engaged; could their tallents be properly cultivated how much they might excel in that delightful art.

8th [9th] day Last night our rest was disturbed by the sickness of brother Layton's wife; the elders were called up to lay hands on her and her little sister who was sleeping in our house was called up to go and see her; it is a native custom when taken sick though they may not consider themselves dangerous all the connexion far and near must be sent for that they may all counsel and sympathize. This morning the female from Raivaivai called and enquired for Ellen; it was her niece who had made friends with E when there; for that reason she called E her grandchild; and land belonging to her niece she called Ellen's land; that is the way when two persons make friends the property of each is considered holden in case it is needed; nothing is too good to be given to a friend; though they may need it themselves never so much it is no consideration, if the friend wants it.

9th day This morning a sister in the church was taken alarmingly ill with the cramp cholic. She sent in great haste for the Elders to administer. Mr P had a few days ago refused to lay hands on her and her husband on account of their using so much tobacco; upon which they were both rebaptized: This morning the elders went at her request; they both having covenanted to put away the use of tobacco entirely. I annointed her with oil and laid warm herbs on her bowels, after which the elders laid hands on her, and she was evidently better: since that I have carried her chicken broth and she tells me her pain is entirely gone: poor creatures: they know nothing about nursing each other; children they are in very deed.

10th day The children are growing very indifferent about learning; they can bear no rigid dicipline; as soon as the lessons are read they wish to be on the run, and it would require more exertion than I should be willing to make to keep them in. I have all I do to keep my own children at their studies; lonely as they are, they do not like confinement; the government of children what a task! blind and deaf to their own interest, they wish only to be let alone: they are more faithful to the children they have in charge than to themselves. As for the natives (I mean the grown persons) they have an idea that missionaries are smart enough to sustain themselves, teach them for nothing, and furnish them with many little necessaries, which they are not in the habit of buying; and all because they are the servants of God, and have more ability to accomplish things than common people; they expect more sacrifice and self denial, they look at the example of the Saviour, and expect us to be like him.

10th day very high winds today, no fish will be taken, so unless we get fowls we must do without meat: another week has gone and I do not feel sorry; the time will soon roll round for us to go home, and I shall be thankful; to be away from all the world is not good, for the mind, it renders it gloomy. I see very little inducement to stay here. neither is there much to stay in any place in this world; there is so little real happiness; surely what there is we ought not to deprive ourselves of.

15th day one year ago this . . . day we left the coast of California, that was the Sabbath . . . this is monday. Little did I then think, what was before me; the extreme sickness and all the disagreeability of that voyage were hidden from me and perhaps wisely; for had I known beforehand what I had to suffer I could not possibly have undertaken it. I hope much good will arise from my coming here though it may not be realized at present. I have endeavored to sew good seed, the fruit may be gathered up after many days. My daughters have set an example of industry and sobriety before the native females; it may result in good. it is a trial to have them in my family, yet I submit to it in hope that the effect may be good: certainly example and precept together is better than precept alone.

[Supper at Grouards]

16th day. Last evening Br Gruard invited Mr P and myself to supper. We had tarrow, cabbage and pork; and the tops of the young tarrow boiled for greens; his wife assisted in cooking the supper but when done would not sit at the table to eat with us; she prefered eating on the ground. in the room of pies and puddings we eate pearies; . . . (that is the dried bananna:) they are equal to figs. . . . spent the evening at Br Crosby's and were . . . ably entertained with the musick of the . . . and accordian which Ellen and her uncle . . . admirably together: the native friends all followed. . . . the house was filled; that is the custom of this place.

Today the weather is cool and cloudy, uncomfortable without a fire. The school is not well attended, so soon does any thing become an old story with the natives. O, how dull every thing is here! I marvel when I think how a few white men have stood it here so long; it would be like being ushered into a new world for them to go back to society: yet their native wives would be a mortification to them.

17th day Cold and rainy. The white brethren all went out early to the reef after fish; returned wet and cold without any. So again we are without meat. Every Wednesday morning we have prayer meeting at the hour of sunrise; this morning the elders being gone, Hoatau [?] led the services: he has a powerful voice and great energy and force in his manner; he has great zeal for this cause; the natives have a great deal of natural oratory, power and warmth in argument.

18th day. The storm has been severe for three days, probably will continue till the sun crosses the line. Spent last evening at Brother Grouard's, he knows not what is best to do; is anxious to go forthwith to California to get a large ship. Mr P is not in favor of his going. thinks it will keep us here too long. O how perplexing to be in suspense!

CHAPTER ELEVEN

The Island Tubuai
A Missionary Family II

Memoirs, 15 September 1851 to 1 February 1852

[The text for chapters 11 and 12 is drawn from the memoirs, which were based closely on the journals Louisa kept at the time. The segments of the journals printed in chapters 9, 10, 13, and 14 are the only extant portions of her original record.]

[Missionary Island Routine]

[September 1851] 22nd day. The equinoctial storm occurred which continued for a week. We are expecting to hear of terrible disasters at sea. Glad our hearts are to see the smiling face of the old king of day once more. In this far off world a dark, dismal day seems intolerable. Sunshine and flowers are our congenial companions.

On the 26th, before the dawn of day, Mr. P. went forth with dog and gun to shoot wild fowls. He was induced to take Frances, our second daughter, with him, with a view to dissipate the gloom that seemed hanging over her. They went two miles to the mountains, and up the clifts, returned with plenty of game. The excursion had the desired effect. This seclusion from the world at intervals is very severe on the children. At such times they resort to rambles on the mountains with the native children, gather wild flowers, decorate themselves and return in fine spirits.

I have witnessed another setting sun, beautiful when going down behind the great deep. All is silent, not a sound do I hear from the noisy world. I know not but it is all burned up and Babylon fallen to rise no more forever. I trust however, that Salt Lake City still remains. How long must we endure this imprisonment. I have one little hope remaining. Capt. Johnson is expected in. He will bring us news from the dear old

147

world, so I will try to live a few days longer. My employment daily is to keep the children at their books. I made a feast for the children under my immediate charge. Fourteen were seated around the table at once. They conducted themselves extremely well, ate with knives and forks, and tried to imitate their superiors. Could I keep them all in the house with me, I should soon have the pleasure of seeing them appear respectable.

Today I called the native sisters together to instruct them in their religious duties. Ellen acted as interpreter and succeeded remarkably well. This she has been able to do for several months. They spoke in turn, each expressing a desire that I might soon have a knowledge of their language, and speak from my own lips directly to them. I shall soon make an attempt to [do] so and having their prayers and faith shall be certain of success.

Oct 6th. Memorable day. Conference convenes today in S. Lake City. The remembrance creates deep sensations in my mind. I sigh to be there, although I do not wish to leave my labors here. Before another month rolls round "Paraita" will be gone to Raivaavai, then we shall still be more lonely. How much it would animate us could we see business going on. See men plowing, sewing grain, driving teams, hear the sound of axes and hammers. See houses building, but here monotony reigns supremely. All I hear is the sound of mallets making native cloth.

8th Wednesday. A party of us went on a pleasure excursion to some small islands five miles distant. We landed on the largest, nineteen souls in all. It is a beautiful island, covered with tamanu, and cocoanut trees. The soil is fine white sand, which contrasts beautifully with the green trees. I walked round the island, picked up shells and some fine specimens of coral. The men caught fish, made an oven in the ground, and cooked us a meal consisting of fruit and vegetables growing on the island. The men threw up a shelter for us with brush and leaves, under which we spread our bedding and slept well through the night. The children explored the island thoroughly, climbed the trees, made new discoveries in shrubbery and flowers, thought it a pity to leave the fertile island alone. We sailed home with a pleasant breeze, passed the village where the workmen were engaged building the schooner. They saluted us with loud voices. "Ia ora na otau to hare ra mui." (peace be to you in returning home.)

I sometimes walk to the opposite village, where the ship is building, distance five miles. I can walk under the shade of trees the whole way, sit down in a cooling shade, rest myself and renew my journey. Thus we resort to changes, trifling though they might be. They serve to enliven the mind.

Mr. Pratt preaches regularly in the native tongue, which I can now understand tolerably well. Baptisms occur nearly every Sabbath. I wrote an address to be read in a female meeting, which Mr. Grouard translated into the Tahitian for me.[1] They seemed greatly to admire it. I read to them the 29th chapter of Isaiah containing proof of the origin of the Book of Mormon. Ellen explained and commented upon it. They inquired if the ancient Nephites were Europeans. I told them they were the ancient fathers of the Tahitians. At this they appeared greatly interested, and wished to learn more about the book. No organ of their craniums is more prominent than marvelousness.

Sixteen of our number remained behind on that island what with those who had been baptized would form quite a branch of the church. The governor of Tubuai was opposed to leaving the missionarys. Said he would be more appreciated on his own island. We had a fair wind home, made the voyage in less than twenty four hours. Found three schooners lying in the harbor. Captain Johnson's was one, and we had the pleasure of again seeing our dear little Mary. Though we were all happy to see her we could not refrain from feeling sorrowful to see her in charge of a mother incapable of training her properly and a stepfather addicted to intemperance. As we hove in sight of our island we saw a crowd of people standing on the beach to watch the approach of our vessel. Our youngest daughter Ann Louise, whom we had left at home with her aunt Crosby, stood with the rest to welcome us.

Captain Grouard immediately put in freight for Tahiti. Our boy Hiram Clark who came with us from S. Lake went with the Captain to learn a little of a sailor's life. The natives made a great feast on our return. We tried to be cheerful to console them for leaving their teacher in Raivavai. The schooners all sailed and left us alone with our native friends, who showed us great kindness.

[Louisa's Birthday]

10th day of Nov 51. This is my birthday. 49 years have I lived, how few attain to that age in comparison to those who come short of it. What a scene to look back upon. Had I known in my youthful days what I had to pass through how faint and feeble my heart would have been when the trials assailed me. They were wisely hidden from me. Often in my youth did a presentment of a fearful future come before me, and bade me beware of taking steps to hasten my doom. But it was written in the book of fate, and therein 'twas written that I had much to suffer for the Gospel's sake. I have said with Job, "the things which I dreaded came upon me." I have endeavored to bear them patiently. Wherein I have failed I look to heaven for pardon. I am not amenable to man neither will I suffer man to judge me. My soul has seen travail, and dark waters have murmured around me, and flood of sorrow have arisen mountains high and burst upon my head. Hunger, cold and nakedness have stared me in the face. Pain of body and agony of mind, false friends have beset me, and secret griefs have fastened their venom on my heart, and threatened to untie the cords of life. But the glorious gospel came, and the light of truth dawned upon my saddened heart, and caused me to sing for joy. Then all my sorrows were forgotten.

Strong confidence in God has ennabled me to triumph in a great measure over every calamity, and this day I thank Him that I have lived to see a glorious work commenced on the earth, although it has introduced me into a thorny path where my feet have been goaded to blood. Christ walked therein before, and the prophet Joseph drank deep of the bitter cup in his life, and died by the hands of wicked men, in a state that boasts of religious freedom. Oh, Illinois! Of you will it be required. In the midst of grief, I now have joy. Afflicted but not in dispair. Knowledge of the truth is now an anchor to my soul. I look for joy in the future to equalize all I have suffered since the fullness of the everlasting gospel has made me a pilgrim and stranger, far away from my kindred and country.

[Teaching by Word and Example]

This morning I went to Mr. Layton's who has a Tahitian wife and she knows nothing about housekeeping. A young girl lives with them who assists in the cooking department. I was anxious to give her some instructions in the system of cleaning house and keeping it in order. I introduced the subject in a plausible manner so as not to give offense. The young girl readily acquiesed seeming to believe it would be a nice affair to know how to keep house like "mau tamahine papa," (Foreign girls). It was astonishing the amount of rubbish we hoed out of one room. Then a fire in the dooryard completely revolutionized the premises. After this, Frances our second proposed occupying the room, teaching two little boys and further instructing the girl in rules pertaining to everyday life.

Nov. 12th. Mrs. Layton had a daughter born. There was great rejoicing among the relatives, it being the first girl in the family. According to their custom they would have it wrapt in a square piece of cloth. I speedily made a suit, dressed it in our fashion, and gave the child my name Louisa. All seemed delighted, and called it a "tamuline papa."

Ellen is an excellent interpreter. I am also advancing fast in a knowledge of the language. I met with a few grown persons for the purpose of reading the scriptures. They had many questions to ask in reference to the meaning of some passages. I attempted in my own way to explain, and really surprised myself, at my success. All present seemed highly gratified. My subject was baptism for the dead, in which they manifest a deep interest.[2] Little do we know what we can do till we make a thorough trial. Past the meridian of life, I learned a new language.

Our three eldest daughters have children under their tuition. They almost feel the responsibilities of mothers. It is a task equal to taming wild animals. Our third daughter, Lois, has a little girl, eight years of age, as near as we can judge. Her parents do not know. Her father is a half breed Frenchman. A sweeter tempered child I never knew. Always submissive to the requirements of her teacher, easily pursuaded to leave off all her unpleasant habits. I should esteem it a great loss of labor and mental exertion to leave her behind when we go from here, and allow her to fall back to her native state, and forget all we have taught her. Ellen has wrought a visible change in the two she has under her care. Oh, what wonders might be wrought here, in the training of these children. Who would be content to be buried from the world to effect it!

Occasionally I have a leisure day, and not having much variety in my reading, I read over my old letters which my mother and sisters sent me many years ago. The sad remembrance of days of sorrow come vividly before me, and I wept. A rare occurance with me. Sister C. said she did not like to read old letters. It brought back memories which gave her pain. But with myself it is an established habit to review the past, and live my life over. It seems sublime and sacred, though it should cause sighs and tears.

Brother Crosby has at length succeeded in delivering a discourse in the Tahitian, much to the understanding of his hearers. In the evening several native brethren came to me for comments on the vision of Daniel. In my broken manner I talked of the "ancient of Days," told them how it was explained by elders of the church. They understood my words, and were satisfied.

The House of Prayer (as the natives call it) is the most comfortable place on this island, built as it is over water, six large windows on each side with slots instead of glass and sash thrown open or closed to suit high or low breezes. In that the heat is never oppressive. There I teach the children at an early hour in the morning: a long class of boys, a few little girls. It is amusing to hear them try to pronounce English words: to repeat the names of the days in a week, the months in a year, to count in English all which they are greatly delighted with, awkward as they are in the exercise. And above all do I endeavor to learn them to hold themselves erect on their seats, a habit they are almost as unacquainted with as our domestic animals. They seem inclined to writhe and twist themselves in all manner of positions. Their hands must be clasped over their heads or on the back of their seats, their feet drawn up under them, any way but the right way. And yet they seem intelligent and shrewd, as other children, having a desire to learn. Oh, could they be taken to America, and placed in a good school! But who are the philanthropists that will advance means for such an enterprise?

Today the queen called to see me. She seemed depressed in spirits; laid her hand on her heart and said, "poiri," meaning darkness. She was complaining that her mind was dark. She says, "little do I know of the Lord and his great work commenced on the earth." I tried to comfort her assuring her that a time was coming when her mind would be enlarged, and she would more fully comprehend the mercy of God towards his erring children. I bade her be comforted; to be humble, and in due time she should be exalted.

Nov 26th. The weather is intolerably dry and the fleas are like the plague in Egypt. Sister Crosby suffers terribly from their bits, poisoning her blood. Yesterday we made a party at the residence of Brother B. F. Grouard, for the purpose of showing his native wife our method or habits of waiting on company. We told them what our design was, that we would help them do the cooking. They were pleased, prepared a good supper. We furnished dishes to set the table, instructed them how to deport themselves. They endevored to imitate us as much as possible, and we had a merry time. In the evening the house being fitted up to look attractive, we had two instruments of music besides the sweet voices of the native women. Mr. Grouard seemed quite proud that his wife had acquitted herself so much to the satisfaction of her visitors. We feasted on melons at the close of the party, the first ever raised on the island.

[James S. Brown Case]

29th. This morning arose early and to our joyful surprise heard the *Ravaai* was in sight, which we had not expected for several days. Brother James Brown was on board, a prisoner, by order of the French Governor.[3] When the schooner landed in Tahiti he was in prison living on bread and water. He was discharged without a trial upon condition that he would remain a prisoner on the vessel till conveyed from out the bounds of the French protectorate. The Queen of Tubuai sent on board and brought him on shore. He appeared in good spirits, intends going to Ravaivai or to some island not under the French flag. The ship brought glorious news from Salt Lake. The glad reception of many letters made our hearts leap for joy. I could not sleep the first night so great was my excitement. Employment now for several days, answering the welcome letters.

The queen is a thinking woman. She mourns over the ignorance of her people, and her own also. They are good readers and could they have books printed in their own language adapted to their capacities what inspiration it would give them to acquire knowledge. I have been reading the history of England in the reign of Queen Elizabeth. I could admire her character but for one foul blot. The execution by her consent of

Mary Queen of Scotts. Oh, how mysterious the transactions of men appear in their political and religious superstitions.

A promising young woman is sick whom I have visited. She needs treatment of some kind. All the medicine I have is a bundle of hops, and a little sage. I use the herbs and encourage them to have faith in their efficacy. I find their faith effectual in many instances. An elderly woman came to me in the night, wished me to go and see a sister of hers who was very sick. I arose from my bed and went with her. She led me through a dark woody place, over an intricate path, but I feared nothing. I prayed and laid my hands on the sick woman. I told her she should be better in the morning and so it proved. "According to thy faith be it unto thee." Consecrated oil, which we brought with us from home, has been blessed to their use often, all on account of the faith they have in it.

Ellen succeeds admirably well in expounding scripture to their understanding, showing her knowledge of the Bible and Book of Mormon, far exceeding my highest anticipations. Frances sometimes appears discontented uttering ejaculations like this, "Oh that I were in Salt Lake City today!" I ask, "Would you like to be there without father to provide wood, and other comforts we have here?" Recalling reminisences of the past, she answers in the negative. I feel sensibly the sacrifice it is to our daughters to be without good society.

Dec 1st. The rain at last is beginning to descend. We hail it as a welcome messenger. Now the streams will rise and everything will be refreshed. The vessel all ready yesterday morning for another voyage expecting in a few moments to spread sail. Suddenly the wind sprung up from another quarter, which will detain them an indefinite time.

Mr. Grouard thinks he has more perplexities than any man on the island, having charge of the vessel besides other duties involves him in seeming difficulties, and some real ones. The native sailors trouble him, have little judgment about their business. He is tired and homesick and has reason to be so.

For the first time the House of Prayer has been cleaned. The seats scoured with sand, new business to the natives, when completed they seemed delighted with its appearance. I told them it must be cleaned every month, that the Lord would be the better pleased with us for a strict observance of cleanliness. The appointed time is Saturday preceding the sacrament of the Lord's supper.

13th day. Profound stillness except when I hear the mallets of the old women pounding bark to make cloth. The vibrations of the beam on which they pound is like the sound of a drum. It breaks the monotony and is preferable to no noise at all. In brother Crosby's dwelling where we often resort at evening we can have musick: Ellen with flutina, Alma C. violin, his father plays flute. It is far from being inferior, though not excelsior.

8th day. This morning the *Ravaai* left the harbor a fair wind for Ravaivai. Brother J. Brown bade us farewell. When the schooner returned from Tahiti last it brought a young lady of suspicious reputation. One of those fearful beings whom everyone has reason to dread unless they wish to be decoyed by her. The woman though a native of Tahiti, dresses herself in a very attractive manner. I feel a terrible dread of her influence over the young men. The king's son is already ensnared. I hope she may be the last of that class that will ever be brought to this island while I remain here. What a world is this we live in. Yesterday I was called on to wash and anoint a little boy who was suffering with the phthisic. He was immediately relieved. There is faith among this people. For a present I received a large supply of food: fresh pork, fish, tarrow, and papoi. No fear of going hungry here.

This morning heard a quarrel between two women. Such a flow of language I have seldom heard. It is the custom when two get offended they pour forth their words in torrents. When all is said that can be thought of, they cease their quarreling, and by their appearance you would not suppose that anything had transpired to break their friendship.

Walking with friends who were leaving the village today I encountered the "Tahitian lady." She passed me looking very demurely; she knows what I think of her. She was dressed in pink muslin, a large full flowing robe, her long black hair hanging down in braids, her heart and mind as dark as her skin, an alluring expression in her sombre countenance which cannot fail to disgust every lover of purity, and bring to their remembrance the words of the wise man, "Her steps take hold on hell." [Proverbs 5:5] I have often lamented not having had a son. I am certain if I had one, I should have to carry him on my heart. I am troubled about the boy [Hiram] we brought with us from Salt Lake, gone on the vessel. I promised his friends I would be a mother to him. I can only pray and warn him of temptation.

Our prayer meetings are all conducted in the language of the island. I long for communion with saints in our own tongue. The elders are scattered abroad.

17th. Last night I was called up from my bed to visit a sick child. I anointed him with consecrated oil, gave him a portion inwardly. This morning he is able to attend school. How the poor trusting souls cling to the promises in the gospel of Christ. There is a disease prevalent among all the islands not known before the whites came among them. There is an old man wasting away with disease, a grievous sore upon one leg. The fruits of sin. Many children are born diseased. Today is the burial of Tutailana, the sick woman of whom I have written. Her sufferings are at last ended. Her disease was of long standing. No skill of ours could reach it.

Dec. 19. I feel a kind of forced contentment. Last night I dreamed the French governor ordered us all away from the island. It would not be strange were it even so, neither should I much regret it. I teach the native children for amusement. Their oddities make me cheerful. Just returned from a visit three miles out, where Mr. Layton is building a schooner in company with the natives. The foundation lies in a beautiful place. A fine growth of a large ito trees completely shade it from the sun. There were twelve of us in company. The friendly people prepared a good dinner for us, and we had a delightful walk home. There was one horse among us so we rode in turns. The tide was out, the beach white, the sand hard and smooth. More than half the way the ito trees shade the beach. Thus does every little diversion help us to bear our solitude, at the best grievous to our children.

[A Grouard Son Born]

We are anxiously expecting the *Ravaai*, and with her the children hope to see their father. Joyful anticipation! Captain Grouard has had a son born since he sailed. There was great excitement among the friends. All interested to be on the spot to welcome the newcomer as soon as it might be presentable. At such times the woman, as soon as the birth is over, is taken to the river and immersed, is never known to take cold. Some females after giving birth to offspring go into decline and never recover. It does not however, appear to result from their common usage as they generally do well. Nature does all for them. Happy would it be for our females if she was allowed to do more.

24th. Today cleaned the house and made preparations for Christmas. The native sisters are preparing food. They praise my house when they see it clean, but do not incline to clean their own. I encourage them by telling them the Lord is better pleased when we keep ourselves neat and clean. What if we do not, we must not expect angels will visit us, for they take no delight in those who are filthy.

[Christmas 1851]

25th. We commenced Christmas by trimming up the house with green boughs and flowers. In the centre of the room a large pillar supports the roof. By the side of it I placed two small trees of ito, of the most livid green extending almost to the roof. The native houses have no loft. To these I attached the long yellow tea [*ti*] leaves, of which the females make wreaths on account of their bright color, and pleasant flavor. Added to these the bright fresh flowers of the bourau scattered about among the branches, forming a pleasing contrast of lively green and yellow.

In the same manner over head and around the entire room I hung boughs, flowers, and branches of the limetree with the fruit on. Our most intimate friends prepared for us a splendid dinner to which they were invited, bringing the food to the mission house. I told them the object was to celebrate the birthday of our Savior. They were pleased. One old lady whom we had not invited, as soon as she learned what was being done donned her finest white robe and made her appearance, I received her as I did the invited guests, knowing she was ignorant of our customs. The natives from far and near thronged the house, looking in at the windows, to admire the decoration. I felt annoyed and asked the chief if he would tell them to go away. He plead for them as a father would for children. They had never seen anything of that kind before, and he wished me to indulge them for once. Another time they should be sent away. I felt that he was right and consented to let them feast their eyes as long as they would.

After dinner we held a prayer meeting. At evening, [we] illumi-nated the house with all the glass lamps in the village. The brilliant lights threw over all a mantle of romance exceeding anything I had ever seen. Brother C. and Ellen made the instrumental musick added then to the sweet melody of human voices made it seem in reality like a birthday of the blessed Saviour. Here now in December the heat is excessive. It is the first time I have suffered with it. Frances I discover is beginning to be uneasy. I pray that the way may open for us to return home least our daughters become unhappy.

28th. After returning from the Sabbath morning service, I was sent for in great haste. Sister Grouard was taken suddenly with a severe chill. She was exercised in a singular manner. The natives exclaimed "tupau pau!" "That is an evil spirit!" In vain I remonstrated, told them she had taken cold; it was an ague chill. They said I was "maro," that is stubborn and hard to believe. As the chill left her they let down the curtains to dress her, a native sister whispered, "Look you under the curtains and see the spirit when it comes out." So great is their superstition. The sick woman got out of bed with a high fever, a little wandering in mind. They eyed her very closely and thought they saw the devil. She is fast recovering.

There is another sick woman sinking everyday. She is in the bloom of life, has six children. O gladly would I save her. She is surrounded by unbelievers in the ordinances of the gospel, even in the same house. It is hard to have faith there. I regret we were not supplied with simple medi-cines when we left home.

[New Year's 1852]

Jan 1st 1852. New Years, we celebrated by making another feast.[4] We dec-orated Brother Crosby's house, made it white with corral lime. "Te fau nehe nehe, te fare, no yona ta na." Many of the natives were invited and seated at the table. Two tables set for seventeen. They improve a little each time. The outside of the house was surrounded with the poor uncouth beings. It is a trial to bear with their extreme ignorance, still a little pleasure to amuse them. They will gaze for a half hour at a picture and you must answer forty questions concerning it. They must know the history entire or not be satisfied.

We all agree in wishing our friends in Salt Lake a happy New Year. We trust they are wishing us the same. On these occasions we dress ourselves in a becoming and tasteful manner, ornament our rooms as we would to receive fashionable and refined company, all for the purpose of example that they may understand our Customs, and to stimulate them to imitation and improvement.

Twice today we thought we heard the cry of "pahii a hoi!" (Ship coming), but were disappointed. The children's ears are open now and will be till the *Ravaai* comes into port. We shall watch to see her tall masts and white sails reeling in the strong breeze which now blows fair for Tubuai. There is no other hope of again being relieved of monotony but the return of the vessel. I have been toiling all the morning cleaning my dooryard. I often do such things to encourage the native women to clean theirs. They will pass along complimenting me in this way, "e hara, Paraita Vahine, faa nehe au a." They seem to think all the little nice habits belong exclusively to Europeans. A few there are who have imitation large. Such if they had courage to excel others would do well, but it is no trait of a native to be above his fellows. With his people there is little division or distinction, even those who do not belong to the church must be treated as brethren.

Today the Elders broke Bread. The brethren came from the other village. Brother Alexander called after the close of the services, talked of his troubles with his native wife. She is a childish girl. It is evident she does not love him. What a pity, that sensible men should involve themselves with these poor ignorant women. They cannot bring them to their level; it is unwise to attempt it. To be comfortable with them they must descend to their level.

5th day.[5] Head winds, no prospect of the ship coming in. Tomorrow we shall go to Mahu for a few days. Walked to the village a distance of five miles, wind very high, did not feel fatigued, made the village at twelve, rested, and went to see the sick woman. She was lying on a mat spread upon the ground, a hard pillow for her head. I saw she was dying, feet and hands were cold. Her husband was leaning over her, apparently the only mourner. I felt distressed to see no one doing anything for her relief. I ordered chicken broth, which she took easily. I heat rocks and applied to her hands and feet. I saw they were expecting her to die, and so sat idly down to await the event. A large pile of cloth lay near her, brought to wrap her in, as their custom is when one dies. She spoke distinctly several times, had her reason well, seemed calm with resignation.

The bell was rung and the children called . . . . [*page torn here and through following paragraphs*] I organized them into a class and taught them to . . . Tahitian words into English: to count reckon. Anything for employment is better than . . . . The white children amuse themselves rambling . . . and gathering flowers. They go often to the . . . places. I cannot be contented without . . . and company. Anything like employment . . . grasp with eagerness. This is a silent . . . noise but the rambling roaring . . . of the sea. Which is unusually loud, our . . . high winds. There is a grandeur in the . . . which seems to soothe the soul when . . . would intrude. It bears witness of the creation, ...

Last night the sick woman died. She was . . . out on clean grass, a white spread thrown over her. Her face was not covered, someone sat with a large leaf to keep off the flies. The coffin was made of a canoe of tamana wood, (island mahogany) in which she was laid after being wrapt thickly in native cloth. A thick plank nailed on for a cover. Outside the coffin unnumbered thicknesses of cloth were wound, native and European. The coffin, being of the most imperishable wood, wrapt in such quantity of cloth, will not in my opinion decay in fifty years. A great feast was made by relatives from which all the people in the village received a portion. The corpse was carried away on men's shoulders, without ceremony.

Last evening we spent two hours in gazing at the moon, expressing our surprise at her singular appearance. One part was red, like blood, emitting no light at all, though nearly at the full. Brother Alexander, being a superstitious man pronounced it a forerunner of evil. Told the family with whom we were stopping it was an omen of something strange . . . take place. So long had we been away from . . . world, and not having seen an almanac in . . . years, we had forgotten there was ever such . . . as an eclipse. When it rushed upon our . . . we were ashamed that we had not known . . . first. We then explained all to the ignorant . . . and their fears were removed. This morning . . . before the day dawned, and went to walk . . . the beach. The moon was shining with . . . resplendent brightness. There was the very . . . of death around me. All in the dwelling . . . just locked in slumbers, the tide had just . . . far on the reef, scarcely a breeze to be felt. . . . atmosphere was calm as the sweet breath of autumn. But oh, so solemn. I gazed over the mighty ocean towards that land so far away and I seemed to feel that I had died, and gone to an unknown world.

I at first thought I would tune my voice to sing a morning hymn, but it seemed an intrusion upon the sacredness of the hour to make the least noise. I felt that secret prayer was more congenial to the deathlike stillness of that little world, in the midst of the mighty ocean. I revolved in my mind the self-denial of my whole life and said "If my Heavenly Father is pleased with the little good I have done all my sorrows will be forgotten.

[A New House]

9th day. Last evening we moved into the house Brother Alexander has been several days preparing for us. It is a large house, all in one room, built in ancient style, round ends. Three pillars in the centre, which support the roof, and these are covered with carved work, curiously wrought. The house is whitened with coral lime inside and out. Long grass laid for a floor, on which mats are spread. Two high post bedsteads curtained around with fine white "tapa [native cloth]." A very large table made from a tree which floated here from New Zealand. The leaf more than three feet wide without a seam. The building [is] almost entirely shaded with trees, large and covered with flowers. Their fragrance is delightful.

[Ancient Remains]

Five rods from the door the grand old tide rolls out and in. No lover of nature could help admiring this situation. Nothing but the want of society is felt here. The good people sent us in food to last us a week, cooked for ready use, nicely tied up in leaves. This morning took a long walk to see an old hollow tree, which is reported to have been in the "taueteni [ancient times, heathen days]," the abode of a man (who was pursued by his enemies) a whole year and was fed by a sister. Nine of us entered the tree together, had room to move about. Two branches of equal size supported by the middle are hollow, and there are openings from one to the other, so the man could change his position when wearied with his confinement.

From the tree we were conducted by Alexander to one of the old "morai's [*marae*]" places of worship in the "taueteni". It consists of huge stones set up in the form of a square room. One very high above the rest they worshiped as God. Flat stones are laid upon the ground under which the heads of their enemies are buried, sacrificed to their Gods. A dense growth of cocoanut overshadowed the place. We rested beneath the cooling shade, drank freely of the water, and pursued our journey, called at a native house where everything was neat and clean. A young woman was seated on a mat with a babe in her arms. We conversed with her in the Tahitian tongue, and she treated us to beautiful fine apples. From thence we started on our way home.

Not far had we gone when a messenger met us with the joyful intelligence that the *Ravaai* was in port, and "Paraita" was on board. The two eldest daughters were far in the rear. The messenger passed on and carried the news to them. Quick and hasty were their footsteps till they reached the house and met their father. Now they exclaimed, "Our wishes are realized." When the house was fited up we felt it would avail us nothing without company. We are informed the vessel has encountered

three severe gales of wind since it left this port, did not make Tahiti, neither the Chain Islands, except Ana [Anaa] and Matea [Mehetia]. The
friends have sent us a great supply of food, consisting of the fruits of the
island, all nicely secured in leaves.

11th day. Paraita preached three times in the native language. The
people all appeared joyful on hearing the voice of their missionary once
more.

[Sailing the Lagoon]

12th. This morning very early went out to the reef in a canoe. It was calm
and beautiful sailing. We raised a small sail and a gentle breeze wafted us
along smoothly. The water was clear, and we could see distinctly the coral
beneath which resembles a garden of vines and shrubbery, beautiful to
look upon. The air was cool, and light clouds shielded us from the sun's
scorching rays. We sailed in and out among the coral to examine the fishing nets. They are curiously woven out of roots, sunk to the bottom where
the water is shallow. The bait [is] put inside; the fish run in through the
small aperture and are secured. Sometimes fish weighing twenty pounds
are taken. We could discover them of all shapes and colors shooting
about and hiding in the cavities of the coral. We stopt on an island of
rocks, struck a fire with wood we carried out, roasted fish, and made a
hearty meal. On our return Brother Alexander dove to the bottom, with
an axe knocked off a large piece of coral which we hung up in the sun to
bleach. Most likely we shall obtain finer specimen to take home.

13th. Started about sunrise to walk round on the beach to Matauru.
The tide was out, the road smooth, the distance nine miles, yet I was not
fatigued at all. The delightful sea air invigorates my nerves. I do not
remember any period of my life when I could perform as much with
more ease. Some little disagreeables in the family has made us all sad.
Frances complains bitterly and longs to go home. The cry of "pahi a hoi,"
has been sounding for an indefinite length of time, and we have high
hopes it may be a vessel that can bear us away to our home and country.

14th. The vessel which occasioned so much excitement proves to be
a schooner from California, Capt. Mayers. He has come for oranges, with
no conveniences to take passengers.

[Socials, Feasts]

15th. Last evening nearly all the Americans were together. The two sea
Captains were present. For amusement we practiced the native children
in performing little acts of courtesy, passing round the room and making
their obeisance to each one, answering questions, etc. Some of them did

exceedingly well. Brother Crosby and Ellen played on their instruments. The conversation turned on the choice of tunes, which excited mirth and did us all good in this old solemn world. What a contrast between joy and sorrow. The newly arrived ship is undergoing repairs, which will detain it several days, a fine opportunity to send home letters, I wish I had time to write a hundred.

Last evening had a music party. The strange gentlemen were delighted, complimented our "band" for their masterly performance. Well might it seem pleasant to them coming off a long voyage and finding on a lovely island a company of Americans, women and children, a joyful surprise indeed.

Mr. Richmond spent the morning at our residence, made us some presents, useful articles for the table, luxuries we seldom enjoy. A kind-hearted agreeable man he is, and meeting him here among the rude sons of nature, makes him appear doubly attractive. For several days my mind has been diverted. I realize the salutary effect changes have on the mind.

17th, Sabbath. After "divine service" we all went to Elder Grouard's to dine. The food purely native, served up in the usual style. All praised the food. King Tamatoa was present, dressed in European clothes. It was the first time I had ever seen him dressed in that manner. I scarcely knew him, so much did he resemble a white man. He even wore shoes and stockings.

[Pages 238–241 of Louisa's manuscript are missing. They were not present in 1947 when the Daughters of Utah Pioneers printed the work in Heart Throbs of the West.*]*

Feasting is a great source of enjoyment to this people. Every little turn in their affairs must be celebrated by a feast, even to changing the Sabbath.

30th day. The feast is going on. Ellen and Frances are preparing to go to Tahiti. The great central Island we have never seen. Their Uncle will take them under his charge and their father has given his consent. It would be more satisfactory could their father go with them but it seems impracticable. He just returned from a long, hard voyage and does not feel willing to embark again so soon.

31st day. Another month is gone. Time whirls on its rapid course! I have for two weeks been dumb with astonishment. When I contemplate [*blank space*] I regard him as a being enveloped in mystery. Things have transpired which have caused me to marvel continually! There are unsound men, as well as unsound animals. How can men of high tones sentiment stoop from their lofty pedestal and descend so low? Where is their pride and self esteem at times so prominent in every word and motion. How can human beings be so variable? Men lay aside their dignity (some do) when they come to these islands. I have been compelled to witness scenes I would never believed possible. I have had nothing to regret in regards to my own, except in the case of our boy. That delusive woman is still on the island, laying snares to decoy the king's youngest son. She has been the author of great uneasiness since her arrival here.

[Ellen and Frances Go to Tahiti]

Feb 1st. Today the *Ravaai* sailed for Tahiti, with a fair wind. She went off before it like a bird. E and F went on board in good spirits. I commend them to the care of Him who ruleth the raging winds! I pray that their minds may be kept in undisturbed repose, that nothing may occur to give them pain or uneasiness. I pray that no delusive influence may be exerted over them, but may the fear of God be continually before their eyes, to keep in awe of every unhallowed thought or deed. Could their father have gone, all would have seemed right, but their uncle is a faithful and just man, under his care I see no chance for evil to befall them. This afternoon the elders broke bread, in commemoration of the Savior's death and resurrection, a great many comunicants. All looked clean and comely. After the close of services I walked with others, went to see a figtree growing, the first I have ever seen. Saw a poor man wasting away with a sore eye, a white man, who has been many years among the islands, has a native wife, (no doubt the fruits of sin).

CHAPTER TWELVE

The Islands Tubuai and Tahiti
A Missionary Family III

Memoirs, February 1852 to 6 April 1852

In the evening had a walk by moonlight. Nothing could exceed the grandeur of the scenery. The moon was near the full, the sky clear as amber. The tall cocoanuts were waving their branches over our heads. Immediately before us the proud waves of the Pacifick were rolling in awful majesty. A strong breeze was blowing to waft the ship that had borne away our children and friends to its destined harbor. It was an hour for reflection and my sister and I talked of the strange things that have come to pass. It seems to have made a deep impression on my mind. Oh, the island seems desolate when the *Ravaai* is gone.

[The French Governor's Daughter]

Have just received under my care a new pupil, said to be the daughter of the French governor on Tahiti, by a native of that island, a lovely little girl, about four years old. I was attracted to her by seeing her play in the water. One morning as I walked out I came near the bridge over the river. A company of children were jumping off the bridge into the water and playing like so many fishes. I stopt to look at them. I espied one diverse from the others. I was struck with the beauty of her form and complexion. I called to the larger children to bring her to me. They did so, and I enquired "whose child is she?" They replied, "Tamahini no Tavana no Tahiti." The daughter of the French Governor on Tahiti. They told me the names of her "mau matua faa a mu," (feeding parents.) I requested them to go and tell the people to bring her to the Mission House, I wished to talk with them. They did as I bade them, and very soon they were before me, and presented the little child.

163

I then asked the woman to give me the child's history. She had been a resident on Tahiti at the time of the child's birth. "The Governor came from France to bear rule among the islands, left his wife at home. After a residence of a few months he took a native woman to live with him, who bore two daughters. At the expiration of two years he went to France, and returned bringing with him his lawful wife. It happened one evening there was a great gathering of the people about the governor's house. Himself and wife were standing in the Piazza above. The lady looked down, saw below, sitting on the ground, a native woman with a white child in her arms. A thought struck her in a moment that it was her husband's, and she said the same to him, which he dared not deny. She then upbraided him for not informing her of the fact before she left France."

She said to him with great candor and firmness, "Had you told me that you had a child here, who had claims on your protection, of whose existance you was the author, I would have taken it into my own family and performed the part of a mother, but inasmuch as you thought to deceive me, and keep it a profound secret, I require you to send the child or children forever from my sight." Like a humbled man he hearkened to her words. They were both sent from that island. The younger was placed in charge of the above named people, who brought her to me. They had the credit of being kind sensible Guardians. I proposed taking her under my charge to teach, which they readily conceded would be desirable and appreciative. Their fondness for the little girl made them conscious that she should be improved.

She wept bitterly when they left her. I took her to my arms as if she had been my own and she soon became attached to me, and was never willingly out of my sight. With a view to learn her she must sometimes stay at home when I went out, I would steal slyly away. Generally before I could get ten rods from the door, I would hear the patter of her little feet trotting behind me, keeping at a short distance, not venturing too near, for fear of a reproof for following when she had not permission. As soon as I felt induced to turn, and with a gently voice speak her name, "Sarah, must you go?" No little wild animal would bound with more lighted feet and lightened heart. I often thought it would be hard to find a more attractive child. Her color was not objectionable. Enough of native to give a tinge not uncomely, her black hair and eyes denoted character, her ideality filled her whole being with inspiration, at the sight of anything beautiful.

Such was her aptness to learn it was a real pleasure to teach her. She had a great fancy for pronouncing English words. We dressed her in European fashion, which caused her the more to admire herself, likewise her guardians, who often visited her, seemed proud, and called her a "tomahini papa." When I left the islands, it was contemplated placing her under the tuition of the English Missionaries. Gladly would I have brought her home, but that was contrary to French laws. Hope has inspired me to believe her father would keep a watchful eye over her, and that she grew up a brilliant woman, there is little room to doubt. Never does my mind revert to the scenes enacted on that "isolated world" but I remember the patter of those little feet, and can see the golden child in the water. I have digressed. I will return to my journal.

[Island Life—"Dull, Dull"]

Feb 3d. [1852] Received presents from little Sarah's "mau metua," as they are called. Kind and agreeable people are they. Last night stood an hour or more on the beach with my sister and a crowd of children. The tide was in and the breakers were dashing upon the shore. While we stood just within reach for it to cover our feet, and then recede to meet the succeeding one, as it rushed forward with a violent effort to impede its course, but in vain, it would mock the power of the receding wave and come dashing on, bury our feet, and away to meet its opponent, carrying with it the loud laughter of the children. The atmosphere was delightful, The stars were looking down in their peerless beauty. The majestic queen of the Heavens was riding on in rival grandeur, and smiling with approbation at creation beneath her. Such is an evening on Tubuai, the little world in this mighty ocean.

Everything is still and quiet no noise on the island when there are no vessels in port with spirituous liquors. Our chief amusement is on the beach at the close of the day, when the air is cool, watching the children play in the water, when the breakers are dashing on the beach. If a little one falls and the wave rolls over him the rest all shout with laughter. In a moment he is up, and ready to venture again.

5th day. Today was our weekly prayer meeting. Ellen being absent, I had no one to interpret, was compelled to rely on my own ability to speak for myself. I succeeded beyond my expectations, and they appeared to understand me well, and were pleased.

This morning I arose early and was surprised to find Mr. P. gone. Searching the house I found his gun, and knew he had not gone in search of wild fowls. I could not conjecture why he had gone without our knowledge. Towards evening he returned. He had walked a long distance to find a spot suited to the production of corn. He had planted with a view to dry it in the milk, to use on our voyage home. This encouraged us to see a move made however small in reference to that most desirable enterprise.

7th day Yesterday was Ellen's birthday. Twenty years has she seen the light of Heaven, and oh! what a pilgrim have I been since the 6th year of her age! How have I traversed creation through! One thing is certain, if for twenty years to come I am required to encounter similar scenes in the struggle of life, no woman's experience will exceed mine. Few are the young women of her years whose lives have been more eventful than hers.

The people are all engaged in grinding limes and making juice for the Tahitian market. Mills of their own construction are in operation. In doing the work they make a frolick, all get together and sing while gathering the limes. They must have a new song at every tree, all their own make. No matter whether it rhymes by rule or not, they can twist the tune to fit the metre. Lime juice is quite an article of commerce. It is a favorite drink, mingled with water in almost all warm climates, but is never used here. The cotton tree is really a cureosity to me; having never seen one before. It produces the finest quality of cotton, grows in pods like a bean. When ripe it bursts open. The tree grows eight or ten feet in height, with many branches.

Today had a feast of reading newspapers from the U. States. It seems cheering to hear from the world. Though all I read is not agreeable but it proves to me the world is still in existance. To be convinced of that fact is better than feeling that a little spot on which I stand in the midst of a mighty ocean is all that is left of the once populous universe. As I sat reading the news a native brother asked "ei hara to parau?" (what is the talk?) Mr. Pratt told what great improvements were being made in America. He replied (in his tongue) that, "men abroad are doing great things; while here they do nothing but eat, drink, and sleep and be idle like dogs." Poor man, he has a true sense of his condition and desires to rise above it.

9th day. All days are alike here, dull, dull. As soon as daylight in the morning, the bell rings and the people assemble at the "Prayer House," to read the Bible. We read and talk a little, dismiss and go to breakfast. Again the bell rings for the children. I teach them to answer questions, from scripture, pronounce English words, tell their meaning etc. Then my own children get their lessons in English. After this, I read, write and sew. How I long for intelligent associations. The few Americans are the same as one family. We meet often and exhaust our subjects of conversation, then our minds reach after variety. We cannot make companions of the natives. They can only amuse us for a little time. It is not desirable to go into their dwellings to remain long, their notions of order are diverse from ours. It would be amusing to see how their admiration would be excited could they go into a well finished and handsomely furnished house.

[Pratt's Land]

10th day. Went to see the land which is said to belong to Paraita, far inland.[1] It appears to be a rich soil covered with cocoanuts and faees [*feiis*], timber somewhat resembling black walnut, but more of a reddish hue. On our way we saw several small improvements, and corn growing, a thing they had never seen before we came here.

[Louisa's Teaching]

What a paradise might be made of this island had the people one spark of enterprise. But that is smothered beneath the rain of ages, and swept away with the knowledge their forefathers once possessed. Now they grope in darkness at noonday. They have a kind of natural religion, pray much and seem to enjoy it. I am sometimes disposed to think they practice it for amusement. In the principles of chastity they seem wreckless. A female though known to be unvirtuous and unchaste in her habits is not denounced as unworthy of a son or brother in wedlock. Although the male may be a fairer type of humanity in regard to morals, it is, however, expected and required when she is married that she be true to her husband.

In consideration of their extreme fondness for children, it is strange they should be so stupid in regard to such principles as tend to procreation. For this cause they decrease. There was on this island at one time 5000 inhabitants. Now they number only 200 all told. My mind is continually occupied in reflecting on the conduct of those men who having had a Christian training come to these islands and corrupt themselves with the heathen women. I wish there could be an example made of a few to alarm others. I sometimes feel such indignation rise up in my heart I could almost see them hung. What are men made of? How can he stain his soul with that indelible mark which will be as lasting as eternity? In my humble opinion he will feel the effects produced by such a course in the world of spirits, memory will haunt him with the reflection, "I sinned against light and knowledge."

12th day. Today was our weekly prayer meeting. I spoke to the sisters twice at considerable length. Every attempt I make I speak with more ease. I told them about the "holy city" of which we read in John's Revelations. "That nothing unclean could enter there." Fornicators and adulterers would stand without and plead in vain for admission. Then said I, "if you are fortunate enough to be among the accepted ones, you will hear wailing and lamentation from those who are rejected." I told them to invite their irreligious relatives to come to our meetings, and we would plead with them to repent and forsake their sins, and be baptized, and begin their lives anew. At the close I asked them if they understood me well. They replied they did, and felt great joy that I could speak their language so well.

13th. Spent the entire day in Prayer House teaching the children and writing in my history. I am surprised at the accuracy with which I call to mind scenes in my early life. Almost every circumstance seems as vivid as the day it transpired. In this way I pass many an hour which otherwise would hang heavily on my hands. Days of silence, and loneliness. This Building is like a cloister where monks reside. A place of retirement and reflection. Here the varied scenes of my life are revived and lived over.

15th. This morning early heard the cry of "Pahi a hoi." A welcome sound indeed. We all run to see if we could ascertain what craft it was. All pronounced sooner than we expected but we thought it must be her. Very soon the news came, "It is not the *Ravaai*," but a Schooner from Raivavai where brother Brown is preaching. Capt. Rutcliff came on shore with seventy passengers.

They all came to see us, shook hands very cordially. They were dressed neatly, looked clean and comely. Two letters came from Brother James B. Great contention on Raivavai about the gospel through the influence of English missionaries. Doors of publick worship closed against him. He is anxious to leave there and go where he can do more good. Those who have embraced the truth are greatly disturbed. Today a great feast is in opperation for the newly arrived visitors, a great dance too, out in the groves. The rain is coming down upon them. For musick they have three drums, and some whistles made of small cane, which makes sweet musick, though very low. The new comers have been walking through the House all the morning exchanging presents with their friends. Every time they pass there must be a salute and ceremony. If they come to your house a dozen times in a day there must be a ceremony "ia ora na oe," meaning life and peace to you. A female came in with a young child in her arms, born on the vessel no more than 24 hours old. She seemed as brisk as her companions showed no signs indicating an event of that nature. I am much better pleased with the appearance of these people than when I saw them on their own Island. There, they appeared careless and slovenly, here they look tidy and respectable. They are aware that the Tubuai natives consider themselves a little higher grade. In coming here to visit they have made an effort to vie with their neighbors. Just now the cry of Pahi a hoi was heard, all thought it must be the *Ravaai*, but the news soon resounded it was a large ship with tall masts, probably a whaler.

I have much satisfaction in endeavoring to expound the scriptures to those who come to me to be instructed. Today I was requested to search out portions of scripture to prove that God exists in a form. This I did with great ease. Hebrews 12th 3d an incontrovertible testimony appears. "Who being the brightness of his Father and the express image of his person." And again, "Who being in the form of God thought it not robbery to be equal with God." Many other portions I sought out, which seemed conclusive to their inquiring minds. Brother Grouard still insists on the expediency of going to California to procure a large vessel to take us and such of the natives as desire to go to the American Coast. All do not accord with his views, reasoning that it would require too much time to accomplish such an expedition.

19th. The visitors still remain here, feasting still continues. All civil, no confusion much to their credit.

We are every hour looking for the Schooner. Wind strong and fair to bring her into port. Last night at dusk, I walked on the beach. The wind was roaring loud, the sea looked angry. The agitated water wore a dark green color. "Oh thou old dread sea, thou art the mother of the continents, the islands thy children." As I listened a trembling thought crossed my mind that perhaps the vessel might be in danger, be driven onto rocks, or in some way endanger the lives of our children. My next thought was He is whom we trust rules the raging seas. As soon as I committed them to His care I felt measurably relieved.

I returned to my sisters house collected all the children we have under our charge, and placed them in a row or class. Ann Louise, our youngest daughter pronounced little B. F. Grouard, the best looking child among them. I gave the preference to little Sarah, the French girl. She is fair, shows very little of her dark blood. Sophronia Grouard has marks of beauty. A bright expressive countenance, dark lustrous eyes, regular features. Alice, the quadroon, wears an open smile which indicates good temper, a lively animated expression, a satisfied air which gives her an affable appearance. I see more clearly how the disposition may be read in the countanance. I feel gratified at the progress I am making in acquiring the language. When I am put to the test, have no interpreter, I quite astonish my hearers. It is good for me to be compelled to speak for myself.

I read from the prophet Ezra his lamentations, and repentance before God, for the sins of the children of Israel, when they were returned from Babylon to rebuild Jerusalem. He rent his garments, tore out his hair, confessed the sins of the people, his shame for their transgressions. I compared the Prophet's sorrow to the sorrow of the missionaries who come to labor among these islands. When a portion of them have turned from their idolatry, broken away from their corrupt and abominable practices, thus causing the hearts of their teachers to rejoice; see them run well for awhile, others seeing their good works are almost pursuaded to join their ranks, when suddenly as though the adversary of all good was lurking in secret laying snares for them, they turn from the holy commandments delivered to them at an incalculable cost, and commence again their livid and dishonorable practices. Then said I, your teachers know the sorrow of the prophet!

They feel like rending their garments, clothing themselves in sackcloth, lying down with dust upon their heads! Such anguish have I felt when I have seen persons, professing to know and be governed by the principles of the everlasting gospel, forget their high and holy calling, and descend to the level of the poor degraded beings who make merchandise of their honor, which should be to them more sacred than the life blood that courses through their hearts. I think of the pure spirits I have known in my life, and ardently do I pray that I may someday see their faces, and bear my testimony to the great truths the Lord has revealed from the Heavens, in this our day and age. This promise has been made me, and by those who have authority; and claim it I must and will. Why should I doubt?

Feb 21st. This is my companions birthday 50 years old. Few men of his years have had an experience more varied. 14 years since he was baptized in Kirtland Ohio, and confirmed a member in the church of Jesus Christ of Latter Day Saints. The last eight years his time has chiefly been devoted to labors in the gospel. His property has been sacrificed, his family reduced to the most abject poverty, sickness and distress in his absence. Hunger cold, and nakedness; houseless and homeless, have they wandered, in dens and caves of the earth! Over deserts and through the howling wilderness! But in the Lord have they trusted, and ere long he will put a new song in their mouths, even praise to our God. On Sabbaths we have crowded congregations; the visitors add to the numbers.

22d. This evening amused ourselves with the children, dressed little Frank G. in boy's clothes for the first time. He walked about with all the importance of an army general, with his hands in his pockets. He performed masterly the ceremonies required, shaking hands and bowing to all in the room. He would not submit to be called anything but a man. Still he wanted his "aunty" to rock him to sleep, as usual. When told that men must not be rocked, he replied, "I am a little man."

This afternoon a great dance and a feast has been going on. A female carried the flag, her companions followed in train, dressed in white, with wreaths of flowers on their heads, and carrying great loads of provission on their shoulders. Their singing has been very loud, drums and whistles besides their vocal musick. The church members venture to go and look on, but do not presume to join them.

Today "te mau metua no toata fran," brought us banannas, fish and fine melons. I have spent the day quite agreably, in reading the political class book.

29th. Last evening the dance was ended. The noise was loud, and to cap the climax they set the dogs to fighting. The visitors brought a number of dogs, no doubt were anxious to know whether they would return to their island conquerors, or conquered. Scenes of a like nature show their wild and untamed habits.

Capt. Rutcliff has just set sail, going to Raiatea after his wife. He has a native woman, like all the other capt's about the island. There is something peculiar about them; all I believe, ran away from home, they now appear to be sober candid men. Capt R talks of his parents in England, being wealthy, his father a ship owner, and he, a wanderer about these isolated islands, and has been for nine years. We begin now to conclude the *Ravaai* has gone to the Chain Islands; probably three weeks will elapse ere she will be announced coming into this port.

Last evening went on a long walk. All had a fine bath in the deep water. Called to see the grave of John Cane, father of our little Mary, who lived with us so long. The yard seems going to decay. He lies alone in the woods. The tall limes and guaver trees hang bending over, reaching to the wind that whistles through their branches, as if to soothe his sleep dust. The spot has been neatly ornamented. A thick coat of lime has been spread over the grave to keep it forever dry. A white board with an inscription. He died five months before the birth of his child, but her mother has taught her to revere the spot where he lied buried. The woman is now the wife of Capt. Johnson. He is a kind stepfather to Mary and a sensible man.

26th. Today spoke at some length in our prayer meeting. It seemed that words were given me as I needed. I could feel that I was understood. Today Lois was taken with a severe pain in her hand. It is badly swolen. We have often marveled at our continual health, when the people in general are so often ill. Transitions with me are all of a mental nature. Transports of joy I seldom feel. Sometimes [I feel] peace and a heavenly calm, at others deep sorrow and unaccountable gloom!

Last evening I ventured a walk on the beach alone. Having never been disturbed in my nocturnal rambles I have ceased to have any fears. The beach immediately in front of my sisters door, the tide having receded, and the sovereign of night presenting her fair face from behind the beautiful clouds, seemed to urge me to venture alone. Everything was so tranquil above and below. I could see the starry heavens in the depths beneath shining up; in the firmament shining down; each vieing with the other in brillancy. I sang some favorite hymns in a low tone. A holy calm stole over me. It seemed the quiet of some soothing spirit so gentle. I thought I should creep softly home and no one would ask where I had been. As I was about to start my husband came in search of me, and uttered a reproof, that I should go out alone. To have told him the true reason would have spoiled the effect, and destroyed all the exercise had done for me. So in silence I made my way to the house, and evaded the subject as much as possible.

28th. Today translated the eight chapter of Corinthians from the Tahiti. A great source of amusement it is to study a new language. Youth is the season to learn everything.

29th. Sabbath. Three discourses today, all in Tahiti. The evening exercise was soul stirring! I understood it better than I generally do. It was directed chiefly to those who having long heard the truth sounding in their ears refuse to obey. They were reminded that "now is the accepted time, and now the day of salvation!" That if now they turn a deaf ear to the call to repent and forsake their sins, the time would come when they would call on God, and he would not answer. It sometimes seems to me a waste of time to preach to them. I wish the labor could be bestowed on those who would appreciate it more. I long to see the *Ravaai* coming into Port! Who can tell but cheering inteligence will again greet our ears, and the way be opened for us to return to our home and country.

The natives still continue their work making limejuice. Of late they grow very noisy. The king is gone, there is no one to restrain them. As soon as they strip the limes from one tree they set up a shout, that is almost deafening, and then they dance, till they come to another. I have often complained of silence, and stillness, and felt as though I were walking among the tombs! Now for a change I must hear the noise.

March 3d. The air is cool and delightful. Every morning I translate a chapt from the Tahitian Bible into English. It does not read the same as in our book, but it is the same in substance. I really admire the language; it is spoken with so much ease. There is not one word in ten, of the English, that these people can pronounce correctly.

Every day I hear the same wild singing. How free from care their minds must be. They carrol like birds, like them do they live, like children playing in the streets, unconcerned about wants, so their lives pass and what will they ever attain to? The human mind is better developed under trying circumstances. In the hard struggles of life, in the stern realities, the mind is more active, it thinks deeper, I never knew a person whose life had been made up of deep afflictions, but from that one's experience there was wisdom to be gleaned. On the other hand there are persons on whom providence has seemed always to smile, and they never have a dozen thoughts in their lives, aside from business and pleasure. When I meet with the good humble sisters in the House of Worship I never fail to wish they could be separated from the rabble, and taken away from the evil influences.

5th day. Translated a chapt in the morning the remainder of the day spent in writing.

Mar 6th. This is Lois B's birthday. 15 years old. She is a tall womanly girl, amiable in her temper. Has two children under her charge: on them she enforces implicit obedience. Fortunate would it be for them could they be brought to maturity under her tuition. They seem greatly attached to her, willing to obey the slightest command. The boy at first apparently had no sense of subjection. If I spoke to him in a commanding tone he looked at one with surprise, and would go his own way. Now he obeys his teacher at a word. The little girl whom we named Alice was much given to telling falsehoods. Lois labored faithfully to teach her to be truthful. Her word now can be relied upon as firmly as any child's in the house.

[News via *Ravaai*: Prepare to Leave the Mission]

Joyful inteligence! The *Ravaai* is in sight. The cry of "Pahi a hoi," is going round the island! Now we are making great preparations to receive our friends. A great feast is being prepared. Since the cry of "Ship," I have caused the Prayer House to be cleaned throughout, had new long grass laid in both rooms of my dwelling, the walls ornamented with green ito boughs, a display of flowers which the native children spare no pains to procure for us. Let them come at any hour we shall be ready to entertain them.

7th day Sabbath. Today broke bread probably for the last time in Tubuai. The word now is that we are to go forthwith to Tahiti. This morning at two o'clock the *Ravaai* came into harbor. The wind which had been high all day died away and the full moon arose. She was beaming forth in all her loveliness when I heard a call at my window announcing the arrival of the Schooner! In a few moments the children were dressed and we were all on the beach. Scores of natives thronged the roads running to and fro, and immediately commenced making ovens to cook for a feast.

March 8th. The sails were all furled and the ship lay gently rolling with the swell. All seemed silent, and we could discover only one man on deck keeping watch. A canoe went off, and aboard, returned with the news that a portion of the company had staid behind, and that we were to go immediately to Tahiti, and make preparations to cross the ocean, and bid our native friends a long farewell. In a short time the passengers came on shore, and we gave them a hearty shaking of hands. They were pleased with the voyage though the vessel had not made the Chain Islands, as was expected, but had been to Rurutu, where they were detained two weeks on account of head winds. Found the people there greatly opposed to the gospel. The brethren who remained on Tahiti have engaged a job of housebuilding for which they are to have $1300. That amount of means will defray all the expenses of a home passage and leave the *Ravaai* for the native brethren to come hereafter.

8th day. A day of consulation and reflection upon a subject of a trying nature. My mind is disturbed. The people seem troubled about our going away. Even the roughs who do not belong to the church, urge us to stay; and although they care nothing about the gospel, they say to us, "if Paraita leaves what shall we do for a missionary?" Little as they heed our teachings, they have great faith in us as missionaries. Gladly would we take the good and faithful ones with us, if means could be obtained. Mr.

Grouard sells all his goods in one day, whether few or many. The people purchase on a large scale, they seldom buy cloth by the yard.

Mr. G. has at length given us his little boy. He is a fine promising child one year and a half old. He will be little or no trouble at present, but will be a great source of amusement on the long voyage.

10th day. Telii came to talk with me about going to California. She cannot be reconciled to have us go and leave her. We told her we would do all in our power to provide a way for her to go. When I see the people look sad I feel grieved that means cannot be had to take them all with us. But many of the church members have relatives who would oppose their going. Hoatau, our good chief, with thoughtful looks, says, "when you are gone the children you have been teaching will go back to the state they were in when you came, and all your labor will be lost."

11th. Today was our weekly prayer meeting. I had great liberty in speaking. I spoke in reference to our leaving, that it was right for us to go. "The work of the Lord is great, and requires us to work fast. We must not stay too long in one place." I said to them further. "We shall intercede to have you removed to the church when we get home. In the meantime you must pray for yourselves and for us." They seemed comforted with my remarks, and reconciled to stay.

Since the return of the vessel I am sad from another source. Our boy Hiram is left on Tahiti exposed to the influences of wicked persons. I sometimes feel that he is lost and undone. Could I know he would go very soon to California where the brethren of the church will watch over him it would relieve my mind of a heavy burden. Oh! the fearful condition of a child left in the world without parents and one not willing to hearken to instruction from those older and wiser!

How terrible to be obliged to mingle with the unholy and profane. I long for the day when a division line will be drawn. Then will be fulfilled the words of Malachi. "Then shall ye return and discern between the righteous and the wicked, between him that serveth God, and him that serveth him not." Brother Grouard's condition is really an unfortunate one. His native wife is stubborn and refractory. She is not willing to go with him to the church, and if she remains here she will not let the children go. Troubles assail him on every side. The natives have imposed on him by putting water in the lime juice. They have had a trial; he compels them to empty the casks and fill them again. It is indeed perplexing to trade with people who are too ignorant to be strictly honest.

Last evening the natives had a long talk which continued till midnight. Some one had named a horse, which proved to be a family name of the contending party. It was grossly insulting their dignity that a poor brute should bear the name of a family relation whereas a sensible white man would not feel dishonored in the least.

The brethren have at last concluded to sell the *Ravaai*. One third its value will be given to the white men for their labor upon it. This will afford us a more comfortable fit out for the voyage. I feel a silent foreboding of consequences which may grow out of certain things which have transpired. I dare not hope for good, and painful it is to expect evil. I cannot look upon a sinful course with any degree of allowance. I must regard it with utter abhorrence! Oh! how it afflicts me, to see those who know the truth turn from it into by and forbidden paths! I think and feel what it must cost them to retrace their steps! Why need I feel that the sins of the world rest on my shoulders? The glorious day is rolling on when the division line will be drawn, and those who love the right will be associated together; and the mouths of the wicked will be stopt!

Our good friend Telii seems constantly grieved about our going away to leave her. She has an adopted child belonging to the Queen, which she would not leave. The Queen would not consent that the child should be taken unless she herself could go. On every hand obstacles arise. Had I the control of the mission, "Hoatau" and Telii should be taken to the church.

Today assisted in finishing a bed quilt for the Queen. Sister C. designs presenting it to her. She has not yet seen it. When she does she will be delighted in receiving it as a present. It is really beautiful! The pattern is "the rising sun."

22d. Today Mr. G. preached a most thorough discourse. He compared his hearers to the hardened Jews, telling them how much preaching they had heard, and how they had turned a deaf ear to it all, with the exception of a few humble and faithful souls, who had received good seed into their hearts, and brought forth good fruit. "Which if they continue will make them heirs of the kingdom of heaven." A more attentive audience I never saw.

Mr. Layton is fearfully sick with the cramp cholic. We are doing all in our power to relieve him, and more than all encouraging him to lay hold on faith, to be healed by the "laying on of hands."

Mr. G. is now alive with interest in Comb's Physiology. Also the lectures of "Horace Mann," which exceed anything I have ever read of the kind. A book of invaluable merit. Banished as it were from the world of erudition we grasp eagerly at anything that feeds the intellectual part, and reminds us that there is a world that is not all ignorance and superstition.

I sometimes feel that I have laid the foundation for a great work among this poor degraded people. The children we take home with us will in a future day (if they are properly reared) remember their own people, and will seek after them to bring out of nature's darkness, into the light and liberty of the children of God. If I can save one poor child from moral degradation, I shall feel repaid for all my labor in coming here. Br. Layton is now able to be out, to help a little about the vessel. Sister C. and I talked at length on a subject of an exciting nature. It is the worst place in the world to throw off an impression made upon the mind by any unhappy circumstance. So little to divert the attention. When a subject fastens itself on the immagination it penetrates into the inmost recesses of the mind or power of thought, and preys with all its force till the subject exhausts itself, and tired nature seeks repose in forgetfulness.

Today Sister Crosby spoke to the native sisters in their language for the first time. She has not devoted so much time to study as I have.[2]

Oh! the long delay in getting the vessel ready to sail. What will those waiting on Tahiti think has befallen us? Frances my poor girl is there, every day expecting the *Ravaai* to make her appearance. Brothers Crosby and Whittaker are there engaged in building. They will pass the time with less uneasiness. We can send them no letters to inform why we are detained. Such is the fate of all who live on these islands: waiting for vessels and wind, all the days months and years!

This morning had green corn for breakfast. It would be a rarity in our own country so early in the season.

March 27th. Likewise fine ripe melons.

28th. Sabbath. Went at early sunrise to morning service. I enjoy religious exercises better at such an hour than at any other. It seems like beginning the day aright. The prayers sound sublime, the singing sweet and heavenly. The exercises seldom last more than a quarter hour, a custom I quite admire.

The natives who own shares in the vessel, begin to regret giving their consent to have it sold. Mr. G. was very angry, talked loud to them with reproving words, for their instability. I do not blame the people for wishing to keep their Schooner. They have been three years in building it, have only had the use of it once. All possible haste is making to prepare the vessel to sail. Time seems more endurable as it wears away; every day is one nearer.

31st. Last evening a long talk was held between a phrenologist and myself, concerning the moral qualities of this people. He argued that in their organization they were wholly deficient. I contended in their favor, from observation. That it was for lack of culture. That almost all brought under religious influences developed conscientiousness and moral principles; they are readily made to discern between right and wrong. Ignorance and superstitions are a legacy bequeathed to them from time immemorial and I can discern inate qualities of mind which shine forth as I teach them; and a love for the good and beautiful. Kindness and benevolence are among their more prominent traits; loving hearts towards those who are trying to do them good.

[Taking Leave From Tubuai]

April 1st. Great joy is manifest. The last stroke is made on the vessel; the cargo will soon be put on board. Today met with the native sisters for the last time.[3] I felt the spirit to bless them. Sister C. and I, also Ellen, laid our hands upon their heads and gave them our parting blessing. They seemed much affected. I said many things with a view to console them. It grieves me to the heart to leave the children we have taught so long. To think how soon they will retrograde, if not cared for, and watched over. We appointed Telii their guardian, and Hoatau, the good old chief to assist her in counsel. Oh! that I could take them with me to the church! Their parents cling to them as they would to life if required to resign it.

3d day. This is the 21st aniversary of my marriage day. More than one third of that time I have lived a widow, or worse, alone, while my husband was on the opposite side the globe. Untold sufferings have fallen to my lot! Deeply have I drank of the cup of poverty and loneliness, with no eye to sympathize or arm to lean upon![4]

Cold and cruel as my fate sometimes appeared, "the fullness of the gospel" as revealed in Latter Days, seemed a balm for all my woes! I could sing myself to sleep when not a morsel of bread was in my house, neither means to buy any: But I knew the promises of God were sure, and that deliverance would come in time to save me and my children from hunger. "Who ever trusted in the Lord and was confounded?" In the course of these twenty one years I have travelled three thousand and seven hundred miles by land, and five thousand by water. And with the exception of two short journies, traveled with my four children without my husband.

4th day. Sabbath. Today broke bread in memory of the Saviour's death and resurrection. This is the last commemoration on Tubuai. I shall never meet the good kind people again in this life, unless some of them should come to America.

It is at last decided that all the children under our care must be left behind. Every entreaty has been used to gain the consent of the mother and grandmother to take the youngest one, but no: they were inexorable! Mr. P. told the Tupuna [grandmother] that if she kept the child and allowed her to grow up in wickedness he would be a witness against her in the day of judgement, and what will be your excuse? Oh, she replies, "I shall have none, but I cannot let her go!" I could almost wish those removed who refuse to let us take the children we have taught with such diligence. The one we are the most desirous of taking (whom we have named Alice) is too good to be left here; it will grieve Lois severely!

6th day. Ann Louise's birthday. We left Tubuai. Early in the morning the friends began to bring in food for the voyage. The friends who refused to let us take their child, gave largely. The old grandmother shed many tears. I gave her counsel and much caution concerning the little girl, to whom she clung with such devotion, and she promised to be true and faithful. Hatau also engaged to be guardian to all the children we had under our immediate care, and preserve them as far as possible from temptation.

We set sail with a fair wind. The people followed us to the beach, and wept much. They "waild" and said "Paraita vahine" was growing old, they should never see her anymore! I told them to be comforted, I would pray that some future time they might come to the church of Christ in America, even to Zion in the valley of the Rocky Mountains! We all wept freely, as we gave them the parting hand; and they waded into the water, along side the little boat that bore us away, pronouncing blessings upon us, "from the true God."

[To Tahiti]

At 4 oclock we went on board.[5] It was long before we were out of sight of the island. The scenery was grand indeed, as it receded from our view! The weather was fine, and I had high hopes that I should escape seasickness; but my hopes were vain. For three days I was not able to sit up, although the sea was exceedingly calm. Our course was slow, but onward. We [had] a splendid cook, and plenty of good food; purely native.

10th day. The men caught a large shark. They were long in tolling him to the boat. He made a grand appearance in the water, which being clear, his whole form and size could be distinctly seen. Monster of the deep! When drawn upon deck he made a great flouncing, was knocked in the head several times with an axe. It was long, before he was dead. The sailors dressed him and ate his meat but it was not given to the passengers.

Sabbath morn at the break of day we were all called on deck, to behold the beauty of the eastern horizon. The sea was calm. Not the smallest cloud was seen in the firmament. At length the great king of day gave signs of his approach, by gilding the eastern sky with his golden tinges. The scene was truly sublime! The whole world of waters seemed lulled to rest! The angry waves were gone! All nature seemed tranquil and serene. Such a scene is favorable to sickness at sea. Monday the 12th the vessel hove in sight of Tahiti. A large range of mountains, overspread with fruit trees and shrubbery in the midst of the watery world, made a most formidable and picturesque appearance. And the reflection, it is forever green! No chilling winter with biting frosts blight the embryo buds. Forever they bloom and bear fruit. The poor dark man is blessed with luxuries. The orange tree and breadfruit are trees of great beauty: natives of the soil. Their delicious fruit, Oh, how tempting to the weary mariner! And to him it is always free, what his appetite demands while on shore.

When we were safely anchored in the harbor our friends came on board, and expressed their great joy at our long expected arrival. Their anxiety and fearful apprehensions for our safety had been great, on account of our delay. We found Frances had suffered much with uneasiness, but it was soon forgotten when she conducted us to her place of residence, and set before us a good supper, of European type which made us feel at home. It was a snug little cottage, at the corner of five roads. A beautiful yard in front of the cottage with flower trees all in bloom, revealing taste and elegance from the hands of some one, we knew not who. We could only gaze in wonder and admire! Tahiti is the garden of the world! The flowers trees which grow some twenty and thirty feet in height, fill the soul with admiration!

CHAPTER THIRTEEN

Retreat and The Voyage Home

Journal B, Part 1, 15 April 1852 to 4 July 1852

[Papeete, Tahiti]

15th day [April 1852]. Took possession of a dwelling house, for which we are to pay twenty dollars per month, rent; the payment divided between four families. We are all quite comfortable here. One large sitting room I have the control of; it has five large windows in venetian Style; not one pane of glass; they make it delightfully cool. Our cook house is placed at a little distance from the main house, so that we are not in the least annoyed by the heat of the fire. The brethren are all engaged in carpenter's and joiner's work, are doing good business; the probability is we shall soon be able to go home.

16th The Raivavai vessel has just arrived, Capt Ratliff. We have now an opportunity to send a message to Br Brown. We have all along expected to procure a permit from the Governor for him to come to this place and get a passage home, but he is absent at this time, and nothing can be done about it; and he must endure his banishment still longer. I sincerely pity him. We hear from Br Hanks that he is very destitute of clothing; has learned the language, and is ennabled to preach to the people. Notwithstanding his destitution, he does not wish to leave. Hard fare the poor elders have who come to these Islands to labor in the gospel. We found on our arrival, that our boy who occasioned us so much uneasiness, had left for California; and that he gave signs of reformation, which has really relieved my mind. I do sincerely hope he will make the best of his way to the Church.

18th Sabbath. Today I am left alone; the family all gone out to walk. I feel really comfortable, and at peace in my mind. It is the first Sabbath for one year that I have not had native children to teach, and to attend on three services in Tahiti. I feel it a great relief. Services in french are held near us but I am not required to attend.

19th day Trouble anticipated concerning the sale of the vessel. The Tubuai natives show themselves really dishonest; they are now trying to cheat the white men out of their share of the schooner: the brethren have trusted them too far and depended too much on their integrity. Should it prove as we fear it will, that a complaint will go to the Governor it will undoubtedly cause a serious trouble, and involve Br G, and perhaps all the rest. I do sincerely hope the cloud will pass over, and we shall be permitted to enjoy peace while we stay, but we know not what is for us. We have only to look to the Lord and depend on him for strength.

20th Today we understand the native owner in the vessel is proceeding against the white men and carrying into the law the disagreement about the *Ravaai*. Last evening they were busily engaged in making out their bills for labor done on the vessell, and for other expenditures; the probability is the bills will more than cover the amount of all they can possibly sell the vessell for. I am sorry they would not act wise for themselves; there is no doubt but they did intend to wrong the white men out of their honest due. Today Capt Ratliffe leaves of Raivavai and permission is sent for Br Brown to come and go home with us; the Consul gave leave upon his own responsibility not wishing to trouble the Governor about it; he cannot however come on shore, without his consent.

21st Today an arbitration was held to settle the dispute about the Schooner; the native owner was very refractory accused Br G of being dishonest, and a long conversation ensued; he became so enraged that he requested the notary republick to record the assertion he made, that no missionary should step his foot on his Island from henceforth; the gentleman addressed, reproved him for his foolishness, and bade him be silent. He was compelled to come to terms, and gave bonds to pay four hundred dollars to the white men owning shares in the vessell. Br G came home in high spirits, said he had not felt as happy for many months; we all rejoiced that the affair was settled.

22d the weather is excessively warm. I can discover a vast difference between this climate and that of Tubuai. It seems pleasant to have our own food, again, though I do not think it agrees with me as well as the native diet; no food was ever more congenial to health, than that of the Islands. Today a boat came in from Anaa loaded with people from that place; the most of them relatives of Sister Grouard and urgent request came for her to visit her native Island previous to her leaving for America She seems bent on going to stay with her sick mother during the remainder of her life, even to the Sacrifice of her children, as her husband is determined on taking all but one with him. She is frequently in tears and seems undecided what course to pursue.

23d Great anticipations about going home: a vessell is lying here bound for California, which proposes to take us for fifty dollars each for the grown persons; but the Bark being loaded with oranges, will not admit our whole company; consequently we must be seperated; on some accounts it will be more agreeable, on others we could wish it otherwise. I could sometimes almost wish to remain here, such is the dread I have of venturing on the sea again. I seem to feel settled, and in a measure satisfied. I have become reconciled to the absence of company. F is extremely anxious to go: her health seems failing. I feel somewhat troubled about her and would hasten on her account.

24th   The bargain was made, and our passage engaged for California. It is decided that part of our company remain, to finish the job of work they have engaged. It is presupposed that no one vessell will be willing to take on so many passengers at once, as they are all heavily loaded with oranges that sail from this port. It would seem more cheerful could we all go at once, but it is not my prerogative to dictate. A silent dread strikes me when I look at ships. I consider how many sick days I must have befor I see the shores of my native country.

25th Saturday [Sabbath] has come again. Tahiti is a lovely place to look upon, the trees and shrubbery charm me, I look upon the flowers and think, they are always in bloom; how different from the flowers that bloom in my native country how short lived they are; for a few days we look upon them, again we look, they are faded away; their leaves are withered and fallen to the ground; here they are in perpetual bloom; the idea is pleasant; a tropical clime, how widely different from the cold bleak regions of the north. Still I would not exchange my own dear native land for this, were it ten times superior; so great are my attachments to it.

26th Sabbath.[1] The day spent at home, we can hear from the house the Catholicks saying mass in french, their musick sounds well. I intend going to see the order of their worship before I leave. O when shall I again hear the voices of our elders proclaiming the truths from heaven; may our heavenly father help us and preserve us from sickness and death.

27th The Bark in which we are to sail for California has gone round the Island to load with oranges, is expected to return in one week then all will be in a bustle to prepare for the departure. O how I dread the confusion; but there is no alternative.

28th   Today called Mrs Howe the english Missionary's wife her errand was to examine a stove she wishes to purchase I invited her to be seated, which invitation she accepted and conversed for some length of time. She appears a woman indeed; she was full of inquiries about our church, our method of travelling, and the way we are supported. I told her we had no salary, depended on our own resources and the benevolence of individuals. I gave her a brief history of our trials in the church since leaving Nauvoo. She seemed quite interested, and invited me to call on her. I intend doing so if I have time before I leave.

29th   Today went inland a half mile or more to a french shoe-maker's. They seemed very polite though I could not understand one word. Br Whittaker interpretted and I engaged shoes for the family. As I came out of the house I lost my veil, came on half way home before I missed it; had to go back sweating in the sun; a frenchman stood by the way side holding it in his hand. I was glad to recover it and came on again quite overcome with heat. Two days since I enjoyed a pleasant walk. Saw the Governors gardens and a fine yard of cabbages; nothing can exceed the scenery on Tahiti; the trees, the shrubbery and the flowers. I do indeed feel loath to leave it, but my fate is to be a wanderer.

May 2d   Two days since Sister Grouard left us as we expected for her native Island; we used every pursuasion in our power to prevent her leaving the children clung to her and cried, she wept and we all wept to think she could be unwise for herself as to leave her two little boys with little prospect of ever seeing them again. She appear'd firm and unshaken about going; her husband gave her money and goods, accompanied her to the boat; she kissed her eldest son when she had taken her seat on board the craft, wiped up her tears, and appeared in good spirits; as the boat saild out of the harbor we saw her with a spy glass sitting in the stern of the boat with the babe in her arms; we bade her farewell, not thinking ever to hear of her more. The following day I went to visit sister Crosby; while there, inteligence came that she had not left the Island; the vessel had sailed round on the opposite side and landed her there, where she was staying weeping and mourning for the children she had left; the following evening her brother came with a request that the eldest little boy might be sent to her, which was refused. Today she has sent for her husband to come and see her, he does not seem inclined to go; he wishes, if she has repented her foolish conduct that she may return without being sent for and make her confession. It is to be hoped she will know her own mind better in future.

Today we hear the Bark which has been several days round the Island loading with oranges is not expected to return so soon as was at first anticipated; it has relieved my mind. I shall now have more time to prepare for the voyage I have all along felt that we should be snatched away in haste, and have nothing as it should be, now I have a better prospect.

Today attended the Catholick worship was quite amused; twenty one sperm candles were burning the ceremonies were long the hymns were all sung in Latin a short discourse in Tahiti which I understood well. The priest exhorted the hearers to call on the virgin Mary in prayer for whatever they might desire that she might interecede with the Son in their behalf. Some nuns were present clothed in black all appeared respectable and solemn.

May 4th A great day on Tahiti. The canon roared for an hour in the morning; the men of war had I should suppose a hundred signals each hanging in the rigging. They made a splendid appearance; next the natives had a great dance. In the evening they had fireworks in the mountains and a theatre on the side of the mountain; a vuranda was erected of scarlet couloured cloth under which the european ladies were seated; from thence we had a fine prospect of the fire works. An artificial frame was erected intended to represent the Governour's house; which when lighted up with powder resembled a large building on fire. Skyrockets were thrown up from the mountains and meeting each other far in the firmament would explode and present an appearance of a thousand stars contending in the air. The fire lights were somewhat obscured by the full moon's rising; but that afforded us a pleasant walk home, and we were delighted with the idea of having seen so much on Tahiti which we had not expected.

9th The Bark has not yet returned. We have every day been expecting her; waiting in suspence, happy shall I be when this tedious voyage is over for such I am certain it will be to me. Could I believe I should not be sick on the vessell my courage would at once revive.

Today sister Grouard came back. Her husband calling and finding her in a poor situation was moved with compassion and invited her to come home with him. She appeared a little embarassed but soon recovered herself. She will now perhaps remain passive till we get started. Today attended Catholick service again.

10th The Bark has at last hove in sight, now all is in an uproar to get on board.

[The Voyage to San Francisco]

15th day [May] Last evening we came on board the *Calio* [*Callao*], which is to convey us to the shores of our native country. Sister C came off with us, we found no one but the Steward on board; the vessell was all in confusion. Our cabbin was not cleaned, and the crew were on shore drunk; we waited till dusk no supper, Sister C went on shore we ate a little bread and meat, drank some wine and water and went to bed. I slept soundly; better than I had done since I landed on Tahiti.

This morning early our friends came on board to bid us farewell, we felt sorry to part with them, as we had always expected to return together; but it has been ordered other wise and I feel to submit. We have bid them a hearty good bye; and now the anchor is hoisting and the voices of the sailors sound cheerful as they pull the heavy chain which will not rattle again till we make the shores of Francisco. May the Lord grant us health is my prayer for Christ's Sake.[2]

16 day Sabbath. Going ahead with a strong breeze but not in a right course too far to the westward. Yesterday all day a calm Children seasick and cross. Last night rain which drove those sleeping on deck below in some haste. I feel the loss of native food we brought nothing on board but cocoanuts. The Capt brought a wild hog on the Bark. Yesterday the sailors killed him had quite an exertion to conquer him. We came away without a cook, the poor steward looks sad, a double burden falls on him; he is a portuguese a tall pale looking man has his own and the cook's duty to do. It keeps him constantly on the move. Yesterday he made pea soup and scorched it the Capt reproved him very sharply, he answered nothing. The latitude today is 16° 12 minutes South.

This afternoon Mr. Nugent related to me a circumstance he heard on Tahiti which shows the native superstition. The queen of a neighboring Island died being put into her grave and remaining unburied for fourteen days she then came to life and told her people what she had seen of the other world. She said at first the evil spirits assailed her and commanded her to climb a cocoanut tree which in attempting to do the flesh was torn from her face and arms. She was walking about with her decayed body, her people all believing that she had in reality been resurrected.

17th The wind is bad for us the little there is. Last night almost a dead calm. O that we might be speeded on our way. How would it rejoice my heart. I feel weak and faint; how tedious it is to have children on board a vessel; they are continually crying and fretting; they deserve pity if they feel as I do. I have a berth above deck and two small windows. I sleep well. A fine breeze bearing a little too much to the westward. I am troubled with forebodings, the future looks dismal and no marvel, when I consider that the past has been so much of that description. O for a resting place for my weary soul. I long to have my spirits cheered once more before I die. All on board seems dull, no life or animation. The old carpenter tinkers away and the Sailors mend sails. The old bark goes ahead and all is of one piece.

19th Going ahead with a strong breeze. Still weak and sick, the children cross and crying; a miserable life for me is a ship life. How can I endure it for five or six weeks.

20th A strong breeze, going ahead, perhaps six knots an hour. Yesterday we saw porpoisses, bounding about in the water, did not come near enough to be taken. Sister G. cleaves to her old practices, lies about barefoot, careless and unconcerned as she used to [be] at home. Today for the first time got her to put on a clean dress and shoes. Last night had a great deal of trouble with the children. The Capt. and owner say nothing in the way of complaint about their crying.

21st This morning in sight of one of the Caroline Islands, now in sight of land. All our mouths are watering for fresh fish and cocoanut water. O to step my feet on land again would heal me in one hour. The weather is fine, all is well with us, but this dreadful feeling of Seasickness. The owner has some fine specimens of coral on board. I intend to . . . [solicit?] one of him.

22d Last evening sent a boat on shore the Island. I entreated them to let me go but was opposed on account of the roughness of the passage through which the boat had to pass. I would have surmounted my difficulty to have had the pleasure of stepping on land. Mr. Nugent and Grouard went off, brought on pahuahs, ninitars and cocoanuts. With great eagerness we laid hold of the pahua's and ate them raw, to the great amusement of all on board. When we came alongside the Island and the vessel was hauled to I changed my clothes and prepared to go on shore; my sickness left me and I felt like a new creature. Sister Grouard remarked that Paraita vahine had a matu upi, that is, a new face. I am certain no being ever felt a more sudden change. When I had eaten heartily of the fruit of the Island I felt almost completely restored. My dreadful faintness left me. I sat up and sang till midnight. Today we are shaping our course due west and sailing with great rapidity. The motion of the vessel operates against me. The inhabitants of the above mentioned Island are from Anaa. Only six families in all came there for the purpose of making money by selling pigs and cocoanuts to the ships that pass; there was a portuguese man living there who appeared to act as their leader; proposed we should wait till morning and trade with him for green corn and cocoanuts which I sincerely hoped would be the case; but the Capt. would not be persuaded and so they hoisted sails and let the old bark go ahead again.

It is now twelve oclock, since last night at eight we have made one hundred miles.

21st day Sabbath.[3] This morning arose faint and sick. It was with much difficulty I dressed myself in my Sunday clothes; I came on deck exhausted, sat down in my rocking chair, the little boy came along took hold of the arm of my chair and as the vessel rolled to the north away I went headlong hurting the boy and making a great parade. Very sick today.

Monday 23d A strong breeze today not able to sit up at all; all longing for fresh fish; no signs of any today, 3 degrees and 5 minutes from the equator, the air is becoming more cool. I had expected it would be to the contrary, many of the constellations appear in a different part of the horizon as we draw near the equator. When we again come in sight of the north star we shall hail it as the harbinger of home. Soon after we shall lose sight of the Southern cross. Last night witnessed the most beautiful sunset my eyes ever beheld; small crimson clouds gilded as with gold; such a sight upon the world of waters is delightful; but nothing charms me while I suffer with this deadly faintness; all mourning after fish; just now the cry of skipjack brought us all to our feet, we thought a feast was on hand at once but they eluded the hook set for them, and we settled back to our old longing again; made amends in part by causing two ducks to be slain and cooked; in the afternoon the Steward dressed a pig. The wind is abating and my sickness abates. Yesterday took some bitters expecting to receive benefit but to my disappointment it produced the most painful effect. I am resolved to keep clear of bitters from this time henceforth.

25th The weather is growing cool Crossed the equator last night, now in the northern hemisphere again. I rejoice in the idea that I am drawing nearer the country I desire; I bid farewell to the Southern Isles never do I expect to greet them again in this life. Should the Saints some future day possess the beautiful Island of Tahiti, I should, were it not for the miseries of the sea, desire to behold it again; there are indeed situations there I covet and would rejoice to see some honest souls who have suffered for the gospel in possession of them. I make a request this day in the name of him who owns heaven and earth to whom all power belongs that the Saints who have suffered for this cause may ere long be in possession of that beautiful Island, and the many ships lying in that harbor be subject to the control of the servants of God; that they carry out the luxuries of my heart.

27th day Last night a serious circumstance arose. Sister G was taken in one of her sulky turns she wept aloud for a long time alarmed the children and made a great disburbance every exertion was made to reconcile her, at length she fell asleep, and in the morning appeared quite calm. The last 24 hours the vessel has sailed 161 miles. She is now going ahead with the greatest rapidity, all sails set. Yesterday one of the pigs were taken sick on rotten oranges the Steward undertook to cure him with molasses. he died under the opperation; he was dressed for dinner. Some would eat and some would not. I myself would eat because I thought any thing fresh better than salt though it were pig that died of unhealthy food.

28th Sabbath 12 oclock last night commenced a several [severe] rain storm the wind was high. I felt the effects of it in the increase of my sickness; it soon abated and we got up and had a fine bathe in the fresh rain water it was reviving. Today the rain still continues. A large quantity has been caught and put in the cask which relieves our fears about growing short before the voyage is over. The time is tedious. F looks sad. We have had a little amusement today in reading the mormon defence written by J Grant mayor of Salt L City. We call it Mormonism, as we have seen it of old. Rather sarcastick it is true be agreable to the spirit of the times O we long to be there!

29th A pelting rain all the day long. I relish nothing I eat.

30th Almost a dead calm the vessel rolls from side to side makes but very little headway I feel sick and weak notwithstanding I have picked over all my oranges and put them up in a condition to keep, have had a hard job of it. The rest of the family have been engaged in washing. I hope to have a more agreable smell in the cabbin now the dirty clothes are removed. Today had the last old duck killed and baked as tough as sole leather it is not a little comical to see the children large and small trying their strength upon it so eagerly do they grasp at any thing fresh.

31st Again in the trade winds going ahead slowly, the little ones are a great trouble and the native woman is enough to kill us all such a temper and spirit I have never seen in a person before She provokes her husband almost to desperation; he is now determined to send her back in the first ship that sails from Francisco after we arrive. This morning have been trying to wash a little; nothing can exceed the weakness of my body. I feel unable to sit up and yet I am tired of lying down.

June 1st Last night the wind arose almost to a tempest the sea was in a great foam. The vessell is going seven knots an hour. This morning while the sailors were setting sails one of the ropes broke and down came one of the heaviest blocks fortunately it hurt no one tho' the children were all on deck. The two men who were pulling fell with great weight to the deck but soon were at their work again. I have been all day in bed and have been miserable.

4th Wind blowing fresh going ahead sick and weak. Last night the cook was taken sick; the Capt said it was all a pretence to get rid of work; proposed giving him a whipping to which Mr Grouard objected and a long debate ensued; the Capt gave way at last went and prepared medicine for him; upon his refusing to take it he gave him a kicking and forced him to take it; the poor fellow is tired of hard work.

5th The cook still continues sick, his successor gives much better satisfaction. "Wearisome days and nights are appointed unto me" The old Bark plunges along through the foaming waves majestically she rolls herself from side to side as she bounds over the proud waves while the appearance of the sun on the water is like ten thousand sheets of silver." I ask for strength to endure to the end of this voyage. What cause shall I ever have to take another like it. Oh for a little peaceful home on land; quietness in my family and an assurance that want cannot come.

6th day. Sabbath. Cold wind; going ahead with great speed. I have tried in vain to have some hymns sung; the spirit does not move; dullness prevails among the passengers. Sister G acts singularly wholly indiferent to her husband. We are in suspense, how matters will end.

7th day. 18 degrees 5 minutes South latitude a cold wind going ahead but not in the right course. the chief Mate says we shall be out twenty days longer, it quite disheartens me. I can now relish nothing but gruel.

8th day I feel truly unwell am forced to lie in my berth and write; the air is cold I have no appetite for any thing done on the vessel. I long for many things which I know cannot be obtained; our last fowl is devoured and I was only afforded one wing it is the last I can have till I see California three pigs only remaining; flour beginning to grow short; all I require is gruel which is weak living. The girls are determined not to work at their sewing on the vessell all dull and spiritless Mr N the owner is quite social and polite we cannot complain of being badly used.

9th Going ahead moderately cold wind; listened an hour to Mr N's history of his travels in Paris, residence in Louis[i]ana; his acquaintance with extensive planters in that State; their method of manufacturing sugar; Scenes in N York and the singing of Jenny Lynn all very interesting; the Capt is not sociable. The cook is a great botch at his business. Good would it have been for us all had he remained sick till the end of the voyage.

10th Long and tedious are the days and nights to me. Another rough day the waves rolling and tumbling; the vessel reels like a drunken man, we have had a visitor today a large bird was caught with a hook and line, the bird somewhat resembles a gray goose though a much thicker neck. he walked about the deck with his long legs much to the amusement of the children; the sailors abused him so much it was thought best to let him go to his home again, riding along upon the billows.

Last night after the lights had gone out the vessel made a lunge and over went the bureau dishes and bottles and all but lodging on Sister G and her babe who were sleeping on the floor; nothing was broken but one mug. It afforded us a laugh when the light was brought and the babe found smiling admidst the confusion Br G reminded us of the mischief it might have done; we told him it was sailor fashion to laugh off an accident especially a lucky one.

11th All days seem alike to me a rough sea nothing for amusement, faint for the want of food; I grudge the pigs their livers as they run about the deck I cannot avoid thinking how good they would taste to me. Last night a very important article was broken through E's [Ephraim's] carelessness. I have a hard struggle to get a little gruel made.

12th Several showers of rain to day strong wind but contrary. The owner objects to carrying so much sail, and heading so much against the wind. The Capt and Mate are against him. I have had a little appetite today. Yesterday the owner gave encouragement that a pig oven would be opened today, and I have been hoping for a meal of liver! But the day is passing away and no signs of an oven. O good news I hear the men saying something like "kill the pig." My spirits rouse a little; what a slave I am to my stomack! Always contriving how it may be satisfied. Mr N has given me a nice jar of mustard, I relish it much I even spread it on my bread instead of butter. The proud waves are riding by and if they were wafting us the right course I should look upon them with pleasure.

13th   This mor[ning] again almost a calm; the sun shines with unusual brightness. I feel quite relieved from sickness last evening; had a glorious meal of liver; I could have eaten all that was cooked for me which was half the pig afforded but I had mercy on my stomach, and well was it for me for I had trouble with what I ate; it seems a decree that I must not eat on board a vessel. Gruel is all my stomach will digest without the help of medicine.

14th   Fine weather fair wind, and steering a right course; great reason to rejoice. Today the latitude is twenty eight degrees' every day bring us nearer the place of our destination a few more days and we shall hear the cry of 'land', how the sound will cause our hearts to leap for joy; the first thing I inquire for will be beef stake and irish potatoes. Some fried eggs, &c. For fresh garden sauce I will entreat; for green peas beats and onions. I am like the man spoken of in the scripture which dreameth and behold he eateth, but he awaketh and his soul is empty. So do I dream at night that food is sweet to my taste, but I awake and loathe the sight of every thing on board the ship. E [Ellen] has at last summoned resolution to commence a little sewing; there seems an unaccountable reluctance on the part of the children to do any thing; for my own part I feel disposed to labor whenever I am able to sit up.

15th   A fair wind going ahead very fast a cold chilly air. I do not feel able to work today; little Edda is unwell. No fish have yet been taken to our great disappointment. Rose early this morning had an interesting conversation with the owner of the Bark he is a sensible man, whatever his principles may be.

16   Today Mr N is overlooking the oranges which are found to be in a bad state from the water's having go[t] to them. He is very unreconciled blames the Capt for not having had the decks calked. The oranges were put up in the best possible order; had they been kept dry very few would have been injured. I find myself very weak and feeble. O why is it I feel so debilitated? The weather is fine and I am ennabled to eat a tolerable allowance tho' without an appetite.

17th   time drags heavily. Rain last night today a calm, which ennables me to sit up the whole day; the clouds indicate a breeze. O for a strong wind to speed us on our way. I long to set my feet on land again; every thing is dull, no changes. Another calm O how much to be dreaded. The ship's flour is just gone what are we to do is the query. The owner is blamed altogher, but the Capt must have known it and should have informed us previous to leaving port. I hope no quarrel will ensue in consequence of it; if we can but endure as good luck would have it we have one can of crackers left F [Frances] is very unwell. The calm still continues, the ennui how unbearable! the weather is fine and I feel less of seasickness but very unreconciled to going so far. This morning I breakfasted in the cabbin made a very lengthy breakfast which served me for the whole day. This forenoon saw an abundance of fish in vain did the men try to attract them to the hook they kept themselves deep in the water, showing that they were apprehensive of danger. O how inviting did their shiny scales looked to me I thought of my poor vacant stomach so loath to receive food; but the pleasure of anticipation was all I was permitted to enjoy.

20th A fine breeze this morning going ahead much to the satisfaction of all on board; the Bark moves off majestically with very little motion. I breakfasted in the cabbin, felt no inconvenience. Last night children and several of the grown persons were sick the effect of eating sour beans. Crying and groaning were heard all night. This morning had a pig dressed, fried liver; I feel greatly refreshed; if this wind continues four days in succession we shall see land; O what a joyful sound!

21st Another fine day, a fair breeze in the morning we have sailed one hundred miles the last twenty four hours our latitude is 34° 45' 7 days more will take us to land at this rate; all our dependence is on the wind and more especially on him who controls it. Our flour is gone we have peas for a substitute I eat regularly at the table but the children are "haa mua" because I eat so long when I eat fast my food distresses me. Br G looks sad today, some ill dream is disturbing his rest, some power of darkness hangs around to molest him, the sight of land I trust will remove it. Last evening the Capt entertained me a half hour with his grievances, complained bitterly of the owner for neglecting his duty I tried to console him by reminding him that such occurrences were common in the business world and that another time perhaps fate might turn in his favor.

[June] 22d day [1852] Today a dead calm. O how discouraging! We have opened our last can of crackers and apportioned out to each one his share we have 16 each.

Ellen Pratt McGary

Frances Pratt Dyer

PART THREE

On Early California

The San Bernardino Experience
1852 to 1857

The Break-up at San Bernardino
January 1858

Lois Pratt Hunt

Ann Louise Pratt Willis

CHAPTER FOURTEEN

San Francisco and San Jose
Journal B, Part 2, 4 July 1852 to 4 December 1852

[In San Francisco]

[The veteran missionaries landed in San Francisco penniless in 1852. "We had nothing," wrote Louisa, "all the earnings of our early lives spent" on Church moves and the mission. "Not an article to keep house with." They found the community of Saints depleted and scattered, but hospitable and generous, answering Louisa's prayers. Fortunately the times were good. The Gold Rush was on. The mines and merchandizing were attracting hordes, creating a demand for city workers.

The Pratts found a small congregation of Latter-day Saints in San Francisco, and another group of Saints at the Mission San Jose, forty-four miles to the south. In Southern California there was San Bernardino, settled in the late fall of 1851 by some five hundred volunteers from Utah. By year's end the founders had built a fort and a hundred dwellings of a most temporary nature.[1]

Apostle Parley P. Pratt presided over the California Saints from 1851 to 1852, when Apostles Amasa M. Lyman and Charles C. Rich were appointed and served from 1853 to 1854. The apostles organized a branch of the Church for the San Francisco Saints in July 1852 with Quartus Sparks as president and one for the Saints in San Bernardino with David Seeley as president; later William Crosby was set apart bishop.

Within the triangle of northern California, San Bernardino, and Salt Lake City, there were pulls and tensions over where to locate. Louisa saw no reason to move so long as there was the demand for labor that paid so well. Still the gathering place in California was San Bernardino. Fundamentally, Louisa always preferred Salt Lake City over any other place. "But", she wrote a friend, "brother Pratt says we are too poor to go, and too destitute to live there if we could go."[2]

It was settlement in San Bernardino for the Pratts from December 1852 to January 1858. For Louisa the five years in San Bernardino were a continual struggle against an array of problems. Life was a fight against poverty. Louisa continued to shoulder family responsibilities out of necessity, whether the husband-father was off on another mission or just taking to the hills to hunt and fish. Resourceful Louisa continued in her life-long custom of caring for herself and family. As she found it difficult to let go, so Addison found it difficult to pick it up. Understandably, personal relations became strained to the breaking point.

For Addison the adjustment from missionary life in Tahiti to the material world was difficult. In the islands it was President Pratt, set apart, carrying full responsibility. He made decisions, led, instructed, initiated policy and practice, conducted meetings, performed priesthood functions and duties. The missionaries did everything until converts were schooled in the ways of the Mormon Church. Brother Grouard stood beside President Pratt in all his performances.

Now, in stark contrast, they had no callings in the church. Addison was called upon to speak in church only to report their missions. (When in Salt Lake City, Grouard spoke frequently.) Nor are we aware of any expressions to them from Church leaders of appreciation and "thank you" for their years of service in a most difficult but highly successful mission. It is as though they slipped into a do-nothing class.

The effect of this on Louisa must have been devastating. She had been so proud of her husband going on the mission, and of his successes reported at conference in Salt Lake City in 1848. She had expectations of recognition, callings, appropriate marriages for her daughters. Nonrecognition, added to criticism from some quarters, intensified her frustrations and disappointments.

Addison Pratt and Benjamin F. Grouard had been closely tied in their lives for nine years now, and while they shared a deep concern for the island Saints, the two men had their differences. There was space between them. They were friends, neither was the other's alter ego. But complaints against Grouard had a way of being applied also to Pratt. And while Grouard was more active and spoke out, Pratt seems to have kept his thoughts and feelings to himself in an endeavor to maintain peace.]

July 4th. Now settled in our own little hired house, quite comfortably. The last day of June we came to anchor in the harbor of Francisco; filled with Steamers and all kinds of sailing vessels; the city was full in view from our little Bark, and our hearts leaped for joy at the sight of our own dear country America; and the idea that we were soon to go on shore and recruit our poor vacant stomachs with palatable food; it was impossible for me to sleep that night, so great was my excitement; my thoughts were too active.

The following morning we left the Bark and went in search of our acquaintance; we found many of them had left the place; a few however received us cordially. We met Br Parley P Pratt and had an agreable interview. The first night we slept at Br Thorp's; the second evening attended a meeting of the brethren and sisters at their house. I endeavoured to make known to them my feelings on again being permitted to greet my native country and being relieved from the horrors of seasickness; my body being exceeding weak and my mind in a state of great excitement; my nervous system was in a tremulous state. I however succeeded much to my own satisfaction in expressing my ideas which seemed to convey joy to the hearts of the little assembly; likewise the testimony of the Brs Pratt and Grouard with regard to the mission and their continuing desires to remain active in the labors of the gospel. A heavenly spirit pervaded the whole meeting the brethren generally expressed their joy and satisfaction that we had been proven faithful had returned in peace giving a good account of our labors. That night I slept but a few moments.

The next day notwithstanding the great weakness of my body I went on board the Bark and assisted in packing up our goods; which was a laborious task; but being all the time under an excitement of mind I performed it with great facility. With my weak and trembling limbs I came up again to Br Thorp's and from thence to a sister Evans, where I slept the third night, almost as little as the two preceding ones; and was on the following day so nervous as hardly to be able to sit quite in my chair.

That day I walked over to the little humble home my husband had procured, which is situated at the far end of the town on the north bench; where is a good landing for ships and steamers. Mr Holenbeck is our Landlord his wife a woman of great faith and zeal for the gospel; a person of bright intellect but of a very peculiar constitution. I have seldom met with a more extraordinary personage. [*Memoir:* She seems conversant with the inhabitants of the spirit world: She affirms that her spirit friends taught her to play an instrument of music. It was true she learned from some source, unknown to her neighbors.]

The little branch of the church at San Hosa [San Jose][3] immediately sent for us to come to their place as they were in want of our daughters to assist them in their domestick occupations and would give them great wages to the amount of fifty dollars for month; my companion and two daughters immediately set out and very soon inteligence came that they were highly pleased with their situations I, myself chose to remain here for the purpose of sending my youngest daughter to school likewise the eldest child of br Grouard's which I have under my charge. [*Memoir:* Our eldest daughter Ellen had a good situation with Mrs. Haskins, a milliner lady . . . for fifty dollars pr month. Thus was our way opened to live. The milliner and dress maker . . . was very fond of Ellen, and allowed her every indulgence she could ask for, besides her high wages. . . . Besides we have friends in the city, of unbounded benevolence.]

Br [Henry] Christy, when we were first from Tahiti, first presented my husband with twenty dollars in money [*Memoir:* before we had time to earn for ourselves.] Br Morris an unfailing friend showed us every attention in

198 The History of Louisa Barnes Pratt

his power with labor and money; which has continued up to this time; he is a gardner and whenever he comes brings me a basket or bag of vegetables, which favor calls forth my sincerest gratitude.

[*Memoir:* We had nothing when we came from the islands. Not an article to keep house with, except one old rocking chair. All the earnings of our early lives, were spent in travelling, wandering from place to place to keep with the church, and away from our enemies.]

Br P P Pratt has remained in our midst continuing to teach us till this present morning [19th] on which he leaves for San Hosa. His preaching has truly been comforting; he is going immediately to Salt Lake City. I feel a thrill in my soul at the mention of the name. I wish I was prepared to go with him; but at present the prospect is dull about going to that place. Br G is extremely anxious to go, my companion prefers the lower country. I feel a degree of resignedness to stay in this place, if it will ennable us to recover ourselves a little from our extreme destitution of means to sustain ourselves. I ask the Lord to bless the labors of our hands.[4]

This morning [September 1852] Br G with his wife and two children left for San Jose which has left me alone with the care of three children I expect to feel the loss of their company. Br G's Tahitian wife is a friendly agreable woman, her little boy three years old is a favorite of us all; the babe six months old is a fine promising boy as I have ever seen; and yet his father often expresses a desire that she would return to her country, and proposed to give her the child or rather consent to her taking it back. Br P admonished her to remain here and go to the church; of late she has seemed disposed to give up mourning for her friends, and now expressed a desire to go to the valley of the mountains. She seems in a measure alienated from her husband and yet her jealousy continues, as I can plainly see when any attention from him is bestowed upon another woman. They are both placed in peculiarly trying circumstances; could they be reconciled to each other my mind would be relieved of a burden I have long borne.

July 24th Invited all the sisters in the place to visit me, made great preparations for them, but to my great disappointment not one came; they all had their respective excuses as the men in the parable had when invited to the wedding. The next day being Sabbath, I went to hear brother Parley preach. Sisters Corwin and Morey came home with me and spent the afternoon. ~~One week after we arrived here my husband Frances and Lois went into the country to assist our brethren of the farming population in their labors; for a remuneration they receive one hundred and 75 dollars per month.~~

I am happy to hear that Frances health has been better since she has commenced in active exercise.

The second week after they left home, a letter was sent down inviting br Grouard to go out and engage in labor on a farm; and brother Tomkins proposed keeping his family free of expense; he immediately made ready and went up with his wife and two children; I was then left quite alone with Ann Louise and the two little Island children; we were so lonely and sad, we knew not what to do with ourselves. The first evening we could not content ourselves to sit down in the house. Mary Holinbeck came in and after having put the children in bed, we walked out went through the gate, and a thought struck us that we might go to the town where Ellen was residing with a Milliner, and have her come home with us. We had no sooner mentioned the subject than we were on our way: we went in haste, and returned, Mary H not wishing her father to know she had been out.

There was a young man in town who had been dismissed from the service of her father for paying his addresses to her; her father was very angry when he found she had been out, concluding perhaps she had gone out to meet him. I was not aware of the suspicions of the parents, or I would not have suffered her to go with me. It was soon however decided that the young man should go to the mountains with brother P. Previous to his leaving, he called at the house when the parents were both absent; presented Mary with a letter, in which he stated that he had been counselled by high authority to prevail on Mary to leave home and go with him to the Valley. She objected to doing any thing contrary to the knowledge of her parents; the letter was put into the hands of her step-mother, and from her to the father, and the seccret was brought to light. The young man soon left the city for the lower country, in company with elder P Pratt; the minds of the parents are now at rest.

After the departure of Elder P. Br Sparks[5] took the lead of our meetings; he has declared his intention to warn the people of San Francisco before he leaves the place of the truth of the great things which have been sounding round about them for many years, of which they are still ignorant. A brother by the name of Morris is in this branch as faithful servant of his Lord and master; speaking boldly of the things of which he has long been a witness. His untiring fidelity is worthy of all acceptation, and of imitation; his benevolence and attention has been great to me and mine; when we were destitute as it were, coming off a long mission, where we were not allowed to receive any remuneration, and landing in a place where money is the God of the people, and where there is very little friendship without it. From the first he manifested a desire to aid us in every way in his power and up to this time his friendship continues the same. I have often said the friendship is better than money; true benevolence will not fail in the day of adversity, but every changing fortune carries (or is liable to carry) away the God of this world and disappoint those who put their trust in it.

I will here mention another friend who has been ready to relieve our wants at any time; a brother [Henry] Christy; he first presented brother Pratt with twenty dollars, then afterwards called on me and gave me twenty more, offering to lend me a hundred if I needed. I feel to bless those who have shown me mercy in a time of need, and I ask God my heavenly father that they may not lose their reward.

August 1st attended a theatre for the first time in my life. I was not so well entertained as I expected to be I cannot say I was pleased with the characters who performed. Mr Booth the celebrated performer was present a most singular and extraordinary personage I disliked the appearance of the females, so many artificial airs have no charms for me. I am not willing to give people money for making a display of their fooleries. I have attended common school exhibitions that pleased me much better.

August 2d I wrote a letter in Tahiti, to send to Tubuai, whether understandingly or not I cannot tell; it will however show to them that we do not intend to forget them. There was no one here who could write better, and I was anxious a letter should be sent; there is one expression they will not fail to understand. that is, "Ia ora na otau."

I am still in the little retired house at the far end of the town, one daughter and the two little Island children for company. We feast ourselves on vegetables and never in my life did I enjoy food and sleep better than I now do. I feel it a blessing. I will soon recover my flesh and I hope look younger; now every one cries out, "how old you have grown;" severe indeed was my voyage across the sea; my flesh almost entirely wasted; but I hope to regain my former vigor in a measure and to forget some of the abominables I have endured in the seven last years of my life.

There is now in the city a great excitement about the new system of communing with spirits by means of electricity. A gentleman of that order came into our meeting last Sabbath evening, asked liberty to speak; I felt interested in his conversation, and would willingly have heard him longer. Br S was not much inclined to listen

5th [3d or 4th] Called this morning at one of the free schools in this city; left my little Island girl under the care of a female teacher whose appearance I liked very much. She told me she emigrated from the State of Maine three years ago; she reminds me of new england. There is a something attached to the manner of a female from that country that distinguishes her from the rude inhabitants of the far west. I seem to cleave to such as my kindred spirits. I feel at home with them.

Money was plenty, wages very high. We had frequent meetings for preaching and prayer, a small branch of the church, composed of as faithful members as ever named the name of God in prayer.

Thursday, evening the 5th [August] attended the meeting Br S spoke very lengthy notwithstanding he at first requested all to speak;

another brother spoke and lengthened out his speech for a half hour; his oddities made us all smile. I thought it better than the plays acted in the theatre; his fist was drawn throughout the whole speech as if to smite some one; his heels were raised from the floor, and let to settle back with great force; the whole a laughable performance.

Friday the 6th Sister Corwin visited me. [*Memoir:* She was Samuel Brannan's mother-in-law.] I spent a pleasant afternoon with her. She admires our little native children exceedingly; said she should suppose brother G would worship his children, but his appearance is that of indifference towards them generally; sometimes he shows a small degree of fondness for them.

Saturday 7th Br Morey called and talked an hour; he is opposed to the idea of bringing the natives of the Island to this country, expressed his surprize that Br G should bring such a family as his from their country. In the afternoon Sister Amanda Evans paid a visit, a very interesting little girl modest and amiable; though very small in stature, she looks like a person of consequence. Saturday night, A L [Ann Louise] gone to a theatre for the first time

8th Sabbath Attended preaching Br Sparks spoke very lengthy upon the falling away of the Chur[c]h from the Apostolick faith; of the renewal of God's covenant in this day and age in which we live. Showing plainly the only way of salvation that it is by observing the ordinances as they were administered in the days of prophets and apostles Mrs Hoskins attended and was much pleased with the preaching.

[A Visit to San Jose]

12th Thursday Left home very early expecting to take the steamer at 9 oclock for San Hosa on coming into the town found it would not sail till 4 in the afternoon put my baggage on board and went to Br Carrington's house where I had expected to be agreably entertained in conversaton Some little word was dropt that offended her [*Memoir:* some doctrine of our church]. She flew in a passion and accused me of being in favor of vice and immorality; said the Saints were vile in their practices; and she compared them to the low and the vicious in San Francisco I told [her] she must not compare me or my people to those characters to whom she alluded; that I had ever lived a faithful and honest life before God and that I knew the Saints to be an upright and holy people that they feared God and loved each other; and that they were not guilty of those things whereof they were accused. I then bore my testimony to her of the truth of the things about which she was contending. Said I "the angels of God shall bear me witness that I tell you the truth; and in the coming of our Lord and Saviour I will be a witness against you that you have abused the character of the poor afflicted Saints, and ordered me out of your house without any provocation and unless you repent of these things you will come under condemnation." I should have no feeling of hardness against her I assured her, and wished to be on terms of friendship that I had ever had a good opinion of her and would not meaningly say anything to grieve or offend her. She softened her feelings so far as to shake hands with me when I left, and her husband being exceedingly mortified endeavored to apologize to me; he was irritated towards her which only made matters worse, and upon the whole it was rather a serious circumstance.

I embarked on board the steamer *Union* and when I went on board found the Capt's family just arrived from the States; a wife and nine children. I was pleased with them, had a pleasant passage up; came to anchor about 9 in the evening, but not finding an opportunity to leave the boat remained till nine the next morning when the stage came from Br Horner's and we were conveyed to his dwelling house. I found Frances in good health and high spirits [*Memoir:* the life of the house]; flying about and accomplishing every thing devolving upon her with great facility; and the family all seemed pleased with her. On Saturday evening she left and came down with me to brother Nichols, where her father and sister were living. Her father had gone to San Francisco expecting to find us there, and bring us back with him; it was a disappointment on both sides, but we could only submit to it and wait his return, which happened on Sunday evening after we were all in bed. There was a meeting of the Saints on the Sabbath at brother Nail's house, not large but interesting; from there, F went to brother Skinner's. Monday and tuesday I spent at brother Nichols'. [*Memoir:* Such a beautiful farming country is seldom found in all the world.]

Wednesday 18th, went in the forenoon to see Sister S [Skinner] and Frances; every thing was in fine order, and we dined with them; took our leave and that evening to Mr Tompkin's where I found brother G and family apparently cheerful and contented; little Frank clung to me constantly while I staid. I learned that more friendship was existing between his father and mother.

The 19th Mr G carried his wife myself and the children, to brother Stark's; I had a fine visit with Sister Loiel [?], an old acquaintance whom I had known in Nauvoo; I was agreably entertained, and after receiving several presents, Br S [Stark] brought me in his waggon to the steamer; it was late in the evening and the people were all in bed; the captain's son got up and showed us where we were to sleep.

20th The steamer started at three in the morning and at 9 we were anchored in the Bay. The steward put us on shore, and we walked up broad way to Mrs Evan's a Sister's in the church. Spent the day and returned after the sun went down to our house. E came over and spent the night with me [*Memoir:* Found the children I had left at home over-joyed to see us. Ephraim in his broken way tried to tell about seeing his two brothers up on the "Plains." The eldest, four years old, clung to me continually, while I remained with them.]

21st Today preparing to move [*Memoir:* to a house in town.]

22d. Today find the people not prepared to leave the house so the matter about moving is suspended; one disappointment follows another.

25th My goods still remain packed ready for a removal; walked to the town expecting to attend the weekly prayer meeting; found on my arrival that I had made a mistake in the day it was one day too soon so I returned just as it was growing dark and the children were pleased as they had expected to spend the evening alone.

[August] 31st 6 oclock the dray was brought to move my goods; took breakfast with Mrs Holinbeck; little Ephraim was very unwell; we walked up to our new home and had to carry him the greatest part of the way; we found the house looking as though hogs had lived in it; we set to work to clean it out; labored hard for two days; we then arranged our things and felt quite comfortable. We now have Sister Evans for a neighbor and her little daughter Amanda, and very agreable they are, kind and obliging.

We are daily expecting the arrival of our friends [the Crosbys] from Tahiti.[6] My lot is still to be alone, my husband always from home. I lay plans for myself, and carry them into execution, and no one says why do you so? my three eldest daughters are from home, the youngest is with me, on her I place great dependence, young as she is; she is my solace and comfort, dutiful and affectionate; Sister Corwin is my friend I verily believe. She has been attentive to me, and had made me some presents; besides she pays great attention to the little native children, and expresses great fondness for them.

[*Memoir:* Sewing was very lucrative employment, I could help myself to any thing I needed; there was no scarcity of money.]

[Family Scattered in and about San Jose]

Nov 28th Nearly two [three] months have passed away since I wrote in my journal; my time has been wholly occupied in sewing to earn a livelihood; not a leisure day have I had I remained one month in the house which I hired of brother Cheney, and which I expect to have remained in untill we were ready to remove to the lower country, but he altered his arrangements and wishing to repair his rooms I was compelled to remove. I felt disappointed; the rooms were pleasant, and I was comfortable and happy. Mr P came home to visit us just as we [were] preparing to remove every thing was in confusion; he assisted us in removing the heaviest articles and then returned to the place of his business. I felt sad when he left I thought how much I had been left all my life with my children. I had but two at home with me the youngest girl and, my little native boy. my third daughter has been employed one month in taking charge of a babe for Mrs Switzer a lady living in the Kremlin a very large boarding house on Stockton Street a most amiable lady and a celebrated singer; she receives $50 dolls pr month for singing in a church; she [Lois] received for one month's service $50 dollars. [*Memoir.* No other employment could have been so agreeable to her. The lady reposed great confidence in her; would permit her to take the child to any part of the city to spend a whole day: carrying with her a little bottle of milk, from which "Francisker" was fed; a name given her by twelve gentlemen, presented her a gold cup with their names engraven thereon.] She is now at home with me. Our rooms are dark and cold. I have pleasant neighbors two sisters in the church live near me most amiable women Mrs E [Evans] the friend of all, Mrs King cheerful and sweet tempered.

Our church meetings have been suspended for some length of time; this evening we anticipate having one, to break bread in memory of our Savior's death. The weather has of late been gloomy, the rains have been frequent, the walking bad. I should have been more disconsolate but for my faithful friend Henry Christy; his friendship has been unvarying, he has been a friend in time of need; and peace be to his memory forever. Likewise Mr Morton a young man who resides with him has shown me some favors. I feel encouraged that he may help me to means when I come to leave to go to the church by making a purchase of some articles I wish to dispose of I hardly know how to dispose of myself; the rooms I live in are unpleasant, besides they are wanted by the owner to be repaired I wish I could be settled once more in my life.

29th day I have arisen this morning long before day being disturbed by our little boy; it is rainy and gloomy this morning. Last evening meeting was held at Mrs Evan's, the Lord's supper administered to a few persons, a long and tedious speech was made by brother Everly; likewise brother Skinner got on the old sectarian tone which continued a half hour or more, none of it seems to be like Mormonism or like the comforting influences of the latter day Gospel; there is barreness, and leaness; O how much these saints ought to be gathered with the body of the church! that their minds may become expanded, and their hearts enlivened. Our friends Mr Christy and Morton called last evening brought us two gallons of wine and some oranges; a present quite acceptable. Mr M has a fellon coming on his finger.

Dec 1st Yesterday received a letter from my husband he writes very discouraging; the rainy weather hinders their business and they are likely to be out of employ. He writes for me to be ready at a moments warning to start for the lower country as he does not wish to stay in town twenty four hours. Last night I was troubled in mind, sleep forsook me. I though of my helpless condition. I felt homeless, my husband discouraged, what arm had I to lean upon thought I. I was filled with tossings to and fro untill the dawning of the day. I then fell asleep and did not awake till near nine oclock. My daughters are all from home. Sister Perkins slept with me. There is a severe rain this morning, dark and gloomy; our prospects are dull about staying in Francisco this winter.

[*Memoir:* I felt annoyed at the idea of being harrassed about so much. My daughters had good situations, were receiving large pay for very light work. I could not see the necessity of being in haste to move. Sister William Perkins was with me, a dear good woman, just returned from a mission to the Sandwich Islands. She sympathized with me. She too was homeless, no abiding place to call her own; and we longed for a quiet habitation, where our weary spirits could repose in peace.]

Dec 2d   Restless and uneasy I have arisen this morning, daylight has not yet dawned, my mind is troubled about leaving this place, it is winter, and the rain is incessant. The mud is very deep here and probably will be deeper at San Pedro. I sleep but little for thinking what I am to do. O how have I involved myself, by taking upon me the support of my family, and my husband by being separated from us for seven years in fourteen has nearly lost all the ability he once had; now in my advanced life I have the care of a large family with no income or means of support. Well I have given my all for the gospel and undertaken to put my trust in God, now let me not shrink from it. I will prove my heavenly father whether he will ever disappoint one who trusts in him.

2d [3d] day Another of my restless nights, four long hours was I tossing and turning. I got up read for some time in the new testament about the sufferings of Christ, it seemed to console me in view of my own helpless conditions, no house or home of my own. The rain still contin-ues, and every thing seems cheerless and dreary, how true the remark of Solomon, "truly the light is sweet and a pleasant thing it is for the eyes to behold the sun." Let me once more be in a house of my own though poor it may be, how much I shall prize it! There was a comical fellow here last night by the name of Cyrus Ira [?]. His conversation was laughable

3d [4th] day Another rainy morning; there is a gloom spread over the face of nature. Again have I been awakened from sleep, by the crying of the little boy. I sprang up quickly with a view to prevent the intrustion of unpleasant thoughts from which I suffer. I snatched an old paper and read a tale of the days of Queen Mary; it diverted my mind. O, I dread these thinking intervals; they are severe indeed. Yesterday I suffered with the excess of severe thinking, and felt the greatest debility, like one recovering from a long illness. [*Memoir:* A sea voyage before me, and the making another beginning in the world. Some of my children I must leave behind. My brother-in-law and sister were not ready to go.]

Last evening Br Christie came in, dark and rainy as it was; my mind was in a measure relieved; there was cheerful conversation, and a ten dollar gold piece presented me; a man with a noble heart how admirable! I pronounce blessings on that man, even the blessings of wealth and health and I ask my heavenly father in the name of his son that the choicest of heaven's favors may fall upon him from this time forth and forever.

4th [5th] day Sabbath evening This evening a meeting was held at Mrs Evans. I took my leave of the brethren and sisters not expecting to meet with them again in this city. This morning took a walk with Sister Perkins called on Mrs Kimball, was introduced to a Lady from Massachusetts; it seems pleasant to meet people from that country. I had been buried in my dark room so long the brightness of the sun almost blinded my eyes. I felt as I stood gazing upon the water and the shipping like one recovered from a fit of sickness; a lingering sadness was hanging about me, the remains of a severe exercise of mental agony which I had been for several days undergoing; my heart has been stricken and stricken again till there is no endurance in it, a circumstance in the least oppressive, casts me down, and from that state it is hard to arise.

CHAPTER FIFTEEN

San Bernardino I

Memoirs, December 1852 to April 1856

[The Move to San Bernardino, December 1852]

Mr. Pratt came down from San Hosa, and we prepared to go on board the *Freemont*, Capt Erskine. We sent our goods to the steamer, the day previous staid on shore to meet our friends again. Mr. Crisman was present, said everything encouraging about the settlement in San Bernadino. It cheered our hearts and made us feel stronger. On Monday A.M. in Dec. 1852 we walked down Broadway to go on board. We met the Capt, he told us we were belated; and only for his having forgotten some item of business we should not have had time to call on our daughter at Mrs. Haskins. She walked with us to the boat. After our having commended her to the watch care of that lady, and receiving her promise, that she would be true to her trust.

Brother Christie came to us at the wharf, helped us into the small boat, the Steamer having been hauled off. He was to accompany our daughter back to her home. We gave them the parting hand and thought to see them no more. After we were seated in the cabbin, to our suprise they both came in! Mr C. said as they were walking back to town Ellen commenced grieving. He then proposed hiring a small boat and taking her to the steamer before she set sail. After having repeated her adieus she went away quite cheerful. Frances our second daughter remained at San Hosa to live with her Aunt Crosby, and come with her to the church [San Bernardino], as was contemplated, the following year.

The first day out I was sick in bed the whole day. The cabbin was full of Spaniards and some were smoking cigars, drinking wine, playing cards. The Capt was very kind and polite. No illness is more unbearable and prostating to the body and mind, than that induced by the motion of a vessel.

The third day out at 9 o'clock p.m. we cast anchor in Santa Barbara. There we lay for three days in a cold rain storm. The Capt had business on shore. The dullness was intolerable! We could not leave the vessel, and constantly in fear of being driven on shore! All the time a pelting storm. The Spanish gentlemen were merry and good humored; urging us to drink wine and lemonade. Little Ephraim was amusement for the whole ship's company. At last there came a bright sunny morning, and we thought to sail again; but the Capt had difficulty on shore and did not come on board till late in the afternoon. The weather was fine the following day, and we had a tolerable trip to San Pedro. We had good eatables, and sick as I was I could sometimes make a lengthy meal, and invariably when cabbage was brought on my appetite would revive.

We tried to amuse ourselves by singing songs to the Capt who assumed to be pleased, perhaps thinking poor music better than none. About this time our little boy was taken violently ill with a fever. For several days he had been unusally interesting. It somehow occured to me that it was an unlucky omen. We landed at San Pedro and Mr Pratt went on shore to find a team to take us and our goods to our destination, a distance of 90 miles; He did not return till late in the day. In the meantime the little boy continued very sick. The Capt. had been trying to learn him to repeat verses. As long as he could speak audibly he would rehearse; at length in a low faint tone he would try to repeat, and crying out, "mumu sick sick."

When Mr. P. returned to the vessel he brought news that forty elders from Salt Lake were at San Pedro waiting to get a passage to San Francisco; going on missions to different parts of the world.[1] It was very exciting news. As I learned that many of them were our old friends whom we had known in Nauvoo, we were in high hopes of meeting them early the next morning; but to our great disappontment the wind arose, the waves ran so high, we could not get on shore. The vessel began to roll, and I was compelled to take my berth, and there remain one painful day and night. The next morning was fine, and we hurried on to shore, met our friends and spent several hours with them. They looked so familiar it brought fresh to mind the days of Nauvoo; the building of the Temple, the fearful tragedy, when the prophet and patriarch were slain! We blessed them in the name of the Lord, and prayed they might be prospered on their missions. Brother Samuel Wooley helped to pack our goods in David Harris' wagon; who had agreed to take us to the camp of the Saints.

[The First Days at San Bernardino]

We then set our faces towards San Bernardino. The first day we made De Los Angelos. Called at a Mr. Hunter's where we met Capt. [Jefferson] Hunt, on his way to the Legislature. We spent a pleasing evening there.

William Perkins and his wife were in our company. The same who had been to the Sandwich islands; they too were going to San B. The little [boy] continued very bad, I had every hour to hold him in my arms; as he would not be contented with any one else. The succeeding day it commenced to rain, and the air was cold and damp. I was troubled with fear that the child would take cold. We rode in the rain, the roads were very bad. At night the rain came down in torrents! We called at a Spanish house to stay over night. The house had neither doors or windows; nor fireplace in the house. What to do we did not know. There was no better place near.

How could I sleep in that damp house with my sick child was a subject of solicitation. We prayed, and commended him and ourselves to the mercy of our Heavenly Father; made our beds on the ground floor and laid down. The next morning was rainy. The Spanish cooked our food out doors and brought it in; we were cold and hungry, and it did us good. We started with fresh hopes that we should be in camp that night and share the hospitality of our friends. The driver left the wagon for a few moments; his younger brother took the lines. There was a deep stream to cross. One wheel sunk in the quicksand; from which it was impossible to extricate it.

The driver soon came up. He ordered the wagon unloaded, the goods carried by the hands of men across the stream to the opposite side; the women and children were carried on the backs of men. The box was taken off and three quarters of an hour of hard tugging was spent in getting out the wheel. The driver said the team should have been driven over in a hurry not giving the wheel time to settle in the sand. Mr. Pratt was not an expert teamster, and the brother was young. When the wheel was raised, it was discovered that the tongue of the wagon was broken. That was "terrible" the driver said for the teams had gone ahead which carried tools to make repairs. I found a shade in some shrubbery and sat down on the ground, my two daughters beside me [Lois and Ann Louise], and my sick boy in my arms.

We waited two hours for the wagon to be mended and reloaded. They had to send ahead several miles for tools. While sitting there I revolved in mind the many scenes of a sinister nature I had encountered in my long journeys across deserts and plains. Well I said, "I can bear it as one bears the pain of an old sore; it pains a little harder for being probed open." We were soon on our way again, all in good spirits. Mr. Pratt was talkative with the boys, and they seemed pleased with his company. We traveled fast, made the Fort at eleven o'c. that night. The younger brother ran ahead to inform his mother of our arrival and have supper prepared. His mother though in bed, made haste to get up, and provide a comfortable meal for us; which we partook of with thankful hearts.

The people in the house were very kind. Some slept on the floor that we might have their bedstead. I laid down feeling comforted that I was among friends, and where I could nurse my poor boy. For several days our goods remained in the wagon, while we were trying to find a vacant room. I was tied to the sick child, and no one seemed interested to examine the goods, which had been exposed to the rain. There were no vacant rooms, every house not inhabited was filled with grain. There was no lumber to build with. The people all lived in adoby forts, roofs covered with willows, straw and dirt. At length a brother by the name of Hiram Blackwell[2] succeeded in getting a portion of grain moved out of a room, so we could barely put our things in, but no place to set up a bedstead. Brother and sister Harris kindly offered us to come there and sleep at night and have the comfort of a bedstead.

Accordingly we did so. After spending the evening at home, I would cross the Fort, sometimes when the weather was cold and damp, to my lodgings; by that means, caught a cold which nearly proved fatal; having a cough seated on my lungs, very severe for two months. We struggled on the best we could with all our things in one room. At length Mr. Blackwell had compassion on us and proposed to sell us his house, which was near ours though not adjoining. It was a large room 18 x 20 altogether unfinished. The price was sixty dollars. I then had a job on hand to get the room finished. Mr. Pratt engaged in farming, had not an hour to spare towards fitting up rooms for comfort. With great exertion I accomplished the finishing of the house, which made it the pleasantest room in the whole Fort. I felt like beginning to live.

Mr. Blackwell a young man from Mississippi was a man of stern integrity. A faithful friend he was to us in time of need. I gave him in part pay for the house $20.00 in gold a present from our friend Christie. Mr. P. gave his note for the remainder, which was redeemed in due time. He presented us with several bushels of wheat for family consumption. The brethren contributed and bought us a cow, which cost seventy dollars. Then Brother Stark who moved there from San Hosa put in a crop for us. Mr. P. asisting some by his labor, though he had neither team or seed. Bro. L. harvested 70 bushels of wheat for us and put it in a bin. It was truly gratifying to us that our missionary labors were appreciated, and that the hearts and hands of the saints were open, to give us another start in the world.

There were colored men in the place from the South country; who though free, still remained with their masters. I made friends of them by sometimes having a little wine or cherry bounce and treating them when they would do me a favor. Leisure days and evenings they would come when their tasks were done at home, and work for me. Sometimes I prepared a good dinner for them. In that way I made improvements without hindering Mr. Pratt from his regular business. I put up bedsteads and cupboards in a style peculiar to myself; fashions I learned from reading journals. I even constructed a table which answered a good purpose, till mills were built and lumber sawed. The people made narrow pine boards split out with a "fro" and mallet; of such we made doors.

I got much credit for my skill and ingenuity in the construction of my backyard and outhouses. I often called to mind the many times I had fitted up places and left them for others to enjoy. At times my heart was ready to fail, but there was no alternative, I could not endure to live in a shabby manner; improvements I must make though I might not enjoy them one year. I made my home pleasant, could invite my friends to visit me and entertain them with satisfaction to myself, and those who were my guests.

[The Grouard Family]

Bro Grouard and family lived in a log room adjoining ours. Mr. G. went to Salt Lake; soon sent a letter to his wife containing a photograph of a person he had chosen to be his second wife. Nahina his island wife seemed in no way displeased. She remarked, "if the woman is not proud and will teach me and the children I am willing." We were all pleased with the spirit she manifested. He at length returned but did not bring the woman he had married; as we were all expecting to be gathered there in due time.

Bro W. Stout was the school teacher in San B. He needed an assistant; and we were induced to send for Ellen to come from San Francisco where we had left her, and engage in the school. She was expected on every boat for six weeks; and great preparations were made for her reception. The time of her arrival being protracted to an indefinate length a male teacher was hired in her stead. We soon however procured a vacant room which we fitted up for a juvenile school, and she taught with great credit to herself, for several successive terms. The number of pupils increased and I assisted her. We drew our pay from the county treasury, which ennabled us to live well. Our school increased to the number of fifty pupils. The children were taught to sing, and some developed sweet voices. The school was visited and highly commended; which was great encouragement.

Our little island boy continued long in a feeble state, but recovered at last. At one time he was so low, the elders refused to administer to him; could not have faith to believe he was destined to live. My husband was preparing to go on a hunting excursion with Lewis Newell. It grieved me that he should leave home at such a time. I said to him what if the child should die in your absence? He replied, "You must get the neighbors to help bury him." He spoke so unconcernedly I felt distressed; and was led to reflect on the contrast between a father and mother even towards an adopted child. He went away, evening came and the child's fever raged terribly! As I stood by his bed I called to mind the blessing Bro Young pronounced on my head previous to my leaving S. L. to go to the islands. He says, "You shall have power over the destroyer to rebuke him from your house and none of your children shall be removed by death, and you shall return in peace." I thought now is the time to claim the promise in behalf of my sick boy! I told my intentions to my youngest daughter the only one at home. She fully coincided, and says, "mother it is right you should claim that blessing." So she kneeled with me, and we called on the Lord. I laid my hands on the head of the child, annointed him with consecrated oil, rebuked the disease in the name of the Lord, and by virtue of the promise I had faith to believe the healing power would descend upon him and so it was. He began to amend from that very hour, and in due time was fully restored.

When Mr. Grouard returned from Salt Lake having married him a wife there, he was cordially received by his first and all went on well for awhile.[3] We at length discovered that his faith was weakened in regard many principles pertaining to the gospel. Some incautious remarks were made by him in the hearing of persons disposed to "make a man an offender for a word." It came to the ears of men who in the absence of the Presidents were appointed to preside, and they spoke of it in publick. Sharp and severe things were spoken and Mr. G's feelings were badly injured. He commenced from that time to manifest a disaffected spirit. At length the Presidency returned and reassumed the reins of government. Those who had chastised Bro G. were reproved, and he was reinstated in the minds of the people; still it did not seem to heal his wound.

He had imbibed a hard spirit, and appeared unhappy. In consequence of this his wife became discontented. She expressed a wish to return to her native country. Jealously on her part increased till she became irritable and angry. Her husband having lost the good spirit could not console her. He went to the leading men, and they advised him to let her go to her island home.

It was then proposed the Bro's Pratt and Grouard should return to their missionary labors and take the woman to her friends. It was a trying time for us all.

[A Third Mission, 1853–54]

[The official call from Apostles Lyman and Rich to Brothers Pratt and Grouard to undertake another mission came in late October. The elders were to return Nahina and baby to Tahiti and strengthen the Saints. But money was scarce. Brother Horner could not help them though with good luck he thought he could purchase "a

small ship and start them off on their missions in a way that they will be safe." But good luck failed them and they went to work to earn passage money. At San Francisco they heard only discouraging words from the islands, that the French opposed foreign influences and that if they landed they would likely be put into prison. Even so, the elders offered to go "at all risks" if sufficient money was raised. But that failed, and without hope for better Franco-American relations the mission effort was abandoned. Nahina and baby were placed on a ship and returned to Tahiti where she married a Polynesian.

While the elders were in San Francisco, there must have been much talk about the missionaries, the mission, the Mormon Church, and San Bernardino. Friend Henry Christie wrote Lousia Pratt from San Francisco that "it was current that Br Pratt and Grouard was dissatisfied with the people at San Bernardino and they were going to try and get there families away as soon as possible . . . ." This kind of talk may have raised notions in some minds about the two missionaries. For this or other reasons, the two were challenged. In conducting a meeting Chapman Duncan called on Grouard to speak. He declined. The meeting went on, and Duncan called on him again. Again he declined. Finally Grouard agreed to offer the benediction, which he turned to a defense of his life and faith. The next Sunday, Brother Duncan repeated his tactic but on Brother Pratt who was ready. Brother Christie reported the meeting:

> *[Brother Pratt] rose up and spoke long and well he recounted all that he and his family had passed through for this Church told them to Judge of the fruits then asked them all Boldly Which of them all acused him of Sin. Said that he had truly sufferd much and in all Honesty almost Prophesyed that Br Pratt would bee a Greet Greet Man And surley he would be a king so Br Pratt console himself with that and all Preasant said Amane; they were all Satisfied with Br Pratt.*

If the Pratts and Grouards were displeased with San Bernardino, were they justified? Louisa concurred. "There are many good meaning people here, and some 'Mighty' rough ones . . . ." She was vehement over one public speaker, "in looks and actions a demon and his sonorous voice and profane oaths make your ears ring with horror, and fill you soul with disgust; while at the same time you have the happy reflection 'I am living among the Saints of God.' . . . I do not love those who profane his name and ridicule the idea of being religious."

As for material comforts, she said, "We own not a roof on earth but a dog and a few chickens." That was 8 June 1855, three years after their homecoming. (LBP to Sister Hutchinson, 8 June 1855, APFP 6.)

Trials of adjustment were overshadowed by the all-consuming issue of plural marriage. Though the subject was of the most profound significance to Louisa, she did not mention it in her journals. Persons in that time could choose from four options: (1) accept the teaching and practice it; (2) accept the teaching but avoid practicing it; (3) say nothing, and do nothing about it; and (4) oppose the doctrine and practice and likely leave the church because of it.

While Pratt was in the upper country he and his friend Henry Christie had many talks on the subject and Christie sought Mrs. Pratt's reflections on the subject. (Henry Christie to LBP, San Francisco, 31 December 1853, APFP 7.)

> *Sister Pratt i should like to hear your opinion on Mormonism as in some of its Peculiar Points. Br. Grouard and I was up at Sister Lincoln's about 10 days ago and Daniel Baldwin was present and the Plurality System came up. We were all of one opinion about it; And that was; that it was a damnable device . . . it is a barbarous and uncivilized Custom.*

He Simply sought her position, wanted all people to be free to think and act as they wished. He wanted freedom of discussion and action. We do not have her answer at this time; this only shows us the widespread discussions taking place, and surely what Louisa's reflections were.

Elders Pratt and Grouard were in the San Francisco area until March when they returned to San Bernardino, taking Frances with them. On 28 April 1854, Christie sent a letter to Addison Pratt who had witnessed offensive behavior of some sort, "not worthy of the name of man." "Who would act such as you say they did?" Whatever the provocations, Pratt remained silent as to his position, unless it shows through in this Christie letter (Henry Christie to Addison Pratt, San Francisco, 28 April 1854, APFP 5):

> *your independence of mind and a consciousness that you have always done you duty; Must raise and keep you at all times far above the Ignorant Crowd; as must have been there at the Mission; But Br Pratt it might have happend for the Best; for it is almost impossible for you to remain Happy, away from the Church and how could you, a great portion of your life has been spent in its service, your intrest your treasure your all is there. Man wants a religion; And i Will say that Mormons as Good as any other; perhaps, a little Better; only i should recommend that in all Cases We should use our own judgement; this to me is the Standard by which our faiths And acts Will be tried; But Br Pratt Whatever religion you Belong to you ar the same to me; I esteem all mankind as i know them; each to perform their respective parts in the Great drama of life i will never ask What is there religion.*

I was not reconciled to Mr. P's going. Mr. G. gave his wife her choice to take her eldest or youngest son, as she could only take one. She chose the youngest. When Franklin saw his father and mother get into the carriage that was to convey them to the sea coast, he commenced to scream. He was determined to follow them; we were forced to hold him with great exertion while his cries were deafening![4]

Oh! how I felt for that mother! Long must those cries have sounded in her ears! Her "first born," was very dear to her. The one that had been given to me, she showed no reluctance in leaving. When they were fairly out of sight I undertook to comfort the poor boy. I led him about the town, took him to the store and bought things to amuse him; after a long time he ceased his sobbing. The boy was then past five years of age. The sister, older wept loudly on account of her brother's grief, but was not so inconsolable. From that hour I have decided against taking children from a mother. Happy had it been for us all had we determined to let the poor woman take all her children, even the step daughter back to their own native isles; where they would have been free as the birds in the air, and never known the want of food or clothing.

They arrived in San Francisco; there they learned that the french Governor would not permit elders to land on Tahiti or on other islands under his protectorate. Accordingly they procured a passage for "Nahina," and they gave up the mission. The two men stopt in San Francisco four months, and returned to the lower Country. Our second daughter Frances came home with her father.

Previous to this event we had taken into our house an emigrant lady, who by accident had her arm shot through; and having traveled five weeks with nothing done for it except to keep on wet cloths, it was in a terrible condition. The flesh was nearly all off the inside of her arm. Dr. Burress undertook the care, and discharged his duty faithfully as skillful surgeon. The lady suffered severely under the first opperation. In coming off the plains the Mormon settlement was the first reached by the invalid lady. She was terrified at the necessity of having to stop with Mormons.

She soon expressed herself happily disappointed; her arm had the best of care, and she grew happy and contented. She could not dress herself for months. Ellen was her constant attendant mornings and evenings, being in school through the day. She was a very agreable lady, seemed much attached to our family and especially to Ellen; always expressing the most heartfelt gratitude for her kind attention, in her helpless condition. At the expiration of seven months her arm was healed, but not strong like the other. She often refered to her happy disappointment in coming among the Mormon people; who were to her like kindred; sympathizing friends in the day of her calamity.

Two months before she left us another invalid was brought to the house. A young man who in crossing had eaten poison berries. The bishop requested me to take him in. I told him there was no man about the house, my husband was gone from home and we already had a helpless person in the family. I went to the wagon to see the poor fellow. Oh! said he, "I'm a poor sick boy. I entreat you to take me in, you make me think of my mother." I was moved with compassion, and allowed him to be carried in. I had a back bedroom where I fixed his bed, and the same Doctor attended him. Two watchers every night, a fire and lights to be kept burning; my rest was broken, the task a severe one. Besides the poor boy had no money, but I believed he would pay me if he ever recovered and was able to labor. In three weeks he was able to wait on himself. Soon went to work and paid me honorably. Always appeared grateful for what I had done for him. Then there came a relief for me. The lady's arm grew stronger, the two little Tahitian boys had both been sick, they were well, and prospects brightened on every hand. Mr. Rankin paid us honorably for taking care of his wife. A present was made to Ellen in the settlement of a beautiful heifer from Mr. Ra'n who was a stock holder from Pennsylvania. It soon made a splendid cow, of great account in the family.

Previous to Frances returning with her father we had heard of her poor health; but had not immagined she could be so wasted in flesh. The sight of her gave me great pain. Her emaciated form spoke plainer than words that the destroyer was aiming at the main spring of life, and marking her for his victim. She would not allow a word to be said about her ill health, or her wasted form. She was full of life and animation, at times, occasionally a look of sadness would pervade her countenance; shades of sorrow would come and go which distressed me to witness. She would never take medicine. She rode horseback, kept in active exercise, sought cheerful company, used the plainest diet, according as the best physicians advised.

My sister Crosby still remained in the upper country on a farm. She was often writing to Frances soliciting her return; as the warm climate was not likely to benefit her health. She went to Los Angelos on a visit. Her friends in Francisco hearing she was there offered to pay her passage on the Steamer, and she embarked without giving me any previous information. When I learned the fact I was surprised and grieved. I felt that a wrong had been committed against me. Soon however a letter came that she was safe with her aunt, and that her return had occasioned great joy.

Mr. Grouard had been gone to Salt Lake three months, and we were looking for him to return with his new wife; amid varying scenes my mind was diverted. The eldest boy Franklin was left with a Mr. Hill, a friend of his father's; he would not be contented, would run away, sleep out all night in some wagon box, occasioning great uneasiness. Whenever I heard he was missing I would search for him; perhaps find asleep in some sly corner. Young as he was not seven years old, he evinced forethought and caution. One night he wandered away, went into the schoolroom, and after securing both doors by placing benches against them he crept into the book box and fell asleep. Finding the doors fastened we forced one open, found him and took him to the house. He continued to cry till he saw me make him a bed on the floor; when his tears ceased at once, and he chatted away as merry [as] a cricket. I would not send him away again, but kept him with his brother, till his father returned with a good kind mother for him. Just before their arrival news in a letter came from Tahiti that Nahina had married a man of her own color and kind, and was apparently contented and happy. This was cheering news to Mr. Grouard. They soon went to housekeeping took the children home and in due time had a daughter born to them. Pure american blood, she was the pride of the house.

[A New House]

In Aug. 54 Mr. Pratt commenced building a house on a city lot which he purchased for $100. He was a carpenter, could do much of the inside work. It was built of adobies. Mr. G. laid up the walls.

We taught the larger scholars, she the juvenile classes. Our school was in high repute. We often had exhibitions to which spectators were invited. The children were instructed in answering general questions, which made them interesting; questioned with regard to their moral and social habits and many things aside from merely their book lessons. It was a labourious task for me; as many of the larger pupils required great attention, and compulsory measures for their advancement.

In Jun 55 we moved into our new house, feeling thankful for our success in once more being in possession of a respectable home. A vineyard was immediately planted, fruit trees of great variety, shrubbery, plants and flowers. No place in town had such beautiful shade trees. I raised a nursery of black pepper trees, which were scattered over the settlement. They grew very high with extended branches, and remained green through the winter. They bore a red berry which enchanced the beauty of the tree, but I knew not how to prepare them for use. Lower California is a delightful climate. San Bernardino was a very desirable location. A better class of citizens could not be found in that state. Two good and efficient men presided. We felt that we had begun life anew.[5]

Fate had decreed that pain must follow on the train of pleasure. A day of sorrow was drawing nigh. In the spring of 55 Sister P.B. Lewis came to us from the Sandwich Islands, where she had been with her husband on a mission.[6] She was a relative of mine, we had been warm friends in the days of Nauvoo. Her health declining on the Pacific isles, her husband had thought it wisdom to send her to California. I soon discovered that the consumption had fastened its deadly fangs upon her frail system, (from a child she had been delicate). She was strong in the belief that she should recover her health; was displeased if any one expressed a doubt. I could see a gradual decline but dared not mention it. The heat being oppressive in the summer she resolved to go to the high mountains, where were mills, and several families living. The air was cool there, and cold spring water to "quench her raging thirst."

I was all the time fearful of the consequences. She was conveyed up the steep mountain in a carriage, on a bed. The families living there were not prepared, if inclined, to give her the attention she needed. Word soon came to us that she was failing. Ellen was disposed to dismiss her school and go to her relief. It was as I feared, she soon closed her earthly existence, and was brought down the mountain twelve miles in her coffin. A few brethren followed, and Ellen on horseback. The procession came up to my door past 9 o'clock p.m. It was a solemn scene! Thus ended her high anticipations, that her companion would return from his mission, she should go with him to the valley of the mountains, where her hearts best affections were centred. While her remains lay in my house I was led to reflect deeply upon her brief but suffering life! Great domestic trials had fallen to her lot! An invalid in her early youth; she had been miraculously healed by the administration of the elders in our church, previous to her baptism. She was an orphan before her first marriage, which proved an unhappy one.

All these events revolved in my mind, and I sorely lamented her fate; that she could not have survived as it was her ardent desire, till her companion returned, the man to whom she was devotedly attached. Her faith in the gospel was firm and unshaken to the last. I had loved her from our first aquaintance, which was in Nauvoo. She left her kindred in N. York state and came to the church when she was but eighteen years of age. I never knew a more energetic, ingenious, persevering girl. Her parents afterwards joined the church, came to Nauvoo before her first marriage, and both died there. It devolved on me to write to her husband.

Her sister in San Francisco afterwards came to the place; the antipode of the dear one gone. To awaken scenes and reflections occasioned by her arrival would be to resurrect long buried agonies and put them again on the rack, to throb and bleed! Let oblivion cover it all, till we meet in presence of her we mourned, and before Him who knows the hearts and tries the reins of the children of men! Brother Ludington, a missionary to India, preached the funeral sermon. He spoke in a most touching manner of the probable return of her husband; and of the uncertainty of all earthly expectations. For days my house seemed like a sepulchre; from which all living beings were departed. At length I resolved to rise above the gloom, and try to rejoice, that my dear friend had gone away to a peaceful home, as I believed. What had she here, to induce her to remain? Nearly all her life she had been afflicted with pain of body or mind. A calm came over me, and I felt comforted.

In Aug 55 the elders began to return from the Sandwich Islands. A sermon was preached in the Hawaiian language. We could understand something by the spirit, and some by the tongue resembling the Tahitian. Then came missionaries returning from India. Bro's Finley and Fotheringham. They cheered us by their company, and their faith. Bro. Davis and wife were beautiful singers. They added much to the life of our social circles. They tarried with us a while, and then went on to S. Lake. At length Brother Lewis arrived, husband of the departed. He seemed at first sad; afterwards considering all the circumstances, her feeble health and prospects of trials to come, he remarked, "it is all for the best!"

[The Crosbys and Frances Arrive, November 1855]

Towards the last of Nov news came that my sister from Francisco, and my daughter Frances were in Los Angelos on their way to our settlement. All was excitement and joy! Ellen and Ann Louisa went in the stage to meet them expecting they would be coming up in the coach. They however had their passage engaged in an open wagon which they must do or wait two days for the stage. Accordingly they all came together seventy miles. It was a time of general joy; they had come to make a home! Now thought I, my weary spirit will revive! My longing desires are gratified; my sister and daughter have come in answer to my prayers. All seemed cheerful for awhile. But my poor girl was not well; there was a trembling at my heart. Memory brings back past scenes of my life so indelibly stamped on my mind. I shudder in view of the reoccurence of similar ones.

[Family Life in San Bernardino]

Dec 25th at length came around. It carried me back to the days of my youth, my father's house, and kindred ties. In those days we were accustomed to have publick worship in honor of the Saviour's birth; there in San B. it was only a dancing party. We were invited to see the assembly, and hear the music. Frances sailed about the Hall like a bird in the air! The music was soul-stirring; I staid a short time, went home and prepared supper for a few persons. Mr. Pratt had no taste for amusements of that kind. To go forth with his dog and gun, and shoot wild game, was more sport for him. There were pleasure parties in all directions, and some to which I was opposed.

One evening Lois went on horseback. After midnight she was brought home in a frightful condition; having been thrown from the horse. I was dumb with astonishment when she was brought in. She could not speak distinctly, her jaw was dislocated, joint twisted, and the sight of her was truly alarming! the young man who had taken her from home seemed deeply concerned. He said the horse had always been considered one of the gentlest kind, but for some cause unknown to him he had taken fright at that unfortunate moment, threw Lois over his head, her clothes caught on the horn of the saddle, tore every thing from her but her under garments. The horse then fell to the ground, with his head against a tree. Frances was terribly alarmed! Was certain she did not breathe for several minutes. She was brought home in a carriage and nothing could exceed F's attention to the injured girl, till she was wholly restored. A physician was called, the jaw replaced, and brother C.C. Rich came and laid his hands upon her head, and blessed her in the name of the Lord. He did not reprove her, but said, "be cautious in future." It was the last of her riding horseback to evening parties, in the dark, and over bad roads.

Mr. Pratt worked faithfully on the lots, pruning grapevines and setting out trees. A young man by the name of Wm McGary came to the place, bought a lot adjoining ours, and began making improvements. He was a tasty workman, the house was roughly built, there was soon a change for better.

A Mr. Grinelle from upper Cal. brought me a little girl five years old. His wife had left him and married another; from her he stole the child. He wished me to take her either as my own or to be paid for my trouble. I advised him not to give away his child, he might repent it in a coming time. I took her under my care. Emma Grinelle was the sweetest and best child I ever saw in my life. There seemed from the first something unearthly about her. Oh! how I pitied her mother! I took her to my arms and felt it was a precious charge. I sometimes feared I could not be watchful enough, as I had never had a tender delicate child like her. She had a cough from the first. I often asked the question to myself why did such a gentle spirit come to this cold hard world? Was it merely to get a body, then suffer and die? The whooping cough came to the neighborhood. As soon as I heard of it I trembled with fear. I tried in vain to keep her from exposure, but a careless girl brought a little one to the house, which did the cruel deed. Ellen dreamed. She saw three little fields of wheat, half grown in height, but fully matured. The reaper came with his scythe to cut them down. It was an omen to me. There were two other little girls younger than mine, but strong, fresh and blooming, all smitten at the same time. Our dear little Emma seemed sensible she could not live. When I would ask her to take medicine that she might get well, she would reply, "I cannot get well." As Ellen was holding her in her arms, She says, "sing to me." E says, "what shall I sing?" "Sing me a farewell song!" Oh! the beauty that is laid beneath the dust! Mother earth takes the lambs to her bosom, to shield them from the storms of life! Her father came, but not in time to see her buried. I gave him a lock of her hair, he took it and went to a retired place. I knew for what purpose. Most sorely did he feel the loss. She would often cry out, "Mother! Mother! come here!" I would run to her and ask what she wanted? She would answer "nothing, go and lie down." Her mother at that time had gone behind the vail; and who knows but she was calling her child?

No human being could be more lovely in death! I gazed long upon her tranquil features, and thought of her poor father! ignorant of the sad event then passing, when his only child would soon be removed from mortal sight! Oh! how we all missed her, but I knew she had gone to add one to the cherubian to sing songs with the redeemed so well did she love singing. I was soon called to the death bed of sister Layton's little girl with the same disease. So fleshy and bright. She said in her native tongue, "that child was the only sun of my soul!" We buried her under the shade of a tree on the lot where they will build a house. The birds will sing on the tree, and change the funeral requium; the murmuring of the rivulet that runs near the grave will often fall on the fond mother's ear a farewell song to the dear one gone and make her think of her island home and kindred. We returned from the burial, and in a few hours another one was gone; and the dream was interpreted.

Mr. Pratt, though unusual for him, was at home on his fiftieth birthday. Feb 21st.[7] We recounted the scenes of his past life, an eventful one it had been, during his short pilgrimage on earth. Travels by sea and land, storms and tempests, hunger and cold; isolation on the islands of the sea, separation from family and friends, and a thousand nameless things. But he says "my health is good, and I hope to live many years."

I went to visit Frances Clark, once the wife of Heber C. Kimball. She had a young babe two weeks old. She had buried her first little girl over two years of age. I had hoped the birth of the second would have in some degree healed the wound. But no, she was still inconsolable! I never saw a more afflicted person. The child was a peculiar one, and very beautiful to look upon! 'Tis such the angels want.

I had thought my own grief great beyond endurance even for a child not mine by birth, but when I saw that mother's sorrow I knew the wound was deeper. We need all our treasures to make our lives here endurable; in this cold and uncharitable state of existance. Oh, will the destroyer be disarmed! When can we shout victory over death and the grave! These lovely children were destined to go early! They are taken from the evil to come. When we tried to exercise faith to have them healed, just when the prayer was on our lips, "Oh, Lord heal them;" with the next breath, "thy will O, Lord, be done." He wants them to replenish his kingdom. There are those around me who have trials, and sorrows more pungent than those caused by death. A man who in Francisco was eloquent, ardent, valiant, in testimony, in declaring the fullness of the gospel revealed to the martyred prophet. Now intimidating his family with oaths and curses! Surely the evil one has possession of him, and leads him captive at his will.

My domestic sorrows I forbear to mention. I carry them in my own bosom, and bear my injuries in silence.

While mourning over my lost treasure there came a brother Owen, from San Francisco. He was full of faith and zeal for the gospel. His conversation quickened my spirit and lightened the burden from my heart. I felt that I could sing a new song, even praise to our God! Brothers Lyman and Rich were good reliable men, and every thing prospered under their administration. Beautiful vineyards were in bearing. Peaches could be had in two years from the pit. The people lived in harmony, so we had no lawsuits, every difficulty was settled by bishops or teachers. Plenty crowned our labors. We had means to help the elders to go out on missions and when they returned we could assist them on their way back to S. Lake.

William McGary of whom I have spoken was a frequent visitor in our family. He was a friendly agreable young man, and a good musician. The 6th of March in 56 was the aniversary of his 23d birthday. Lois was 19 the same day. So I made them a dinner, and invited company. Lois was inclined to be merry, while he was silent and sober. I knew now why it was, but learned afterward. He had entertained hopes which were likely to prove fruitless. We had depended on him for company, were cheered with his music, and I regretted that any thing should have transpired to mar his peace, and make him moody and silent. He at length went to San Francisco on business, made a short stay and returned; soon went to houskeeping with his Aunt Morse, appeared reserved and melancholly. Brother C.C. Rich had a very sick child; he called for Mr. Pratt to go with him to the council House; where was an upper room dedicated to prayer; where the brethren assembled in cases extraordinary, when great faith was required.

Thither they repaired to call on the Lord, and seldom did they fail to obtain answers to their prayers. At length came the 25th aniversary of our wedding day, the 3d of April 1856. Mr. P. was very sick. There was an oyster supper at Wm McGary's but he could not attend. So we brought some to him, of which he is very fond, and it did him good. The day was spent in deep thought on my part. I reviewed my wedded life, and marvelled that I had been enabled to endure so much! I thought of the covenants I then made at the altar; had I fulfilled the promise, to "love honor and obey?" I had done what I could. Why should we be required to make solemn promises when it depends all on circumstances whether we can fulfill them. No woman ever felt a stronger sense of duty, than I have.

The 6th of April, was an important day. Ann Louisa's birthday. 16 years old. We remembered it with interest for its being the birth day of the church, of Jesus Christ of Latter Day Saints. When it was organized with six members, in the town of Palmyra State of N. York. A L's uncle made her a present of a beautiful little work box. Many years should she live, she will keep it as a mememto. That day the Church was 26 years of age. A conference was held, I reckoned how old I would be should I live 26 years longer, 79 years. I said, "should I live to that age I shall see much of the gathering of Israel, and the enlargement of the kingdom of God." Who can fathom its progress, through blood and tears! Who can tell the numbers that have been made to rejoice, that the Lord the God of Israel, has spoken from the heavens in this our day!

CHAPTER SIXTEEN

San Bernardino II

Memoirs, 14 April 1856 to 8 February 1857

[Addison Pratt's Fourth Mission]

Mr. Pratt was appointed to go again to the island. I did not feel reconciled, but I bore it as patiently as I could. Brothers Rich and Cox came to
give him a parting blessing. It was great and good! They also gave me one.
Said I should be blessed in the absence of my companion, with the necessaries and comforts of life, that my mind should be buoyed up under trials. They also laid hands on Ephraim who had then a sick turn. The 14th
day of Apr my husband started on his mission. The two eldest daughters
accompanied him to the foot of the mountain. Mr. J. Dyer came with his
team to take him on his way. So we were left again, to struggle on with the
ills of life alone. Not knowing when the "father" would return, or whether
he would come at all.[1]

[Charles W. Wandell]

Brother C. W. Wandall was then installed as school teacher.[2] My two youngest
girls were attendants. He was a competent teacher, and they improved
rapidly under his tuition. There was a celebration for "May Day," appointed;
to be held in a grove several miles distant. Lois was chosen for the May
Queen, although a young lady grown. She was required to make a speech
before the audience; which was expected to be very large. She felt the undertaking to be enormous in its nature; but when she found there could be no
excuse, or permission to withdraw, she went forward with a self reliant air
and performed well her part. Joseph Hunt addressed the Queen in a most
dignified manner. The whole affair was published in the San B news.

[Grouard's Disaffection]

About this time Mr. Grouard commenced to lecture in the place, on science and natural laws. Spiritual philosophy was bearing with heavy weight on his mind. I wished much to hear him lecture, but he being considered weak in the faith of the gospel, and leaning towards spiritualism, the sisters did not attend his lectures, for fear of publick remarks. At length he moved two miles out of town, and commenced farming. It was a poor looking place in the woods. The rabbits destroyed everything as fast as it grew. How much out of place he seemed there! Designed by nature for a public man, then spending his time to no good effect. His last wife was an inteligent agreable woman.

There was a report in circulation, that Mr. Pratt did not intend returning to that country, that his intention was to spend his days on the islands. Neither myself or daughters believed the report, had any foundation in truth, yet it was not agreable to hear it. It was enough for us to be left again without hearing evil prophecies.

"May Day" came, and our minds were diverted. Every thing was arranged in good order beneath the shade of large embowering trees. The children flocked together like doves to their windows. More than a thousand people were assembled. The fairy queen appeared with her maids of honor. A platform was erected and on it she was seated in a large armed chair covered with some emblem of royalty, then the two maids of honor crowned her with a beautiful wreath of roses. The first maid addressed the assembly in a very becoming manner. Next Mr. Joe Hunt addressed the queen, in a brilleant style. Lastly, the queen made a speech to her subjects, informing them what they had to expect during her reign. Mr. Wandall conducted the whole affair in his graceful and easy style. The picnic was spread sumptuously. The band of music poured forth their loudest strains and dancing of the children closed the exercises.

Shortly after this I received a letter from Henry Boyle containing inteligence from Mr. Pratt. Brothers, Pratt, Boyle, Layton, and Potter, had taken passage on board the Steamer *Sea Bird*, and were badly treated. There was something relating to the voyage of which I had reminded Mr. P. previous to his leaving home; and when the ill usage was administered I think he would give me credit for having a little foresight. Again it devolved on me to manage my own business, and provide for my family.

Brother Wm J. Cox was my unvarying friend. If any thing was likely to go wrong, I went to him for counsel. If my cattle strayed, he was the one to send his boy and horse to find them. He never denied me a favor which I asked of him. The Saviour's words were, "Blessed are the merciful, for they shall obtain mercy."

During the month of May a circumstance transpired which affected me sorely. A new graveyard was fenced in, and many of the dead had to be removed. Sister Lewis who died on the mountain, her child which was buried in Los Angelos and our dear little Emma Grinelle were removed to the new burial ground. I could never endure the thought of disturbing the silent slumbers of the dead. The sad scenes of the past were all brought back. Whenever my mind was afflicted I resorted to outdoor exercise. I had my garden to till, and though the task was hard, it often prevented my giving way to despondency. How much the mind needs change, as well does the body to keep it healthy.

[John Eldredge]

Important scenes were often transpiring. Missionaries returning from foreign countries. My house was open to receive them. Then my heart would be cheered by hearing of the spread of the gospel in the old world. In the spring of 56 Bro John Eldridge returned from his mission to Australia. I felt rejoiced to see him return alive and well but Oh! the sad tale he had to tell us![3]

The vessel on which he embarked was wrecked. In a furious windstorm the vessel parted in the centre and five persons were drowned, two mothers and three children were washed out of the cabbin. The part broken off was then carried by the waves, and one end touched the reef, so the remaining passengers were taken off and their feet set on the rocks. Previous to this, a rope was stretched from the vessel to the reef and tied to the rocks. Some were saved by letting themselves down into the water and clinging to the rope, thus making their escape to the Island; which was uninhabited. There they remained three days and nights without food or drink. They were then taken off and conveyed to another island.

On that Island without inhabitants, they found fish and turtle on which they lived two months. Then a vessel came to their relief and took [them] to Tahiti, where they remained for one month. Then Bro's Graham and Eldridge embarked for San Francisco, leaving the other passengers to come after. Bro' Eldridge spoke in publick with a humble chastened spirit; made beautiful remarks; in regard to the miraculous manner in which his life had been preserved. At times he appeared abstracted and melancholy. The cries of the poor perishing women were ringing in his ears.

The two Elders soon left us and started on to Salt Lake. With them four teams went, loaded with provision for the poor saints in Utah. Emigration being great, there was danger of suffering. There were no rail ways to convey supplies speedily; but a whole season was required to make a journey to the frontiers and return.

[Ellen's Marriage to William McGary]

Previous to their departure an important event took place. On the 26th of May 1856 my eldest daughter was married to Wm McGary. Bro' E'e was invited to attend, being as he was a very old acquaintance. When I informed him of the approaching ceremony he appeared pleased; which gave me a little encouragement, although I did not feel quite happy over the affair. There was a cloud in the horizon, which though far from threatening, was not like the clear blue sky, serene, and inspiring bright hopes of long sunshine. The event had been kept private from the public, and even from the nearest neighbors. After the ceremony which was performed by Ellen's uncle Crosby, and refreshments were served, our spirits revived; and as toasts were offered in abundance, the scene closed with mirthful conversation. Great surprise was manifest in the community when the fact was known. In general it was not fully approved, I cannot say I am in favor of private weddings.

A few days passed ere the secret began to be divulged. Then a wedding party was demanded. The guests invited did not know for what occasion they were to assemble. At the opening of the exercises the newly married couple were introduced. It was a surprise to nearly all present. There were great congratulations; and the party was a merry one. E's father was then on Tahiti; her sister Frances was in Los Angelos. That they could not be present at the first wedding in the family, was a source of regret.

[Louisa's Island Boy Ephraim]

I had daily cares pressing upon me. My fruit orchard and garden required great labor as nothing would thrive without irrigation. My little island boy was some comfort to me; though on my mind a constant anxiety; early showing the habits of his race, a constant desire to ramble about, could not bear confinement. When no more than six years old he would wander away, and then like his elder brother sleep out in some nook or corner, whereever night overtook him. I could never lie down at sleep till I found him.

When interogated why he did not come home, his excuse would be a fear of being corrected for staying so long! I did not mean to be severe, but thought it my duty to break him of his wandering propensities. How nature shone out in those two boys! Bright shrewed, and witty, with loving dispositions; but their Indian traits it seemed impossible to overcome.

[The Fourth of July]

About the first of June Sister C. and I were summoned to attend a court, for the first time in our lives. Y.L. Sparks and wife had seperated, both sueing for divorse. We were questioned and cross questioned, heard many disagreable things. Our testimony was in favor of the woman. We answered the questions as quick as possible and withdrew. The case was decided in favor of the wife, and a bill of divorce obtained. An artful woman was the first cause of the unhappy affair.

Lonely indeed is a woman's life if her husband must be always gone from home. Besides the burden of providing for her family there are hours when her heart longs for sympathy, and her children cannot supply the place of a husband. There was a woman whose name I forbear to mention, who did me a great injustice. My spirit was deeply wounded, but with her I could not reason. I had never wronged her, and at different times in her life I had sought to do her good. Her conduct towards me was the sin of ingratitude. Let Him who knows the secrets of all hearts, judge between us.

The Fourth of July drew nigh, and I helped to make a new flag for the occasion. Eight yards in lentgh, and five in width. Mr. C. W. Wandall was the director in chief. He treated the ladies employed to make it very politely; brought in dainties to help out the dinner, which Sister Lyman prepared, and served.

Mr. Woften [?] made one in our family circle, and at our social parties. He was fine looking and very intellectual, often entertained us with the history of his early life. He had seen great sorrow. He had married a wife in his youth every way calculated to make him happy; their love was reciprocal. In the gold excitement he went to California. She did not freely give her consent. She left Nauvoo and went to her friends in N. York City. While in Cal, his relatives wrote to him that she had clandestinely left there with a strange gentleman. For several years her place of residence was unknown to him. At length he heard she was married and settled in Florida. His daughter wrote him a letter with full particulars. This cast a shadow over his whole life. In the midst of mirth, and scenes of joy a close observer would discern a shade of sadness on his brow.

The Presidents of that branch of the church Amasa Lyman and C.C. Rich were highly respected by our unbelieving neighbors, although it was well known that they had four wives each, all living in that place. They did not seem to think it their business to interfere with out domestic relations so long as the leading men sustained good business characters, were moral, temperate, and industrious; helped to improve the country, by building mills, and making lumber to build up other settlements. They seemed proud to have us for neighbors. Mr. Lyman was renouned for being an eloquent speaker. Mr. Rich for a wise counsellor. And the whole people for being honest, upright, cheerful, and progressive. On the "Fourth" we had a grand celebration. A score of flags and banners were waving in wind. I had charge of the young school girls and arranged them to join the procession. "Mothers in Israel" with banners. Fathers, and all classes; every thing in the best style, and order. C.W. Wandall delivered an oration.

In one respect we were disappointed. We had expected the stage to arrive from Los Angelos on 3d day with Frances and the Misses Smith. The coach did not come in, neither the ladies. They however came the following day, made a short visit. Frances was not well. How it afflicted me to see wasting away her form once so elastic and energetic! Like a deer she would bound; her spirits bouyant as a bird's that glides through the air; fearless of all beneath it. The climate there was too oppressive in summer for her weak lungs. I would sometimes walk out in the middle of the day, as necessity would demand, and so excessively hot would be the earth it would injure my shoes; and almost blister my feet. Such heat, with such a rich soil, and kept moist, there is no bounds to the growth of vegetation.

[Mr. Ball. The Twenty-Fourth]

There was an interesting incident which I had forgotten to mention, which happened about the third year of our residence in San B'o. There were several young men in town who were accustomed to call often at the house and spend the evening in singing. Mr. P. was then at home. Our eldest daughter played the flutina, & often sang to entertain company. It was reported that a celebrated singer had arrived from upper California. The young gentlemen acquaintance were authorized to invite him to call. Accordingly they came on a certain evening and presented the stranger; introducing him as "Mr. Ball." I thought the name sounded familiar, but not an inkling came to my head that he was the son of an old friend. We soon found he was a comical fellow, and also a good singer.

In the course of the evening I asked him what state he hailed from. He replied, "Massachusetts." "ah," said I, "my native state." "Indeed, and when did you leave there?" "In 1829. I kept a sewing establishment in Athol, and boarded with a family by the name of Ball. The lady was my particular friend. She had three children, the eldest a boy named Francis, at that time four years old." He stared at me, and says, "was your name Miss Barnes?" "It was." "That lady was my mother, and I am that boy!" No suprise could surpass mine! There was the boy I taught to sing songs when only three, or four years old. He could repeat correctly the childish songs I taught him; for the singing of which he earned many a cent, as he went about the shops and publick places. He still continued the practice earning money by his musical talents. He was afterwards a frequent caller, and we had long conversations, about his mother and the family.

A correspondence was then opened between his mother and myself, which revived reminiscenses of days long past and gone. The old familiar names of our acquaintance were often refered to, and their history would occasion alternate joy and sorrow, as I learned the good or ill fates that fell to their lots. Over this young man the mother had great anxiety; although possessing a brilliant intellect he was not in all respects a pattern of sobriety. To be a renouned humorist was his highest ambition. The characteristics of his childhood were fully developed in his youth.

Mr. Grinelle came and spent a few weeks with us. Oh! how he mourned for his lost child! His last tie to earth is broken. He is not only a widower but childless. When we talked of her last illness, of all her endearing words, of her attractions, her sweet temper, her loving disposition, how our hearts throbbed with grief! That one so lovely must be torn from us who prized her so much; when other children with comparatively no charms to bind them to their kindred and guardians, are permitted to live and grow, to mature, and come even to old age. The ways of providence how mysterious!

A deep solemnity rested on my mind. I walked the house and tried to pray. As I walked in the dooryard a calm spirit came over me. I thought of my utter loneliness, which none can know what sympathy it demands unless similar trials have fallen to their lot. Wm McGary who often helped me in my labors, started on a three months tour among the Spanish settlements, with a thresher. On the 24th July there was a military ball in town. Bro' Cox invited me to be his partner, his wife not being able to attend. I felt reluctant in accepting the invitation, but concealed my real feelings and consented to go. It was a crowded assembly; and all things considered, it was a grand affair

[Pages 325-327 are missing from the manuscript. They are also missing from the Daughters of the Utah Pioneers transcription.]

[Social and Domestic Affairs]

In Sept. 56 Elder Fleming returned from Australia where he had been on a mission. He was our neighbor in Nauvoo and we were pleased to see him once more. He spent several days with us and gave us an interesting account of his labors in New South Wales. Previous to his leaving S.L. he had taken a second wife; her name was Nancy Henderson. Ellen had received a letter from that City that said Nancy had broken her marriage vows and married a man who did not belong to the church. We were in company where all were cheerful, when it occurred to Ellen the news she had heard. Without due consideration she related the curcumstance to Bro' Fleming. A shadow came over his features like a storm cloud in the sky, his cheerfulness was at an end. For the evening and indeed for succeeding days. I was very sorry that E should have been so thoughtless.

From that time Bro' F seemed in a reverie, and in haste to go on his way home. We learned afterwards that the girl's choice had not been a wise one; but she was not restored to fellowship in the family she had left, and where she was honored and respected.

There was an excitement in town about the exit of Dr. Burress. He had left pretending to go to San Francisco to buy drugs and return. Soon news came that he had embarked on a steamer bound for U. States. He had borrowed money of different persons, a gold watch of one, left a few debts standing out, but no agent to collect them. He was a man we all had confidence in! We were led to marvel what could have induced the man to forfeit the good opinion of a community where he had been so much respected.

I had my lot to tend and to irrigate. Frequently my turn would come to water in the night, that to me seemed very hard. I thought the men should consider me a lone woman, no husband or son, should give me the water in the day and they should take it at night. I sometimes thought men had not sympathy for women whose husbands were sent away; no salary that they could send relief to their families. My Nephew Alma Crosby a young boy sometimes assisted me when I was obliged to irrigate in the night. My vineyard now began to bear grapes in great abundance, thus rewarding me for all my toil. Lois was an assistant in Mr. Wandall's school had twenty dollars pr month. I had many things to be thankful for, but there seemed a seated malady on my heart. My eldest daughter was comfortably situated. Her husband was ambitious and enterprising in his way, but he lacked that high culture, so very desirable in a companion, he often made rash speeches. Oh, how admirable is a becoming form of speech! a happy method of conveying ideas and sentiments. What an accomplishment! but how few possess it in this rude and wild country. I harden my heart; and try to be reconciled to things for which I have no attraction or affinity.

There were southern people belonging to the branch, who had come there with colored servants; they employed me to write letters for them to send to their kindred and sweethearts in Salt Lake. They had a peculiar form of inditing which I was required strictly to observe. Many a favor in the way of labor did I obtain from them as a reward for writing their letters; besides the merriment it afforded, to read over the letters and observe their simple style, so peculiar to that race of beings.

Having many things to worry and perplex my mind I often had sleepless nights. For that reason I contracted the habit of sitting up in my bed and reading till a late hour; thus inducing sleep. One night I was arroused suddenly by feeling heat through the bedclothes. I had been holding the lamp in one hand and my book in the other; falling asleep unknowingly my lamp had tipt over, the oil spilled out and the spread caught fire. It being woolen it did [not] flash quickly; and I awoke in time to save my bed from being consumed. That was a warning to me to avoid reading with a lamp in my hand. We had a beautiful place; but it required energy and great care to keep it in a flourishing condition. I once complained to Pres't Lyman that I had so many years been left with the care of a family to manage my own business out doors, and in, a husband always gone from home. "Well sister Pratt you have lived, have you not?" "Most certainly I have," I replied. "Then what does it matter?" said he. "The struggle for life is our business here."

But my reasoning was, that it was hard to have our energies taxed to their fullest extent, and that continually. That the raising of a family devolved naturally on a united head, not all on the weaker one. He showed me that I was called to make sacrifices for the gospel of Christ; that if I bore my burdens cheerfully great would be my reward.

[On the Spanish Settlements]

We often took rides to the Spanish settlements, where we were hospitably entertained; feasted on grapes and wine, and fruit of various kinds. Although the people are kind I dispise their manner of living. They generally build their houses on an elevated spot. The road runs through their towns on low land, their buildings are on very high points. Nothing disgusts me more than an old spanish building. Themselves their houses and cattle, are all of the same type.

Oh! the contrast between nature in her primeval state and her condition when highly developed and cultivated! How desirable is progression! On the Islands of the Pacific I was charmed with nature. There was a simplicity about the natives, and their manner of life that seemed in keeping with their isolation, buried from the world as they are, it is not strange they should have habits peculiar to themselves. But it is not so with the Spanish; for centuries they have lived on the borders of civilization; and yet they will keep their old native traits of character. They build their houses of adobies the walls three feet thick, no glass in their windows, a close shutter to be closed at night, when necessary; a ground floor solid as rock. Their beds are made of wool; pillows the same. You might as well lay your head on a log of wood for softness, as on one of their pillows. But they look attractive. In the first place they have cases made of pink silk; then a cover of fine muslin trimmed with lace. Invariably white counterpanes.

At their "Fandangoes" they will treat you to wine, whiskey and tobacco. They will pass around first what they call sigarites. Each lady is offered one. The Spanish ladies will accept, as a matter of course. The American ladies always refuse. When they all commence smoking you may breathe if you can. The ladies wear rich dressing, and their shawls are beautiful.

[Apostles Rich and Lyman, John M. Horner]

Oct 8th. 1856. Bro' C.C. Rich returned from San Francisco, brought letters from Mr. Pratt and Frances. The former had just returned from Tahiti, the french would not allow him to preach there. He was greatly suprised to find our daughter there. She had gone from Los Angelos unexpectedly to us all, the circumstance had caused me great uneasiness, as I knew she was in failing health. But when I heard her father was with her my mind was relieved.

Mr. Lyman was a renouned preacher of righteousness. He often expatiated with great energy on the condition of females in the married state. Their incessant labors in raising a family, the indifference with which many men treated their wives. He would set forth in a clear light how their condition might be ameliorated with proper forethought on the part of the husband. The reader may perhaps ask whether he practiced what he preached? I believe he did. He was never known to be a tyranical or fault finding man. His exortations to his wives were to help each other, bear the burdens of life. To be kindly affectioned one to the other, thus lightening the cares devolving on each separately. Bro' C.C. Rich was not counted so great a reasoner, but distinguished for wise counsel in all difficult cases, a peace maker; always encouraging charity, and brotherly love. Under the administration of these two men we had a peaceable, industrious thriving community.

It is my testimony gained by experience, that people living in a good climate where the necessaries of life are easily obtained are not so selfish, or covetous. They will help each other from a principle of gratitude feeling thankful that providence has placed them in propitious circumstances, where they can accumulate means to provide for their own wants and help others. I remember the liberality of the saints in San Francisco in the year '50. They had money plenty and it was disbursed to the needy as free as water. To the company of Elders, we met at San Pedro as we were moving to the Lower Country, (men sent on missions to foreign countries,) the brethren in Francisco gave seven thousand dollars, 7000. John M. Horner gave $1000 from his own purse. Times changed in that City, and he became bankrupt. After a few years he measurably redeemed himself.

Mr. H'r was a man who wanted to make business for every body. He would hire men by the score, give them all the highest going wages; then take their money to oblige them and pay them interest on it. His liberality would never have injured him had he been farseeing enough to have apprehended a reaction in financial affairs. His wife was more cautious, and often reminded him of his danger. She could see breakers ahead; and safer would it be for men in general if they were more disposed to hearken to the counsel of a wise and prudent wife. Mr. J.M. Horner was a resident of San Hosa valley, where fortunes were sometimes made in one year, raising potatoes. There came a time when their price would not pay for digging. Thus were fortunes reversed.

In the lower country the market was not so fluctuating. Floods were not common as in UC [Upper California]. The rust on wheat was what we had to fear. Heavy dews in succession were the main cause. I saw two hundred acres in one field, a large heavy growth, all ruined with rust; so the owner never entered it with his reaper. The Spaniards had a way of preventing the dews from injuring the grain. They would tie a larraette between two horses, then gallop the animals through the grain; the rope would switch off the water settled on the heads. It is an old saying, that "one part of the world know not how the other portion live." It is very true. A more delightful climate for flowers cannot be found on the continent, as far as I know. A mile from town Col. Jackson's lived. He was a lawyer, but his wife was a horticulturalist. It was a favorite resort to walk from town in the cool of the day; there to regale on fruit, admire the orchard and flower garden.

Mrs. Jackson cultivated the garden, raised the vegetables, the fruit and flowers. Her husband scarcely knew what there was growing on the premises. She was a romantic woman, with ideality large; therefore strove to have everything beautiful around her. It was really enchanting to take a botanical review of her roses! such a variety! Oh! the beautiful boquets that were sent to town from her garden! Besides her floral predilections she was a fine singer! Her music to all lovers of that art attracted as many as the flowers. She had an instrument called a seraphina; that in a new settlement attracted as much attention as a grand piano would in an older place. The Col. was a polite gentleman, and they had two pretty little daughters. What heart so stoical as not to admire such a place of resort? I endeavored to imitate the ladies example in the production of flowers, but had not her skill in fruit growing.

[Trip to Los Angeles and San Gabriel Mission]

Oct 21st [1856]. Ann L. and myself took the coach for Los Angelos. We staid at the "half way house" the first night; had supper and breakfast, paid $2.00. The next day we went to Mr. Tompson's at the Monte. A publick house. At the breakfast table I heard a long exposition of Mormonism, from Judge Drummond, a noted Federal official.[4] I looked upon him with indignation! There were several gentlemen at the table and I was not introduced, consequently I did not feel free to reply to his remarks. I thought of the words of Job in his affliction. "My spirit burned within me, and I kept silence even from good words, but it was pain and grief to me." In reply to his slanderous epithets, I could have told him about his leaving his wife in the States and taking a woman from Philadelphia and bringing her with him to S. Lake; there introducing her as his wife. Was soon exposed by a letter written from his lawful wife to a friend in the City.

The following day we pursued our journey to San Gabriel, where was a Catholic church. A huge ancient building. I would judge it might have been standing a hundred years. We visited Mr. Strickton's orchard. It filled me with admiration to gaze upon the immense pear trees loaded with fruit, and such enormous sized pears. I had never beheld till then; having never seen them growing in a climate so congenial to the growth of all kinds of fruit. While in San Gabriel, I attended a Spanish funeral. Such a scene was entirely new to me. The cannons roared a dozen times. Small arms and fire crackers, loud singing and praying. The floor in their Temple was laid with rocks. I kneeled on them for such a length of time that I became very weary. A great many candles were placed around the edge of the coffin, as the large procession paused at every few rods singing and reading prayers. At length they entered the ancient building all falling on their knees. Back of the altar hung the pictures of Christ and the virgin Mary. St. Peter and some others.

Four bells there were belonging to the house, which were rung so often one could scarcely endure the noise. I visited a Mrs. Hall from Mass; her husband Frank Hall a trader in San Gabriel. It seemed pleasant to meet a lady from my native state. I felt at home with her. She was not a member of the Mormon church, neither was she an opposer! She treated my religion with respect; and when I taught her the doctrine of healing the sick by faith, she seemed deeply interested; being subject to frequent ill turns herself. We at length made our way by coach to Los Angelos. We stopt with Mrs. Picket and her two interesting daughters. The lady was formerly the wife of Don Carlos Smith, (the prophet's brother:) who died from exposure when pursued by a mob. She afterwards married a young man, a Mr. Picket.[5]

Mr. P. [Picket] at this time was in San Francisco, in the printing business. Sister P sustained her family by dress making. She was highly esteemed by the people of that City, and largely patronized. By her second husband she had a pair of twin boys. Respectively named Don Carlos, and William. Her youngest daughter Josephine was naturally gifted as a writer of poetry; was unfortunate in her marriage, was separated from her husband which caused her deep affliction. This gave pathos and sublimity to her poems, awakened the tender sensibilities of her nature; she wrote with an inspiration which aroused the sympathies of the publick, they aided her in her endeavors to sustain herself. She improved her education, became a popular teacher; was enabled to help her mother. The eldest daughter married a sheriff, who was killed by desperadoes. Mrs. Picket moved to San Francisco, where her eldest daughter went, to visit, died, and was brought to Los Angelos and buried by the side of her husband.[6]

There were daring deeds done in that county. I passed a house where an old man was robbed of a thousand dollars. The robbers entered his house tied him hand and foot, took his money and left him bound. In that position he remained for a considerable time, untill a neighbor fortunately happened in and liberated the poor man! No clue to the robbers.

Nov. 9th we returned to San Gabriel. Stopt with Mrs. Hall to wait an opportunity to go home. It was decided that A.L. should remain with her for a few weeks and I must go home without her. I reluctantly consented. The following day 10th was my fifty-fourth birthday. Mrs. H. [Hall] thought we should do something to make it memorable. So we resolved to take her new babe only two weeks old, and go on a visit to Mr. Stockton's where the great pear orchard was located.

There was no conveyance at our disposal, so we started out to take our chances. We very soon hailed a Spaniard going after wood. He kindly took us on, and conveyed us safely to the place. We passed a pleasant afternoon. Mr. S. [Stockton] and myself held a discussion on Mormonism; I found him a sensible inteligent man; not prejudiced against our religion. He took Mrs. H. and I home in his carriage at evening; and thus passed my fifty fourth birthday. I was led to review my life, and the scenes through which I had passed, all my sufferings and sorrows. And although they had been many and great, yet I could see how the hand of the Lord had been stretched out over me to preserve my life in times of danger; how my children had been spared to me, and I felt there was more to be thankful for, than to complain of.

I began to prepare to go home and leave my daughter. Mr. and Mrs. Hall were extremely kind, did all in their power to make our stay agreable. The place was settled mostly with eastern and southern people. But oh! the Spaniards were too many, for me to admire the place! I cannot endure them! To see the dark dismal looking beings dressing like the whites, adopting the airs and habits of a superior race, and yet so unlike them. I can look upon the poor Indians with more complacency, because they are unassuming; they make no pretentions to civilized life, I can pity them. From the others I turn with feelings of repugnance!

On the 12th day I left San Gabriel in company with Mrs. Burns, a friend who was going home with me. We came to Thompson's hotel called, Mrs. Lewis was there with several children, one pair of twins. They had just escaped from a fire, the night previous; their house and everything in it was burned.

That unfortunate lady was Mrs. Tompson's daughter. In her infancy she fell in the fire, and was terribly burned. Her face was greatly disfigured, but as she grew up with good nature, and good sense, she was fortunate in marrying a good substantial man. It was indeed a sorrowful sight to see her with such a family and think what a foe fire had been to her! We travelled on by moonlight that night. The Coach driver was a merry fellow and there were other lively gentlemen aboard; so our journey did not seem tedious. We lodged at the "Half way House," reached home at three the ensueing day. I had presents for my little Island boy, and he was delighted to see me come. Ann Louise was left behind, but Mrs. Burns was an intimate friend of my daughter's. An evening party was at once proposed, guests invited, which came off the same evening, to the satisfaction of all concerned.

[Frances' Marriage to Jones Dyer, Mid-November 1856]

Soon after my arrival, a letter came from my daughter in San Francisco, containing inteligence of her marriage! This created suprise and excitement! I could not say I felt pleased, neither did I allow a sensation of displeasure. A solemnity rested on my mind, and I secretly uttered a prayer to my Father in heaven that it might result in the health and happiness of my dear girl! I knew the young man Mr. Jones Dyer, to be an honest industrious person; had a good business character, and a considerable property. She would be separated from me, her father was with her then, but would not long remain. She would be located away from all the family. She wrote a hopeful letter, said she was happier than she ever had been, or ever had expected to be, that her pathway had hitherto "been strewed with thorns;" the future she said "wore a brighter aspect." I restrained my tears, and wrote a cheerful letter to Mrs. Hall, and my daughter in San Gabriel. The weather was unfavorable to a cheerful state of mind, for there was a terrible wind storm!

[William J. Cox]

Wm J. Cox was appointed President over the temporal affairs of that Branch of the Church, in the place of David Seeley, who was removed for convenience, and not for unfitness, as I understood. They were both good men. Bro' C was the man I have mentioned often in my history as being my unvarying benefactor, in the absence of my husband; when cares crowded heavily upon me. In the midst of the great windstorm I have spoken of, I went in to see Sister Cox who also, as well as her husband, was a kind benevolent being, full of sympathy for the sorrowing. A woman in feeble health generally. I found her at that time in a sad plight. Being in an open house, there was no escape from the dust! Sick in bed, the wind blowing at intervals a complete hurricane; her situation seemed truly pitable! But there was no remedial, till the wind ceased. I prayed that the old tornado might stay his fury! I remained an hour, nearly suffocated; then between the gusts, ran to my house; which was not so accessible to dust. I thought any condition preferable to being buried alive!

High winds in that country were frequent, but not often so fearful! Mr. Burns, the lady's husband who came up with me from San Gabriel started just before the storm to come after his wife. The dust blinding himself and team, he lost the road, and had it not been for some horseback men who came to his assistance, would have been in a sorry condition! The country was subject to drouth; consequently we had to resort to irrigation. After a severe gale of wind we might expect a gushing rain, which happened at the time above mentioned, and it proved a blessing to the country, causing the grass to spring, in time to save the stock. About that time I received a letter from Salt Lake, with cheering inteligence. The Saints were rejoicing in the Lord, and praising Him continually.

Shortly after receiving the cheering news from Salt Lake that the Saints were prospering, another letter came from Emeline Rich to T Swartout, giving an account of the terrible sufferings of the Hand Cart companies! Two were still back on the plains, or had perished with cold. Those who had survived and had made the valley had camped without wood to make fires often, a great scarcity of bedding, short of provision, yet they succeeded in reaching the settlement; but as the letter expressed, "the most heartrending sight that ever was seen!" How quickly pain follows pleasure! One day we rejoice, the next we are called to mourn. I was led to reflect what this gospel had cost! What did it cost formerly? Why should it cost less in this our day?

[The Grouards]

On the 28th Nov [1856] Sister Grouard came in from her lonely retreat with her little daughter, where whe had been confined two months, suffering all that a human being could for the want of society. I was happily suprised. Such is her destiny since her husband has become disaffected in the church.

They have turned their attention to spiritualism, but that does not seem to be an anchor to their souls, sure and steadfast; they miss the fellowship of the Saints. The poor woman started home 2 1/2 miles, drawing her little child in a carriage. It seemed lonely to see her go.

[Religious Experiences]

I was at the time every day expecting Ann Louisa home from San Gabriel in the stage. At length word came that she was detained on account of the severe illness of Sister Morse's daughter, who had come on a visit to Mrs. Hall's and was not able to be moved. She had gone from San B. to that village to stay in a friend's family; was a companion of my daughter's, was visiting her, when she was taken violently ill. I went immediately to see Mrs. Morse and inform her, carried the letters I had received, read them to her sons as she was not at home. When she returned, and heard the news, she was greatly alarmed! As soon as possible she made preparations to go to her child. She felt timid about going alone. Her niece Harriet H. consented to go with her, and they started amidst our prayers and blessings, that they might bring back the "sick girl" alive! Word soon reached us that the physician had given her up; they requested that the Saints would pray for her life to be spared. I went to the store, got a bottle of olive oil, with a view of having it consecrated for the special benefit of the afflicted girl. Bro Cox came to my house, with a few others who felt a sympathy for the sorrowing mother, and we united our hearts and voices in prayer. A more fervent petition I never heard than Bro' C. offered up; every word was full of meaning. I felt a witness that the prayers would be answered. The oil was consecrated and sent to them. The young lady had returned who went with the mother, bringing no encouraging word. I wrote to A.L. to come by the next stage if she could be spared, and to sister Morse to be of good cheer, for we were all praying for her daughter's recovery.

Christmas day was drawing nigh, so I made a star to represent the star of Bethlehem. Dec 25th. The aniversary of our Saviors birth, was celebrated, by firing guns and making a noise in the streets; many not even knowing the meaning of the term, Christmas. In the evening I went to a confirmation meeting. Fifty persons were confirmed. Mr Lyman lectured; spoke loudly against the use of whiskey and tobacco. The coach came in but my daughter was not in it. I learned the reason however; the carriage was filled before it reached her place of residence. On the 28th, while at the dinner table a carriage drove to the gate, and behold, Ann Louisa allighted! great was our suprise and joy. She brought the good news that the "sick girl" was mending! rehearsed to us the particulars of her dangerous illness, which was painful to hear; yet we rejoice, believing that our prayers would be answered.

Jan 1st 1857. There was a New year's ball across the street from my dwelling; the music seemed inspiring, but I felt solemn: my husband far from home, I was full of thoughts, trying to immagine what might come to pass that year! I opened the bible to see if a promise would meet my eye, it fell on the 23d psalm. The Lord is my shepherd I shall not want. I felt comforted believing there were blessings in store for me the coming year. The Stage came in and brought news that the "poor girl" was still weak and low; none but those who had faith in the promises of God believed she could recover, but we would not doubt. At the same time the mail came in from Salt Lake and brought me a letter from my old friend Constantia Hutchinson. She complained of sore trials and secret griefs: She is one whose soul is formed for high enjoyments, but fate marked her in early life for a victim of disappointment. She needs the grace of God to sustain her, and I pray, she may have that grace!

Prayer meetings were frequent, and the youth seemed to be awakened to the need of reform. There was a time appointed for the renewal of our covenants; and many of the Saints went to the waters of baptism. I went with my daughters, and fifty others at the same time. It seemed "a time of refreshing from the presence of the Lord." I had been reading of the persecutions of the protestants in France in 1500. I felt to thank my Heavenly Father that we lived under a Republican government; that those fearful times had passed away, and the votaries of religion were more free from danger. On the 8th day a boy came to tell me that one of the young oxen his father had in keeping for me breaking to work was very sick. I went on horseback a mile from town to see him, carried medicine in a bottle. He was one of the most beautiful animals I ever saw. The man had worked him when the weather was too warm. As I gazed on his noble form I said, "every thing lovely in nature must die!"

And so it proved; he being of finer mold than his mate, must die first. The following day there was a tremendoius earthquake! It terrified me exceedingly! While it lasted I could not stand on my feet. I thought the world was turning over! the house appeared to rise a foot from the ground, and swing from east to west. It was several days before the earth was still, and I was constantly in fear of another shock! It affected me something like the rolling of a vessel; as it did several other persons.

Mr. and Mrs. Grouard came into town preparing to go to upper Cal, concluded to leave the eldest daughter with Ellen McG'y. The little island girl was willing to stay. I felt sorry they were not contented to remain with us. The reason was they had changed their views in matters of religion. By the impression of the spirit I said, "it is not a wise move," and thus it proved. Sorrows came upon them, and they were away from sympathizing friends.

At that time the preaching was warmly devoted to the wants of the poor Hand Cart companies. Our sympathies were all excited in their behalf. I never felt a more willing heart to give. Wagons were soon loaded with boxes of clothing and bedding, and taken to Salt Lake.

On the 16th there was another earthquake. Causing one woman to be convulsed, and another complained that her hearing was affected.

The earth shook for one minuete, but it did not affect me as the first did. The earth looked wavy, like the waves of the sea. What convulsions there must be beneath us, and what danger is liable to overtake us at any moment!

The same day Bro' C.C. Rich called; he always had a comforting word for any one. I read to him a copy of a letter I had written to Mr. Pratt; he seemed much pleased with it, said it could not be changed for the better. My mind rested on that subject. I had been fearing, that I had written something I ought not. I then wrote to my daughter F's and explained to her satisfaction, what before she did not fully understand.

In 57 Jan 3th there was a great excitement in the country about Robbers, plundering and murdering! We were alarmed for the safety of our friends in Los Angelos. Mr. Peterson the sheriff at Los A, had been killed. The Dragoons were in pursuit; report said thirty mexicans had been killed by them. The people began to talk loudly about going to Salt Lake. A vigilance committee was organized, several mexicans were hung, near San Gabriel. Every one was excited and telling some new thing. Just then the papers came from Salt Lake all dressed in black! Bro' Jedediah Grant was dead. Two very touching discourses by Pres't Young and Heber C. Kimball were recorded in "Deserett News." Previous to his departure he had an important vision, concerning that world to which he was hastening. Every thing he saw there, was typical of things here, only more etherial, far more beautiful! It was of deep interest to us all. He related his vision, and soon closed his eyes on all earthly scenes.

Brother and Sister Hammond who had been on a mission to the Sandwich Island and returned, had been living more than one year in that place. They were pleasant agreable persons, and we all felt much attached to them. But their faces were set towards the mountains, ever after the earthquake. And the terrible depredations by the robbers in the adjoining counties made them still more anxious to go to the body of the church. She was a dear good woman, and full of sympathy for every troubled heart. When I was unjustly censured by the "cruel woman" I mentioned in a former chapter, she was my soothing friend. She knew I had aimed to do right and when my spirit was wounded by an act of ingratitude, she reminded me I must look for redress; and that I should banish every feeling of ill will towards my enemy.

[The Grouards Leave San Bernardino]

Feb 8th. The last evening before Bro' Grouard's started on their journey to the Upper Cal, they spent at my daughters, Wm McGary's, Mrs Jackson the floral lady, was present. Mr. G. was very silent. There seemed a spell upon us all. We had all been (only a few months before,) on terms of great intimacy, now there was a restraint laid upon us. Our spirits did not harmonize. We felt unwilling to refer to the subject. We all knew the cause of why our friends were leaving; that they had believed in a doctrine which we denied as being the doctrine of Christ; and they believed it was in advance, and several steps in progression. They took a sorrowful leave of us, and we saw them no more. From California they went to Illinois. Death removed some of their treasures; and whether they are happier in their new faith, and more resigned to the events of providence is a matter of great doubt. I cannot believe they are.[7]

CHAPTER SEVENTEEN

San Bernardino III
Memoirs, February 1857 to January 1858

[Personal Experiences, Reflections]

In an adjoining Co, there were horrible things told of the robbers. One, a mexican by birth had his head cut off, carried about and exhibited. I would not sanction such a deed.

The time came to make a garden. I must oversee it, and do what I could. I hired an Indian to spade up my ground. I sewed the seeds and watered it. Mr. Pratt was then in San Francisco, and I could not learn when he intended to come home.

Mrs. Morse at length brought her daughter home in a state of convalesence, to our great joy and thankfulness. She was soon able to come to my house, staid overnight, and slept with me. I had strange feelings! I looked upon her as one raised from the dead! So near death's door had she been. Her face was palid white, and her large blue eyes stood out with such renewed expression! She seemed to feel that she was newly born; and we gazed upon her wasted form, and felt to thank the Lord that she had been redeemed from the grave, to bless her poor mother!

The girls mother was one who had been subjected to great domestick trials. Her husband had turned away from his faith in the fullness of the gospel, broken his covenants, in the church, and had grown cold and hard towards his wife. How cruel it seems when in an advanced period of life, a poor woman has to be chastised and abused by one for whom she has sacrificed every thing even the peace and contentment of her soul. By whom she had stood steadfast through the storms and whirlwinds of her mortal life: faithful and true, in the role of poverty, laboring to sustain herself and children: and who will thank an unloved wife for all this? As I pondered these reflections in my heart the words of the prophet Isaiah came in remembrance. "Behold I have called thee as a woman forsaken

243

and grieved in spirit, and a wife of youth when thou wast refused, saith thy God!" Then the succeeding promise is so comforting. "For a small moment have I forsaken thee, but with great mercies will I gather thee." "In a little wrath I hid my face from thee for a moment, but with everlasting kindness will I have mercy on thee, saith the Lord thy redeemer!" [Isaiah 54:6–8] So when the afflicted woman rehearsed the story of her sorrow, I refered her to the precious promises which had been fulfilled to her in sparing the life of her daughter; and which she realized with a thankful heart:

I had a great amount of hard work to do. The work on the lot was laborious, besides the care of providing for my family. I often felt it was a blessing to be thus employed. I had not so much leisure to dwell upon past scenes in my life, the remembrance of which brought pain to my heart.

It seemed to fall to my lot to console with sisters who had family trials. With regard to these of whom I write the reader might immagine that poligamy was the cause of their afflictions, but it was not. The latter of whom I shall speak, though her husband had another wife besides herself, yet she was the loved one. Her name was the same as the above mentioned, though not a relative. E. Morse's husband was a drunkard; and when in liquor, which was frequent, he would abuse his best friend. She had no hope of his reform, and she wished to leave him with his first family and go to the valley of the mountains. I sympathized with her, and fully approved of her plan. When offering my condolence to others I measurably forgot my own sorrows. I could see in many instances their condition to be worse than mine. For though my husband was invariably gone from me, and seldom sending me any means, yet he was esteemed an honorable man; and not a disgrace to his family.

I had a kitchen built on to my house. Mr. Grouard laid up the walls before he left the place. When I undertook the finishing, the brethren were kind. Bro's Crosby and Mills laid the floor grates. I had friends in that place, and I never knew of but one enemy. A man from the upper country bought sheep in that county, and gave me a hundred weight of wool. Of that I made beds, and felt quite proud of them. My little island boy began to be a little help, I could send him on errands, although he was not as trusty as I could wish. The 6th of March was my daughter Lois' birthday. The 20th aniversary, I reviewed the years of her life, I said, "few have accomplished as much in the time as she has." She had journeyed three thousand miles by land and 7000 by water.

I was continually subject to turns of melancholy, restless and tired of every thing about me. There was something uncongenial to my natural disposition. My companion was always gone from home, and I was required to maintain the character of a married woman. I felt it measurably unjust; but I endeavored faithfully to discharge my duty as father and mother both in one; and those who knew me best all praised me for raising my daughters in a manner to be respected and beloved. I had pleasant society, kind agreable neighbors. With industry and good management I could keep my family above want. My eldest daughters were competent teachers of the common branches, and could do well for themselves. Still they were under my care till after their marriage, and I felt responsible for the course they might pursue.

Daniel Stark's were my intimate friends. I often visited them. They built a fine house in San B. Bro' S was an ingenious carpenter. I was at his house when he was putting on the finishing strokes. I told him I wanted no such house in San B. for I did not intend to remain there always. My face was set towards Zion in the mountains. For there said I, "my friends my kindred dwell, there God my Saviour reigns."

But to return to the subject I left unfinished. I commenced speaking of [Lois] my third daughter's birthday. Besides her lengthy journeyings, she had been a teacher for one year and a half in the islands of the Pacific. Eight months in San Francisco she earned from thirty to fifty dollars pr month. Four years in San B. she had been the main dependence in household matters. She was strong and healthy, and now bids fair to live long on the earth. We made a good dinner for the occasion, fourteen were invited guests.

[Ellen's Baby Emma Francelle]

Two days later which was the 8th of Mar Ellen McGary was delivered of a daughter. My first grandchild. I immediately thought of a name, but I scarcely dared mention it lest the father might not be suited I wished much to have it named our loved and lost one Emma Greville. There was no objection to the first name, the second they prefered to have Francelle. I consented and the child was named at once. Little Ephriam amused us greatly by his expressions showing his ideas of the event. He seemed impressed that an important event had transpired. The father of the child was a tobacco smoker. Ephraim says to him, "you will leave off smoking now, wont you William, now you have got a child?" We all smiled, and thought the father might feel reproved, when a boy only seven years old realized the responsiblility of a man becoming a father. He laughingly answered, "I suppose I ought to."

There was something new for us all to have an infant in the family. Not a particle of clothing had the mother prepared. I had taken the precaution to prepare a suit otherwise we might have had to wrap it in a piece of cloth, as the islanders do their new born. Then there was sewing for all hands to furnish the remarkable child with changes. It was dressed in a "slip" I embroidered for her mother before she was born. My four children had worn it for a first dress, and also for a christening dress at four weeks old. It was a dress any mother might be proud of. Mr. Grevelle came in from over the plains, when the child was only a few days old. When I told how we had named her, he was affected to tears, said he would make the child a present. Emma G. had then been gone one year, and yet her image was continually before me. She was always on my mind when alone. I thought of her sweet looks, and disposition; and could not forbear sometimes exclaiming. Oh! cruel death, how could you lay pros-trate one so lovely!" Why not take away one less beautiful! Then the whole scene passes before me!

Then came letters from our relatives in Canada; they had just received Daguerotyps of Sister Crosby and myself; and many comments were reported as having been made over the pictures. Many years had intervened since they had seen us and they could only say whom we most resembled. I was like my mother, and sister like our second brother. Time they thought had stamped his image heavily upon us. "No doubt we shall think the same when we see them or their portraits." Near this time Orson Whitney came in from the Sandwich Islands. He congratulated Ellen on receiving such a treasure as the infant appeared to be, and her own extraordinary strength and vigor. He made us a short visit, and pur-sued his journey to the mountains. We made daily use of tepid water for ablutions, in treating the mother and child; which proved of signal bene-fit to both.

[Domestic Affairs]

Wm Mc [William McGary] was a man for improvements. Everything about his premises bore marks of taste and neatness. The ground was so productive it was a pleasure to bestow labor upon it. The second year from planting a peach pit, you would begin to have fruit. Although I did not expect to make that a permanent abiding place I felt inspired to make all the improvements in my power. I meant to leave a mark that those who came after me would know some active being had been there.

Mar 18th I dreamed a singular dream. I thought some one showed me a box, and told me there was a serpent shut up in it; bade me beware of it. I heeded not their counsel. I took off the lid and caught the serpent by the head; he ran out his tongue and then bit my hand; but so closely did I hold his head be could not bite to hurt me. I [held] him so awhile then shut him up in the box again. I made my own interpretations to myself.

I toiled in my garden every spare moment I could steal from my new "grand baby." The best indians I ever saw to work are in Cal. They were a great help to me. The same month I dreamed another dream, more sin-gular than the first. I thought I was invited to a feast, where two white

horses were cooked whole, with saddles painted on them and they standing upright on the table, ready to be carved, and served around. I marvelled, and expressed my surprise, I was told their meat was extremely
good. I did not eat of it myself, but saw a company seated at the table. I
wondered what strange thing was about to take place!

There was a disturbance threatening. The disssenters and some outsiders had been jumping land on the Ranch. Mr. Lyman and Rich had
bought the land and given their notes for it. These disorderly men began
to fortify, expecting to be routed; placed cannon near their retrenchment. The rightful owners took no notice of it, let them make what
improvements they chose.

A circumstance transpired in the neighborhood causing great excitement and regret. A mother of five daughters, mostly quite young, was
found intoxicated, and senseless with liquor. It was indeed a most sorrowful sight. The little ones crying, the father not at home. My sister took the
younger children home with her, and kept them till the mother recovered
her senses. She then conversed with her, and asked to know the cause of
her reckless course! Oh she was unhappy, and did not love her husband!

What a futile excuse for a mother to make, for drowning her senses
and ruining her character; when she had a family of good children to set
her affections upon; and a husband kind, even if not so brilliant as she
might desire, he was not an angry man neither a drunkard. I was led to
exclaim, alas, poor human nature!

[Addison Pratt's Return to San Bernardino]

In the afternoon of the 1st day of April [1857] Mr. Pratt came home, after
an absence of one year. His health was good but he did not seem as cheerful as I had hoped to see him. He had been the long voyage to Tahiti, the
french governor would not permit him to visit the adjacent islands. He
could only visit the branch of the church on that Island but dared not
make his preaching at all publick. It was an expensive voyage, and but little accomplished. His family were pleased to see him safe back again, and
he was delighted with his little grand daughter!

He had much to tell us that was new and interesting about the saints
on Tahiti. How rejoiced they were to see his face again, and how they
regretted the restraint laid upon him, in not being permitted to visit the
churches on other islands. Some of the chiefs came to see him and tried
to pursuade him to steal away and go privately with them. But he told
them it would soon be made known and the french would bring him back
and imprison him! Well, said the old chief, what if they do, it will be no
more than the apostles of old had to suffer for the gospel's sake!" A more
daring elder would have gone, but Mr. P. was one of the cautious kind. He

encouraged us that Frances would come on the next stage, that however proved a failure.

Brothers Lyman and Rich were called from head quarters to go on a mission to England! were to take their families and leave them at Salt Lake. The event seemed to inspire us with new desires to go with them; we felt the place would be lonely without them.

Soon after Mr. Pratt's return, a brother Alexander called to see him, he had come from the islands with us, left a native wife there, married a white woman in San B. He had much to inquire about the natives; expressed a desire to be there and live the easy life he once lived. I discover a little something wrong in his spirit, it could not harmonize with mine. It made me feel unhappy. It seemed to me that I carried the church at Tupuai on my heart; and I felt an inexpressible desire for their salvation!

Oh, how grevious it seems to see those who have known the truth, and borne a powerful testimony, been sanguine in the cause; to see them waning away, as if they were tired of serving the Lord, and are ready to ask, "what profit will it be to us to sacrifice so much?" I am ready to believe they have done some misdeed that has grieved the spirit, and driven them into darkness! From such a dilemna I pray to be delivered! Or rather saved from falling there in!

The 6th of Apr. came, and conference commenced. Mr. P. gave an account of his mission, in publick. There was baptizing in the p.m., and I kept the new babe while the father and mother went to renew their covenants in the church; and I felt a spirit to pray earnestly that they might prove faithful while they lived and always honor God and his cause, and pursue a course that will exalt them in His kingdom![1]

[At Home, the Pickets]

It was the 17th aniversary of Ann L's birthday. Preparations were made, company was invited, a great many toasts were drunk, and blessings pronounced, to which we all said amen!

There was another woman came to me to enlist my sympathy; (besides the two I have mentioned in a preceeding chapter) She was an old veteran in the church, almost from the first. Her husband had turned to be a swearing drinking man. She was bound to leave him and go to the church in S.L. She requested me to write a letter to some of the leading sisters of her acquaintance and ask them to unite their prayers, that the way might be opened for her to go! Accordingly I wrote and solicited their sanction, that she should escape from her persecutor, and flee to "the stronghold," in the valley of the mountains. She received encouragement, and went, according to her desire.

On the 9th Apr. The Stage came in from Los Angelos and brought Agnes and Ina Smith, (nieces of the prophet Joseph) but to our great disappointment Frances was not with them! No one knew the cause. Miss Josephine was a player on the guitar, and sang very sweetly. Several musicians called, and the house was full of company. They were very interesting young ladies, attracted attention from all the young people. After the death of their father their mother married a young man by the name of Picket, and located in California.

On the afternoon of the 11th the rebellious party from "Fort Benson," (as they were pleased to call their rendezvous) came into town under arms. It was reported that Mr Sparks had come to take his children from their mother, who was then separated from him by law. But the children were secreted, and after sharp words passing between the parties, they left town. It was counted a trespass against the civil law.

It was a time of great drouth. Oh how earnestly we prayed for rain! The weather was very warm, the earth seemed groaning with thirst! There was quite a sensation created on the arrival of Dr. McIntyre's son, from the upper Country. The Dr.'s were our particular friends, and we were expected to be partakers in their joy; and as was most natural to help entertain their only son a dashing youth who had made his debut for the first time in that City. A party at Mr McGary's was the first introduction. Mrs. McIntyre and her son were invited, and treated with all due attention. The Doctor was not a party going man. Mr. Pratt did not much incline to them, but would sometimes go to be obliging. Mr. Wood, a companion of Mr. Mc was a splendid violinest. The presence of the two young men together with the company of the lady visitors from Los Angelos made quite exciting times.

[Withdrawal of Apostles Rich and Lyman]

To which was added the departure of the Presidency, and a considerable company for Salt Lake Valley. A company was made up to escort them to the Cajone pass, where they were to camp the first night. The visitors in town, my daughters, a number of the citizens, composed the escort. They camped with the traveling company, joined in singing and prayers, wished them God speed, and returned.

It was long before Mr. Pratt could enter fully into the spirit of leading out in managing business, and providing for the family. I had so long been accustomed to cares, that even though they bore heavily upon me, I knew not how to throw them off.

We began by this time to have grapes in abundance, and they seemed a great luxury, and a blessing. So productive was the soil that I felt repaid for all my toil. My pepper trees began to attract notice, being the only nursery of the kind in town. I was proud of my beautiful trees!

There were threatenings of a mob when the company started north, but it all fell through, and the escort returned in fine spirits. The stage Coach agent offered the visiting ladies a free passage home. They had received a missive from their mother where in she complained of feeble health; the eldest daughter, one of the most dutiful girls in the world, resolved to go immediately would not be enticed to stop a day longer, not even for the offer of having a young gentleman to accompany them home. "Duty before pleasure," was her motto. It occasioned quite a disappointment, when the young gentlemen called and found "the singing birds had flown." Every Stage coach that came in we looked for our daughter Frances; her father assuring us it was her intention to come soon after he left. But we looked in vain.

[Ephraim]

I often had great trouble with Ephraim, had to punish him severely for telling lies. It gave me great pain, for I loved the child, and desired above all things to be merciful and forbearing towards him; but I felt it a solemn duty to teach him at any cost to be truthful! It grieved me sorely when any of the family lost patience with him, and would petulantly remark, "There is no prospect of making an honest boy of him." I had hope, and so I struggled on. I thought of the long weary years I had watched my own children, and with prayers and tears had labored to stamp upon their hearts a love for truth, and justice! To teach them to regard others rights as their own. Without a father to aid me, (except at short intervals.) I had brought them to maturity, and they were not likely to disappoint my hopes. I felt assured that I could take a child even of another blood, and by a similar training make him even as my own. A son of my own had been denied me, and I felt I must have one in him! I was the only being who had natural love for the poor boy, and when I saw others show a hard spirit towards him it had the effect to draw him nearer to me. He clove to me with all the ardor of childlike affection that any of my own had ever done. But waywardness was woven in his nature. You could not make him understand that there was any sin in taking fruit from a persons trees without leave, if they had plenty left. "Why," he would say, "They have enough, they'll never miss so few!" I saw plainly that I must be held responsible for the child's nature, for his organization as though I had made him myself. I had nursed him in infancy had taught him to lisp his first words, carried him in my arms as though he had been born my own. Not so with his "father Pratt," he saw but little of him, his own father nothing.

[May Day, 1857]

We were accustomed to make excursions in large companies to City
Creek, six miles from town; where was a beautiful grove of trees, and a
good place to catch fish. On May day in 57, Mr. P. and some others went
on the day preceeding, camped over night to catch fish for the whole
company. Each family provided a variety of cookery, of a most excellent
flavor, which when spread on the ground beneath the shade of the towering oak trees made a delightful appearance! We all seated ourselves on
our blankets while we partook of the luxuries, which had been provided
by many different hands. President Cox gave thanks to our Heavenly
Father, for his signal mercies the past year; in bringing us together again
on a similar occasion, to acknowledge his bounties bestowed upon us;
and that so many of us were still alive to give thanks!

After the ceremonies were over the carriages were arranged in
order with the musick ahead to drive home. As we drove into town the
bystanders raised their hats and made their most humble obeysance,
cheering us and admiring our imposing appearance! There was a grand
ball at night at Mr. Daley's opposite our dwelling. Dr. McIntyre's called,
and we all walked over to see the party. A splendid supper was set, everything in high toned order.

On the 6th the two young men Wood and McIntyre called to take
leave of us and to express their extreme satisfaction in regard to their stay
with us, and promised another visit in the fall. They went away cheerful,
with their hats trimmed with flowers; said they should preserve them till
they reached their home near Sacramento. William McGary took leave of
his family, and went with them with a view to get business more lucrative
than could be obtained about home. We were sorry to see him go.

[Visitors and Visiting]

The departure of the three merry hearted men, made a great breach in
our social circles. The vacancy was partly filled by the arrival of Mrs. Hall
from San Gabriel: with a beautiful little boy, named Obed; and a Spanish
servant girl, to wait on him. Mrs. H. had never been in the place before,
and we had enough to do to escort her about to see the wonderful
improvements that had been made on that "Stock Ranch," in so short a
time! She admired every thing. We felt paid for presenting scenes to her,
she had so just an appreciation of every thing in nature, and art.

Mr. Worden a very scholarly gentleman, had been teaching a writing school; he closed, and Ann Louisa got the premium! We had not
expected A.L. would win the prize for being the best writer. It was not

awarded for the perfect style of writing alone, but for the entire neatness of the book; not a blot had been found. The prize was a beautiful picture! So her friends were all pleased.

Mrs. H. had her own carriage, and we rode over the Ranch. At Mrs. Jacksons the floral lady's retreat, she was more than delighted. The whole botanical realm seemed spread out before her, and called forth her loudest admiration! Sabaath day dawned and we took her to the house of worship. Capt. Hunt held forth in his usual style; not refined, or systematical, but appropriate and very energetick. The lady found no fault with our preaching although she was not of our faith. After the services were ended, we took a ride to another beautiful flower garden! A family by the name of Dodge, from Boston Mass.

They lived in a low small cottage, neatly whitened outside, and almost hidden from view by the tall shrubbery and fruit trees. Then the flowers in such variety, and abundance! The people were not at home, but as we could not afford to lose our trouble in going there, we gathered each a boquet, and thanked them for the same. We felt as little Ephraim did when he took fruit without leave, "they had enough left." On the 12th the carriage was brought to our door for us to ride. The horse tied by the reins to a shade tree. He pulled backwards, till by some process the box was hauled over the tree, and broke off all the large branches; yet the carriage was not broken. We rode over a rough road to a friend's house. Every bridge and mud hole, Mrs. H. would tremble with fear; and entreat us to let her get out and walk over.

Again as we were riding out when more than a mile from home, the tyre run off one wheel unobserved, till we had gone a considerable distance even till two spokes were broken and the fellies were scattered in the road. Mrs. H. at this accident was much excited! Mr. P. had stopt behind, and sent the ladies ahead to be their own teamster. There was no alternative but for us to leave the horse and broken carriage and walk back. This we did carrying the "little ones" till we met Mr. P. (hastening on to overtake us) and informed him of the disaster; at which he smiled aloud, and remarked, "it might have been worse," counseled us to walk on, and he would bring up the rear with the horse and carriage. The following day found us exploring for wheelrights and blacksmith's; to get repairs made as soon as possible, that the lady might be on the move towards home, before another accident would occur.

The carriage was at length repaired, Ellen concluded to accompany Mrs. Hall to her home; a gentleman engaged to drive, and they started in fine spirits. After they left us we felt lonely, so we visited Mrs. McIntyre; to offer our condolence in that her only son who made her home so cheerful while he staid, and who was the idol of her heart, had gone back to his home in Upper Cal, and we all felt the loss of his company. Mrs. Mc was a remarkably cheerful woman, when things went well with her; and she even had the tact of concealing a breaking heart beneath a smiling countenance. The Dr. her husband, was a low spirited complaining man, who really felt the need of more sympathy than is generally bestowed on one of that type.

A few days passed and I received a letter from Ellen and Mrs. Hall, containing an account of their journey to San Gabriel. Little "Obed" had cried terribly! Mrs. H. had been sick on the way, but they arrived safely; sent a pressing invitation for me to come in the next stage. I felt not so much inclined to go, as I had cares at home that seemed to tie me there. Mr. P. from having been from home so many years had out grown the practice of bearing the burden of providing for the family. We were accustomed to having a great number of visiting people at the house; often to spend several days; there was a necessity for a frugal manager to keep supplies on hand and see that the table though not furnished luxuriously, was at least respectable. I however after counselling with my family concluded to go.

Accordingly on the 10th June I left San B. in the stage for San G'l arrived safely the 12th found Ellen and her babe at Mrs. Hall's well, the latter very sick, or rather with a hard cough which seemed threatening. We sweat her with sage teas put bottles of warm water in her bed which relieved her. The stage came in from Los Angelos and Mrs. Picket was aboard going to San Bernardino, and Oh, we wished so much to go with her! but we were not ready, and did not like to leave our friend in her low condition; so we promised if possible to go the next train. Accordingly we took leave of the family where we had been kindly entertained and went on the way to Thompson's Hotel, to await the arrival of the Coach; but when it came in it was loaded to the brim! and though great were our entreaties, we could not be taken! We were sadly disappointed, but made the best we could of it. Mr. Hall hearing we were detained, sent his carriage for us to return to San G'l.

Mr. Hall was one of the most faithful men in the world, to a wife! No mother could be more attentive to an infant in sickness, than he was to his wife. I formed a resolution at once to make an effort to have something effectual done for her recovery. Being a great believer in the cold water practice, I immediately resorted to that: praying earnestly that the means used might be blessed. As the lady was weak from her long illness, we took the chill from the water, making it about blood warm, at the first; bathed her in a large tub. I never in my life saw any thing have a more visable effect. She began to mend immediately. We followed the application for three days and had the pleasure of seeing our friend decidely improved. On the 17th the coach came in without passengers, and we had everything in readiness to go.

I had almost forgotten to mention how much we were amused with the two children. Mrs. Hall's little "Obed Nye" was a perfect beauty; past one year with the exception of my deceased, darling Emma Grinelle, he was the most brilliant and attractive. Ellen's little girl Emma Francelle, nearly the same age, was almost his equal; and what interested us so very much, was their attachment to each other. The delight they would manifest when brought in contact, was the common subject of remark. We considered it an omen, that in some sphere, either in this world or another their fates would be linked together. We reached home in safety, found all right, with one exception; the weeds had overrun my garden. I had lost time, but felt not to regret it, as I was assured I had done good to my poor friend. So I set about clearing my garden, and soon saw a commendable improvement.

[The Marriage of Lois to John Hunt]

Sabbath, June 28th [1857], as I was sitting alone in my room, Mr. John Hunt called, and asked my consent to marry my daughter Lois. It was a shock to me though I had reason to expect it. How thought I can I give up my main dependence. Lois had been a faithful daughter to her parents, and I knew how much she would be missed in the family. But as I believed the young man was honorable and true hearted and that he was her choice, I could not refuse. Preparations were immediately made for the wedding, which was to take place on the Fourth of July. Some "unpleasantries" transpired in the intervening time, though trifling in their nature served to grieve Lois, and spoiled all the enjoyment for myself; proving the old proverb true, "The little foxes spoil the vines." Something touched my sensibilities and I felt my spirit fall. I went to Sister Cox's and spent a few hours, felt a little relieved. Bro and Sister C were both so filled with love and sympathy. There was something soothing in their voices and words; they were like the rays of sunshine in a cold and stormy day.

On the memorable Fourth the people assembled early at the Bowery. Every thing looked cheerful. The tables groaned with luxuries, a great many toasts and speeches, cheers succeeded and dancing brought up the rear. What I enjoyed was, walking about, and saluting old friends. The exercises closed at five and we returned home and Lois was married in the evening. The house was crowded with guests, more than could be seated. Lois chose her father to perform the ceremony, but at the instant required he was attacked with pleurisy! so violently, he was not able to stand. Pres't Cox took his place. There was one blunder made. Ann L. was in her room finishing her dressing, expecting to be called in time, but was forgotten! We were all very sorry about the mistake, as she should by right have been brides' maid; but the groom's sister being older, and her intended present, the honor was confered on them. Ann L. seemed grieved and displeased; did not recover her usual cheerfulness the whole evening. There was a grand supper across the street, at the young man's sister's; everything in the best style. Lois' father was not able to attend. I could only go in for a short time, as he needed my attentions every moment, so severe were his pains. Bro' and Sister McIntyre spent the evening with us, which made the time more endurable. It was sad, when contrasted with what should have been. The scene closed, and I realized that I had but one girl left; to help bear my burdens, and to be my companion when her father went from home. She then seemed doubly dear to me.

[Women's Natural Rights]

At that time a new book was advertised, entitled "Mary Lynden." I was soon in possession of it, and it seemed written expressly for me. I drank into the spirit of the author, who by intuitive perception saw a brighter future dawning for woman! Wherein she would be permitted to live a higher and a purer life; and be the owner and controller of her own person; understand the laws of her being, and be protected in her natural rights; never compelled to violate the best affections of her heart, for the sake of conformity to a false custom. The author professed to have written a true life, both private and publick. How few have done that! I had female friends who had secret sorrows, and who often came to me for sympathy; to them I read in my new book, and they felt inspired to hope for a happy future wherein children would be born pure; which the gospel also promised us, and it made our hearts rejoice!

We rejoiced that woman dared to speak in defence of her sex; to utter sentiments pure as breezes from the world where sin cannot enter, bidding us hope for the day when men and women would know the laws that should govern their lives and be constrained to abide those laws, that they may give life to pure and holy beings: "Sons and daughters of an everlasting redemption!" How many females have suffered martyrdom to pure and holy desires! Their best and holiest affections have been crucified! We glorify our Father in Heaven that he has set his hand to redeem us in these "Last Days". That light has come to the world and we have been the happy partakers! Woe to those who reject that light! and greater woe to those who having acknowledged and accepted, turn, and trample it under their feet! From such men let innocent women be delivered!

From hence forth I live devoted to reform, in the social condition of my poor unfortunate sisters of humanity! My three daughters were often together with me, and we mourned for the absent one, who did not come as we had expected.

[Troubles Abroad and at Home]

Just at that time the sorrowful news reached us that bro' Parley P. Pratt had been assassinated by the hand of an enemy![2] We met in groups and mingled our sympathies for the church and his families in Salt Lake City. A mighty champion in the cause of truth had fallen! We talked of how much he had preached and written! How many hearts had been made to rejoice at the sound of his voice, souls redeemed, which had it not been for his indefatigable labors, might have remained in darkness forever.

We rejoiced that though gone from our sight he yet lived in his writings! which would be glad tidings of great joy to many honest hearts, seeking after truth! We believed a happy reception met him in the spirit land; and we exclaimed, "peace be to his memory forever!" I read his jubilee song and reflected on what a vast amount of labor he performed in fifty years; both mental and manual. He was impressed that a season of rest awaited him; in his song he bids a thankless world farewell, and said he should labor no more abroad: now he has gone to have a great jubilee, with the martyred prophet, and all the faithful saints who went before him!

On the 12th of August I was sick with a fever. Likewise Ellen had an attack near the same time. Immediately we resorted to the pack sheet, and cold baths; a most effectual remedy for a fever. In two days the fever was broken.

While I was quite weak a letter came to me from my husband's sister in N. Hampshire, couched in bitter terms against our "leaders," and the doctrines taught by them. Even rejoicing at the death of Parley P. and justifying his murderer! The letter was calculated to wound me, but I knew it was her ignorance and the natural enmity of the human heart towards the things of God; and I would not allow reply; that was, to remind her that the same spirit crucified the Saviour, and put to death the apostles and holy men of old; that we should be cautious about condeming any thing we did not fully understand. After some reasoning, her spirit softened a little.

The weather was excessively warm; the heat sometimes seemed too intolerable to be endured! Mr. Pratt was never at a loss for amusement. Although generally employed at his trade, when at home he invariably found time to go on all the hunting excursions. To hunt bear, deer, turkey, ducks, any kind of game. I could never rejoice in taking life. If a squirrel is on a tree, and I see him skipping from branch to branch, although I know his flesh is good for food, I do not wish him molested. I choose to let him enjoy his liberty, and I will dine on vegtables, without meat. We had human life in all its varied forms and features; plenty smiled around us, we had beautiful fruit.

A brother Haskins came from Salt Lake, a great singer of songs! Songs of a most amusing character. Many pleasant evenings were passed in his company. He called his songs "the songs of Zion!" although many of them were comical.

Pres'ts Lyman and Rich were gone; the place was lonely without them. I had a sister living near me; she generally had a cheerful spirit; viewed the hand of the Lord in whatever took place. I could say with the psalmist. "Mixture of joy and sorrow I dayly do pass through." When for a few days things moved on smoothly, and I felt that heaven was smiling upon us, then some poor friend would want my condolence; some unhappy scene had transpired; a beloved perhaps an only child would be snatched away and Oh! no sorrow wax ever like theirs! Then I must weep and pity! Go with them to see their treasure deposited in the silent grave: pause to read the inscription on my dear Emma's headboard; feel for days like a being walking among the tombs! Then again the sunshine of peace would come into my heart.

Aug 21st mail came in brought letters from Frances P. Dyer, and Wm McGary. An urgent request for Ellen to go to upper Cal. to join her husband. I could not by any pursuasion consent to have her go. She would not have courage to go alone with her child; her father would be constrained to go with her. The money was sent to bear her expenses, but I could not endure the thought that she must leave me and take the dear child from my sight! I felt that I had no treasure to part with; it was all I knew how to do to make life bearable with what I had. I wished to encourage William, but he had a good home there, could do well in San B, and it would be so much happier for us all. Mr. Dyer owned a house and 25 acres of land on that Ranch. The house furnished with every necessary article, yet he had gone and left it, because he could get more lucrative business in San Francisco, and the region round about.

They requested their furniture sold, and the money sent them. I took the responsibility on myself, and disposed of it to their satisfaction. The house was left long without an occupant, the indians had broken in, carried off what they wanted and damaged the furniture. I often passed the dwelling, and wondered why people cannot be satisfied to do well; without that restless desire of doing better! I often went to visit my eldest daughter whose husband was absent and desired her to come to him; but the more I was with the child, I felt devoted to her more ardently! I would look into her bright blue eyes, listen to her happy noise as she caroled when I went to the house, and felt that all the gold in California would not tempt me to part with her!

I had two daughters to visit. Lois' home seemed rather pleasant, her husband's sister Harriet H. boarded with her, a very interesting young lady; which made the time pass more cheerfully, as Mr. Hunt carried the mail to S. Lake and was gone much from home. His mother was my friend, a woman full of faith and good works. We often held sweet communion and walked to the House of God in company.

Oct 2nd Lewis Newel came in from Salt Lake brought letters from my old friend C. Hutchinson.[3] She entreated us to come up to the mountains, and be gathered with the Saints; that fearful things were anticipated; our enemies were laying plots for our overthrow![4]

The same messenger brought news of the terrible calamity that befel an emigrant company coming on their way to Cal. A band of Indians had pursued after them, massacred the whole company! The news caused a terrible excitement![5] Unbelievers began at once to blaze about, that the indians had "Mormon allies;" and a few began to be vindictive towards the saints in that country; as though they could be confederate when hundreds of miles from the scene! On the 6th Oct. at the time of our Conference Bro' Wm Mathews just in from settlements, gave us a full account of the horrible deed; perpetrated by the Indians, according to the best of his knowledge. If he believed they had "white allies," he was careful to conceal it. Had he intimated suspicion of that nature, our indignation would have known no bounds!

In the midst of our horror and astonishment, Wm McGary returned from Upper Cal; and our minds were a little diverted from reflecting on the unhappy circumstance. Wm having learned that his wife inclined to stay at her own home, made a speedy return.

He appeared happy and satisfied; pleased with the improvement of his little daughter, who had gained suprizingly in size, wit, and beauty, in his five months absence. The fruit and shade trees had grown so much; he was delighted with every thing, and thought in future he should appreciate home.

Then came Sisters Cannon and Sargeants from San Francisco bound for Salt Lake. The latter I had heard of for twelve years, but never saw till then. She sail'd from New Bedford, with her former husband Mr. Lincoln, on the ship *Timoleon*, with Mr. Pratt on his first voyage to Tahiti. Mr. L died returning to the coast of Cal; was brought into San Francisco for burial. His widow married Mr. Sargeants; who being an unbeliever in our faith was not disposed to go to S. Lake. Next landed a vessel at San Pedro, from Australia; with a large company of Saints to join our ranks.

[The Utah War and the Call: "Liberty to Act Free"]

The general topic of conversation was, of events which seemed presaging in those days. One and another prophesied, that we should all be called to leave that place before a year passed away. The Australian brethren had lively faith; they made our meetings spirited and interesting. Elders were in the company whom I had known in Nauvoo; and had not seen their faces for twelve years. Old memories were revived!

The publick prints began to team with slanderous reports about the church at S. Lake, which annoyed us to hear, although we believed every statement false! There were whisperings of impending ills; some were troubled, others felt secure, trusting wholy in a divine providence which had so many times delivered from danger and death! To be in suspense, and feel unsettled, is terrible, to one who has not a firm trust in the great Deliverer![6]

The 1st day of Nov. two elders from Australia preached to the people. Their discourses were comforting and instructive; filling our minds with animated hope. At the close, a stranger, calling himself Potter Christ arose, called on the people to listen; proclaimed he was the "Ancient of Days!" Said he was immortalized; had passed from death into life; that he should no more taste death. He further said, in sixty one he would lead the elect back to Jackson County, Missouri, and build the Temple there; then the tares and wheat would be separated. The people listened to him for a short time, and then turned away; believing him to be insane. He succeeded in getting a very few to believe on him, and soon left the place.

[The Breakup of San Bernardino]

People began now to advertise their places for sale. The prevailing spirit was, "sell out and go to the vallies of the mountains." I looked over my beautiful place, and thought of the hard labor of body and mind it had cost me! How in the darkness of night when all eyes in my dwelling were closed in peaceful slumber, I had gone out alone to water my trees! Now they were just beginning to reward me with luscious fruit, and cooling shades!

Must I go and leave them! There was no compulsion, every one was at liberty to act free; either to go or stay. I felt my heart bound with cords of love to the church! With the Saints I must go! The organization would be broken up, there would be a community of strangers. My heart was filled with tossings and sleep departed from me! I could have borne all cheerfully, had my husband felt valiant and brave. A spirit of melancholy seized upon him, which bowed him to the earth! I was compelled to assume a cheerful courageous appearance to comfort and sustain him; which I tried to do, when my heart felt like a withered leaf![7]

There was continual excitement throughout the entire settlement. Trouble was anticipated at head quarters. The counsel was for the scattered branches to gather in. Report said, government was plotting against us; what our destiny would be was not clearly shown, but we knew, that no weapon formed against us would prosper, however much we might have to suffer for the cause of Christ. I was not alone in my troubles, others there were who needed sympathy and encouragement. Sister McIntyre's heart was divided between her husband and only child. The former bound to go with the church; the latter owning a Ranch in the vicinity of Sacramento, could not leave without great sacrifice. She seemed between two fires! duty inclined her one way, parental affection the other. Such was the state of her mind she could be no comfort to me.

My children would all go but the one in San Francisco; and when she heard we were going, her grief knew no bounds! Her husband though a member of the church, did not realize the necessity of going at a sacrifice. It was rumoured that Buchanan would send an army to Utah to extirminate or drive the people from the Territory; that they would explore till they found a hiding place; even the "secret chambers" which the prophet alludes to: or would they stand their ground, resist their enemies, and depend on the Lord to fight their battles? Mr. Pratt was a warm, patriot. He could not sanction for a moment any thing like rebellion against a "republican government!" But where was the boasted liberty, if we must forever be harrassed on account of our religion? The sorrow on his mind deepened, till at length be declared his intention to send his family and remain behind.

Entreaties were vain; he forbade our pursuasions. He would go to San Francisco; encourage Mr. Dyer to come with him and bring our daughter the ensueing year. He would not ask us to go with him as he was not fully convinced that it would result in the best good for us all. I then commenced my entreaties that he would keep the place in his possession, and fit us out with the other property; let us go with the relief teams sent from Utah to help the people. To that he would not consent; as he wished to go from the place, and hold no interest there, when the present inhabitants were removed. The house and two lots, had cost us sixteen hundred dollars. $1600. Six hundred was all we could get offered for it. That was better sold than many places, even at that low price I could think of nothing but a great shipwreck at sea! To see the beautiful furniture packed on to old Spanish carts, sold for a mere song, freighted off by those uncomely beings who had no use for such things, in their old homely dwellings. Oh that oblivion might forever cover that scene! As Job prayed that the day of his birth might be blotted from remembrance, so have I prayed that the trying scenes of that disolution of an organized body of honest industrious citizens, who had made themselves happy homes by hard labor and economy, might be succeeded by something so great and glorious, that memory would deny it a record in her archives! And if the blame is found to rest with a threatening Legislature, let them pay the debt; and it will be a heavy one! Mr. McIntyre came from the Upper Country to help his father and mother prepare for their journey across the desert. He prevailed on his mother to go home with him, and wait till he could settle his business and go with her. He had become the suitor of my daughter Ann L.

PART FOUR

On Pioneer Living in Beaver

Beaver, Utah Territory
1858 to 1880

Jonathan Crosby

Alma Crosby

CHAPTER EIGHTEEN

Fateful Move
San Bernardino to Beaver, Utah

Memoirs, January 1858 to January 1859

[For the hundreds of Saints now leaving San Bernardino, the break-up was a crisis of major magnitude. Families sacrificed years of hard labor and money invested in homes and fields and turned their backs on their dreams of the good life in California, ready to begin all over again, to build new homes and villages, to reclaim the desert. There had been forced moves before; here was repeated the whole-sale disruption of life and the creation of tragic situations for hundreds of families. For the Addison Pratt family the consequences were great. The Big Move marked the end of the Pratts' unity and family life. Louisa and Addison separated: he remained; she and her family traveled Zionward.]

[The Separation of Louisa and Addison]

A great company started; a hundred teams, all strong and reliable. It was a grand sight; all white covered large wagons. Another company was ready, not so large; in that my two married daughters were to go.[1] I was not ready. There was a tremendous mountain to pass over [Cajon Pass]; on the other side was a camping ground, good feed for animals: the latter company were to remain there to recruit their teams, and till I should overtake them.[2] They took my sacks of flour, sugar, and heavy arti-cles to lighten my load over the steep mountain. Bro's McIntyre and Pratt were to accompany us till we came to the camp; see us safely started and return to San B. Accordingly we set forward at the appointed time, took a last lingering look at the dear old place; traveled on with a carriage, and loaded wagon, with two yoke of oxen. There were a few other teams, by the help of which we ascended the mountain. We traveled on, came to the camping ground, but behold the company had gone![3]

Astonishment, and consternation seized upon us! What did it mean? Another small company were camped near the place, they had heard by a messenger that the company were annoyed by Indians, who commenced driving off stock; the Capt would not wait another day; it was not safe for one or two teams to remain alone, and my daughters were compelled to go and leave me. Even little Ephraim had started with Ellen, expecting us to overtake him. Ann L. cried with grief and anger! Her father was obliged to go back, he had brought nothing with him for the journey; husband and lover must leave us to encounter the endangers of passing through an Indian country. Mr. P. committed us to the care of Capt Tinny; a good man, had a small company of poor slow teams.

We had a good teamster, kind and obliging, but terribly afraid of Indians! The parting scene was over; a promise that the next year we should see them in the mountains; we were conscious of an uncertainty, and our hearts were too sad to hope for anything. The old slow company started; scarcely one family with whom we had been acquainted. There was one, a sister Taylor from Austrailia, a widow, who had seen great sorrow; a grown son was with her; was dissatisfied and determined to go back; she had left one in Australia. She had three daughters, two had gone ahead with the first company. So our families were separated and we communed together, and talked of all that had befallen us, and of the goodness and mercy of God who had brought us safely through many dangers. For days we walked and wept as we crossed the barren desert; think of the loved one behind us, and of those who had gone before.

Often as we let fall our tears by the way side I thought of the promises of the Lord to the poor Israelites, through the prophet. "With weeping and with supplication will I lead them, for I am a father to Israel and Ephraim is my first born!" We understood the meaning, of Ephraim being called the first born. Ann L's eyes were seldom dry, till we overtook those who had gone and left us.

[At Las Vegas]

When we reached the Los Vagus we found Ellen and Sister Crosby, with their families, camped in the old Fort, waiting with the Indian missionaries for us to come along.[4] Ephraim had been watching for days on the walls, for us, his joy was great when he saw the team drive in, and knew to whom it belonged. Seventeen wagons were crowded into the old Fort. The mountain Indians were likely to steal the cattle any hour, if they were not closely guarded. Those immediately under the care of the missionaries were a little more honest and civilized.

We felt our hearts revive a little, when we had overtaken our friends; still the remembrance of the bitter cup we had been forced to drink, in leaving those behind who should have come with us, at times pained us severely! Often times before leaving San B. when it was decided what my fate was to be, when sleep departed from me, I would arise at midnight, walk about my house, and repeat the words of the poor Saviour in the garden of Gethsamane! "Father, if it be possible let this cup pass from me." With the next breath I was compelled to repeat, "nevertheless, not my will but thine be done." I had undertaken to drink from the cup held out to me, and however bitter, I must not let my courage fail, till I had drained it to the dregs.

Untill we reached the Los Vagus we had no organization of our company, no chaplain appointed, no prayers at night or morning! All the anxiety was to watch the indians, and guard the stock. I never so thirsted, and longed to hear prayers!

At the Vagus we found father Wade; who had come from the settlements to the lead mines.[5] The first night we had a meeting in the Fort. The old veteran arose with such dignity and assurance; prayed for the poor travelers through an indian country; it seemed to me that I heard a voice from heaven, speaking peace and comfort to my soul! He said when we went on our way, we must have order; call on the Lord for his protecting care, and every day return him our thanks. We all knew it was the right way, and said amen, to every sentence. The brethren were faithful in guarding at night, till at length they laid down and left no one up to watch. The mountain Indians on the alert drove off one of brother Crosby's best oxen; slaughtered it, and in the morning when they went out to drive in the stock, they found him roasted and half devoured!

The owner realized the scripture injunction: watch and pray. He was fortunate in being supplied with another ox to fill his place. We were all waiting there to recruit the teams; and if we had gone straight forward on our journey, we might have saved many valuable things which the Indians took from us at night. They would cut holes through the covers of the wagons, take out whatever they could lay their hands on, and the sleepers would know nothing of it till morning.

[From Las Vegas to the Muddy]

Tired of watching and waiting, I determined to go on; and not wait for the main company who were expecting relief teams from the settlements. Accordingly my teamster Mr. Coal, and Wm McGary my son in law resolved to start. We took a friendly indian with us for a pilot, entered on a seventy miles desert! It was a fearful undertaking, but we thought anything better than staying in that old Fort, and having our goods stolen. Bro' Crosby had gone ahead of us in company with a missionary. So with our two lone teams we wended our way across the great desert, till we made the old "muddy river!"[6]

The greater part of the indians had gone on a hunting tour. There were only a few, and they seemed friendly. The men thought they might venture to trust the cattle for a few moments while they ate their suppers; which they did in great haste; but it was time sufficient for the red men to drive off two of the best oxen! Nothing could be found of them; the chief feigned ignorance he knew nothing. I never saw two men more excited, but they were not brave enough to follow the tracks into the canyons; though they had pistols and ammunition; myself and two daughters would have staid by the wagons undaunted, but they had not courage to venture. That was the most horrible night I ever spent in my whole life! We were not afraid of being killed, but of losing the other cattle, and being robbed of our provisions.

The cattle were brought and tied to the wagon wheels, and a double watch set over them. Not one moment did we turn our eyes from them the whole night. Our teamster walked to and fro, apparently under the deepest excitement! A more severe windstorm I never knew. It was all we could do to keep the covers on our wagons. We prayed for daylight to dawn upon us! Even then, what should we do for sufficient team to haul the goods. We gathered flags to feed the animals, and started very early. The indians followed us for several miles, begging for food; we gave what we could spare and told them to go back. The good friendly fellow who came with us from the Vagus continued with us, showing signs of real sorrow because we had lost our animals. One giant ox whose mate had been stolen, had to wear a short yoke, and pull alone; it made us feel sad to look upon him.

[From the Muddy to the Santa Clara]

We dragged a few miles the first day, through deep sand; walking the most of the way. The dear baby would stand at the side door, crowing and playing as though nothing had happened. Night overtook us at the foot of an exceeding high mountain. We knew our teams could not haul the loads over it. So by a pale lantern light we dug a vault in the road, took out all our heavy articles, stove, books and dishes, cached them there. As the dirt fell on the boxes we felt solemn; for we feared every moment the Indians from the mountains might see our light and come upon us. We told our red friend he must not tell the piutes where we had buried our things; "no, he would not, they were "Catch wino!" We fed the cattle and watched them till morning; then carred many articles up by hand, put all the cattle on one wagon, hauled it up quite easily; went back for the other; and when on the summit, saw two men, with teams, coming!

They were brethren from Sante Clarra,[7] going to the lead mines. At the sight of them our driver fired his pistol, and shouted, "Glory to God!" They came up, and we ate and drank with them. Bro' Hamlin then wrote a letter to Bishop Crosby at Sante Clarra, and sent our red friend, whose name was Amasa to cary it. He told us to give him a little food to last him on the way, that if he had much, he would not go so fast. It was seventy miles. He started on the run, went like a mule till he was out of sight. In the meantime we dragged ourselves along wading through deep sand, putting all the team on one wagon, drive a few miles, and go back for the other. At length we reached the summit of the Rio Virgin Hill.[8] While on a small desert five miles from the river, our water gave out. A young Indian came to us; we told him we had no water, he made signs that we should give him a bucket, and he would go to the Virgin and bring some to us; left his bow and arrows for security.

Away he went bounding like a deer! In a short time he returned with the water. We praised him, gave him food; and he staid with us till we came to the hill top; where a friend came and helped us down, with a team. There we camped, to wait for the company behind to overtake us. A small tribe of Indians lived near. The chief whose name was Isaac, was friendly to our people. He came to see us, and we told what troubles we had met on the way, that our provisions were scanty. He pitied us, and staid by us over night, to keep the indians from begging and stealing from us. While there a beautiful little ox, whose mate was stolen at the Muddy, died from exhaustion. Oh, how it grieved me to see the savage creatures tear him in pieces!

The faithful boy we sent with the letter never stopt to sleep till he reached bishop Crosby's, presented the petition, that he would send a team to meet us, and some flour, to last us to the settlements. Accordingly the bishop's son came back with the boy, with team and flour; found us camped on the Rio Virgin under the protection of Isaac the chief. Amasa felt that he was of some consequence; he walked about the place, after we had dressed him in shirt hat and pants; thought he must eat with us, after having done so good a deed. He went back with the man and helped take the things from the cache, all safe. The camp behind came up and we started on our way again. We urged the good boy to keep with us; which he would gladly have done, but the Piutes, and Utes were at variance, and he was afraid the Utes would kill him. The company let us have an ox to help out our team, and we went on to Pinto Creek. We were sorry to leave the good faithful boy!

[Pinto Creek and Mountain Meadows]

Our son in law J. Hunt, having made the settlements and hearing of our misfortunes, came back and met us at Pinto C'k. At that point our ears were pained at the rehearsal of the awful massacre! Indeed, we had passed over the ground, counted 50 sculls, which the wolves had dug up from their burial, where they had been lightly covered with earth. My daughter, in walking over the ground picked up a gold watch; which she keeps to this day. We made our way along till we came to a camping ground on Shirts Creek; there was mother Hunt, and my daughter Lois. It was the 8th of April 58. We encountered a severe snow storm. I had not set my feet on snow for eight years. We were camped in wagons. There was one little log cabbin, with a fireplace, into that thirty persons crowded to warm by the fire.

[Granddaughter Ida Frances Born to Lois]

There my daughter Lois gave birth to her first child.[9] No Dr. or midwife; but mother Hunt with energy equal to any emergency officiated and it proved a happy deliverance! A beautiful daughter was born! Born by the high way side, in a loaded wagon, not as roomy as a "manger!" Long, long, to be remembered, will be that birth place! We were twelve miles from Cedar city. Six from Hamilton's Fort. To the latter my daughter was moved as soon as she was able; and there she was made comfortable.

[Cedar City]

I went to Cedar City and rented a house.[10] It was lovely; myself, daughter, and the little Island boy, were alone; yet I did not feel like a stranger. We found kind neighbors; brothers and sisters in the gospel. Six miles north my sister C. lived. Six south my daughter Lois; eighteen north my eldest Ellen McGary. It would have been more pleasant could we have all been located in the same place, but it was nearly impossible to find a vacant house.

　　The people in Cedar had built a new town, close to the brow of the mountains. Having been troubled with floods thought best to build on higher land. Their buildings were adobies, some very high and nicely finished. In removing they had taken out the wood work, and left the walls standing. It looked so doleful to see so much labor wasted. Two storied walls nicely laid up with lime mortar all left to go to ruin, to me it looked sinful. I could not account for it. When I inquired, the answer was, they were counselled to move the town; it was easier to make new dobies than to take down the old walls. Then the loss of their beautiful shade trees, grown so exceedingly high; I could never cease thinking of the waste of labor! Here and there a lone family remained. A Potter by the name of Moore lived half way between the old and new town.

Isaac Haight was the President, a very agreable family, he had.[11] Mrs. Moore an English lady was my companion from the first; she treated us with respect and attention. Ann L. did not incline to make new acquaintances. She chose retirement. When she would go to visit her sisters, spend a week, then I was left lonely; no one but my little Ephraim, to keep me company. Sometimes in spite of prayer and faith, I would fall into severe fits of despondency. I felt that I was cast alone on the tempestuous sea of life; running against a current that rolled mountains high! Struggling at every pore to stem the overwhelming torrent! Almost on the point of giving up and letting my bark go down amidst the waves! Then again I would rally, lay hold with fresh courage, and say, I will fight the battle of life, and come off conqueror! I mourned the loss of my beautiful home, in the genial climate! there it was cold and frosty! I made a little garden; but the soil was poor; it did not pay me for my labor.

Numbers of San B. brethren located in Beaver.[12] I paid them a visit, and concluded to move there. Ellen McGary taught school in Parowan; and little Emma Francelle was permitted to stay several days with me, at intervals. At length to my great sorrow Wm McGary resolved to move to Ogden, where his parents lived. So then the dear child must be taken far away from me! They entreated me to go with them! Why I did not incline to go, I knew not, but the spirit did not thus prompt me. I felt it was better for them to stay, as we were continually hearing that the whole church north were preparing to move south. Great was the poverty of the people in Cedar City. Every day my house was thronged with women, wanting [to] buy groceries, cloth and every thing I had. I never saw a poorer dressed congregation than assembled every Sabbath day in the House of worship. In the course of three months there was a visible change. The people brought goods from Cal, and exchanged with the citizens for provision. Thus were they mutually benefitted. They had been trying five years to make iron; till every person engaged in the enterprise was reduced to poverty. The old iron works spread a gloom over the whole place![13]

[From Cedar City to Beaver]

After a residence there of six months, I moved to Beaver, hired a house of C.W. Wandall, a brother we had known in California. We were quite comfortable with him, as he was a lone man, kind and polite, and hired his board with us. Many of the San B. brethren were located in Beaver, which made us feel quite at home again. We could not however avoid feeling keenly the contrast in the two climates. The soft genial atmosphere, and luxurious soil, was exchanged for cold hard winters, and ground imbeded with rocks.

Many an old friend called on us while we lived in Cedar City, and Oh, how their presence gladened our lonely hearts! One Sabbath morning in the month of May, we were joyfully surprised by the entrance of Elder John R. Young, just home from the Sandwich Islands.[14] He had been with us in San B. for quite a length of time, as he was on his way to the destined mission; and several years had passed since we parted. We had lengthy experiences to relate; and we thanked the Lord even for the dark days, from which we had gleaned wisdom; and for delivering us in times of great danger! He cheered our hearts, and went on his way to S. L. City.

Wm McGary went north to visit his kindred, but did not take his family; they were left in Parowan, where we could visit them in his absence, and there my daughter, his wife, taught a flourishing school.

After his return, he seemed more contented to remain in the South country; having learned for a certainty that the whole body of the church in S. Lake were moving South! That Johnson's army were camped on Ham's Fork, a tributary of the Platte, designing to make an entrance into the S. L. Valley. It was generally understood they were coming with hostilities bringing "sealed orders." It was the firm resolve of the saints to leave no traces of improvements behind them. They would apply the torch to every building, flee to the "white mountains," far away from the abodes of their enemies, to such a forbidding retreat, no Federal officials would presume to follow us! So our minds were harassed continually.

Before moving from Cedar I came to Parowan to visit my daughter; bringing with me Ann L., Ephraim, and little Emma, who had been left with us a week to relieve her mother while attending to school duties. The child's mother met us outside the town, rode in with us to her residence. We were affected to tears to witness the joy of the child on meeting her mother! Instead of rushing to her arms, she hung down her head; and waited for her ma to extend her hands inviting her to come! She then commenced to admire every thing she wore. She kissed the flowers on her dress, and in broken dialect talked of the beauty of her ornaments about her head and neck. So exquisitely happy did she appear that we marveled that she had been so contented while she staid with us. I went into school as an assistant, while I staid, I admired the looks and behavior of the children, 56 in number; but my heart ached to see how poorly they were clad, and how much they needed books!

As I have before remarked we could find no house to rent in Parowan. All expecting their friends from the north. The Indians we learned were very troublesome in Beaver. They had driven off a large number of cattle and horses. The men were in pursuit, with little prospect of recovering them.

Just at that time letters came to us from California, from a family living in the house I had left, with so much regret. They expatiated largely upon the beauty of my trees and flowers; how delightful every thing looked about the place; how abundant was the yield of grapes they wished I was there to enjoy them. I knew they had no intention of awakening sensations of regret for the sacrifice I had made; but in a moment I was transported there; and the trying scenes all passed before me in dread array! That, I rembered was the sixth time I had been broken up; and seen many of my hard earned articles of comfort and convenience wasted; and never till then, had I mourned over any loss I had sustained, on account of my adherence to the fullness of the gospel!

I was advanced in life, and my companion was not sufficiently fortified with a brave heart! Beaver was a rough newly begun settlement. A good range for stock, and a most delightful stream of soft water! A few wild plums and currants, was all the fruit we had, except when the indians brought us wild berries from the mountains. A large block building in the center of town, which served us for a house of worship, a social Hall, a Schoolhouse, general mass meetings, theatres; assemblages of every kind. I purchased the best dwelling house in town; a hewed log house, an acre of ground attached. Here I commenced making a new home, with my youngest daughter, a faithful girl, and my little island boy, then eight years old.

As we were on our journey to Beaver the first time the team (young cattle) was driven by Elder Wm H. Sherman; who was not much practiced in ox driving, though a very inteligent young man from NY City. We met some Indians, the oxen took fright and commenced a stampede! I had my little grand daughter in my arms. The cattle turned out of the road, and galloped over the sage brush. The Indians knowing they were the cause, laughed heartily. We knew not how or where we should land; but the driver succeeded in getting them cooled down, and turned into the road, and we went on our way rejoicing.

The Bishop in Beaver was Philo Farnsworth.[15] To my surprise on making his acquaintance I found he was one I had known when a young man, in Winter Quarters. It was a pleasant discovery, as he would take an interest in our welfare; greater, for having known us in the dark days of adversity! Where the ague chilled our blood, and the scurvy crippled our limbs! And thus it proved; he was a good man, and was our friend. Then we found Ross Rogers,[16] a young man we had known intimately in Indiana. He had moved to Beaver with quite a large family. I bought ten acres of farming land; I had a good team, and two cows. I got my house repaired, and hope sprang up in our hearts, that the absent members of the family would come to us; and we should redeem our lost treasures! One day as I was walking out with a friend we called at a Mr. Hoad's. They recognized me at once, though I had thought them entire strangers. When they reminded me of their place of residence in Nauvoo, I remembered they were my neighbors; I knew their history, they were no longer strangers. After the excitement was over, I looked around the room.

To my joyful surprise there sat my daughter Lois; just arrived from Hamilton's Fort. She had kept silent, waiting for me to notice her presence. I was more than rejoiced, because so unexpected. She had come to Parowan, and meeting Bro' Hoad, found it convenient to come to Beaver with him. I thought my prayers were beginning to be answered. She spent several days, and returned to her home at Ham's Fort. She brought with her the little girl born as we were camped on Shirts' Creek, in the snow storm! Then a beautiful child several months old; named Ida Frances. We made new acquaintances, revived old ones; meeting frequently with old familiar friends, whom we had not met for eight and twelve years. Oh, how such events would carry me back to the fiery ordeal in Nauvoo, when our beloved Prophet and Patriarch were slain! One circumstance comes fresh to my memory.

While living in Cedar City, there was a great celebration of the memorable Fourth, July appointed at old Harmony; where the famous John D. Lee presided! The people far and near were invited. Bro' and sister Crosby from John's Fort my soninlaw and daughter from Parowan, came along, and we all went to the celebration. It was a great feast; almost wholy at the expense of the afore said President. Living in that Fort we met the Sister who as we were crossing the plains, fell from the front of her wagon and broke a limb; having at the time an infant only four weeks old. She was swung up on a frame to the bows of the wagon; and for several weeks was a great sufferer! It was a sorrowful affair! But we all tried to do the best we could to relieve her. My Ellen, then seventeen, was alive with sympathy for the poor woman! She seemed to feel it a duty, to watch at her bed side, by night and by day! And the infant was her special charge.

The sister appeared agitated, and quite overcome at the unexpected meeting, after a separation of nine years. With tears flowing, she embraced Ellen, exclaiming, "Oh! you are the dear girl that saved my life! She said, "I have ever been impressed that had it not been for the watchful care of that young girl, I could not have endured the fatigue and suffering I was doomed to bear!"

We spent a cheerful day and night: (in the evening a grand ball) returned to our homes feeling refreshed in body and mind. Bro' Wm H. Sherman went out with us to the feast. He was an interesting young man, full of faith in the gospel. In his society time passed cheerfully; but it was of short duration; he soon left us and went on to Head quarters. Sister Moore proved a faithful companion while I remained in Cedar. She was not happy in her wedded life, though her husband had no wife but her.

Her heart seemed buried with her first husband who died in England before she heard the sound of the Latter Day Work.

I heard occasionally from the father of my children; and ever that his mind was to come. At length we received three long expected letters, from California. One from our good bro' Christie, in San Fran'co, full of interest for our welfare. From J.N. McIntyre, to Ann L. and from my daughter Francis L. Dyer, expressive of her grief when she heard we had left San B. and she could not be with us. Moreover she declared her reluctance to coming, and her full design to detain her father if possible! Nothing could have grieved me more! My heart was torn and "my spirits flagged like withering grass!" There was my child who once had faith to be healed by the laying on of hands! Would ask for the elders to come and administer, whenever she was taken ill! Now wedded to the world; her mind darkened, in regard to the great things, that so concerned me!

The contents of the letter I locked in my own bosom. When questioned by those interested in Bro. Pratt, I would answer, that he was not quite ready to come with his family, but would come the ensueing year. It was too much to say, his courage failed, because dangers threatened, and "iniquity abounded, which caused the love of many to wax cold!" Soon a letter came from him directed to Ellen, not flattering our hopes by any means.[17] It weighed heavily on our hearts! Still we trusted in God, and prayed earnestly that He would overrule events for our best good and His own glory. Ann Louisa was generally cheerful; although our condition was lonely; she would not complain; but would attend faithfully to every duty. Ephraim would have been a blessing, but for his restless disposition. Quickness to learn from books, a good intellect; but the Indian traits were prominent! a desire to roam about. He would go from home; promise to return at a certain an hour, perhaps be two days gone. Correction was of no avail. He needed a father to encourage him, and keep him employed.

[The Utah War Ended]

The whole population moved out of S. Lake City, crowded the settlements South. At length a treaty of peace was made and the people returned to their homes.[18] Many however sold their possessions, and went not back again. The spirit pointed South; which paved the way for settling that forbidding country, on the Sante Clarra and Rio Virgin. By this time Wm McGary had resolved on moving to Ogden. Another trial awaited me. Ellen would not go willingly, but would yield to pursuasion. I kissed my darling child, and a sensation pervaded my mind, "you will see her no more!" They entreated me to go with them; but the idea of moving again, caused a solemn dread! If I went I must leave my sister, and one daughter behind. I shrank from the undertaking.

[Ida Frances Hunt]

My friends from abroad sent me the kindest letters, full of love and sympathy. They soothed my sorrowing spirit and made me hope for brighter days. I began then to love my other grandchild who was not so far away. Ida Frances was lovely to look upon; her yellow hair and fair skin, were beautiful to me! Born was she by the way side, as we came on a fearful journey! But I feared to set my heart upon her knowing that my images of beauty were wont to be torn away; I thought of the lines I had often repeated, "I ever thus from childhood's hour Have seen my fondest hopes decay, I never loved a tree or flower, But they were first to fade away!" But the heart yearns for something to twine itself about with devotion; and we love God more, when surrounded with lovable objects which have power to awaken the divinity within us!

We were continually hearing of families moving back to California! I was not pleased. I thought we should be steadfast and endure hardness as good soldiers; and not be like the Israelites looking back to Egypt for the leaks and onions. On the midst of our darkness and gloom there were often lights breaking in upon us. Cheering news came that Mr. Hunt my son in law had returned from a trip to Cal, and brought his sister Harriet. We were pleased, for we knew she would bring us letters and presents and would come quickly to see us. Accordingly she came, and Lois, with the darling child! We were more than glad. She had much to inform of what had transpired after we left, of the new settlers, and misfortunes by floods &c. She had come to spend a year, would visit S. Lake, and her relatives who lived far to the north.

[A Home in Beaver]

My first business in Beaver was to make repairs about my house and its surroundings.[19] I had a few indiferent fruit trees. So late did frost come in the spring, that I was induced to cover the trees with sheets and blankets to save the fruit. Currents and wild plums, was all that could escape the frosts. Our two cows were inclined to stray, and we could not depend upon our island boy to guard them. So when they were gone we would go to Bro' Cox! he was the one to search, and bring back the wanderers.

10th Nov 1858 was my 8th 7th year [8 X 7 = 56]; the most eventful year of my mortal life! I was strong and healthy; able to tend my own garden with a little help.

That same month my sister and her family moved into Beaver, and took up their residence near mine.[20] Thus another light dawned upon us. It was a matter of rejoicing. I then had an own sister's house, to which I could resort when tired of the monotony of my own.

There was no mill, or carding machine yet built. Our grain was carried to older settlements to be ground. We often carded our wool and cotton by hand cards, as in olden times. We could realize something how our grandmothers worked before we were born. There were workmen in the place who made wheels and looms. We were proud of our home manufacture. We generally made diversion of our carding. We would assemble in numbers; each lady with her cards in hand. The hostess whose carding was to be done would prepare a sumptuous feast, of which we all partook freely. Sometimes a few gentlemen were invited. Many a pleasant day did we spend in that way. And even after machinery was introduced, lightening our labor would we refer to "the good old times we used to have," Then all the pride we knew was to excell each other in planning colors, stripes and checks.

Sister Cox was to me a faithful companion. Our spirits ran together notwithstanding the contrast in our domestic lives. She had no child born her own, but had three adopted at different periods. She had a companion wholy devoted to her; even anticipating her wants and wishes. Whereas I was one who had been "called as a woman forsaken and grieved in spirit!" had raised my four daughters under the most trying conditions of life; and with inexpressible anxiety of mind, had I brought them all to maturity! All married, and gone from me but my youngest one; and she was a solace, and a blessing; a companion and the staff of my declining years.

Often were we surprized and gratified by unexpected calls from Elders returning from missions; whom we had not seen for many years. One came from the Sandwich Islands who was my schoolboy in Nauvoo. He had grown to manhood, I could not recognize him till he told his name; then I remembered him a little boy whose father, Warren Smith, was killed at "Hauns Mills" in Missouri. I exclaimed, Oh! what changes time brings about! There was the boy who was left for dead by the side of his slaughtered father! Now holding the priesthood, and appointed a "swift messenger" to the nations; to bear the glad tidings, that the Lord had set his hand to gather his people for the last time; and to establish His kingdom on the earth!

Bro' Amasa Lyman was a local preacher in the southern country. His coming was ever hailed with interest by all the people. He expatiated largely on high toned morals. Declaimed loudly against the practice of some, in dealing less kindly with "outsiders," than with members of the church. Taking advantage of a stranger's necessity. "Israel from their being strangers, were to know the heart of a stranger."

On the 14th Dec [1858] Mr. Wandall commenced a school. Ann L. and Ephraim attended. He was talented and a competent teacher; often sad and moody, however, on account of the separation from his family;

not being able to learn even their place of residence, that he might write to his children. What grievious things some seem destined to bear! 26th My soninlaw and daughter came in from Hamilton's Fort; likewise the sister late from California was with them, and what was most pleasing to me my darling granddaughter was brought to my arms once more! I found her greatly improved. The meeting was a merry and happy one. The following day great preparations for a picnic and party at the Tabernacle were made. The choir and Band were engaged, accordingly the tables were arranged in the evening, and everything conducted in good order. The House was crowded, with persons of all ages. From gray hairs, down to barefooted schoolboys. Variety was the order of the day; or rather days. Select parties were only occasional. Generally parents took their children.

It was a new settlement, with few inhabitants; we counted ourselves all of one class. There was however variety in dress. Some English ladies of London celebrity wore fancy dresses, of the finest texture, and tastefully made. They formed a striking contrast when parading the dancing Hall with the mountain boys, dressed in red shirts and buckskin pants; fringed with the same material. A garb of which the boys were proud. It never once occured to them that their dressing was any thing unsuitable to lead out ladies attired in silks and muslins. Those were pleasant days; pride had not assumed her dominion; we were only characterized by our faithfulness in the cause of truth. Our amusements were considered necessary inasmuch as they were mingled with the worship of God; with prayers and exhortations. An elder holding the priesthood was appointed to preside. He would call on the Lord, and keep order.

Chapter Nineteen

Settling in at Beaver
Memoirs, January 1859 to July 1860

Jan 4th . . . 59. Nearly a year had passed since we left Cal to return to Utah. I was settled in a house of my own, and felt comparatively reconciled. It was announced that our visiting friends were to start early in the morning to return to their home. I felt agitated, not knowing when I might see them again; and more so because the dear child would be taken from me. They started, and we wished them a safe ride home.

[Pioneer Settlement of Beaver]

At that time the Beaver Creek overflowed the town; and freezing made one solid body of ice. Then commenced the skating amongst the young people. But I could not walk about at all, without some one to lead me. Brother Amasa Lyman built a house in Beaver.[1] He went into the Kanyons himself to oversee the workmen in getting out the lumber to build it. It was a severe undertaking; on account of the extreme cold weather, and the bad condition of the roads. Some of the brethren froze their feet, broke their chains and wagons; and sensibly did they realize the exchange they had made in climate and conveniences, in leaving California and coming to this forbidding country! But they made no complaints, and took every thing cheerfully.

When perplexities crowded upon them, when the Indians ran off their stock, and the wolves killed their calves and lambs then they had recourse to amusements, to dispel their unpleasant reflections. They would beat the old bass drum long and loud which was a signal for the people to gather to the tabernacle. All who desired to go thither they hastened; some dressed in homespun, and others in silks and satins; equality was the watchword; dress made no distinction. There we called on the Lord, to bless us in our diversions, to help us to refrain from evil thoughts and words; that we might banish from our minds our annoyances, and be refreshed in body and spirit, that on the morrow we might be better fitted for the duties of life.

After the introductory ceremonies, those who chose to go forward in the dance, did so in the innocency of their hearts feeling that they were upheld by the servants of God, and those who kept the faith. No doubts rested on our minds whether the Lord was pleased, we all felt fully justified. At such entertainments we had songs, both comical and sentimental and of a religious character, appropriate to the condition and experience of the people. There was a good brass band; our musick was not inferior to that in older settlements. At first some lived in very low cabbins some in what was called "dugouts." There were two english ladies who had been accustomed to fashionable life, and who came to America wholy for the gospel's sake; they were subjected to the necessity of living in cabbins, which in their own country would not be tolerated even for pigs to live in. They could bear the change cheerfully, looking for better days ahead, because they had come here to serve the Lord.

They were my neighbors, and often cheered me by their faith and zeal for the cause, for which we had all sacrificed so much! Although we were forced to live in cabbins even in caves of the earth, as the ancient saints did, yet we tried to maintain as far as possible the habits of our more prosperous days, so that strangers coming amongst us might discern that we were not persons of low origin, but had been privileged in early life with culture, which had stamped our characters with honest principles, and a respectable bearing. To me, a great source of enjoyment was a continued correspondence with distant friends. Although I had embraced a faith they did not understand, they were not disposed to discard me; but continued their sympathy in all my trials, though believing that I was the author of my own misfortunes!

At the first, our mails were irregular and far between. At one time in Beaver after waiting and longing to hear from the old world the U S mail arrived with eight letters for me! What a feast I had! My good neighbors were called in to rejoice with me. How the contents carried us back to the scenes of former life where we enjoyed a high order of civilization and refinement! But we felt that our minds had been enlarged with light and knowledge, sufficient to reward us for all the worldly sacrifices we had made! I often met with sisters of the church who had been members almost from the first; who had been through the mob war in Missouri; driven out in the winter; lost all their accumulations for years; came into Illinois destitute of food and clothing, shared the hospitality of the people of Quincy, which they remembered with the deepest gratitude! These sisters, to whom I refer, administered comfort to my sorrowing spirit.

They seemed to count it all joy that they had been called to suffer for the truth; seemed not in the least disheartened; all their anxiety was that they might have grace to endure to the end, and receive their reward. The burden of Mr. Lyman's preaching was to inspire the people with courage, and above all else to treat strangers well, even if we had reason to believe they were our enemies.

The place was healthy, very few deaths occured. I remember the first that affected me. A little boy two years and a half old, an only child. The affliction seemed doubly aggravating, on account of some alienation between the parents and their near relatives. The young man went to his father and entreated him with tears, to come to the burial of his child; but he refused; it was supposed through the influence of a step mother. On that ground he could not be justified. Strangers endeavored to supply the offices of kindred, and showed pity to the afflicted parents! I remember the remark, and exclamation of the poor man as the rocks were being piled on the grave of his boy! "Oh! I long for the day when the archangel's trump will sound, and my dear boy will come out of the grave!"

About that time the 27th aniversary of my eldest daughter's birthday came around, and impressed me with deep thought and reflection. I was then far away from my parents and kindred, and felt myself a stranger. She was now separated from me, 250 miles, with her husband's friend in Ogden. Mr. Wandell still lived near us; an agreable inteligent gentleman, but at times, oh, so sorrowful and lonely! He could get no inteligence from his lost family.

Ann L. made acquaintances in the adjoining settlements, kept up a correspondence with her former associates in Cal. and appeared comparatively happy.

We made our own garden; in which we took great delight; but we were continually annoyed with breachy cattle. Men were careless; they did not realize how hard it was for poor women living alone to be aroused late in the night to drive stock out of their enclosures, and the broken down fence to repair. Little Ephraim was some help, when we could keep him in sight, but to play truant, was as natural as the hair on his head.

[Visits and Visitors]

The first winter passed away, an exceedingly cold one! March was ushered in, boisterous as the angry waves of the ocean! On the third, Mrssrs Wandell and Swartout myself and daughter started in a carriage to pay a visit to Lois H. my daughter, living at Hamilton's Fort. We were under way an hour before daylight. It was a calm morning, and we were anticipating a pleasant ride to Parowan; but early in the day a tremendous wind storm arose! We however reached Parowan safely, spent the night with our friends; started early on our way; soon the wind commenced to blow in a most terrifying manner! Several times we came near being overturned; but we pressed our way through and made the desired haven a little before sundown.

Miss H. H. [Harriet] the sister, was there; all were pleased to receive us, and we were highly entertained. That night the snow fell five inches; but as we had intended a lengthy visit, the snow did not interfere with our enjoyment. Little Ida Frances noticing the expressions of joy, passing from each to others joined in the general mirth, as though she understood it all. The 6th day was my daughter Lois' birthday. Suitable demonstrations were made. The 8th was the first aniversary of the granddaughter's [birth]. So we prepared a picnic and rode six miles to her birth place. The snow had melted away, and we spread our repast on the ground, and while partaking, reviewed the scenes of the year that had passed, and conjectured what might transpire in the succeeding one.

Sports of different kinds were introduced, and we spent a cheerful day. Brother Wm Cluff made one of our number, a returned missionary from the Sandwich Islands. It was also his birthday, so we partook of brandy, peaches and nice cake, in honor of the two illustrious personages. The next morning we started for home; made calls in Cedar and Parowan; came on to Johnson's Fort; passed the first night. I do not remember ever being more chilled with the cold in my life; but meeting a friendly reception, we were soon made comfortable and happy. The following day we proceeded on our journey, called on our friends in Parowan. Friends of "long ago." The meeting of them revived old memories: Crossing the plains, the deserts, walks by moonlight, and buffalo meat.

We took leave of our friends, and drove five miles to Red creek spent the night, and the following day drove home in good time, the weather being favorable; found all safe, all felt our hearts lighter than when we left home to go. What is there that sweetens life so much as friends and friendships? Immediately after our return the weather turned cold and the freezing was like midwinter.

On 16th Mrs. Moore set out on horseback to come to Beaver from Cedar City; a distance of sixty miles. It was a brave undertaking, and had the weather been agreable she could have made the journey in two days. But the second, she was compelled to camp with a train of freighters; all strangers, and not a lady in the camp. She was at first greatly embarassed; which they discovered, and being humane and generous they reassured her, promised her protection; fitted up a wagon where she could be retired; fed her animal, gave her a good supper and breakfast, and in the morning she rode into town in fine spirits!

She amused us much with the relation of her adventures; and we all rejoiced, that she was so fortunate even in her emergency, to meet gentlemen! Truly so for had they been otherwise, her case would have been a sorry one! Sister M spent a week with us, started back; seemed excited in view of her journey. I learned from some remarks she made, that she felt a dread of meeting her husband; as he was a forward man, she did not know what humour she might find him in. I saw in her countenance a troubled look, which made me pity her. Oh, what a blessing is an amiable gentle spirit! It spreads sunshine in the home circle, and makes the most humble abode more desirable, than a gilded mansion, where sourness and hatred dwell! Freezing weather continued to the end of March; it went out like a lion!

The 1st of April we were agreably surprized by unexpected callers from California. Two young men Merick and Abbott. The latter I had not met for many years. I remembered him a small boy, when his mother and I were pleasant neighbors. He had been taught by her to respect me, and for that reason called, to inquire of my welfare, and take from me kind words to his mother. He also made me a present of a box of tea; which was very high in Utah, and very acceptable at that time. So all the little bright spots in our every day life helped us to bear the monotony of the place, and to remind us that our days were not all dark, but sun and shade were alternate. Letters full of loving words came to us from all directions, so our hearts had not time to sink irretrievably, ere some kind hand would grasp ours, and say, "be comforted!" Bro' Lyman occasionally preached doctrine the people did not fully understand, and appreciate. We were told to say nothing about it, but to ponder it in our hearts.

Teams began to roll in from California, with goods for Salt Lake City. Often did they bring good news, and presents from our old tried friends. We were frequently reminded of Solomon's words. "As iron sharpeneth iron so the face of a man brighteneth the countenance of his friend." April came; too cold to plant any thing. Strangely did it seem to us, having been accustomed to make gardens in Feb. More sensibly did we realize the difference in the climate we had left, and this icy one in the tops of the mountains! Even to the 10th of Apr stern winter held her sway; the cold north wind shook the frail coverings on the cabbins, and made us long for spring once more! The 11th I remembered as being the birth day of the dear sister who died at my home in the state of N. York; of whom I have written. The reason why I was so impressively reminded of that event, was the raging of the elements! The same as on that sorrowful day, when my brother and I followed her remains, (her only relatives) to her long home!

The same day arrived my son in law, and daughter Lois with Miss H H on their way to S L City. Again I was permitted to see my granddaughter. A severe snow storm over took them here, and they were forced to remain over one day with us. They started on, cold as it was, to face the north wind; and I was troubled on their account. Letters came from my husband and daughter in Cal; few were the words inscribed, to inspire a hope that ere long they would be with us. Myself and daughter continued to improve and labor on our Lot; contended for possession with our neighbors' stock; which claimed a right on account of poor fences: owners seemed wholy unconcerned. My son in law and daughter returned from their tour to S L City, left "the sister" to spend the summer.

I had expected Ellen McGary to come with time, but as disappointment seemed always to be my destiny, I learned to bear it, and even to welcome it; and say with Kirke White, "Sad monitor, I own thy sway; thou art not stern to me." The returners were in great haste would not stop to visit at all. Lois encouraged me to expect her in a short time to spend several weeks. That reconciled me to their flying call.

Soon after the U.S. Troops passed through the place from north to south. There were thieves among them. Fowls were stolen, Cooking utensils which people were accustomed to leave outside their dwellings, were taken away, to the great annoyance of some who were scantily supplied. A few articles were recovered, by following the camp, and appealing to the officers. By the time they returned every thing was made secure.

[Ephraim]

My Island boy still continued in the habit of "running away." So I adopted a new plan to prevent him. I put so little clothing on him he was ashamed to go on the street. That would do in warm weather. Unfaithful as he was, I had a mother's love for him; and could not endure to see him punished by one who had no legal right to do it. Mischief had been done in my brother in law's garden: it was at once laid to Ephraim's charge. The man came angry to my door, took the boy by the hair of his head, and with a stick in his hand administered severe blows! The boy knew not what it was for, only being told it was for mischief in the garden; which was after words ascertained to have been done by the sheep. The circumstance affected me very much. I felt that great injustice had been done the child, but I could see no way to have it righted. The boy had been often sent to drive sheep from the man's lot; but ever after would refuse to go. I would not compel him. I felt myself injured, by having to witness such an out burst of passion! It weighed heavily on my mind for several days; but I asked for no redress.

[Lone Louisa]

Ann L. soon left me and went to S L, intending to visit her sister in Ogden. When she was gone, I had no child in the place. Oh, the utter loneliness that came over me! I was taken sick soon after A L left me. My truant boy ran away; so there I was alone, not able to help myself. True, I had kind neighbors, but that did not satisfy me. I wrote to Lois, informing her of my condition; and she came immediately. Never was I more thankful to see any one; I so much needed her help and company. She brought the dear child, and staid several weeks. Her husband had gone north at the time, and a friend came on purpose to bring her. I felt to thank the man heartily, and I told him he should be blessed!

Unwelcome news came to me, that Ann L who had left home to visit in S Lake had through some inadvertent act, had sprained her ankle, was quite helpless; had been taken from S L City to Ogden, on a bed. She was with her sister, slowly recovering. I was also informed that my son in law was about moving his family into S L. It was sorry news to me, as the injury would in all probibility retard her return. I had hoped to see her at home on the 24th of July, the 12th aniversary of the entrance of the Church into S Lake Valley. We had an interesting course of exercises in Beaver.

The 30th Mr. Hunt came from north, and my daughter Lois had to leave me. His sister H. had been married to Mr. J Mayfield; and they were all resolved on going back to California. So I must give Lois up to go so far away! I nerved up my heart, and thought I would see how bravely I could bear it! I walked out, went to my sister's house, kept tolerably calm, till the shades of evening drew around me.

I then returned to my own deserted dwelling. I could not there remain; walked out into the street, looked north and south. A sense of my sudden despoliation rushed instantly upon me, and I gave vent to the fullness of my burdened heart! I exclaimed! What cruelties do I have to bear! Every child I have is gone! My last and only one I can claim, is disabled and cannot come to me! I went to my bed with an aching heart, and my eyes swolen with weeping! In the middle of the night I arose, went out into the bright starlight and bathed my head in the cool running water; It soothed me, and I laid down on my pillow and fell asleep. When I awoke for a few moments I felt calm. Then suddenly my grief returned! I complained in my spirit! "new sorrows are constantly springing up in my path!"

I had a pet sheep, we named him Bill. We thought him very knowing. He yielded us 7 pounds of wool at one shearing. He was almost like a child about the house; would come in when allowed and eat off the table. One dark night I heard a noise of something running. I arose dark as it was and went to the coralle found my poor old Bill was gone! I remembered hearing the bars in front of the house shake as though something was trying to break through. I then knew it was "Bill," fleeing from some ravenous beast; and Oh, how I regretted not running quickly to the bars, to let him in; he would have rushed into the house in an instant, and been saved! I returned to my bed, but not to sleep. I arose at the early dawn and went on the street. Not five rods from the house lay my poor pet lamb, torn in pieces by a cruel wolf! I mourned the fate of the poor thing! which after being loved and petted so long must come to such a cruel end!

The following week a large company went to north Creek for a ride and picnic. Returned at evening; and had a cotillion party in the schoolhouse. I attended, with others, and assumed a cheerful air; but it was false coloring. I was doubly alone! Even Ephraim was gone. I had sent him to help Lois make preparations for her journey. So I communed with myself, and resolved to set my heart lightly on every thing liable any moment to be torn from me! I dwelt in immagination on that exalted sphere, from which I felt that I had fallen, in coming to earth! and contemplated the time when I should regain that lost estate. I sometimes thought my annoyances of a domestick nature relieved my mind of too much deep reflection, and varied the channel through which my feelings ran, and made them more bearable.

In the height of my mourning over my absent children, and my losses, I must be aroused in the middle of the night to drive stock out of my garden; perhaps a dozen head, breaking down my corn just in the milk, and ready for use; trampling my vines into the ground, destroying the young squashes and melons. Then instead of chastened sorrow, a feeling of resentment and indignation filled my mind, to the extirmination of every thing else. The owners I denounced careless and unjust, to allow their cattle to destroy the labors of poor lone woman! The cows understood letting down bars with their horns, which sometimes were secured with pins and chains. I would go to the owners of the stock, they would promise to take care of the breachy animals; perhaps the following night the trespass would be repeated; till the Bishop would interpose, and peremptorily forbid a repetition of the offense. I felt there was one command I should fulfill. "Work out your salvation with fear and trembling." Certain I was that my temporal salvation would be wrought out to that effect. After an excitement of that kind I could not sleep quietly for several nights.

[Ann Louisa at Home, Lois's Family in California]

The 27th Aug. Lois my daughter from the Fort, and the newly married sister, Mrs. Mayfield, came to pay us a farewell visit, before starting to California. I was pleased to meet them once more. As we were enjoying a picnic at sister Crosby's, news reached us that "Mother Hunt," and Ann Louisa, were in sight of town; coming from the north. The former, to see her children before they left, and my "lame girl" coming home! Great was our surprise and joy! The carriage soon drove up to the door, and we had them by the hand. The following day the visitors made calls, took leave of their friends. I bade Lois farewell, as cheerfully as I could; gazed long upon my little girl Ida, and thought, how much she would be changed, when I saw her again.

On the 10th Sept. Mrs. Hunt returned, having bade her children farewell at the Fort; they to go south, and she to journey to the north. She was a tender mother, warmly devoted to her children. She bore the separation cheerfully. I would try. I was every day expecting my daughter Ellen to come from Ogden. Frequent opportunities were afforded; she seemed never to be in time. I was vigorously engaged in gathering and securing what I had raised; and often refering to the losses by breachy cattle. Ann L was long afflicted with lameness in her sprained ankle, which caused the heavier burdens to fall on me. The 6th of Oct. came; the elders South went to Conference in S. L., and returned; brought cheering inteligence from the saints; how the spirit of the Lord was poured out in such effusion, that the participants wept for very joy!

A large company of the people of Beaver went up to receive blessings in the House dedicated for that purpose; I felt that I could run on foot behind their wagons, so anxious was I to go with them! But I could not leave my poor lame girl, to take care of everything. I got a new floor laid in my house and continued making improvements; the better to keep my mind occupied. I was often led to exclaim, what a struggle is life! The moment we stop combatting obstacles, our living runs out. One must rise early and late take rest, and eat the bread of carefulness. Dr. McIntyre sent me a letter, complaining of enui, and unhappiness: he had like myself left his companion in California, she choosing to remain with her only child. I wrote in reply, and endeavored to cheer his heart with comforting words. I can say soothing words to others when I see them cast down, even when I need comfort more than they.

10th Nov. was my birthday. Fifty 7th aniversary. Bro' and Sister Cox came to spend the day, and I went out to buy beer. Returning, I met Mr. Wandell; invited him to call, and partake of the refreshments; he did so, and drank a toast. He would not quite desire that I might double my years on earth, but as long as I was permitted to remain, he hoped I might be hole and healthy, and have plenty to eat and drink. Bro' Cox also drank, adding to the aforesaid, many hearty expressions of genuine friendship. Other friends contributed, and the time was merrily spent.

[Ellen's Tragic Loss, Return to Beaver]

A few succeeding days passed peacefully. When lo! Another dark cloud arose. Ann L. went to the P. Office, returned with two letters. I grasped them eagerly! One was a yellow envelope trimmed with black! Where the letter was sealed, was imprinted a heart with thorns entering it; a true emblem of the heartrending tidings the letter contained! From my children in Ogden.[2]

Their dearly loved and only child had died! She had fallen backwards into a tub of boiling water! The same little tub in which she had regularly been bathed almost every day of her life! Her mother had only turned her head for a moment, not thinking her so near; when the fatal accident took place; which brought anguish deep and lasting, to every heart who had known and loved the darling child! The agony of that hour in which I read the sad inteligence will be remembered while my thread of life is lengthened out! The grief of my poor afflicted daughter sank deeply in my heart! The whole night through, I wept incessantly! I felt my spirit wandering away above the earth, in search of the little bright cherub; inquiring among the angels "had they welcomed my darling to their blest abode!"

She was three weeks lingering after the accident and they would not inform me; hoping she might recover. I blamed them, for had I known it I could have taken the Stage and gone immediately! The poor child cried for grandma to come and see her! She was two years and eight months old. When friends called to inquire how she was, she would answer, "poor Emma is all burnt up!" My mind seemed inflexibly moved to dispair, to think of the poor little form having to be laid away with sores! I felt, that could she have died a natural death, I could have borne it with christian fortitude. But to dwell on the form I had so much admired, and see it despoiled of its beauty, ere it could be committed to its sacred resting place; too far it led me to compare the animal and vegetable kingdoms, and to exclaim, what is humanity more than these!

Word was sent, that the sorrowing mother was coming immediately home. The 7th day of Nov was the day of doom, the child's decease! The birthday of my daughter Frances, then in California. The 10th of the same month was my own, when I had visitors in my house, all trying to make merry; congratulating me for having lived so long! That day the sorrowing parents were inditing the letter to send me, and calling it the sadest day of their lives! Little do we know when we are indulging in mirth whose hearts are breaking, at the very moment!

December had now set in, it was fearfully cold! The Creek had overflowed its bounds; up to my door and all around the premises was solid glare ice! Every night we listened till a late hour to hear the rumbling of wagon wheels; Long did the time seem to us, and still more tedious would it have been but for warm hearted friends, and pleasant neighbors.

I could not forget the impression I received when I last embraced the dear child in Parowan. It was prophetic. A spirit whispered, "you will see her no more." Dark as our days were, they were not all darkness. I had an own sister to console me; sympathizing and kind; full of faith in a merciful providence, which all things for the best good overrules. She helped to bear the sorrow. Two kind english ladies, sisters in the church, (of whom I have written,) respectively named, Willis and Bettenson. They were women of character and faith in a bright future; always ready to partake either of joy or sorrow, with their fellow beings. Our blessings were not under valued; neither did we murmur, and complain that God was not merciful; but with the Psalmist we affirmed, "Though He slay me yet I will trust in Him!"

The singing of spiritual songs had a soothing influence. St. Paul said, "if any are merry let them sing psalms!" I have proved it good to sing when afflicted. The 21st Dec. my children arrived from Ogden. I was rejoiced to see them alive and well: I scarcely dared trust myself to speak of the absent one! My daughter nerved her heart to comfort me; and by so doing was measurably consoled herself. After the first interview we were ennabled to converse on all the particulars relating to the solemn event, with a tolerable degree of composure. For some cause, I could not tell why, I felt the blow was aimed at me! I felt that my heart had been too much set upon the child; and long had I been convinced that the Lord was not angry with me for sinning against His righteous laws, for I had been willing to sacrifice all the day long!

Christmas came around; we attended religious exercises, and heard many comforting things spoken by the elders of Israel. We were invited to the Bishop's, to spend the evening. A small band of musick, with an elegant supper, were chiefly enjoyed. My soninlaw Wm McGary, was a skillful musician; my nephew Alma Crosby, a good violinist. Ellen, played the flutina admirable! Bro' Crosby played the flute. On New years the Brass Band came from Parowan, and there was a great concert, held in our Tabernacle. The songs and recitations were delightful! All these amusements helped us to recover our former cheerfulness, and enabled us to bear life's burdens a little longer.

[Teaching School]

On the 3d of Jan 1860 my daughter Ellen McG commenced teaching school, assistant to Wm Paul Smith. Employment was good for her. Her husband went on a freighting expedition to California, with Capt Hunt. So E. boarded with me. Shortly after I engaged in the same school. It was a severe task. The children in the great moves had been sadly neglected; how they will be redeemed is unknown to me.

At that time there was a continued shaking of the earth; A rumbling as of distant thunder, for some days. Several females were greatly terrified!

There was a continual passing and repassing from S. L. to Cal; which afforded us many opportunities to renew old acquaintance. Strangers would call upon us, whom we had no knowledge of at first sight, and after a little inquiry find them to have been the children of some dearly remembered old friends, who of all others we desired the most to hear from! Such scenes were among the bright spots, which enlightened our pathway.

When sister McIntyre in Upper Cal, heard of our great sorrow, She wrote us a letter of condolence. And well could she sympathize having had a dear boy thrown from a horse and brought home dead! In pitying her, I half forgot my own pain. A loving gentle spirit has power to comfort and bless. She was a dear good woman; to bind up the broken hearted, was her chief delight.

The school wore heavily upon me, both in body and mind. I undertook the task with a firm resolve to see an improvement in the children, both in their studes and common demeanor. I was not disappointed.

On Feb 21st Mr Dibble exhibited in Beaver the paintings representing the assassination of Joseph and Hirum Smith in Carthage Jail, Ill. Likewise the scene of the Nauvoo Legion when last assembled in that City, and the Prophet making his farewell address, previous to his leaving for Carthage; where he was slain. I had not seen the paintings for many years; and the busts which are an exact likeness, I had never seen before. Oh! how vividly it brought back that awfully solemn event, when those mighty men fell.

Intelligence came to us that Mr. Pratt was leaving the Upper Cal; and coming to San B. He would meet my soninlaw Wm. McGary, and Pres't Cox: they would be certain to encourage him to come up with them. Hope sprang up in our hearts! Ellen struggled on with her school; looking forward to the close, when she would be relieved of a great burden; groceries were scarce, and sold for high prices. A present sent me of a pound of tea, rejoiced the hearts of all the elderly ladies in my circle. Sugar we used very sparingly. Molasses we had plenty; made from our own cane. A blessing it was in those hard times. Truly we called ourselves, "Pioneers of Latter Days!"

On the 21st of Mar. [1860] I closed my department in the school. I had the satisfaction to know that my exertions had been blessed; that my pupils had made a creditable improvement; and what I had done was appreciated. I felt weary and worn, and thought to rest and refresh my mind. But it was not good for me to have leisure. When my energies were not taxed to their fullest capacity. I thought too deeply; lived over my past life, and groaned over my bereavements. I blamed myself for repining. I knew it was wrong; yet I would not admit that I was responsible. I said, I might as well be held amenable for being born into a world subject to so many ills; In that I had no agency. How could I help mourning over the fate of a fallen world! To mourn was my meat and drink! I was not afraid the Lord would be angry with me, "He was merciful, and full of pity, to those who loved and served Him."

From my husband's sister in N H I received a letter expressing her surprize that I should come to Utah without my companion! I read the spirit of the letter, which I felt bordered on reproof. I replied in a most pathetic manner! Assuring her that if she knew all the circumstances attending our removal to this country, and all I had been called to suffer, that no chastising word would ever escape her lips! But to the reverse; all the powers of her feeling heart would be employed to comfort and console!

Mr. Mc Gary returned from Cal with Capt Hunt's train, but Mr. P. still remained, to breathe sea air, where he desired to be. The train camped in front of my door, and there was a barrel of whiskey rolled out, and offered for sale. All the sons of "Bachus" in town rushed to the spot! I never was more disgusted than I was, to see sensible men pay such devotion to an article, which causes wise men oftentimes to act like fools.

[First Trip to Salt Lake City]

Myself and daughter E. had been preparing to go to S. L. with William Mc when he returned. The train moved on, and we were to get ready, and overtake them. Every thing packed in ample order, thinking we were the same as started to our chagrin, and surprise, one of the mules was found to be missing. Wm traveled perhaps forty miles, made diligent search, but all in vain, finally concluded an Indian had taken him off. After much perplexity we got under way traveled nearly the whole journey alone; had some interesting visits on the way. At Provo I met Mrs. Mary A. Pratt, Parley P's first wife whom I had not seen for twelve years. She recognized me in a moment, and we had pleasant conversation together then she bore us company to Battle Creek, where she had a daughter living. After an interchange of many endearing sentiments we parted; she remained, and we went forward on our journey. Made Mill Creek, in due time, where I had a distant relative, who pursuaded me to stop and visit my old friends in that region.

My children were opposed to my staying, but arguments prevailed; I remained; and went to see my dear old friend. Mrs. Daniel Russell. She had been to me a loving neighbor in Winter Quarters, when cold and hunger stared me in the face! I could never forget her; and in my long absence she had buried a kind husband and was then a lonely widow. So I went to her house and that day May 7th [1860] was ten years from the day I left S. L. City to go the north route to San Francisco. Sister R. went with me to the City eight miles, and we took lodgings at Bro' Horace Eldridge's and from thence visited our mutual friends throughout the town.[3] In reviewing old acquaintance I was often reminded of the resurrection; when we shall clasp the hands of those whom we had not expected to meet.

On going to the Tabernacle and listening to voices so familiar to my ears ten years before strangely was my mind exercised! I was bewildered with joy, mingled with solemnity indescribable! The same honored men stood up in the defence of truth, testified as I had heard them a hundred times, that the great "Latter Day Work" was begun on earth; which prophets long ago foretold; which would in time make an end of sin, and bring in everlasting righteousness! I gazed at their familiar faces, saw how their locks had whitened, and yet their faith in God was firm and unshaken. I felt that I had been to another world and come back to tell what there was behind the veil. I went to Pres't Young's and spent a day. The house was large; wholy built in my absence. Mrs. Zina D. Young took me through all the apartments. At evening I was invited into the large parlor for prayers. There all the wives and children were assembled.

No place ever seemed more heavenly to me! Pres't Young then offered up petitions in behalf of his family and the church. After which he took a seat and conversed a long time. He inquired with apparent solicitude about "Bro' Pratt." I gave him an account as favorable as possible. He talked of the state of affairs as they then were. Of the resolutions before the House of Congress: which was to send commissioners to negotiate with the Mormons, buy out their possessions and let them go out of the Republick. But said he, "we shall not sell our possessions, but remain upon them, and trust in the Lord to protect us!" He invited me to make a long visit in both houses. That night Ellen returned from Ogden, and I was happy to meet her; so lost and lonely did I feel, when my children were all gone from me.

Every day revealed old acquaintances, almost passed our of mind, amidst the multitudes of new ones I had formed in the ten years. I walked over that City, wondered and admired! When I left it, not a house was built, worthy to be called a house. Then the lofty buildings were towering up in every direction. Large orchards on almost every lot. A flourishing populous city. I was led to exclaim, "what cannot the hands of men accomplish!" I also learned of much that poor women had done, who had like myself been left alone with young children; their husbands sent on missions to the four quarter's of the globe! Their faithfulness will most certainly be rewarded. Mrs. Eleanor Pratt was then living in the City; the last wife of Parley P. Pratt, and the one who was traveling with him when he was assassinated.

I made her acquaintance: an interesting brilliant minded woman. She gave me a full account of the sad tragedy in Kansas. Likewise of her troubles with her first husband in San Francisco. Mr. Mclain was a violent opposer to the "Fullness of the gospel," which she assayed to believe in, and did embrace. He took her children from school without her knowledge, put them on board a vessel, (though very young,) and sent them to New

Orleans; to his relatives. When the fatal news came to her ears, she was like a distracted woman! She immediately took another vessel, and followed them. She remained with them one year: attempted to steal them away; was followed by policemen, and they were taken from her on the sea. After several years she went again; recovered her children, was on her way home; when a mob came upon her, slew her husband, and took her children!

My daughter E and I had many seasons of joy. Our friends were never weary of hearing us rehearse our experience on the Island of the Pacific. Amidst our joy we must of necessity have sorrow! As twin sisters they go hand in hand. Our dearly loved Irene Pomroy died suddenly. She was brought in from a country residence for medical aid, died the third day; even before we had an opportunity to see her. Her right arm had been amputated. And there was the end of our lovely and gentle friend! Youthful and blooming was she, though the mother of eight children. It was a solemn sight to see her husband approach the sacred spot where lay the lifeless form of his faithful and devoted wife. He arrived too late to receive her parting blessing. Her arm which had been preserved in ardent spirits, was brought and laid in its place. And Oh! She was lovely, even in death! Her mother, and her family of children came to see her buried. Many tears were shed, over the group of little mourners. The grandmother was a blessed woman, and she pittied and consoled the children. The deceased had suffered two years with a cancer on her wrist. But in her death there was peace! She had remembered her creator in the days of her youth.

Afterwards I went with dear sister Whitney to the Endowment House. It seemed a peaceful retreat, where every commotion of the soul is hushed! I felt that I could hear the soft whispering of angel voices in mortal ears! I met many whom I greatly desired to see, in that house. I had a severe cold, which seated on my lungs and weakened my whole system. Brother Joseph Young with several others laid their hands upon my head; and pronounced upon me the blessing of life, health and strength! It was the promise I most desired, and I went away with a light heart, and elastic step. The following morning I felt quite well.

We soon took leave of our friends, and started for home. Ellen came with me, Mr. McGary went to Montanna. With one exception we had a pleasant journey. A terrible hail storm came upon us. When we were quite a distance from a settlement. Our carriage cover was a poor protection, when the rain was comming down in torrents! We were drenched through, but we found large hospitality in Payson: dried our wet clothing, and resumed our journey. Made home in six days. Ann L. was alone, and rejoiced to welcome us. The neighbors were all eager to hear us rehearse our adventures. We left S. L. on the first day of July, with Mrs. Samuel Woolley. I rested two weeks, and commenced teaching school.

CHAPTER TWENTY

Beaver and a Trip to California

Memoirs, July 1860 to December 1864

[The Pull of California]

Ann L. and Ephraim had raised a crop of vegetables in the garden; had taken care of the cows and been faithful in all that was entrusted to them.

News came from my daughter Lois H. who had gone back to Cal. that she had another daughter born to her. I could have rejoiced, had she been near me, but she was far away, an intolerable journey between us; I had no prospect of seeing her or her child, in any definite length of time. No encouragement was sent that the [my?] husband and father would soon join his family, to comfort and bless. All was uncertainty. To live in suspense, was inevitably my doom! So I said, "The Lord shall be my portion forever! My strong hold, where unto I may continually resort!" I was comfortable as for means to live; wheat had been raised on my farming land, sufficient for a year's supply; but all that and more, could not fill the aching void in my heart! In Sept. Wm McGary returned from his tour north, bound for California.

Another trial was on hand for me. He used every pursuasion in his power to have his wife go with him! She was not inclined to go, and I was decidedly against it. Her health was delicate, and her conveniences for traveling would not be suited to her condition. After earnest entreaties we prevailed on him to give up the project, and remain with us. He went to work and seemed reconciled. He built a small room adjoining mine for Ellen's accomodation, worked with apparent contentment one month. He then determined on going and leaving his wife with me. To that we consented. The 15th Nov. he left us. The winter was before us of which we had a dread; less however than we should have had, had he not supplied us with wood. Of that we had plenty, and Ephraim was able to chop it for the fires. When he arrived in California he made complaints that I had prevented his wife from bearing him company on the journey. Ellen's father and sister were inclined to blame me; which grieved me exceedingly! But when I stated to them the nature of the case, they saw it in another light.

I closed my school, had a short vacation, and commenced again. The second term in my own house. I had forgotten to mention that Ann L. went with the company to visit her sister in San Bernardino. She had gone to Parowan on a visit with no intention of going further. There were ladies in the company and finding her there, prevailed on her to accompany them. A messenger came in great haste, to obtain my consent, and get some of her clothing. I was greatly agitated: was undecided what to reply. I wrote her a long letter, telling her of my fears; giving however a partial consent for her to go, if she promised to return with the company. The same she was willing to do.

I was seized with trembling after the departure of the messenger. I felt to regret I had given my consent. I began to fear A. L. would be persuaded to stay and go to the Upper Cal, to see her sister there. Such an event I felt would be in keeping with my fate. Christmas came; E. and I being alone, we proposed a picnic, and had quite a cheerful time. A terrible snowstorm soon after occured! We were fortunate in having visitors: a gentleman and his wife, came to spend a few days; so we got through the storm much easier, on their account. On the 29th Jan. [1861] Ellen had a daughter born, which accounted to our friends in California, the reason I was not willing for her to risk such a fatiguing journey. We had with us a faithful experienced female friend, for several weeks who was both a help and comfort. The 17th Feb closed my second term of school. I had an exhibition, gave the children an entertainment. Every pupil was presented with a written certificate; which contained some worthy maxim or choice sentiment. I felt resolved to have a long rest.

[The Family on the Move]

On the 7th of March Ann Louisa returned. I had often passed sleepless nights through fear she might not come with the company expected. Capt. Shepherd came ahead on horseback. I ran to meet him; was afraid to ask if A. L. was in the company: he anticipated my inquiry, and informed me at once, that she really had come! I went on a bound to the house, to communicate the news to the inmates. There was general joy, and we set about preparing "a feast of fat things." We had in the midst of doubts, hoped that Ann L. would pursuade her father to return with her. But it did not so prove. As she expressed it, "he was not ready." In the mean time a letter came announcing the death of my husbands mother. 81 years old. She was prepared to die, having lived devoted to God, and her family.

April 6th 1861 A L's birthday. In honor of it I invited a party of ladies the majority very aged all widows. One widower. Father White, an inteligent English gentleman. He was appointed president, and chairman: to wait on the ladies, and make time pass agreably. There were present two aged sisters from India. They could sing in German and Hindostan. The President was a very mirthful man; and having seen much of the old world and some of the new, was well qualified to entertain company. In the evening we had music and anecdotes: the obliging gentleman escorted the ladies home. Again my labors commenced in my garden. Continual exertion to learn my little untrusty boy to be faithful and help me. It told on my patience and I feared doing wrong. My wisdom seemed exhausted.

Bishop Lunt went from Cedar City to S. L. Conference. My friend "Mrs. Moore" went in his company. On their return they called on me. I was happy to meet them. Bishop L. preached in the evening, a most enlivening discourse. One would infer from his remarks, that he thought the world all joy, light and peace! He blessed us on leaving, and counselled us to be faithful in calling on the Lord. Mrs. Spiking, whose name was Moore when I knew her in Cedar, had obtained a bill of divorce from Moore, and assumed her former name. She seemed much happier than formerly, although she had heard nothing of her long lost son. I felt relieved from school duties, but my labors were incessant in my garden. I found physical exercise necessary to the diversion of my mind. When weary and worn in body, the agitation of a restless spirit was soothed, and "nature's sweet restorer balmy sleep," would steal over my senses, waft me away to dream land, and drown in forgetfulness the cruel things that had fallen to my lot. The house of worship where I taught school was a dread to me; so neglected and out of repair did it appear.

I often had my doubts whether the Lord would hear our prayers as readily ascending from a place like that, which had not the credit of even cleanliness. It was however improved a little by the vigilance of the women in the community.

The President and his suite passed through went South and returned. We prepared a publick dinner for them, set tables in the dilapidated meeting house, which contained so many varieties of dainty food, and that arranged in a style so commendable, it threw a shadow over the deformity of the house, and won for the entertainment the character of respectability. I accosted President Young, in reference to my husband, inquired what he thought of his remaining so long in California? I said, "will you not write to him?" He replied with an impatient tone of voice, which pained me exceedingly and I regretted having mentioned the subject to him.

I continued laboring with great diligence in my school; using every possible effort to make the children learn; and as reward I had the pleasure of seeing them advance rapidly, in the primary branches. But a want of suitable books was a constant annoyance! How often I thought of persons I had known in the world, who spent their means for that which did them an injury; and I wished, Oh, so ardently; the poor children in Beaver, could have some of their money to buy books!

At that time a second comet appeared; similar to the one two years before. It was seen in the north, traveled towards the east through the night, the rays streaming to the west in the morning. Every night higher in the heavens. I often arose at an early hour to gaze upon it and wonder!

In July 61. Hiram Blackwell an old friend came to the place. I had been troubling what I should do for help? I had more burdens than I knew how to bear. Ann L. wished to go north for a short visit, and little boy was not much to depend upon. This young man was very kind; he helped me in various ways; and greatly relieved my mind. So it often happened to me, deliverance would come in the time of my greatest need. Thus I was taught to trust, and wait on the Lord. The second little grandaughter [of Ellen] began to [be] near a year old; she was twining herself about my heart as the other little unfortunate had done. I feared to love her much. At length her father wrote from California that he was coming home. He was humble enough to acknowledge that it was wiser that his wife remained with me. He returned in Oct. his habits much improved: having renounced drinking and swearing: we tendered him a hearty congratulation!

Ann Louisa went her tour north S. L. met with no accident and returned. Wm McG. left the effects he had brought from Cal. at his father's house in Ogden. Came home with the intention of moving his wife and child there to live. Ellen was not pleased with the arrangement, and for a time seemed dejected. At length Mr. McG decided to go to San B. Cal. for a load of merchandise: would go to Ogden and bring home the things he had left, and leave his wife again with her mother. Accordingly he started with his wife and child to visit his people, and bring home her goods.

[The Cotton Mission]

In the meantime there was great enterprise going on. Three hundred families were called on by the Presidency in Salt Lake, to go South; settle St. George, and the region round about, in Washington County. The event proved an agreable excitement. The movers came along in companies at different times through the fall and winter. They all camped in Beaver over night, and sometimes for a day or two, to do their washing in the soft clear water. We made it a point when we heard a train had arrived to go at once and see who among the crowd were our acquaintances. We could invariably find some. It was pleasant to invite them to my home, seat them at my table, hear their familiar voices after a long separation: recount to each other the toilsome scenes through which we had passed, and all our blessings which had been mingled with the sufferings to make life endurable. Sometimes we would go to the log meeting house where they would camp at night, and spend the evening with them. The bishop provided them with wood, and took every precaution to make them comfortable.

There were generally musicians in every company, besides good singers; so they could entertain their visitors very agreably. They knew they were going to a forbidding country, of little timber and little water, except for those who located near a large river. But they seemed merry as the birds. The climate was a warm one, they could soon have grapes, and fruit of various kinds. But Oh, to hear the explorers give a description of the place, was enough to dishearten any one who had not the bravest heart. They said they would give it no false coloring, and those who went must go in faith, trusting in the Lord to open up springs in the deserts; to direct them in their researches, in developing the resources of a country, hitherto unexplored. They found it even better than they had anticipated, and soon made happy homes.

Never would I have known the sweets of friendship had I not been shifted from place to place, often being in conditions to need attention, which when bestowed on me by strangers endeared them to me; and though years many might intervene in our separations, my heart was warm towards them when fate brought us together; and we clasped hands in remembrance of scenes long past and gone!

[Disasters]

But to return to my chilren. My soninlaw and daughter with the little one, came back safely before the holidays commenced. So they were present to contribute with their music to the entertainments given on those occasions. On New years I went two nights in succession with others of my years and staid until 4 o clock. It seemed to revive my spirits. I did not miss my sleep; but was able to rise in the morning and attend to my customary duties, eagerous and active. Wm McG. started on the 5th of Jan 1862 for California. I sent a present by him to my grand daughter Ida Frances Hunt; but he disappointed me, and left the little "favorite dog," in Parowan.

When I heard of it I was quite displeased. It was "a little thing:" but to be faithful in little things is something great. At Christmas time bro' Joseph L. Haywood on his way south, called and made us a visit. I had a picnic at my house which he seemed to enjoy very much. He was full of faith and zeal for the cause of truth. He prayed with and blessed us. The following day pursued his journey with a cheerful spirit. He had not gone far when news overtook him that his eldest daughter had died, with the putrid sore throat! She was a beautiful child, ten years of age. We all felt sad, knowing how aflicted he must feel! But he was a man of God, and would turn to Him for solace and comfort.

About the middle of Feb, news came to us that Wm McGary was drowned! There had been a great flood on the Rio Virgin; swept off buildings and orchards. A great excitement prevailed. We made inquiries, and the report was changed. He had not been drowned, but was killed by Indians! This was equally excitable. Again we made inquiries; which resulted in the certainty of his being alive long after the flood, and pursuing his journey unmolested. Thus our minds were relieved. The train at length came in from Cal, having encountered a terrible flood on the Mohave! They were obliged to remain four days in camp; wading about in water nearly two feet deep; all the time in fear of its rising higher. That year floods were every where. A distressing account reached us of a flood in San Bernardino. Nearly one hundred families lost their all; buildings swept away, land literally ruined; and the owners narrowly escaped with their lives:

We were glad to hear that my soninlaw [John] lost only fifty dollars worth of fencing. He was among the favored ones. Mr. McG arrived safely, suffering no serious loss by the flood he had passed through. He then seemed reconciled to remain in Beaver, and soon purchased a house and Lot. He was appreciated in the community, being an ingenius mechanic, and having great musical talents. It is pleasant to meet persons who combine the useful and ornamental. How admirable when the organs are all well balanced. Mr. McG possessed interesting qualities; but he was restless, and impulsive, stability of character was very low in his organization; his wife being the opposite temperament, sometimes occasioned conflicting views and sentiments, either expressed or understood. When things went smoothly with him, we all were cheerful. His abilities to accumulate were above the medium; all that was requisite for peace and contentment was a steady purpose. I have spoken much of the above mentioned as it will appear in the future how much his variable turn of mind affected the peace of my family.

[Louisa's Trip to San Bernardino, July 1862 to 1 May 1863]

In July 1862, having a generous offer of a free passage to California, to visit my daughter Lois in San B. I accepted it; reluctantly in some degree as it seemed unpleasant for Ann L. to be left with the care of the little untrusty boy. But her sister lived near, and they were both willing I should go. It was a serious undertaking to cross the deserts in July. But other ladies were going and I summoned courage to go. The weather was excessively warm. I passed through St. George in the Southern part of Utah, called on my old acquaintance, took a view of their city, which told largely for the industry and perseverance of the people: but such was the intensity of the sun's scorching rays that the corn had the appearance of having been scalded with boiling water.

I asked if it was possible it could revive, and come to maturity? They assured me it would change its appearance when the sun went down; which was true. I crossed the deserts with less suffering than I had expected. When we camped at noon, to rest the team and get refreshments, the driver would turn the wagon, (which was heavily covered, in the direction for the wind to blow through, and exclude the sun. A young lady traveling with me suggested the idea of wetting our clothing in the heat of the day; which we did, and found it a comfortable method to avoid getting overheated. We wore wet clothes on our heads, and wet our undergarments. So we made the journey with comparative ease. I went wholy unexpected to my daughter: great was her surprise and joy! There was the house I had left with such reluctance; the regret had worn out of my mind. I looked upon it with indifference.

I had often thought that should I ever have occasion to pass the dwelling place where I had expended so much labor of soul and body, I would go a half mile further to avoid the sight of it! But my feelings were entirely changed! I had attractions else where; that one spot of earth where once my hopes lingered had lost its charms. It had been neglected; the trees looked withered for the want of water. My daughter lived three miles out of town; a pleasant retreat it was. There I met my dear grand child Ida Frances, then four years old; two others were added to the family. There were some of the old citizens remaining, who had not been to Utah. They were not so valiant in testimony as they once were, but they were kind to me, and paid me all the attention I could ask for. I received a pressing invitation from our old friend "Christie" in San Francisco, to go there by Stage and Steamer and make him a visit; that my passage should be paid there and back.

The proposal seemed very desirable; but just at the time the small pox broke out, and was raging terribly throughout the country! I would not have feared it for myself, but my friends were opposed to my going, not having the confidence in vaccination that I had. In one instance I had proved it a preventive and for years had felt secure. Mr. Pratt was then living in San Jose Valley, with our daughter Frances and her husband Mr. Dyer. As soon as they heard of my arrival, Frances resolved taking passage on board a steamer and coming immediately to San B. Accordingly as early as the 1st of Sept she made her appearance with a little son, aged two and a half years. Seven years had rolled into eternity since we had seen each others faces, and we were both changed.

Reminiscences of the seven long years crowded upon our minds in rapid succession. Over some events we mourned over others we rejoiced. That she had recovered her health and become the mother of a beautiful child was an occasion of joy. That her father did not share the burdens of our changeable adventurous and migrating life, was a source of regret: although he had been a comfort to her in her separation from the rest of the family: but sympathy for her mother and youngest sister made her wish it had been ordered otherwise. Sometimes we were very cheerful. I had two daughters there, and four grand children. We thought and talked often of the eldest and youngest in the wilds of Utah; of baby Nellie too; and how we wished that fate had so decreed that our homes had been located near together.

We had pleasant visits with our old friends, who five years before had been our neighbors. "Mother Hunt" had two daughters living there, they were my soninlaw's sisters; kind and agreeably attentive to us. They had pleasant families; sons and daughters of considerable age. The place had built up and improved, with fine buildings and orchards; but our homes were not there. One must go far to the west, the other to the north; barren deserts would lie between us, and no one but the "all wise," could tell or know whether we should ever meet again. Three months passed away, and Frances began to talk of returning to her husband and father, for they were thinking her absence long. Mr. Hunt sometimes talked of selling his farm and moving to the Upper country; but my faith and prayers were against it.

I had my heart set on having my daughter and family come home with me. I remonstrated against going so far from the place designated and appointed by revelation for the saints to gather in the last days; that they might be preserved from the judgements which were foretold should come on the wicked, and all those who rejected the gospel of Christ. Mrs. Daley (Mr. Hunt's sister) although she did not incline to come then to Utah herself, encouraged her brother to come, for my sake, that I might have my daughter with me, in traveling on the journey home, and then to be located near me. I felt to thank her for her thoughtful solicitude. The project of moving further west was given up, and the Rocky Mountain country began to be the theme.

Mrs. Jackson the "floral lady" was still living there, firm in the faith of the Latter Day Work, and determined to go to the mountains, where the Saints were gathering. Her beautiful home of fruit and flowers, had not sufficient attractions to induce her to remain there. Mr. Dyer still owned a home in San B. which had cost him $500. It was situated two miles from town, exposed to injury by Indians; the timber on it was stealthily taken off: my daughter thought it would go to decay and be worth nothing, she sold it for fifty dollars. I felt sorry to see property wasted in that way. She seemed destined to make sacrifices. When she left the steamer at San Pedro, took the coach for Los Angelos, (as she was coming to San B.) She left her gold watch in her berth under her pillow. As soon as she got on shore she told the captain.

The Capt. sent immediately to the steamer, made thorough inquiry, nothing could be found of it. No doubt the cabbin maid knew where it was, but it was never found by the owner! Her name was inside. We were sorry for her ill luck; it was a beautiful time keeper; she had carried it for years. The cabbin maid was dishonest, or she might have recovered it. She bore the loss bravely; said she would not complain if she got the dear boy back safely to his father. We parted, and the little fellow thought it was wrong to leave grandma behind. When he saw us grieving, he wept, and says, "grandma I will let you go!" I gave his mother credit for having taught her child habits that made him every where admired. He was wholy submissive to her commands, never showing in the least a stubborn will.

Mr. H. [Hunt] soon sold his home in the country and moved into town; and we commenced making preparations for the arduous journey. I am certain I never worked with better courage or higher hopes. When Frances met her father and informed him of the fact that Mr. H. with his family was preparing to move to Utah, he decided at once to join us in the enterprise, and bear us company to the valley of the great Salt Lake. He wrote a letter to that effect, to which we responded, congratulating him on the welcome reception he would meet; and accordingly he was soon with us; lending his assistance with a hopeful spirit; though at times seeming to dread the journey. Mr. Dyer assisted him in procuring a good "fit out," every thing to make him comfortable. A carriage was purchased for the family to ride in, and a span of white ponies, which Lois would drive.

There were two other teams, and loaded wagons; a small company besides Mr. Hunt's train, sufficient we thought to guard against any attack from Indians. We brought a variety of grafts and vines, for southern Utah; having heard that Wm McGary had bought a place in Harrisville. Which he did, and made a commendable improvement. But his desire for change would not allow of his remaining there till we could reach him with the fruit trees and vines.

When we first set out on the journey Mr. P. assisted in driving one team. The animals were not all well broken; they made trouble, were very refractory. At the head of the Mohave he began to feel disheartened. There we met men from Beaver going through to Los Angelos for freight. I overheard Mr. Pratt saying to bishop Shepherd that he regretted having started; he was fearful the animals were not reliable, he wished himself back, rather than undertake the journey with them. Bro' S. encouraged him to be resolute and firm, he determined to go ahead, in spite of obstacles; assuring him if he did thus resolve he would surmount all difficulties and made the journey a success. He was always a poor traveller by land, perfectly at home on water.

With renewed energy we pursued the journey, with very little difficulty, except being kept awake at night with the children's coughing. Unlucky it was for us, just before we started on the trip they were all exposed to the whooping cough. We made the best of it; they did not seem to be the worse for being so much in the open air. We traveled on quite well till we came to a point where two routes were discussed, the old and new. I had a terrible horror of the old route. It so happened that I laid down to sleep, while the council was held. When I awoke I found the company had been traveling a considerable time on the old route, of which I had such an abhorrence! Never did I feel more unreconciled! Words were vain, they would not turn back for any pursuasion of mine, as I only knew the route by information. Terrible as it was, report said, there was more feed and water for animals. We had not gone far when we found alkali springs. They were not so strongly impregnated but the horses could drink a little without injury. The rocks were the next, they baffled description! For miles on miles not one rod of smooth ground. I recollect thinking as we rumbled over them (expecting every moment the wagons must certainly break down) that if the country could be settled by human beings there would be rocks enough to fence all the land into City Lots, and lay up walls for their buildings. If any poor weary mortals were ever thankful for deliverance out of difficulties, our hearts beat with gratitiude when we saw and felt the wheels rolling on bare ground.

All the way behind the carriage was tied a beautiful little mare, for which Lois had sold her household furniture. Those of us who occupied the carriage had become so accustomed to her we really enjoyed her company. As we drew near the mountain springs, a point known far and near to be a rendezvou for Indians; the men counselled together what plan should be adopted to keep the animals from being stolen? They decided to hire them to herd the stock, but neglected to keep one of their tribe in our camp for security.

The sun rose in the morning, our breakfasts were over; it was drawing near the time to be on the move; no Indians made their appearance with the animals! The men looked at each other as if they would ask, "what do you think?" They started off over the hills. They had only gained the top of a little mountain when lo! there was the little pet mare killed and roasted! The brisk frolicksome colt, no where to be seen, probably devoured before its mother. Mr. Hunt's indignation knew no bounds! There was only one savage fellow remaining near the spoil, and he had laid down to sleep. He jumped and ran when he heard footsteps: like a deer he bounded down the hill; as pistol shots rustled about his ears! Whether to retard his speed in the distance, the men did not know and less did they care. They found their animals grazing alone, the herdmen had fled.

From that point we hurried away; not with much brotherly love for the red men. Oh, how we missed the pet mare and her colt! The children mourned, and felt lonely. On we traveled, not speaking many words till we reached the white settlements, and were out of danger. At St. George many old friends greeted us with kindly salutations, and welcomed "Bro' Pratt." At Hamilton's Fort where Lois had lived nearly two years, on terms of great friendship with that family, we were received with warm expressions of joy, that we had returned in peace; and greater than all, "Bro' Pratt," was with us! Six miles further brought us to Cedar City, where we met Mrs. Spiking with whom I had intimacy during my residence in that town. She was loud in her congratulation. As we had gained the settlements where everyone knew us, it was proposed that Mr. P. and myself should occupy the carriage and drive ahead.

Accordingly we did so, taking the eldest daughter Ida Frances, of whom we were proud. We made a few calls; and when we were half the distance from Cedar to Beaver we met Pres't Young and company: a train of seventy carriages and baggage cars. Ann L. had come out with the company expecting to meet us. Nearly the first carriage after the Pres'ts we discerned her smiling face; more radiant as she saw her father! Brothers Young and Kimball allighted from their carriages came to ours and saluted Bro' Pratt in the cordial manner; congratulated me on my success in having been to California, and returning had brought my husband with me. They blessed us in the name of the Lord, and went on their way. We came on a few miles and met a company of ladies coming out to escort us into town.

My sister Crosby and my eldest daughter were in the crowd. It was the 1st day of May, they were all decorated with wild flowers. When they hove in sight their colors made quite a display. They took an umbrella for a flagstaff, on it they hung a red silk handkerchief, a blue apron, and a white napkin. Ann L. was riding with us, had informed us the ladies were on the way. They pressed brother Pratt to take a seat in their carriage, and ride into town with them. He readily complied; and several of the sisters rode with me. Lois with the little ones was riding in the loaded wagon, but immediately with us, a partaker in all the ceremonies. We drove into town a merry party. Some of the neighbors had assisted our soninlaw Wm McGary in ornamenting the place. The front yard was decorated with green cedars. Large tables were set, loaded with comfortable refreshments, and some luxuries; we all partook with thankful hearts.

[The Family United: Addison in Utah, 1 May 1863 to November 1864]

My daughter Lois was soon settled in a comfortable house near me; her husband took a load of flour and went to Montanna. Mr. Pratt, seemed measurably contented, although it was hard for him to become accustomed to the great inconveniences we had to bear with. There was no fenced pasture for the stock, and when the working cattle were wanted, they had to be searched for on the range. The wayward Island boy was a heavy tax on his patience. He had not been with him from infancy, and learned to love and pity him for his unfortunate organization. The boy was very obedient to him when directly in his sight, but if he wished to send him on business, even a short distance, his faithfulness was an uncertainty. We tried to make his burdens as light as possible considering the many years he had been free from the cares of a family. Ann L. and I had worn the harness continually; it did not irritate us so much.

Mr. Pratt had tolerable health through the summer; but when winter came on he was afflicted with rheumatic and other chronic complaints. He tried to brave the cold climate, so diverse from the torrid zone, but it oppressed him severely. We had many meetings, and social evening parties, all of which he made an effort to enjoy. With hard struggling he wore away the winter. In the spring Wm McGary like a bird of passage decided to sell his house and lot to Mr. J. Hunt and move to Ogden; where his relatives lived. The opportunity was a favorable one for Mr. P. to visit S. Lake, and salute his old friends. I consented to resume duties of out door exercises, and have him go to Head Quarters; believing it would revive his spiritual strength, and give him fresh courage to battle with the ills of life, in a hard country.

In Salt Lake City Mr. P. met a most cordial reception; not even receiving a rebuke for having unnecessarily remained away so long. Brother James Brown, his fellow missionary to the Islands received him with great respect; being comfortably located there with a large family, generously offered him a home, to share with him in whatever his fortune might be. He had claims on a Lot which was surveyed to him on our first entering that valley; and we were hoping he would take measures to recover it, make a home and send for his family. He spend a few weeks there, but did not attempt the recovery of his Lot. He went to Ogden to visit our daughter Ellen. Mr. McGary had opened a cabinet shop, hired an experienced workman to learn him the trade. He carried on a flourishing business. Mr. P. being accustomed to the use of tools was able to assist him. He spent the summer and returned in the fall to Beaver.

When he parted with Ellen he expressed his full intention to remain in Beaver as long as her mother and sister decided to make it their home. We were glad to see him back, feeling well, and apparently in good faith. In the time of his absence, Mr Dyer our soninlaw from California had been through the Territory, with a load of wine and fruit for Montanna. Late in the fall he returned. He stopt in Beaver to spend a few days, when to our surprise and grief Mr. P. announced his intention to go back with him to the warmer climate; feeling assured he could not endure another cold winter. We remonstrated against it, all we thought was reasonable; we saw a change in his health and spirits as the cold increased. So I tried to crush the rebellion in my heart, and asked the Lord to give me a will to be resigned to every event of His Providence.

[Alone Again]

When "the father" had gone, the mother and daughter sat down lonely, to review the past, and plan for the future. The little adopted son wishing to console us, suggested what he could do to aid and assist us. We had a good team; he could go to the canyon in company with boys older than himself, get a load of wood and chop it for the fires. Ann L. was willing to assist in teaching, though it was never a favorite employment, as it had been with me in early life. She had many offers of marriage; and some in accepting she would have had my hearty approval; but for some unknown cause they were declined. So we taught school, rented [out] the farming land to raise our bread, had cows to supply us with milk and butter; we plodded on the journey of life fully equal with our neighbors. It was pleasant for me to have three little granddaughters in my school; they were studious and quick to learn.

By this time we began longing for Frances to come from California and bring my eldest grandson. Mr. Dyer occasionally freighted to the northern mines; he would come directly through southern Utah. We hopefully received encouragement that she would accompany her husband as far north as our settlement, remain with us while he journeyed to Idaho, and returned. Our hearts were lightened with anticipation. In the mean time our city was building up fast, for an inland town. Elders were every year going forth to preach the gospel; and when they returned they brought "their sheaves with them." These were scattered through the varied locations; and some were good and faithful saints. They had left their country and all their kindred to be obedient to the gospel of their Lord and Savior. My sister and I had done the same; we were the only two of a large family who had come to the mountains.

CHAPTER TWENTY-ONE

Beaver and Family

Memoirs, January 1865 to December 1869

[A Second Trip to Salt Lake City]

In the year 65, I went the second time to S. Lake City, taking with me my grandaughter Ida Frances, and my Island boy, then able to drive the team. Ida F. was eight years old. She had yellow glossy hair, of unusual dimension for one of her age. She was self possessed and amiable, neither bashful or rude; always obliging. If she was invited to sing she would never wait to be urged, as little girls generally do, but would seem pleased to contribute something to the enjoyment of the company she was in. We spent a week in Pres't Young's family; he called her his girl, because of her complexion; she so much resembled several of his children. Ellen came from Ogden to meet us, and we went home with her and spent the summer. I went to visit my kind friend Abigail Abbott. At her house I was taken sick. For a week I was not able to be removed to my daughter's. Her married daughter then the widow of Capt. James Brown, lived in the same house. They both bestowed on me unwearied attention; and assisted Ellen in doing every thing in their power for my recovery.

As soon as I was able to ride I was taken to the river and baptized for my health. From that time I began to amend. In the mean time Ida Frances was visiting her relatives in Ogden Valley. She came to me before I was quite well, and began to inquire when we could go home? Her father thinking her absence too protracted, sent for her to come with some friends, if her "grandma" was not able to undertake the journey. To do that she could not be pursuaded. With grandma she had come, with her she must go home. Mr. Dyer my soninlaw was then in Idaho. When he returned, we had a comfortable way to come with him. So we started joyfully, with good courage, and had a prosperous journey.

One annoyance we had on the way. There was a miner in the company, who rode on horseback and carried his baggage in Mr. Dyer's wagon. He was a terrible opposer to the mormon faith; was frequently cursing the Leader's more especially those who held the doctrine of "plural marriage." The man was too low bred to be conscious of his impoliteness; was unwearied in his endeavors to confer favors on the two "lady passengers;" and when he felt that he had offended us, he would resort to his methodist hymnbook, and ask us to unite with him in singing; which we would sometimes do, with great aversion; with a view to soften his hard spirit, and calm his warring passions, towards those who had never wronged him. Mr. Dyer though not a great believer was a gentleman, and would not ridicule any person's faith, because it differed from his own.

We met a "brother Clark," from Parowan; camped with him a night. As we were seated by a cheerful fire, Ida F. and I took our seats near him feeling that we had a protector, who would help us defend our rights. The opposer soon commenced an argument. Our champion put him to silence with few words; reminded him that the world was wide enough for us all; if he did not feel to fellowship the people of Utah, there were other territories where he could go and find his own class of spirits. He seemed to acquiesce in the justness of the remark, and was less disposed to cavil the remainder of the journey. We came to springville, where lived good "father Parish," my benefactor in Nauvoo. We slept in his house, (I with my little girl,) nothing was left undone to make us comfortable. The house and its surroundings wore a garb of comfort.

It was near the last of Nov. when we left S. L. City. There was every prospect of stormy weather; and our friends feared we might suffer with the cold. But they blessed us, and said they would give us their faith and prayers, that stern winter might not overtake us on our journey. Sometimes we failed to make a settlement before night drew darkness around us; then we stopt and made camp fires, had food prepared, and our beds in the wagons. At such emergencies the "miner" would restrain his unruly tongue, and see that the coach cover was closely fastened down, and every precaution used to keep us from the cold; thus proving that though he was like a rough stone from the quarry, there was kindness in his nature.

I knew many people in every town we passed. It was a marvel to the poor friendless miner that I received so many cordial invitations to be entertained free of expense. He finally concluded that though the doctrine of the people was wrong, their brotherly love was truly admirable! As we neared home, the weather having been mild all the way, I refered to the promises made in S.L. by the faithful ones, that no evil should come upon me, and I should reach my home in peace! Well Mr. Dyer says, "Inasmuch as you believe in prayers, you must invoke blessings on me till I reach my home." To which I assented. When the town broke upon our vision, Ida Frances was in extacies! She was certain she could see the smoke from her "mother's chimney!" A messenger went ahead to announce our arrival, which caused no little excitement; for we had been absent four months. The children were delighted with the tales their sister could tell.

The same night we reach home a snow fell. Mr. Dyer went on his way South, nothing daunted by the approach of winter as a hundred miles would take him to a warmer climate. He left us a promise that the next time he came his wife and child should come with him. Ann L. and Ephraim had kept the home in good repair; and I soon commenced teaching school in my own house. The winter though cold and hard had its charms. We had Theatres; our own young people the chief actors. Lyceums, and publick entertainments; in which all were partakers. The aged by mingling in amusements with the young, were mirthful and kept free from moroseness, and stupidity.

[Hiram Blackwell]

There was a circumstance transpired of an afflicitng nature the winter Mr. Pratt staid in Beaver, which I have failed to record. I will here give it place. In a preceding chapter I have spoken of a young man by the name of Hiram Blackwell, who was our patron and friend. Although he had been raised by an aristocratic uncle in the South, largely he was industrious; willing to labor, with those who were compelled to labor for their own support; always ready to lend a helping hand in time of need. His habits were however repulsive to some who did not fully understand him, and especially among the youth on account of his peculiarities he was often treated with disrespect. This excited the sympathies of those older and wiser, and had more knowledge of human nature. Such persons could discern traits in his character worthy of the highest respect. He felt that he had warm friends in Beaver, and he clove to them in his heart. In the year 1864 being in California, he came up the South route to Utah. He had an attack of pneumonia on the way; made all possible haste to reach Beaver. Passing several settlements in company with others on horseback, after his disease had gained with great force upon him, he still would pursue his journey; determined to reach the point where he believed his best friends resided, and throw himself on their care and benevolence, either to live or die! When he reached Parowan, he found teams coming to Beaver. To some young men he appealed to give him a seat in their wagon, in exchange for his riding animal. They not realizing his alarming condition were not inclined to grant the request, and in his extreme weakness he had thirty five miles farther to ride in the cold. When late in the night he reached the habitation of his faithful friends Wm J. Cox's, the heads of the family were gone from home.

This was a grevious disappointment to the distres't man! He requested to see "Sister Pratt;" the younger members of the family knowing that I had been for sometime indisposed, failed to acquaint me of his arrival, in a direct way; so I was not informed of the sad state he was in, till the day preceeding his decease. I was not able to walk to the place; I rose early in the morning and watched the approach of the carriage with the greatest impatience; but Oh, it came too late! Sister Celia Hunt was with me, she greatly desired to see him alive, that she might disabuse his mind in reference to a painful subject in which he thought she had been at fault. Death waits not for grievances to be reviewed when the fatal moment arrives. Those who refused to oblige him in his distress were led to reflect.

A poem containing allusions to his heart sorrows will be inscribed at the close of these memoirs, as a tribute of respect to a faithful friend, and a devoted advocate of the true Gospel. A few who knew the lone man best mourned his untimely end!

[Visit from Frances and Son]

I now return to the winter Mr. Dyer brought me from Ogden with my little charge Ida F., left us with a promise. True to his word the succeeding spring he came up from California, brought his wife and an only child, a son, seven years of age. The inteligence reached us before the train arrived and we hastened to meet them a few miles from town. They had a safe journey through Indian country, and we all felt to thank and praise the Lord. I now had three daughters together. We thought and conversed of the two absent ones; the father and the eldest sister.

[Ann Louisa's Marriage to Tom Willis, June 1866]

Mr. Dyer went on his way to Montanna, on a trading expedition, left his wife and son to spend the summer with us. As pleasure rarely comes unattended with pain, we had one thing to annoy us. Ann L. had contracted an intimacy with a young man her friends thought wholy unsuitable for her. We however had hopes it would not result in a permanent attachment, and we managed to pass the summer in a pleasurable way; the little boy being the light and joy of the house. His cousins were very proud of him; he had a sweet voice to sing, and was not backward; he could sing songs of the war, alone, or with his mother and cousin Ida Frances. We contemplated a visit to S.L. and Ogden in the fall, and time was actively employed in making preparations. Frances was much interested in arranging Ann L.'s wardrobe in a creditable manner, to appear respectable in S.L. City, among the associates of her earlier days. Disappointment was her only reward.

The day appointed for starting on the journey dawned upon us, and we began packing our trunks. We noticed a hesitancy on the part of Ann Louisa to get her trunk arranged in order. I felt surprised and inquired the meaning of it. Frances appeared silent, as if expecting a disclosure, and dreading the effect it would have upon me. A. L. then announced her intention to remain, and enter the bands of wedlock with the person we all disapproved. I was dumb with anguish! My thoughts so overpowered me I could neither reason or implore. When I had partially recovered I should loudly remonstrated, but Frances objected to my opposing her sister's choice, as she was of age, and should be considered sufficiently wise to choose for herself. Reluctantly, yea mournfully, did I submit to her reasoning; for which I ever after blamed myself, knowing by prophetic inspiration it would prove an unfortunate union.

The carriage was driven to the door, our trunks were put in; we looked upon her who had occasioned our great disappointment, and a feeling of commiseration thrilled through the centre of my inner life! For in my immagination was portrayed the trials of the future that awaited her! Frances was at the time in failing health, she could not well endure my sighs and tears. I was compelled to smother my grief, which made it more painful to endure. A hundred times I asked myself, "why did I leave home?" I could only answer, "there is a destiny that shapes our ends." We made the best of our way to Ogden; made short visits on the way. The friends had all expected A.L. to come with her sister; expressed surprise at her nonappearance. To tell the true cause we could not, except to Ellen, whose heart throbbed in unison with ours, in prospect of the dreaded event!

From my daughter Lois I received inteligence that the nuptials were solemnized the ensueing Sabbath after I left, by Wm J. Cox; in presence of their uncle and aunt Crosby, herself and Mr. Hunt, several of the young man's relatives, at Ann L.'s home. But her mother was not there! which restrained hearty congratulations; as all present knew of the scene enacted at the hour of my leaving home. Bro' Cox also wrote me a letter; endeavoring by consoling words to reconcile me to the sad event; which he hoped might not prove as unfortunate as my predictive fears. The young man had a respectable parentage, was connected with the Cox family; but his education had been neglected: being deprived of a mother's counsel at an early age, he had led a wandering life; and accumulated nothing. No trade or profession, what could he do with a family?

Ann Louisa's father wrote a letter of condolence. He would bid us hope and turn to the brighter side. He had known the young man, had discerned in him a good native talent, and as he believed an honest purpose; he might yet attain to something honorable and praiseworthy. There was one point, and only one, on which I hung a hope! he was a believer in the gospel, as revealed in "Latter Days." If he did but cling steadfastly to that, he might rise even to eminence in the scale of beings, redeem his misadventures, and prove himself worthy of the woman who had consented to unite her fate with his. We at length resolved to trust in Him who can bring order out of confusion; who has power to "cast down the mighty, and exalt those of low degree." Our spirits revived, and we contrived to pass our time pleasurable, with old and new acquaintance.

[Trip to Ogden with Frances]

Mr. McGary was building an addition to his house, and doing a prosperous business in his shop. The little Californian was delighted with all he saw and heard. He was remarkably attentive to preaching. Not having been accustomed to go often to a place of worship, the exercises seemed to make a forcible impression on his mind. I took him to a fast meeting: as it was the custom to bless children I sent him forward to the stand to claim a blessing with others. Manfully he walked to the stand, where the bishop and high priests were seated, answered promptly all the questions put to him, telling his name, and that of his parents, his birth place, all correctly. Bishop Herick laid his hands upon his head, and as if inspired by a spirit of prophecy, promised him life, light, knowledge and great wisdom, to choose the good and refuse evil; that he should be known far and near for his inteligence and his integrity; and if he desired it, and sought after truth in early life, he should be a swift messenger to the nations; to carry the glad tidings of salvation to those who sit in the region and shadow of death!

Many other things, which the child sought earnestly to comprehend. His father was then in Montanna. He ran to meet him on his return, and his first words were, "Oh, Pa! I have been blessed!" His father refered to the ordinance of baptism, required to make him a full member of the church; yes, he answers, "when I am eight years old I will be baptized!" Ever after he seemed to have a reverence for bishop Herick. He would run into the street if he saw him passing, accost him in the most courteous manner: "I know you sir, you are the man who blessed me!" The bishop pleased with his ingenuous manners always had a kind word for him; and the boy was a favorite with all who knew him. We visited in S. Lake City, and Mrs. Dyer renewed her acquaintance with her old schoolmates, of fifteen; then, women with families, like herself.

[Dyer and McGary in Business in Ogden]

It was at length decided that Mr. Dyer should remain in Ogden and engage in business with Wm McGary. Sales of furniture could be made to great advantage in the country, by a good salesman, and money was the ruling principle. There were doubts in my mind as to the success of the scheme. Mr. Dyer had a thousand dollars to invest, to stock the shop. I could have said, "keep your money," but the old maxim would be the reply, "nothing venture nothing have." The sequel will show if my impressions were wrong.

[Return to Beaver, Fall 1866]

Late in the fall I returned to Beaver, left my two daughters comfortable situated in Ogden. Ann L. and her husband were living in my house. I endeavored to be as affable as possible, but the man's policy was at antipodes with mine. He was of southern extraction, his domestic and social habits were of a different cast, and though good nature and good sense restrained contention we mutually agreed to be separated a small distance.

They moved to their own place, and we lived on terms of peace if not of intimacy. In process of time A. L. had a son born; her health was miserable, for several months. There was no defect in the child, as we had feared from his father's eyes being extremely sensitive to light; but strong and brilliant in the shade. The boy was beautiful, and lived one year and eight months. By this time a daughter was born to them fair as the lillies of the valley; lived nine months and died. At this juncture some misfortune in the generative organs brought on a weakness from which she has never recovered; although she has borne four sons, all living.

[Ellen's Troubles]

The succeeding summer after my return from Ogden, I was engaged in school teaching. Everything was moving on prosperously when a letter came from Ogden. It was not an annoucement of death, but alas! more terrible! My eldest daughter was in deep trouble with her husband. He had proved treacherous to his marriage vows, had become involved with a young woman separated from her husband but not divorced. He was under censure both by the civil, and eclesiastical law. Business was suspended, and confusion assumed her right to rule. The transgressors were in terror and dismay, the man's creditors were alarmed, he was dreading the vengeance of the woman's brothers; there was general distress and dispair, among all parties concerned. Thus proving true the proverb,

"The way of the transgressor is hard." My daughters were anxious I should come to their aid and comfort; though they knew it was too much to ask. I wrote them my counsel was to be calm, to be merciful towards the offenders; let them repent; it was not the first crime committed in the world, neither would it be the last.

But "Wm, was distracted and would not attend to his business. The creditors were threatening to lay an attachment on the property, which would involve Mr. Dyer." I knew not what good I could do by going, only to soothe their troubled minds. I counselled with her friends here, it was their opinion it would be better for her to leave there till the excitement was allayed, her situation being such as required tender concern, in order to keep her mind calm, and tranquil as possible. Bro' A. Farnsworth and wife had contemplated a visit to S.L. kindly offered me a passage with them. I dismissed my school and made arrangements to go. They too would bring me home, and Ellen with her children, if she decided to come. We made S.L. in good time, I left them there and went on to Ogden. My feelings on meeting my sorrowful daughters can be better imagined than described.

When I met the fallen man who claimed sympathy and forgiveness at my hands, words would be too powerless to describe what either felt. By his own rash and impulsive measures the suit had been instituted, carried forward unadvisedly contrary to the wishes of his injured wife. She had petitioned for a length of time to prove whether his penitence was truly sincere, before consenting to a full reconciliation. To an indefinite time he would not concede; it must be specified, and not reaching far into the future, or the final separation must take place. When counseled by the bishop to be deliberately cautious, be patient and forbearing with the aggrieved one, accede to her proposal, and let time the healer of all curable wounds perform its accustomed office. He would for the moment acknowledge the wisdom and justice of such a course; the next hour his frenzied immagination would urge him on to seal his own doom, and consummate an act he must forever regret.

When all was done, signed and sealed, his consciousness of right returned to him; and he fully realized what he had done. In repenting of one error he had committed another. He was truly an object of commiseration. His business matters were in a state of confusion; his creditors stood ready to divide the spoil. I recalled the premonition I felt when Mr. Dyer announced to the copartnership in which he had entered. The shop was closed, work suspended. We heard not the lively sound of the saws and hammers; all was still, as if death had been there. Mr. McGary went to his father's to board, a distance of one mile and a half. Mr. Dyer went to Montanna to raise money to pay the indebtedness of the Firm. The once cheerful establishment was clothed in gloom; old acquaintances though full of sympathy seemed barren for words to offer condolence. It was at length decided that Ellen should come home with me, and bring the two children.

We engaged a man to bring us to Salt Creek for $50.00. The day was appointed for us to start. The morning dawned, we expected a scene, which was realized. "Wm" came to take his last farewell of his wife and children; as to him it seemed the last. He gave vent to the fullness of his heart; tears flowed in great profusion from all eyes present. I told him I believed the time would come when his family would be restored to him, if he remained unmarried, and acted an honorable part, in reference to such an event. He replied that he would not marry in ten years, if his wife remained single for that length of time. We parted. The McGary family showed a kind spirit towards Ellen. We came to S. Lake City called on our friends who were full of sympathy and kindness towards us. Sometimes as we were traveling along a shade of melancholy would sit on Ellen's countenance and her children would notice it.

William Addison four years old, would look wistfully in his mother's face, and ask; "What ails you mama? You mustn't feel bad; aint your little boy right here with you?" She would then be forced to smile. We stopt in Salt Creek with a bro' Timothy Foot, and our teamster returned to Ogden. Bro' F. was very kind to us, made us welcome to his accommodations; Said he, "any of Bro' Pratt's family will always be made welcome at my house." We telegraphed to Beaver and my soninlaw John Hunt came to meet us with a team. We reached Beaver safely, and Ellen in meeting her sisters and old friends seemed comparatively happy. The little boy showed his love of nature in his admiration of the large trees and shrubbery that grew about the house. Playing in the shade, he would exclaim, "Oh, I love the trees. I don't want to go back to Ogden to that old shop!"

We had left Frances in Ogden to come late in the fall, when her husband would return from the mining country. We trusted in the Lord and called on Him to give us aid and comfort. We had no other resource; no earthly arm to lean upon: that caused us to cleave more closely to our Almighty Friend.

I commenced teaching school in my own house. The little girl and boy were brought under discipline, were fond of their books; which encouraged their mother. The boy unknown to us had the habit of wading in the cold creek water! He caught cold, which seated in his bowels, and produced canker. We were not aware of his alarming condition till it was too late to effect a cure. We employed an english "Root Doctor," who did not understand his case. He treated the child for worms, and knew nothing to the contrary till the canker showed itself in his mouth! even penetrating his head! When he saw it, he acknowledged his ignorance of the case. It was too late to conquer the disease!

Twelve days preceding his decease, his mother was confined with a daughter! Five months from her separation. The poor little boy grieved terribly when he had to be put from his mother's bed. Although able to sit up he took no notice of the babe; but seemed to feel that he was supplanted in the attentions of his mother. The night previous to his final dissolution, he was placed at the foot of his mother's bed. The moon shone on his head through the window. She discovered a deathlike palor, and was yearning over him with anxious looks; he was roused, as if he understood her fears, and said to her, "don't cry mama, I will not go and leave you!" The elders were sent for the following day: they had not faith for his life, but blessed him with a happy entrance into a brighter world, and a part in the first resurrection. That he should have an easy death, and pass away without a struggle!

The sympathy of friends around us soothed our breaking hearts! My daughter was able with her babe two weeks old to ride to the burial ground where was singing and prayers, and everything said to console and comfort the mourning and sorrowing heart. We laid him in his lowly bed and returned to our lonely dwelling! Then was the hour when his father and grandfather came more vividly in remembrace! We said, "did they but know at this hour how much we need their sympathy they would fly to our relief!" That same evening the brethren and sisters living near us came in to pray, and sing; and to offer words of condolence. So we bowed our heads in submission; and hushed each murmuring sigh! The newly born grew in beauty, and we felt she was given to us by some kind angel's hand, to heal our wounded spirits! When a few months old she was my constant care. We named her Frances Aurora. Her mother belonged to associations, for mutual improvement; often had calls to go from home; then the child was invariably left with me.

Almost imperceptibly did my heart twine about the beautiful child, for thus she was in my eyes. Long evenings, when she was past one year old, even when alone with her I could not feel lonely. But the destroyer was lurking about, to mark his victims, in the form of "scarlet fever!" A few days and all was over! The little bright star that illuminated our dwelling from our sight was veiled, and we could see it no more! But to return to her early infancy. When but two months old, Mr. Dyer came from Ogden with his wife and son, on his way to California: hoping to retrieve his losses there, which had accrued to him in coming to Utah. Our meeting was a solemn joy, if so it might be termed. Frances had loved the dear boy, and deeply did she feel our loss.

She admired the infant girl, and much did she wish it might live to solace the heart of the bereaved mother! She seemed loath to leave us. I saw a struggle in her mind; and but for her husband's interest she would have remained with us. We followed her on the way for several miles, then bade her farewell and returned. She wrote us from Sante Clarra what passed in her thoughts as she travelled on. When walking behind the carriage alone, she had to strive against the temptations to turn and follow us home! It was a fierce struggle with a sense of duty that impelled her onward.

[Frances's Return to California]

More than that, there was a premonition; a dread of something fearful before her! And the event was realized in the breaking forth of a flood, on the Mohave river. Mr. Dyer had started with a small company of miners. His animals strayed, and while searching for them, the company moved on and left him.

He was in Indian country, dared not go beyond the settlements alone. He camped three weeks on the Clarra, waiting for a company of "mormon boys" to come along. Well he knew their method of traveling. If a brother's animals had strayed, the whole company would wait till they were found; no going on to leave one behind is ever seen in their programme. We heard of their being detained, and felt great anxiety; but we could not go to them; though within a hundred miles. About the time they started on, a fear came upon me that something would befal them. I was impressed to pray much. I had a friend near me, who often joined me in prayer for some special blessing. I called on her to come and unite with me in supplication, that they might be delivered out of all difficulties, and not fall by the hands of the Indians: When we next heard, it was a thrilling story!

A flood over took them on the Mohave. Without a moment's warning the water rose to the beds of their wagons. My daughter and the little boy were carried in the arms of the taller men to a little hill at a distance; hither six wagons were hauled with all possible haste! There they passed a day and a portion of the night constantly expecting to be washed away; as the water continued to rise till up to the waists of the tall men. Frances in her account of the fearful event described the anguish of her poor little boy when he saw the water gradually rising, till they had not a dry spot for the soles of their feet! She wrote of the signal service rendered them by a tall stranger, who came to them from a camp of Soldiers, going from some Fort to Los Angelos to bury an officer. This same stranger came to their camp fire as they were seated around, entered into conversation; when suddenly the flood burst upon them!

A providential occurence it seemed indeed! He being a tall man could stand firm in the deep water, and assist in hauling the wagons to high land. When he saw the suffering of the poor boy he proposed taking him on his back and wading through the deep water to the camp of

Soldiers, who had gone high up on the slope of the mountain. There was a man in that company, whom the child knew, and he was willing to be taken to him to have his life saved. The stranger took the boy on his back, assuring his mother that if she saw the water up to their shoulders, she need not fear; for he was a good swimmer, and would carry him safely through. She saw them ascend the mountain!

I quote her own words, in the letter. "When I saw them rise to the acclivity, above the water, and knew my child was safe, I lost all fears for myself. I had given orders that if I was drowned he should be taken to his grandpa in San Bernardino. It was Christmas eve! We knew not our destiny; the water continued to rise till midnight. Suddenly it stood still! In a few moments it began to fall! Joyfully we clasped each other's hands and wished a merry Christmas!" There were fifteen souls on the little Island, my daughter the only female. Early in the morning the stranger returned, to assist the company in moving to higher ground. They went in search of their animals. Mr. Dyer found one of his, a very valuable one, drowned. He felt the loss, but had no word of complaint, inasmuch as their lives were all saved.

When the water retired they went on their way rejoicing! They reached their home in due time, and told the story of their adventures to their wondering father! The boy could never forget the night he spent in the camp of soldiers, away from his mother; fearing he should never see her again! When she went to him on the following day, his excitement was painful! The transition from suspense to relief, was so great! Mr. Dyer is a very short man in stature, which made it difficult for him to encounter the deep water, and render assistance to others. When the account came to me I recalled the presentiments I had near the time of their trouble; the wrestling I felt when calling on the Lord, in their behalf. Then I believed, some guardian angel had impressed me to pray earnestly, that they might be delivered from danger, and death!

When safely they had reached their home, found their father alive and well, they remembered their great deliverance; and all their losses were forgotten. The succeeding Christmas, when all were assembled around the festive board, they remembered with tears of gratitude how they were delivered from terror and dismay, and carried on their way rejoicing!

[Death, Again]

As soon as Ellen's last born was of sufficient age to be left through the day, she engaged in teaching. The child was left in my care while the mother was absent. It grew, beautiful in our eyes! The care of it seemed no burden to me. News came that Wm McGary was married. It was a surprise to

Ellen, in consideration of his promises made unsolicited, that he would remain single ten years, if she did not enter the married state in that length of time!

The inteligence did not appear to affect Ellen much, except at times she seemed more meditative and abstracted in thought. Little Nellie often spoke of it seeming conscious that something was wrong. She requested me to write a letter for her to send her father; when asked what she would have said to him, she replied, "tell him I don't care anything about the woman he has married." She was a thinking child though but seven years old. The babe had whooping cough during her first winter, which alarmed us; but she bore it well, and recovered. The months rolled round and her first birthday came. Oct 2d. It was a time for fruit. The children belonging to the family were invited to come and partake of dainties prepared.

Her little cousins helped her sister; and they dressed her for the occasion; plaited a beautiful wreath of flowers for her head, seated her in a high chair; and to her were presented first, all the dainties on the table. She seemed to understand that she was the object of interest, mainly, as all the attentions were directly to her. Wild with joy she would clap her hands and respond to all the signs of mirth! I looked upon the happy group around the table and thought, "Little do they know what lies before them! Who can tell what another year may bring to pass!" The elder daughter then seven years of age, seemed entranced in admiration for the child! The brother was gone, and her very existance seemed blended with that of the little one. She was the star of promise and centre of attraction!

Oh! how vain are all earthly hopes! Four months had passed in comparative contentment when the destroyer came barking about, searching for the brightest gems, to fasten his cruel fangs upon. The scarlet fever was announced: a most unwelcome guest! Assiduously did we endeavor to guard her from exposure; keeping her closely indoors; but vain were our attempts. A child knocked at the door; our fears for a moment were forgotten; the mischief was done! Oh! how fervent were our hopes and prayers! Four days of suffering told the sad story! Lonely our hearts and our home! But we dared not murmur! We had one, only one left. Her grief knew no bounds! To see her ideal of beauty laid prostrate! her prattling tongue forever silent! And to be buried out of sight! All our sympathies were enlisted for the bereaved girl.

We told her of the pitying angel; of the bright beautiful home the lovely child would have in the Lysian world where dwelt our Saviour who when on earth took little children in his arms and blessed them; saying, "of such is the kingdom of heaven!" In comforting her we consoled ourselves. Ellen's friends rose up to comfort her! They enticed her from home, to join their associations; that her grief might not fasten too deeply on her mind. They forgot in part that I too needed pity, as well. When she went from the house Nellie and I were left alone. I was wont to think of St. Paul's injunction. "If any one is afflicted let him pray, if merry, let him sing psalms," I have proved singing to be a heavenly antidote for a sorrowful heart! When cheerful company is not at hand, let the mourner sing! Writing was a solace to me in affliction; and reading books which led my mind away from scenes of cruelty, to the time of everlasting redemption! When Christ shall have put all enemies under his feet; and triumphed over death and hell!

Time the great healer of wounds bound up our broken hearts, and we began to be cheerful. Nellie learned to love her Aint Lois' little ones, and grew happy again. At intervals her grief would return. She would sometimes come from her sleeping room in the morning, weeping sorely, because she said, "we had to let the prettiest ones die!"

[Ann Louisa's Troubles]

Ann Louisa my youngest daughter had one boy, of a year's growth at the time; he was fair as a lilly, and we looked wishfully upon him and wondered if we dared to love him! Eight months passed away, and we began to feel comforted in view of our bereavements. Ann L. had a daughter born. When but a few weeks old, the "scarlet fever" smote the little boy; and before there was time to administer relief, he was gone! The elders were sent for in great haste, but to his mother's astonishment, they pronounced him past recovery; and he breathed but a few moments; having had but twelve hours illness. We began to feel that the Lord was trying us as he did Job, to see if we would acknowledge his hand, and say with him, "The Lord gave, and the Lord hath taken away, and blessed be his name! The mother was calm, and seemed to feel that he was taken from some "evil to come." She had failing health; and the succeeding summer moved to a place where in wet weather the water flooded over the premises; causing the atmosphere to be damp in the house. The result was, the infant girl was attacked with pulmonary complaint; and being exceedingly fleshy, the disease soon bid defiance to all medical skill, and the parents could not exercise faith to save her!

Their last gem was torn from them; but they bowed their heads in humility and tried to feel that the Lord had taken her to add one to the seraphim who surrounded the throne and chant his praises in hymns of joy!

The parents moved with their fleshy child one mile and a half from town; to a low damp place; the result was, the mother and babe both took cold; producing with the latter inflamations of the lungs; with the mother a swelling of her breasts; thus rendering her incapable of nursing the distressed infant as she desired. Ellen was engaged in school; yet went to her assistance as often as was compatible with her duties. The child's breathing was greatly obstructed. It pained me sorely to hear her breathe! I would walk away from the house at night a distance of several rods, still the heartrending sound would reach my ears! But it did not long continue; and she fell asleep more beautiful in death than in life. Not in the least wasted in flesh, no sign of decay about her features, till we laid her in a cold bed, decked with flowers, white as the new fallen snow! It was a marvel to many why she did not change color, having apparently suffered so much!

The mother seemed calm and resigned; her last gem was taken, but she uttered no murmuring word. That our days on earth are numbered, and we cannot transcend their bounds to me seems an incontrovertible decree. Else why in some instances can we lay hold on faith, and claim the life of a child, in answer to prayer; by virtue of the promise. "Whatsoever ye shall ask in faith, believing, asking in my name saith the Lord, it shall be granted." I have proved it verily so. If I pray, believing without doubts that I shall receive, my desire is granted. But we read, "faith is the gift of God." Then first of all we should examine our grounds for faith, and if we cannot command it, is it not vain to utter our requests?

CHAPTER TWENTY-TWO

A Railroad Trip to East Canada

Memoirs, Winter 1870–71 to December 1871

[Ellen, Ann Louisa's Baby]

Ann L. soon after the death of her last one, left the unhealthy location and returned to town. Ellen went to Ogden to recover the property awarded her by the court when her separation from her husband took place. She there encountered *him*, though she did not meet his wife. Their meeting, as she told me, was of a painful nature. To her he confessed his rashness; and though he had a devoted wife he was far from being happy. She spent the summer with her friends there, having with her her only child; which left me lonely, with one exception, I had grand daughters to be with me, and was teaching school in my own house. Late in the fall Ellen returned bringing with her means, in goods and money to supply her wants through the winter.

During the winter my youngest daughter had a son born. She had long been afflicted with a weakness common to females, which deprived her of much enjoyment. Her husband though disposed to treat her kindly, (according to his version of the term) was not successful in accumulating; and her feeble health prevented her administering to her own necessities.

The winter of 1871 passed cheerfully away with me having in contemplation to visit the home of my childhood; in the cold region of Canada East. I had by this time increased my stock of cattle to a sufficient number to ennable me to dispose of some, and make myself a comfortable fit out for the long journey. My old friend Mrs. Spiking in Cedar City proposed to accompany me to Omaha; having a long lost son in the state of Missouri. We conjointly had great anticipations! Her son had been lost to her, more than fifteen years.

She learned by accident his place of residence and determined once more to set her eyes upon him. I had been separated from my kindred thirty eight years: many among them had passed away and to think of meeting the living ones, gave me strange sensations: knowing how much they must be changed! To think of meeting my own brothers and sisters with whom I was reared under the same roof, and finding them so changed that I could not recognize them, was a solemn dread to me! yet above all other earthly things I desired to go. My friend came in time to assist me in making the necessary preparations. Early in May, we took leave of our children, admonishing them to remember us daily in fervent prayer, that we might have a prosperous journey and return in due time.

We hired our passage to Salt Lake with Bro' J. Hall. At the first onset an obstacle arose to dishearten us. We started in good spirits rode a little distance called to bid Ann L. Willis a good by: found her with a very sick child; The physician had pronounced it dangerously ill with inflamation of the bowels. The mother was greatly alarmed; the father was away from home, though not out of town. What was to be done? The child unless immediately relieved would perhaps not survive the coming night. Must I go and leave my daughter in such distress? The teamster could not wait for us. My daughter said, "go and promise me you will pray for me, and for the life of my infant." Sorrowfully we turned away and started on our journey. We both had heavy hearts! Sister S felt deeply for Ann Louisa.

We were very silent, as we traveled on. I thought how shall I endure, till I can hear whether the child lives through the night? We must reach some point ahead where a letter could be sent us: no telegraphing news, at that time. We counselled together; and agreed that we would inquire of the Lord: believing He would make it known unto us. As we rode along a strange lady was walking by the side of our wagon. We asked her to ride as she appeared to be going some distance. She was conversant, and we saw she was a believer in prayer. To her we communicated our intention. She fully endorsed our belief, that the Lord would hear our prayers. The men belonging to our company retired a little distance, to camp for the night; leaving us to ourselves. The strange lady was still with us.

She kindly offered to unite with us in prayer, making the case her own. Our request was that the Lord by a dream, or vision, would make known unto us whether the child survived the night; was yet alive, and would he continue to live? We prayed in faith, believing the Lord would hear us. That night I dreamed I had the babe in my arms, his eyes were unusually brilliant, his face was fair, and he looked healthy; but on one cheek there was a little sore. I told my dream, and Mrs. Spiking says, "behold, I can interpret it! The boy is well, with the exception of one ailment, he is cutting teeth!" Had a thousand pounds rolled off my shoulders it would not have lightened me more! When a letter reached us in S. Lake, the words written were the same. "He is well, but cutting teeth!" The Doctor says, "great caution must be observed." I then wrote to my daughters how the Lord had blessed us and they rejoiced, and were thankful.

[Across the Country by Rail]

We tarried two weeks in Salt Lake City, visiting our friends and receiving their blessings. We went to the House set apart for holy ordinances, and attended to baptisms for our dead. Before leaving home I had written to Mr. Pratt informing him of my intention to visit our country; suggesting the plan, that he would take shipping at San Francisco and meet me in Canada or N. Hampshire; where his kindred lived. But his health was not firm, and he had not ambition to undertake the journey. We took the cars at S. L. and went to Ogden; made a short stay. I had an acquaintance there, who was in someway associated in business with the R. R. commissioners. He offered to assist us in securing a passage across the plains at reasonable rates.

There were three ladies for whom he would buy tickets to Omaha. Accordingly he got our fare reduced to $40.00 each, on first class cars; which we considered good fortune to begin with. I had never seen a R. R. Car in motion till near the time I was ready to take passage, at S. Lake. They looked frightful at first sight. I had read of so many disasters, it was natural I should fear. But when I was seated and commenced to look about me I saw the company all appeared composed, no signs of fear; so I soon felt safe; and quickly did I realize the improvement from ox team traveling. I was filled with wonder and admiration! I felt that no other method of conveyance was worthy of notice. I seemed to scorn the idea of riding after a common team. I felt as though I were a bird flying through the air, soaring above all danger.

I had not conceived an idea that any thing could cause me to feel so elevated! I had all my married life been emigrating farther west. From Canada to the "Holland Purchase" in [New] York State: thinking then I had got too far *West*! From thence to Indiana, into the howling wilderness, where the tall maples grew closely at my door. From that point to Illinois, on the Mississippi, and on, on, to the Rocky Mountains! Keeping ahead of Rail Roads: till at last they overtook me! I rejoice that I have lived to witness the ingenuity of man; in the construction of any thing so wonderful! I was greatly amazed on the cars, in discerning the variety of spirits. A place above all others to study human nature. As soon as it was announced that there were ladies from Utah in the Car, a curiosity was at once excited. Some few there were who would shun me. Others were attracted, would draw near, show a desire to converse.

The gentlemen generally railed me about our peculiar doctrines. The principle of polygamy they were loud in condemning. Then I would ask them if they believed the bible. "Certainly we do," would be the reply. Well I would say, you read the Psalms of David, and you honor him in every sentence: the holy effusions of his soul poured out are like the teachings of the blessed Saviour. You do not pause to think how many wives he had: and that it was said of him he sinned not, except in the case of Uriah's wife, because he took her unlawfully. And even in that case the Lord was merciful, and blessed Solomon who was her son, more than all the wise men of the east, and instructed him in building His House.

I found it the better way to avoid argument as much as possible, but would testify boldly to what I knew to be true. I was constantly thinking of the improvements that had been made in the years that had passed since I crossed the plains in 48 with an ox team, being nearly four months on the journey. Then I could go from Ogden to Omaha in two and a half days. The tunnels through the mountains astonished me! the scenery, the beautiful fields of grain, the little gardens coming almost up to the Rails in some places, filled me with admiration! I felt that I was in a world of enchantment! I would exclaim, "What can not hands of men do?" Then I remembered how men of old commenced to build a tower to go up to heaven! and the Lord said, "Let us go down and confound their language, and hinder their work," As though there was a possibility of their accomplishing their design.

A bridge over the Mississippi at Rock Island a half mile in length, excited my wonder, and amazement! Another specimen of what men can do! Crossed the old Missouri at Omaha, in a flat boat; the waters muddy as ever. I called to mind how I dreaded to drink of it when sick at Council Bluffs! Nothing on earth at that time seemed so desirable as clear cold water! At Omaha I parted with my friend Mrs. Spiking and she went to Unionville, Missouri. Chicago was in her glory, I greatly admired it. I made the acquaintance of a widow lady who had come from California, belonged in Rochester. We had much conversation; and she introduced me to a Presbyterian Clergyman. As soon as he learned I was from Utah he was very reserved and silent. I could see prejudice in his eyes, and on his knitted brow, so I took no trouble to draw him into conversation; as the lady had expected.

I was alone, without a protector; yet I felt safe, and perfectly at home. The conductors were kind and attentive. I reached Rome, NY where I had to remain over night, and change Cars. It was eleven p.m. when I went to the Depot. I knew not where to find a hotel, there was no coach waiting. As I was talking to a lady passenger in the Depot, a gentlemen standing near overheard our conversation. He accosted me in a kindly tone and offered his assistance to conduct me to a hotel; where, he assured me, I should be well entertained and brought to the train in due time in the morning. I queried a moment, "shall I go out on the street with a stranger at this late hour?" I looked intently at him, I descerned in his countenance an honest expression; and said to myself, I can trust him; for I am advanced in years, and he is young man; he can have no other motive than showing kindness to a lone woman.

And so it proved. He told the landlord my history; that he must see that I was conducted to the train by 6:00 in the morning. I had a beautiful room, conveniences for bathing; and every necessary attention. Was called in time, a dish of tea prepared, a coach to take me to the train. So I went joyfully on my way.

At a Depo where the passengers were detained an hour or two I met some very talkative people. A lady who said she lived in Palmyra NY, at the time Joseph Smith found the gold plates. She had never any doubts of the truth of that. She knew the plates were found, as was reported; but she had never before seen a mormon that belonged to the church which originated in the finding and translating the characters on the gold plates. She was pleased to meet me.

At the same place there was an elderly gentleman who seemed disposed to ridicule every thing pertaining to the marvelous work, as believers esteem it. I heard him for a few moments. I then gave him a searching look and said; sir, We all hold our religion sacred, no doubt you do; we do not like to hear our religious faith ridiculed! I can assure you my religion has cost too much for me tamely to submit to hear it maligned, and contemptously spoken of!" The man felt the rebuke and apologized. He said, madam, I beg your pardon; I am glad I have met you, and heard the explanations you have given on the subject: it has removed in some degree my prejudice." The same gentleman asked me if I did not feel timid considering the advanced period of my life to undertake so great a journey and no immediate protector?

"Oh no, I replied, "I have trusted in the Lord all my life and he has taken good care of me, I am willing to trust him longer." And now said I, "I will tell you what my faith is. If a disaster was hanging over the train, I believe I would have warning, either by a dream or vision in time to make my escape." "Well indeed," said he, "that is first rate, I am glad you have such faith." So we parted in friendship, after what I considered the insult.

At Ogdensburg on Lake Ontario, two ladies came on board, bound for Boston; respectively named, Mrs. Melissa Branson, Mrs. Joseph Heart. They came to my seat when they had learned that I was a "Mormon woman," from Utah." We entered into conversation, and they became much interested. The first mentioned requested me to write her from Canada. Accordingly I wrote to her from Dunham, and gave an account of my meeting with my relatives after a separation of thirty eight years. She replied in a most friendly manner, and I regret to say, I did not continue the correspodence.

[Greeting Relatives and Friends at Home: Dunham, Canada]

When I reached St. Albans V T. I began to meet people who knew my relatives in Canada. They seemed pleased that I was going to visit them, after such a succession of years. The Cars took me within fifteen miles of my old old home. Then I took passage in a stage coach that conveyed me to my eldest sister's door. I passed the old homestead where she lived when I left the country. Her son owned the place by inheritance, and then occupied it with a large family. Every thing looked natural about it. The fruit and large shade trees I so much admired in my early childhood. In that dwelling my sister's two sons were born.

Reminiscences of early life rushed upon my mind in a rapid succession as I rode along, gazing eagerly at every inch of ground. The Coach driver understood how long I had been absent, and that I wished to surprize them, by my sudden appearance. He knew Mrs. Baker's place of residence, and having a curiosity to hear the salutation when she would find me out, alighted from the Coach and went in. My sister hearing a knock at her door, arose from her bed and bade us walk in. I could see but one natural feature; and had I met her in a strange place we might have remained as strangers for an indefinite length of time. She had met with an injury by falling from a carriage and being run over by one wheel, which dislocated her collar bone; causing it to protrude giving her a stooping posture.

I said to myself, "can that be the bright agile woman I once knew to be my eldest sister? Oh the ravages of time!" I addressed her in a cautious manner, saying, "Madam could you permit a poor traveling woman to stop with you a short time to rest herself till she can find where her friends live, and send for them to come?" She replied very faintly, "I am a widow woman in poor health not able to wait on any one. I fear you would not be comfortable." I answered, "Oh, I will not make you any trouble." By this time I had taken a seat and she was seated near me! The Coachman stood in the door, I stept to the table and we talked about the fare and I paid him, exchanging a few words, Mrs. Baker then inquired, "what are the names of your relatives that live in this town?"

I said, "I have a brother here whose name is Joseph Barnes." She stared me in the face, "Joseph Barnes indeed!" Perhaps you are Louisa Pratt! are you?" I replied, "Yes, Levina I am!" She burst into a flood of tears, and caught me in her arms! The coachman took his leave. She confessed that at first she felt suspicious that I might be an imposter, and while I was talking to the driver she thought silently, "that cannot be a bad woman, she has a pleasant voice." She seemed chagrined when it was known among the friends that she had treated me coolly at first; but she lived almost alone and was very aged.

It was soon made known in the neighborhood, that "Mrs. Pratt had come from Utah," and the friends came crowding in to see me. They were all certain they should have known me, any where; but I do not believe they would.

I met those who were my companions in youth; some, I might have remained in their company a week, without the least supposition that they were persons with whom I had once been intimate, unless it had been betrayed in conversation. My eldest sister's husband had been three years in the spirit world. Half the pleasure of my visit was lost because his place was vacant. He was a man greatly beloved: had he been living, he would have spared no pains to have made my visit pleasant. My sister was a hearty mourner; would dress in nothing but black; though professing great resignation to the events of Divine providence, a sure and certain hope of a resurrection to eternal life! The Episcopal house of worship stood on the same spot where in early childhood I was wont to go on Sabbath mornings; rebuilt almost the exact type of the ancient one; doors fronting the same direction.

Near the South door as I entered, I saw the great white marble stone inscription, "Sacred to the memory of Stevens Baker," "Blessed are the dead who die in the Lord, from henceforth, for they rest from their labors, and their works do follow them." That stone and the spot where it stood, seemed of more value to this bereaved woman than all the world beside! Through the grave yard I walked reading on the head stones the scores of names once familiar and dear to me. Some who had been buried from sight twenty and thirty years. I could remember when but a few tokens were to be seen on all the ground where the departed ones lay then, multitudes lifted their white caps, as if saying, "here we lie sleeping!" From the graves of my father and mother and a dear sister I plucked leaves and flowers, pressed them in a book and brought them with me to Utah. Sacredly will they be preserved, while my lamp of life holds out to burn.

A few days passed in reviewing antiquated places about my "old old home!" My youngest brother was living in the house my father built when I was but twelve years old. He was a youth but eighteen when I saw him last; now a grey headed man an emblem of the ravages of time. He was a bachelor, with a widowed niece to keep his house. The house inside had undergone repairs; outside it appeared the same, except showing signs of decay. Oh, the old familiar haunts! The foot paths where in childhood and youth I was wont to stroll, cull the wild berries, all so vivid in my recollection, I could not think it possible that three score years had passed into eternity since first my nimble feet tripped over the pleasant grounds, and then almost two score since my eyes had rested on them.

To the woods I went where my father and brothers made maple sugar, as far back as I could remember. I sat upon the same old rock by the side of which they hung the large iron kettles to boil the sweet water extracted from the trees. The old rock was covered with moss; which told how many springs had come and gone while it had faithfully been serving its owners. Thousands on thousands of pounds of sugar had been made against its impregnable sides, and it not the worse for its usage.

I looked at my brother, and thought how he had grown old alone; no wife or children to call his own. It seemed to me he would have borne his age better, had the spontaneous affections of children been mingled with his own love. He was not willing to admit that his life had been less happy; reasoning that his freedom from care had measurably supplied the want of connubial felicity. I could not appreciate or endorse the argument. He partially consented to the proposal to come to Utah with me when I was ready to return, but the dread of so great a journey appeared to dishearten him; so accustomed had he been to home life. He was highly esteemed for his honestly and benevolence. He seemed kindly disposed towards me, notwithstanding my strange views and belief as he thought. So with many others of my relatives and early acquaintance.

I met those who were pupils in my school when I was young. They had grown grey headed, had large families, children married. They treated me with great respect, invited me to their homes to be entertained, introduced me to their children, and grandchildren. I was amazed and interested. One, a bachelor, had preserved a school ticket I had given him in his childhood, 45 years. Keeping it in his bible for a place keeper.

[In Defense of My Faith]

I went regularly to the church where I was accustomed to go in my youthful days; heard the same lessons from scripture read, which were as familiar to my ears as the alphabet; having heard them nearly every Sabbath day for twenty years. The old Episcopal priest whose name was Charles Cotton, had long been gone to the better world; and another in his stead whose name was Godden was installed. He was cold and unsociable with me, because my religion differed from his. My aged sister was a favorite with him, but towards me he was cool and reserved. There was a Sabbath school celebration, conducted by the said Clergyman; I went with my kindred. I availed myself of an opportunity to converse with him upon the subject of our faith. I accosted him in friendly tone and drew him into conversation. I began by refering to the circumstance of his having shown an unwillingness to admit me to the communion table, when I had come to the altar by my sister's request. His reply was, "oh, we cannot fellowship mormons." I said to him. "Sir you do not understand our doctrines, if so, you could not possibly condemn them without denying the scriptures!" I can assure you the doctrines of the Latter Day Saints are purely apostolical. You my dear sir, do not preach the fullness of the gospel; you only preach it in part. You do not say as Peter did on the day of Pentecost, when the people cried what shall we do to be saved? Repent and be baptized for the remission of your sins, and you shall receive the gift of the Holy Ghost. You do not tell them that the signs shall follow them that believe: that they shall heal the sick, cast out devils, speak with new tongues, take up serpents, and if they drink any deadly thing it shall not harm them."

"This sir, is what the Elders of my church preach; promising everything in the Lord's name, according to the faith that is exercised." I then went on to tell him of instances I had known where the sick had been healed, the lame made to walk raving maniacs restored to reason, bearing my testimony faithfully, to the truth of the great "Latter Day Work." He seemed softened; said he believed I was a true christian, and that the Lord would feel after me and in his own due time bring me back to the only true church. I replied, "should I return to your church I should turn away from a great light to a little one." Our interview ended; he treated me more cordially ever after.

Meeting with persons contemporary with myself in youth, it was admitted by all that I had borne the wear of time better than they had. I had gone the world over, endured all the toil and sufferings it would seem possible for a mortal to pass through and live; they had remained permanently in their own native town, seldom having been more than fifty miles from home, and yet I was both physically and mentally more active than they. I had kept pace with the spirit of the age was not so sterotyped and old fashioned. My health had been preserved by observing the laws of life. I had never weakened my nerves by dosing with drugs and patent medicines. Cold water had been my remedy for all diseases, diet, and fresh air important preventatives. Besides my religion was a more cheerful one than theirs. I had sought to keep my heart mirthful in the midst of my greatest sorrows.

Although my friends did not receive my testimony in full, in regard to the coming forth of the "Latter Day Works" yet they were pleased to listen to my rehearsals, where in the power and goodness of God in delivering his people in times of their great distress had been clearly manifested. They dared not deny the promises of God to those who trust in Him. And yet, how could they believe that a people so dispised and maligned by the christian world could be the heritage of the Lord! Whom he had gathered out of every nation from the power of their enemies, and planted them in the vallies of the mountains in a hiding place, while His indignation is passing over the earth abroad! Why could they not remember that the ancient Saints had all manner of evil spoken against them?

I went to visit my two brothers living in adjoining towns: the elder two years my senior, was a methodist local preacher. He looked old was very grey. He did not however, like some religionists manifest a spirit of prejudice and unkindness. In all his conversation with me he showed a truly christian spirit; with one exception. I thought it his duty to investigate the work, which I testified to him had been revealed from Heaven, in this our Day; even the "Fullness of the everlasting Gospel." He showed no disposition to find fault, but was contented to go on in his old way. His fourth wife, (three dead) was an adventist. That sect professes the belief that the Saviour is liable to make his appearance at any hour. Whereas the Latter Day Saints believe the time is drawing near, and great preparations must be made. In a special manner, must a Temple be built, in Jackson County, Missouri.

They say, "he will come as a thief in the night." And so he will to those who do not believe in modern revelation. The apostle says, "we are not children of Darkness that day should overtake us unawares." The wise virgins will have their lamps trimmed and burning and be ready to go forth to meet Him, even at the dead hour of night. But to return to my brothers. The above mentioned is Cyprian Barnes, the second son born to my parents. The third, Lyman Franklin, B lived in the township of Broom; the same that married the friend of my youth. Our meeting seemed a strange scene; we knew not what to say. What I felt most impressed to exclaim, would have been, "why how strangely you look! Can you be my very old friend?"

After a few days friendly intercourse they began to seem a little familiar; but their manner of life had been so widely diverse from mine, we could scarcely sympathize on my subject. Their children pleased me. They were types of their father and mother as I had known them forty of fifty years before.

[An Accident]

I was delighted with one source of enjoyment in Dunham, where I was reared. Almost every family owned a horse and buggy. I had great pleasure in riding about. My youngest brother, (Joseph by name) kept a splendid animal to drive. Emily Barnes my niece, who was house keeper at the old home could drive, and take me wherever I wished to go. The roads are exceedingly narrow in that country; not more than half the width that they are in Utah; Besides they are thrown up from the sides to the centre; to drain off and make the roads dry.

My niece and I had started on a tour to my methodist brother's residence. A furious dog came barking and frightened the horse, and he gave a sudden start, threw the carriage off the elevated ridge and down we went below. I was badly hurt, but not seriously. A thought occured as I was going over, "my children have forgotten to pray for me this morning! It was an injunction I had left with them, that they should not forget me in their morning and evening devotions one day in my absence. Fortunately for us we were near a dwelling; the man came out and righted us, and we pursued our journey. We reached my brother's and told of our misfortune. I was very lame. I could not call on my brother to administer to me by the laying on of hands, so I asked him to pray; which he readily consented to do.

In his prayer he said nothing concerning the accident, and my injury: it was purely spiritual. He appeared to be addressing a being who did not understand temporalities. I afterwards told his wife, that I believed in telling the Lord what we wanted; and I wished the prayer to be an importunity that I might be speedily healed of my lameness; and sustain no permanent injury by the accident. She agreed with me, that it should have been thus indited, to be appropriate. Remedies of various kinds were applied and I slowly recovered. I wrote to my daughters and grandchildren what had befallen me, and I think they acknowledged that they had sometimes been remiss in their duties, which I had so explicitly enjoined upon them.

[Nephews Admired]

My aged sister had two sons, her only children. One lived on the old homestead his father occupied when I left that country; but my sister had a home delightfully pleasant in the village. A farm of six hundred acres was the portion of each son.

The elder son Wm Stevens Baker lived three miles from his mother's residence. Many a pleasant ride did we have over a beautiful road to the country seat of that son, who had wealth and comforts around him; an excellent wife, and seven children, nearly all full grown, and living at home. It was an agreable sight to see them all seated around the family table. I looked at that father, and thought what admiration I felt for him in his infancy! The first time my eyes ever beheld him perhaps I thought he exceeded in beauty all the infants I had ever seen! I was then fifteen years old, and he was the first grandchild born in the family. I was his first teacher; from me he learned the first rudiments of his native tongue. He had come to middle age with correct habits, and a mind well stored with useful knowledge. His wife an amiable inteligent lady; his children finely organized and well disposed, disciplined, and educated. I could tell of his childish pranks whereby he amused me so much in his childhood; and with mirthfulness we recounted the scenes which years multiplied had not been able to obliterate. The scenery between his residence and his

mother's was picturesque and delightful. Such a growth of large trees
along the road, besides orchards and cultivated fields. A few old buildings
remained the same in outward appearance. My mind was constantly filled
with thoughts; reminiscences of the past crowded my imagination.

Three months and a half I spent in visiting my relatives and old
neighbors; recounting to them my great experience in the different
countries where I had lived; my joys and sorrows, trials and tribulations
through which I had been called to pass: and out of which the Lord had
brought safely to rejoice with them again in the home of my early life.

It was marvelous in their eyes, and they were constrained to say, "It
was the Lord's doing! They all seemed rich in this world's goods; many of
them in splendid buildings grandly furnished; beautiful pianos; children
all taught the art of music. I told them I was richer than they were. I felt
that in free thought, knowledge and understanding of the laws of God I
was far richer.

The time drew near that I must leave. My poor old sister looked sad;
She was certain we should never meet again in this world. I tried to avoid
a scene: proposed returning after going to my brother's to pack my
things, when there concluded to write her a farewell letter and start on
my way. My youngest brother accompanied me to Swanton V T. I took the
Cars to Malone N Y.

Sept 25 1871. I left the old Cedar House. I turned and looked
behind me as I walked to the carriage and secretly I said, "farewell old
habitation; the abode of my father and mother thirty five years! Farewell
old trees, whose branches shaded me when my heart was young and felt
no care. Year by year your petals will put forth leaves to gladden the birds
that sing in your branches; but I shall see you bloom no more! The sweet
songsters that will sport among leaves will greet my ears never again."

As I have said, my brother brought me in his carriage to Swanton,
on the side of Vt. When I took my leave of him I felt sad and more like
weeping than at any other parting. I considered his lonely life; how his
years would wear away, and when he came to the close of his earthly pilgrimage he would leave no progeny to bear up his name.

[At Malone, New York]

I had relatives in the City of Malone, whom I designed to visit. Children
they were of my respected friends Simon and Clarisa Stevens: of whom I
have written in the early part of my history. I met a lady on the cars who
knew the families I wished to find; she kindly offered to conduct me from
the train to the residence of Mr. George Stevens; whom I remembered a
boy fifteen, then a man past fifty. I contemplated a novel introduction.
The lady, my guide, did not know my name, it would devolve on me to

introduce myself. It would have something romantic about it. As we neared a stately building walking and gazing at the surroundings, a gentleman accosted me in these words. "Are you not Mrs. Pratt from Utah?" I replied, "if I am how should you know me?" He answered, "kindred spirits always know each other."

The lady was dismissed with thanks, and the gentleman conducted me to his dwelling and presented his cousin to his wife and daughter. He was living in ease and affluence, I knew he inherited nothing from his father, that he had acquired all by industry and economy. We soon exchanged histories, and he told me how he came by his wealth. He refered to the integrity of his father, of his struggles to sustain a large family in a hard country. He had worked faithfully for his father till of age, went to California in the gold excitement, made the best use of his acquisitions. We then commenced to discuss our religion. He wished me to give him an unvarnished account of the origin of my faith, in all its varieties. "The Latter Day Work" as it was called, which the world was so ready to condemn.

Accordingly, I did, and when he had heard me through, he pronounced my religion "a good one." He says, "I can see nothing wrong or unreasonable. Your religion is as good as mine." He seemed to have an established belief, although belonging to no sect. Every thing was directed by a wise overseer, who would bring good out of evil, order out of confusion, and every man to his proper level, All affliction was designed for good, in the economy of our all wise Father.

This man had two brothers and a sister living in the place, to whom I was introduced, and who treated me with great respect, as a kindred of their beloved and revered parents. Mrs. Lawrence the sister whom I remembered when a little child five years old was then a responsible lady, mistress of a large mansion, presiding with dignity over a well trained family. Mr. Lawrence was in the mercantile business, thriving and properous; a kind genial companion: they seemed like kindred in very deed. The two younger brothers had pleasant homes and agreable families. They seemed to regret nothing, except that their parents could not have lived to see their children all comfortably situated. I assured them their parents would look from the spirit world with complacency on their well doing and rejoice that they were virtuous prosperous and happy. The mother of Mr. Lawrence, an amiable widow lady was living with her son. She was much interested in all I told her concerning the "marvelous work," in which I was engaged. It was truly gratifying to me to converse with her, and feel how free she was from prejudice, and what a spirit of charity she had for her fellow beings!

While in Malone I went to a County Fair. Besides exhibitions of almost every kind to be thought of, there was a balloon to ascend. I had never seen one before, and the size of it astonished me! The floral Hall exceeded anything I had ever seen of the kind in beauty and variety. Seven thousand people were on the ground. I was so wrapt in admiration that I wandered away from my friends and lost sight of them. They were searching for me while I was inquiring for them in vain. We could not find each other. I took passage in the coach going to the Depot, and was taken to my friend's door. I found there had been great inquiry after me, and even concern; but the lost was found, and the event afforded a subject for merriment during the evening.

[At Moira, New York]

When ready to pursue my journey Baker Stevens accompanied me to his eldest sister's residence in Moira; a distance of ten miles. She was the eldest member of that family. She had been twice married, fortunate in both choices. Her first husband died in middle age. She wedded another, twenty years her senior; but so kind and indulgent, in her failing health, with a competency to keep her above want, he was entitled to her highest respect. She had in childhood and youth been a favorite in my father's family, and an example to all who knew her. Her early piety was remarkable, and her obedience to her parents won for her the highest esteem. She had a brother and sister living in the place, with large families; all esteemed for their high toned morrals, and well ordered lives. It came to my mind, that this family of children were blessed for their faithfulness and submission to their parents. The younger sister had been named for me; and in infancy when she was initiated into the Episcopal Church I was her Godmother. She inclined to me, and listened to my teachings; and when I testified of the things which had been restored to men on earth in this generation, she treated the subject with candor and consideration. She gave me encouragement that she would some day join me in the valley of the Rocky Mountains, where she could be more perfectly taught concerning the "great Work of the Latter Days."

[En Route Home: The Chicago Vicinity]

I took my leave of my kind relatives and came on the cars to Chicago; three days after the first great fire. Oh! it was horrible to behold; There was no Depot; and the flames were still ascending from the beds of coal, which mocked the power of the engines that were playing upon them. The eldest brother lived forty miles from Chicago, at Bristol Station. The 11th of Oct I took passage for that point, and reached there in the dusk of evening. My aged brother and family were seated around their supper table. I enter alone and silently. In a moment my brother exclaimed. "It is

my sister Louisa Pratt!" He was expecting me to come having heard I was
in Canada: otherwise I cannot believe he would have recognized me. He
looked strikingly natural; more so than my other brothers did. I felt
inclined to keep my eyes riveted upon him, so pleased was I to see how
well he had born his age. His children were gone from him to homes of
their own, except the two younger ones, a son and daughter. Every thing
appeared prosperous around them. Their eldest daughter married and
living near; her husband a responsible inteligent man. I thought within
my heart, "here is another instance of a child being blessed for faithfulness and obedience to parents."

Such was the character of my elder brother [Horace]. When he was
forty years old he married a woman twenty three, by whom he had eight
children. She was an inteligent lady of good parentage; and proved a dis-
creet and prudent wife, and mother.

My second sister lived eighty miles on the Illinois Central. My
brother and wife proposed going with their traveling carriage to convey
me there. Accordingly we set out. The country on the way was delightful.
Beautiful farms and orchards; the scenery was enchanting! After two days
travel we arrived; found my aged sister much changed in appearance,
being very hard of hearing. Her sons and daughters were grown and had
large families except the youngest one, a daughter, married and living
with her, and had no child. They had named her Ellen, in honor of my
eldest daughter. I admired the daughter for her amiable and loving temper, but she had failing health. For several years she had been laboring
under an incurable disease, the asthma. Oh, how my heart yearned over
her! How much I wished that she could come home with me, become a
believer in the fullness of the gospel and have faith to be healed by the
power of God, through the administration of those holding the priesthood! But I knew it would not do to urge such a thing, her friends would
not consent to it. My brother and wife went home and left me to return on
the cars. I sisisted her eldest son whose name is Frederick Lockwood. Well
did I remember the time of his birth, his infancy and early childhood. He
was termed "a crying child." We talked of the sleepless nights he caused
his mother to pass. He remarked, that he believed he was born to mourn,
and forever have a sorrowful life! He was a thriving prosperous farmer;
abundance crowded his labors! But his wife the glory and pride of his life
was torn from him by death! Afterwards an idol daughter, an only one.
Then a son grown to manhood, his chief dependence for help and comfort, was struck down by lightening insight of his house! A sadness of heart
seemed seated on his countenance. I could not avoid thinking how much
he wept in infancy! He seemed more inclined to listen to my teachings
than many of my kindred, more attracted to me; and for him I felt an abiding sympathy, as for an own son. He had married a second wife; had made

a wise choice. I endeavored to convince him that notwithstanding his bereavements he had been blessed; that his experience would benefit him in the life to come.

It was a source of regret that I could not converse with my sister understandingly, on account of her deafness. What a joy would have come to her heart could she have understood and believed my testimony concerning the "Latter day Work." Her husband was less inclined to avail or contend than she was; wishing the subject treated with respect for my sake. Prejudice which had before borne great weight on their minds was measurably removed; and I had a peaceful visit with them. We laid aside our creeds, read the bible, sang and prayed together. I bid them farewell with very little hope that I should ever meet them again in this uncertain life.

I took the cars for Chicago, arrived there after an absence of two weeks. There were a thousand men at work; clearing away the debris and preparing to commence building. Bones of children burned were found in the ruins. There was no Depot; a blunder was made, partly my own inattention and I was taken seven miles out of my way. I took the coach and went back. A gentleman in the coach learned the mistake I had made and took the liberty to counsel me. He says, "madam, if you are traveling alone you must be on the watch; know where you wish to go and see that you get started in the right direction; remember the cars never wait for any one." I thanked him, and he engaged a man to conduct me to the street where my trunk was left, get another coach and take me two miles, where the cars would start for Bristol Station, the town where my brother lived. I was set right at last, and went on my way rejoicing that the mistake had ended so well. I reached the place in good time, found my brother and his wife waiting to receive me as I stept off the Car.

A few days I spent with them, conversing with my brother on the subject which most vitally concerned me and which he could not gainsay; even the ushering in of a new and last dispensation, to bring about the gathering of Israel and the restitution of all things spoken anciently by the prophets, and again in these days confirmed by the voice of the Lord, authorizing men to speak in his name. My soul yearned over him as we communed together! I besought him never to utter a reproachful word concerning this "great work", but to pray earnestly for a witness in his own soul of the truth of it, that he might not remain in doubt and uncertainty. He assured me he would not contend against a doctrine whose adherents clung so fervently to the scriptures as did the Latter Day Saints. I took an affectionate leave of the family, and embarked on board the cars with my face set towards home.

I had relatives on the way whom I desired to visit. The first, not a great distance, and I had hoped to reach there before night set in, feeling doubtful about finding the lady's residence. On the way a shaft was announced broken; an hour passed while making repairs. I was very anxious and uneasy. I immagined myself alone in a strange place in the darkness of night searching for the house of a friend. A young man sat near me in the car, stept off before me; was standing near and helped me down the steps. I inquired whether he could direct me to a Mr. Trouslot's? (a French gentleman to whom my cousin was married.) He commenced by naming the streets and corners I must pass. What a predicament to be in thought I! No coach at hand. The young man remarked, "madam, I fear you would not find the way alone, I will conduct you there, and assist in carrying your baggage." I had ordered my trunk put in the baggage room, but woman like had quite a load of other things. I gladly accepted his offer, and thanked him heartily, although not willing to ask the favor of him. I found he was acquainted with the family, and felt that he was doing them a friendly turn by his politeness to me.

I was soon ushered into the presence of my relative whom I had known a young lady in Nauvoo. Her husband I had met once before, a cheerful friendly gentleman. The joy they both expressed on seeing me, amply repaid the youth for conducting me thither, as he affirmed to them, in return for their repeated thanks to him. I learned his name was White, and I wrote the incident in my journal. I had a delightful visit with my friends, left them with many blessings exchanged, and came eighty miles to Osceola, Starke County [Ohio].

In that town I had a relation by the name of Lois Thompson. She was a woman dear to my memory and I had not seen her for twenty five years, having parted with her during the fiery trials in Nauvoo. She was living two miles from the R. Road. I was directed to call at the store of a Mr. Blazzard, who would procure for me a conveyance to the residence of my friends. I did so, and found the merchant a kindly disposed man. He left his brother who was acquainted with persons in Utah, to entertain me, while he went out to engage a passage for me; found an agreable one, and I was soon on my way, feeling grateful for the kind attentions paid me by strangers.

I was joyful on meeting my relative, for she was a believer in "the fullness of the everlasting Gospel," as it had been revealed to us in this era of the world. She had been prevented from coming to the mountains through an unbelieving husband. I spent several days with them; had sweet communion with my friend, and her amiable daughter, their only child left of six. Mr. Thompson though an opposer to our religious faith, was kind and agreable towards me. I had a happy visit, bade them farewell, with an assurance from my relative that she would never relinquish her claim and desire to come to the gathering place of the Saints, whenever the Lord would open the way. That was my last stopping place. I had paid my passage to Omaha. Mrs. T'n came with me to the Depot, saw me on board the cars. Willingly would she have consented that her daughter should come to Utah with me, that she might marry among the Saints; so great was her faith in the Latter Day Work! But her father would by no means consent. I could not blame him, she was his only child.

[To Omaha and En Route to Ogden]

I came to Omaha, where I must buy my ticket to cross the plains. I went to the agent at the landing; he would give me a pass for $75.00 to S. Lake. I told him I could not affored to pay that price, my means would be expended before I could reach home! that I had a long hard journey to perform after making the trip to S. Lake. Well, said he, "I have not the power to reduce the fare, but you go to the Superintendent Mr Sikles, whose office is two miles from the Depot; the coachman will take you there for one dollar; that gentleman will readily reduce the price when he learns your circumstances." Accordingly I went, allighted before a spacious building, walked up two long flight of stairs, was ushered into the presence of a kind benevolent looking gentleman, who immediately noted my appearance, and accosted me in a courteous manner. I told him I had come to present my claims before him, as a pioneer of the Union Pacific Rail way. I had crossed the plains in 1848 with men who were searching out the best location for the great enterprise. I had helped to make the first settlement in the great Basin of the Rocky Mountains! I had grown old in hardships in helping to subdue the soil of a rough country, "ought I not to have some privileges, at least to travel the Road at a moderate price?" He replied in a most kindly tone, "Indeed madam you should have; and what can you afford to pay? I answered, "I came from Ogden to Omaha for forty dollars." "You shall return for the same; on a first class Car." I thanked him and bade him a friendly good morning.

I could afford to pay the coachman one dollar when I had saved thirty five. I was soon on my way with nothing to regret, but the disappointment in not meeting my friend Mrs. Spiking to return with me. She had been unfortunate in visiting her long lost son; She found him hardened against the truth, and the faith for which she had endured many things. In her zeal and earnestness to prevail on him to return with her, she irritated his mind by pressing the subject of her religion to warmly upon him, thus exciting opposition, amounting to persecution. He even burned her books, which she testified to him were truths revealed from heaven by the ministraiton of holy angels in this dispensation, of the "fullness of times." She was detained in Missouri, having loaned her son money, which he could not refund at the required time. Application was made to Pres't Young, and he sent for her to come with the emigration train.

I had a safe and speedy passage to Ogden, had several conversations with persons unacquainted with the private history of the Latter Day Saints, as a united body. A Mr. Lathrope from San Francisco had been to N. York and was on his return. We conversed long together. I told him of the great deliverances the Lord had wrought out for the people: how they had lived by faith and trusted in an almighty arm which had been streched out continually to save from dispair when threatened by their enemies. The special incidents I related to him seemed deeply to interest him, and he remarked emphatically, "I think the subject demands the attention of every candid and sensible man!" He affirmed that I had enlightened his mind more in regard to "the marvelous work," as it is termed by its adherents than any other person had done, since he had heard the sound of "new revelation," by the mouth of one claiming to be a prophet of the Lord. (I pressed the subject of investigation upon him.)

I reasoned that a man of understanding like him should not suffer a subject unheeded to remain, which was creating such excitement throughout Christendom as the one I had been endeavoring to elucidate. He acknowledged the truth of my remarks, said he would visit S. Lake at his earliest opportunity, and make the acquaintance of the leading men in the Church. We parted at the Depot in Ogden; and I went about to visit my friends in that City; who were all apparently delighted to witness my safe return, to listen to the adventures of my journey. After a few days I took passage for S. Lake, again had the pleasure of greeting old friends, and hearing from home.

[Salt Lake City and Home to Beaver]

I spent three weeks in S.L. City, was there on my 69th birthday, at the dwelling of J.A. Browning. All complimented me on the physical improvement apparent in me; all decided that I was ten years younger. The rest from labor and care, the excitement of change, combined to enliven my spirits and give vitality and animation to my nervous system. I had accomplished that which I had contemplated for many years, learned something more of my genealogy, obtained names from my kindred, which would be desirable when I was permitted to perform a work for the redemption of my ancestors, who were called from this life before the Latter Day glory dawned upon this benighted world!

There was a City Lot which had belonged to Mr. Pratt before he was sent the second time on the Island mission. In the time of our lengthy residence in California It had passed into other hands. I went to President Young, to solicit his influence that it might be restored to me. It was occupied by an aged brother who had for several years held peaceable possession. Pres't Young said he would see that half the Lot was given to me; that the occupant was old and he would not like to have him expelled from his home; the land had not then been purchased from government. I consented to the proposal, likewise the occupant was satisfied. I put in my claim at the Land Office, appointed an agent to do the business for me.

I was preparing to come home; it was late in the season and the roads were never worse. It was expensive coming in the stage coach, besides I would be obliged to ride three nights in succession. Mr. Musser Super't of telegraph line, was sending a man on business for the line, and offered me a passage gratis.

The traveling would be slow, but I would have the privilege to visit my friends on the way. I thought the offer a generous one and accepted it. The young man was in no hurry, was hired by the day; kept with his team free of expense at the bishop's in the settlements, I had all the opportunities I could desire to call on my old acquaintance, but the journey seemed longer than to go round the world on the R. Cars. Never was my patience more exhausted. I reached home the eleventh day late in the evening. The night being dark the driver had difficulty in finding the way to the street where my residence was. My daughters were expecting me, were assembled with neighbors and friends, to greet me with a hearty welcome home! They assured me they had been faithful in remembering me in their evening orisons, had prayed that the Lord would return me to them in peace and health; and thus had it come to pass; and we thanked and praised Him for the same!

CHAPTER TWENTY-THREE

A Variety of Activities

Memoirs, December 1871 to December 1875

There was joy in the house among the children. I had presents for them all. Maple sugar was a luxury that had never seen or tasted. Many grown persons raised in this western world had never seen the article. The fact of its being brought so far, and some of it made from the same trees which yielded sweet water in my early childhood, and from them I had helped to make sugar made the flavor more exquisite, and the sweetness doubly sweet.

[Ellen's Affairs]

In my absence Ellen had taken in a widow lady for a companion, and to assist her; and likewise a gentleman boarder, with two children. The latter had been unfortunate in harmonizing with his wife, and she had absconded, leaving him with the children on his hands. An unnatural thing for a mother to do. The gentleman and one child remained for awhile as boarders after my return. The young man had married at a very early period of his life, before his mind had been cultivated and matured; wedded to a mere child in years, lacking culture, wisdom and judgement, but excelling in domestick qualities; could spin and weave at fourteen; thus launching on the broad arrea of life with no preparation, not even a common school education. The young man possessing good natural talent, notwithstanding his limited acquirements evinced commendable aspirations; determined to push his way and support his children. He had once had an honorable standing in the church; but by some inadvertent act, and afterwards want of humility he was disfellowshipped. This was his condition while an inmate my family. Between my daughter and him I could discern a growing sympathy. Their situations were measurably assimilated. To me it was a great source of uneasiness. He was her junior by many years, besides

340

his uncertian position in the church made me fearful of his future course. She had been unfortunate in her first marriage, how could I endure to see her make an unwise choice the second time? Her daughter Nellie watched every movement, seemed suspicious of every polite attention paid her mother. It grieved me to witness the yearnings of the child, over the only parent she had to whom she could look for love and support. The intimacy became more visible, and my heart grew more saddened by the prospect of a final result. There was a little hope! The man was of good origin; his father had died firmly established in the "Latter Day Work," left his dying injunction to his children, to cleave to it all their life time! I knew the young man, loved and revered the memory of his father, and yet towards that subject which his honored parent had in his last moments declared to be of incalculable importance, he manifested a visible indifference.

[Report on Addison's Health]

The winter passed away pleasantly with a few exceptions. Towards spring word came to us that Mr. Pratt's health was failing. He had long been troubled with serafula in his ankles, causing irritation terribly annoying! There was great anxiety on his account. The humors could be removed but the consequences might be fatal.

[William McGary's Proposal]

Mr. McGary wrote from New Mexico in the Spring of '72, to his former wife and daughter, expressing in the warmest terms his abiding affection for them; desiring to learn if by any means a reconciliation might be made, between all parties, and his lost ones be restored to him. Ellen did not return a favorable reply, as all her friends desired. She knew he had been lawfully married to another than herself, and she feared there might be two wrongs, which would not make a right. Our minds were harrassed and perplexed. She desired at any sacrifice to do that which was the nearest right. He declared himself a changed man, having learned wisdom from a bitter experience. A reunion would probably have been affected had E's mind been free; and could it have been done righteously to the satisfaction of all parties concerned, happy would it have been for us all. But fate had ordained otherwise. The spring passed away in suspense.

[Beaver Developments, Cricket Infestation]

In the meantime Beaver grew and multiplied. A factory had been built, we were no longer obliged to spin and make our own cloth. Improvements on every hand were increasing. The grasshopper war was ended, which lasted six years. Although the ravages of the destroyer were terrible, yet deliverance would come to us from some source. When the crops were cut off in one portion of the territory, in some other part there would be a small surplus. Through all the years of anxiety and dred, I did not feel alarmed! When the insects would light down in swarms upon my garden, there was in my heart a secret faith that enough would be spared to me. In Nauvoo, Elder John Taylor blessed me, and I remembered his words. "When there is famine in the land, there shall be bread in thy house, and to spare!" This promise kept me from dispair and doubt, when to all human appearance a scarcity was at hand. "Whoever trusted in the Lord and was confounded?" We were told that we should have the insects seven years: but the Saints prayed fervently to have them removed, and they left one year in advance of their time. No people were ever more thankful to have the plague removed, than we were to see the pests take their flight before laying their eggs for the coming year. My garden was planted in good faith, with every prospect of a bountiful crop.

[Louisa's Illness]

On the 4th of July I went out to a celebration, feeling well and cheerful. I was unfortunate in being seated near a north window, and there was a strong breeze. I felt the danger, but still kept my seat. I walked home, and towards evening was taken with a chill; a violent fever followed, and I was pronounced a sick woman. I resorted to the pack sheet and bathing, and in three days my fever was broken. A cold storm ensued. I took a relapse; my daughters were alarmed, and friends advised to call a physician. It was not my design to have medical treatment. I had long denounced drugs, and depended wholy on cold water applications for fevers, and hygienic rules for general health. It was insisted upon that I must take medicine. A score of powders were left. I had no faith in them, but would take them to be submissive to those who had the care of me. I grew weak continually, untill I could not bear my own weight upon my feet. It was my belief it was the effects of the medicine that weakened me. I said I would take no more. The Elders were called in to administer. Bishop J. R. Murdock[1] laid his hands upon my head, with several others, and declared in the name of the Lord that I should live! That I should have health, and see many good days. I believed every word, for I knew it was a prophetic declaration! Had it not been given him by the spirit he would not have dared to utter such a prophecy! I began to mend, and was soon able to sit up. I could see from my window how the weeds were gaining prominence in my garden. I asked bishop Shepherd[2] to walk out and see what he thought of it. It worried my mind to see it neglected. He came in, saying, "it must by some means be plowed, and hoed; I will attend to it. My mind was relieved, I knew it would be done. Accordingly the Teachers in the Ward came and cleared it of weeds; which changed its appearance so much, it gave me strength and courage to look out upon it. A dear old friend lived near me whom I had known for 25 years. It was her calling to administer comfort to the sick. When my family were doubtful about my recovery she sat by my bedside to assist my faith in the power of God to heal me. My experience enables me to testify that the exercise of a determined will, faith in the willingness of Him who has all power to remove disease, is more effectual than all the drugs and patent medicines the world ever knew. I was soon in a comfortable state of health, able to [take] over my business.

[Death of Addison Pratt, 14 October 1872]

My daughter Frances wrote from Cal. that her father was fast inclining to dropsy. I wrote to his friend Dr. Winslow then in S. L. City asking his advice and sympathy, as he had known Mr. Pratt many years; having sailed on the same vessel to the Pacific Isles. I knew he would feel interested, and would at least write him a letter of condolence. He replied to me expressing deep interest for his old friend, but doubtful whether any thing could be done but to afford some relief during the short time he might remain. He also wrote to Mr. Pratt prescribing soothing antidotes, and assuring him of his unvarying friendship, all which would have been comforting, had it arrived in time. The grim messenger waits not on the wishes and desires of kindred and friends, unless there is an exercise of strong faith in the power of God to rebuke the destroyer! When the needy one is surrounded by those who would scoff at the idea of administering through the holy Priesthood in the name of the Lord, he is not likely to have strength to lay hold on faith to be healed, when no help is near! Two days preceding his final dissolution he wrote a letter to his family: equally as well constructed as any he had written in health. It was highly expressive of his entire resignation to depart this life and enter upon the untried scenes of another; with a firm conviction that all would be well with him. He felt that he had lived a long life and accomplished much; had no desire to remain unless he could be insured good health, and a living with his family. He knew his end was near! That he lingered on the brink of the "dark valley," but he feared no ill; He wrote of the faithfulness of the daughter who was ever at his side to soothe and comfort him, and prayed that she might be blessed.[3] Another letter soon followed which announced his departure! That he fell asleep like an infant in its mother's arms, without a groan or struggle. Happy was it for the sensitive daughter who was alone with him at the moment, for no person ever had a more solemn dread of nature's great last change when brought to pass by extreme suffering! She told of the loneliness of her habitation when he was gone. To us all, the world seemed more lonely!

[Teaching School]

The succeeding winter Ellen went to Cedar City and taught school. Nellie her daughter remained with me, and I taught in my own house. My room was crowded, and the task was heavy on me. The larger boys sometimes inclined to be idle, which was a great annoyance, and called forth remonstrance more than was agreable to either party. Towards the close of my school I had a heavy fall; bruised my shoulder, and lamed my side. We were preparing for an exhibition the last day. It required great energy on my part to see that the pieces were well learned. The older boys seeing this that I was feeble, offered to assist me, and acquitted themselves creditably. Accordingly I went on with my school, brought it to a close, had the exhibition, all through the careful consideration of the boys.

[Ellen's Marriage to J. M. Coombs, 1 January 1873]

The 1st day of Jan. 73 Ellen was married to Mr. J. M. Coombs. The following week she started for Cedar; to fill an engagement she had made to assist a lady in her school. They not being ready for housekeeping engaged in business while making preparations. I had serious objections to the match, therefore the nuptials were not solemnized in my presence, neither in presence of the daughter. But when the step was taken and could not be recalled we concluded to make the best of it, and affect to believe it all for the best. I considered that greater mistakes had been made in the world and even ended well. My heart and home felt lonely when my last daughter was gone from me, and would have been doubly so had not my third one lived near me with a family of daughters, the eldest a modest sensible girl, a choice one to me from her infancy, of whom I have frequently made mention. She measurably supplied the place of her whose loss I mourned so deeply.

Spring returned, Ellen closed her term of school, and moved to Parowan; where Mr. Coombs fitted up a dwelling place. A portion of the time the daughter remained with me. In the fall Mr. C. sold his place in Parowan, and purchased one near me in Beaver. Things now began to look a little brighter. I had three daughters with their children to visit me.

Beaver grew and increased in population. Unbelievers in our Faith crowded in among us; drinking saloons became common, an unhappy influence was prevalent among our young men. The bishops and

Teachers labored faithfully to restrain them from irregularities and there were some who remained uncontaminated.

[The Beaver Female Relief Society]

I have delayed the mentioning of one important event. The organization of a Female Relief Society 1870. It was organized in my house with six or eight members. In less than a year it numbered two hundred. The eldest lady in the city was appointed President. I served as Secretary and counsellor about two years. Then being prepared to commence the building of a house it was deemed advisable that younger women should take the lead. Great good was done in relieving the wants of the poor, in the visitation of the sick, in fasting and prayer for the unfortunate. When one of our members were sick it was, and still is our custom to fast and pray for their recovery. To wash and annoint them, lay our hands upon them and rebuke the disease. This to the unbeliever in the restoration of the priesthood might seem a daring thing for women to assume a right to perform. But when the Savior said, "these signs shall follow them that believe in my name they shall cast out devils," &c, He made no distinction of sexes.

There was at a certain time a man in our ward, (a good man too,) who from some cause became deranged. His family feared him, he had to be confined away from home, with men to watch him by night and day. He would not allow the Elders to lay hands on him. A council was called, it was resolved that the whole body of the church should fast and pray untill the evil spirit would depart out of the man. Accordingly we assembled. Great sympathy was felt for the poor brother and his family. Many fervent prayers were offered up. At the close of the meeting the Elders repaired to the room where the insane man lay bound; he was humble, did not resist their laying hands upon him. They commanded the evil spirit to depart; and lo; it was gone!

The man "was clothed and in his right mind." He was conscious that an evil spirit had troubled him. Three years after I asked him if he felt the influence of that spirit about him? He replied he did not; that his mind was calm. He had however an attack sometime after: was taken to prison and confined. After intercessions were made in his behalf he became a little calm; when inquiry was made of him whether he would permit the Elders to lay hands upon him he replied in the affirmative, but asked the privilege of choosing such persons as he had faith in. He chose three Elders and one aged sister, known for her exceeding faith in administering in alarming cases. They repaired to the prison where the poor maniac lay in chains! At first he trembled and struggled to resist them; but when the foul spirit was commanded in the name of Jesus Christ to depart, and go to his own place, it obeyed the summons; and the man was led home to his family; who received him with joy, in that he was himself and not another.

These incidents came under my own observation, and I testify that the power of God has often been manifested among the Latter Day Saints in rebuking diseases and casting out unclean spirits; and the glory be to Him who giveth the power.

But to return to the Relief Society. We built a good house, on a Lot we purchased for the purpose, all by our own economy. We dedicated it to the Lord; and in it we held our meetings, publick and private. At the first celebration I was requested to compose a song for the occassion, and also to deliver a lecture on the subject of plural marriage; which I did, much to the approval of all parties concerned.[4] Our celebration was a creditable affair.

When a Bill was before the House of Congress, known by the title of the Cullam Bill, in which the rights of this people were to be shamefully abased, our Society arranged an Indignation Meeting. We drew up a document, wherin we protested against the measures instituted in the Cullam Bill. Chose a committee, formed resolutions, wrote a petition to send to congress; wherein was portrayed the sufferings it would bring upon the people, should such a bill be sanctioned and become a law! It was dispatched with many names of petitioners, praying the Bill might be abrogated. During our exercises Mr. Cullam's name was by no means held sacred. Many toasts were contributed by the ladies; each endeavoring to excel in the ludicrous. We had no gentlemen at the meeting; felt free to speak our sentiments, having every thing our own way.

I had the honor to be appointed Marshall of the day, as I was the eldest lady except one, and she was needed for chaplain. We had been acting in an independent capacity until we knew well how to organize a meeting without the assistance of the gentlemen. The reader might ask whether our petiton elicited attention at head quarters? We believe it did, for "the bill" was not passed in its original form, and we heard no more of it. But ere long another was announced, bearing the name of "Poland."[5] By this time we felt too elevated to notice that; we were established in the belief, that no weapon formed against us would prosper; that every tongue that arose in judgement against the people of the Lord, would be condemned! The Federal officials crowded hard upon us, hindering men from their labors, but no great harm was accomplished.

When our brethren were under arrest and courts were in session; the faithful sisters would assemble and pray for their deliverance. Asking the Lord in all earnestness to make a way for their escape! That the wisdom of their enemies might be turned to foolishness. And so it proved whether in answer to our prayers, we know not, but it was done, and we gave God the glory. There were men among us who claimed to be of us, who when proved guilty in the highest degree of criminal acts either by bribes or some other means escaped punishment at the hands of the U.S. officials. It seemed the sole aim of the Prosecution and Judges to incriminate the authorities of the church, when that could not be done they seemed indifferent as to individuals on whom the guilt rested.

There came a Judge in 1873 whose name was Hanley. He wrote to Head Quarters advising that a Regiment of Soldiers should be sent to Beaver Co. urging it as a necessity in bringing criminals to justice. It was generally believed that it was done through a purely selfish motive. In obedience to his request the Regiment came. Some of the officers were honorable men; the soldiers with few exceptions were intolerable drinkers of ardent spirits. It was terrifying to hear them on the streets at night! Our city was a changed place: from peace and quietness, there was riot and confusion in our streets. There were men who came with the army, lawyers and traders, who disregarded the rights of the citizens. Land which we had fenced and improved for fifteen years, they went on to and built cabbins.

Several of these gentlemen had in a publick meeting expressed great sympathy for the women of Utah: promising them aid and assistance whenever they chose to break their bonds, or bondage, as they presumed to call our domestic relations. So when they had laid claim to our land, and were convened in their cabbins, we, a company of the Relief Society, went in carriages to present our complaints to them: alleging that our rights were infringed upon; that the ground from which our children's bread was raised was wrested from us, and we had come to them for redress. The very men who had promised their assistance to redress the wrongs of the "poor women," (who asked no favor at their hands,) when appeals to only to prove what they would do, replied to us, "you are too late ladies, we are engaged for the other party."

We gave orders for them to remove their cabbins from off our land, otherwise in a few days we ourselves would be there with a force sufficient to remove them. We assured them we should submit to no such indignities, for we knew the law was on our side. They showed no signs of resentment, and we bade them "good day" and rode away. Soon after they quarrelled among themselves and one of the party was shot. It was reported to have been done by the citizens, and two or three were arrested and kept in prison for some considerable time. It could not however be proven, and circumstances were stronger against their own party. Accordingly the persons under suspicion were set at liberty, the main witness having absconded: and to this day the affair remains in doubt.

One year had scarcely passed away ere two of the party died with the immoderate use of ardent spirits. Men they were whose natural talents promised better things. The third was taken sick, took an overdose of morphine and awoke no more. Soon after, our land was entered at government price, made secure, and we had no further trouble. The cabbins were removed in due time, and we had reason to believe the intruders were ashamed of the undertaking.

[In 1873 leading women of Utah organized to win the suffrage, civil and women's rights, and published the Woman's Exponent. *Louisa enthusiastically lent her voice and pen to the movement. During the next seven years there appeared more than a dozen articles over her name. She spoke to and reported her talk before the Retrenchment Society, and spoke out in the mass meeting of 13 December 1878. She spoke to a sisters' conference. She led in petitioning the Territorial Legislature for their rights. Hon. John Murdock, on Monday, January 28, 1879 presented a petition from Beaver, signed by Louisa B. Pratt and three hundred and eighty-two others, asking for the removal of the political disabilities of women, and making them eligible to office.[6]*

At the time she was writing her history, the Exponent *published selections from her diary, for a series of installments titled "Scenes on the Island Tubuai, South Pacific Ocean." She told of her native son Ephraim, and reported her association with him, his rearing, and his running off. A touch of humor graced such articles as "Advantages of Being Old," or "Ending Faults with Old Folks," "Speak Gently to the Aged," and "Filial Affection." Louisa's writings and reports of her activities reveal her as a leader in the women's rights movement in Utah.]*

[Renewed Contact with Benjamin F. Grouard]

About this time I learned the where abouts of B. F. Grouard, our companion in the missionary labors on the South Pacific Isles.[7] I wrote to him sending the account of Mr. Pratt's decease, in California. He replied in a most friendly consoling manner, and moreoever gave us a statement of his views in regard to a future state of existence. He was a confirmed spirtualist. Knowing he believed in obtaining information from spirits, I requested him to inquire what had become of his Island children? After a long time had elapsed he returned an answer that he could learn nothing concerning them. I greatly desired to know the fate of my poor boy, who had left me to go to Montana as a teamster, his employer promising to bring him with him on his return to California. The gentleman did not return; wrote me a letter stating that Ephraim had left his employ and he knew not what had become of him. So my child on whom I had lavished many prayers and tears was lost; Many a sigh and groan have I uttered in thinking what might have been his doom! Wayward in his nature associated with rough men in a mining country, I have feared he might have come to an untimely end, and better that I should not know.

[Comments: Families of Ann Louise and Caroline]

At this time my youngest daughters husband Mr. Willis had sold his house and Lot, and invested his means in establishing a saloon. The town being full of Soldiers and miners he did not lack customers, and for a while made money. The business however was soon run to the ground there being too many engaged in it. He again sold out not having secured himself a home. My daughter being in failing health with an increasing family began to feel the stern realities of life. To be shifted from place to place and feel no where at home, is a painful situation to an ambitious mind; hands tied with helpless children, retarded by feeble health from making any exertion to help herself to the necessaries of life; hard times in busines opperations disheartening men, many a poor woman is led to exclaim, "hard fate of mine!" It is a truthful proverb, "The Lord helps those who try to help themselves." And in my own experience I have invariably found it true. Never have I failed of success when in times of dread and dismay I have called on the Lord for wisdom to direct me: thus confirming the words of the great apostle. "If any man lack wisdom let him ask of God, who giveth to all men liberally and upbraideth not, and it shall be given him!" Altho! my life was monotonous yet I had some variety. I had a sister and three daughters living almost within calling distance. Some of my grandchildren were constantly with me. The eldest Ida Frances began now to be a young woman in mind and manners, a lover of books with which my house abounded. My sister's son her only child, being married, was fast accumulating an interesting family. My nephew though a very exclusive man, in a general way, is very inteligent and companionable. It requires tact and ingenuity to draw him out and understand his qualities of mind. When that point is gained, one feels that he has found a hidden treasure whose resources are not likely to fail. Few there are who lean to him and appreciate his company. My sister who had no daughter born to her, now had five through her son.

[Correspondence with Samuel R. Wells]

I had for seven years an esteemed friend in the person of Samuel R. Wells of N York celebrity. I was his agent for the A. P. Journal, S. of Health; likewise in the sale of his books.[8] A correspondence opened between us which continued up to the period of his decease. His letters had become household words, the reception of which was hailed with pleasure and interest. Although not a full believer in the doctrines of the Latter Day Saints he ever manifested the most forbearance and christian charity towards them. In our lengthy correspondence, he never uttered a railing word, or attempted an argument to convince me that my religion was a delusion. When I set forth a principle and affirmed it to be true, he would never utter a contradiction, but would commend me for frankness and honesty, thus proving himself a gentleman in every sense of the term. On the 31st of March 1875 he wrote me a letter, with a phrenological chart drawn from my photograph, which I had previously sent him. It was highly satisfactory, and even flattering; which I was about to express in my reply when the mournful inteligence reached me that he had departed this life, on the 13th of Apr. So soon after writing the letter, in which he said nothing of ill health. The shock to me was a severe one! A man in the prime of manhood as it were, only 57 years all told, with a firm constitution and in the midst of great usefulness. I was led to reflect on the mysterious events of Divine Providence! It seemed to me the whole world had sustained a loss! Why I was led to ask, with his great knowledge of the laws of health and life could he not apply them to the preservation of his own life? In the removal of the buildings which he had occupied for many years, there was a profusion of miasmatic dust which affected his lungs; his excessive labor in the removal of every thing from his office and replacing them in another building, wrought upon his nervous system. Pneumonia and typhoid bore him away in their unrelenting arms, not heeding the appeals of a loving wife, who had worked by his side more than thirty years; and who had not a child left to comfort her! So cruel death always marks for his victims the most lovable objects, and those to whom the most hearts twine around as if his conquest would be greater, the more he can render inconsolable! Well, let him triumph a little longer, the day is hastening, when the true followers of Christ will sing the song of redeeming love, and shout victory over death and the grave! Then the song will be "Oh grave; where is thy victory! Oh, death, where is thy sting!" My desire is to live till the Saviour comes in the clouds of heaven, with power and great glory! I long for the day, I cannot fear! I have the promise if my faith does not fail. Ah! there it is; something is left to me I wanted the Patriarch to say. You shall live! and be among the wise virgins, who with their lamps trimmed and burning go forth at midnight to meet Him, and shout hosannah at his approach!

[Routine of Life]

My life went on in an ordinary way in doing what good I could in conjunction with my sisters of the Relief Society; to relieve the wants of the aged sick and needy. We made bedding and garments for such as were not able to make for themselves. We made bedding and garments to sell, and by other means we contributed five hundred dollars to the building of the Temple in St. George.

1874 the 10th of Nov. I celebrated my 72d birthday. I made a feast for those who were my friends of long standing. Some who had known me in the days of Nauvoo; had known my trials and tribulations; my endurance through all the calamities that had befallen the church. A meeting was organized and I was called to the chair; a secrtary appointed. The company then spoke in order dwelling with interest on the past, wherein we had glided down the stream of time together; our friendships remining unbroken. One lady present whom I had known for 30 years, was ten years my senior; she could relate our experience during the firey trials in Nauvoo. She refered to many incidents of deep interest in our early acquaintance and events of a more subsequent date related with clearness and precision, when we considered her advanced age, made her speech attractive. Many toasts and congratulations went round, all which the secretary recorded and it was published in our local paper. The succeeding winter [1874–75] passed pleasantly having company and help in the house. I was not compelled to go out in cold stormy weather to provide wood and do marketing. An evening school was kept in my house, which was instructing and amusing. There was unusual socialbility in the neighborhood, all conspiring to render life agreable to those who would condesend to be partakers; but such as stood aloof and were cold and suspicious, were deprived of much enjoyment they might have shared with others.

[Revision of the Journal]

During that winter I commenced revising my lengthy journal of fifty years standing. I had some assistince in the beginning, but was soon convinced that it would not be practicable to trust it in the hands of a second person as there were abridgments and alterations to be made. I saw at once the task must devolve wholy upon myself. Since then I have continued to write at intervals; having 9 quires of paper written fine on both sides to review, besides manuscripts of considerable amount. If there should be mistakes either in rhetoric or grammar, I trust the reader will be forbearing in criticism, remembering my advanced age and the hard life I have lived.

The following summer my garden went untilled. I immagined myself too old for the undertaking; although the aged lady I have spoken of planted her garden and tended it with great success. She also being ordained to visit the sick among her own sex to administer blessings and annointings. She lives by faith, trusts in the Lord, and her strength is equal to her day.

[A Two-Month Visit to Salt Lake City]

The first of Oct. [1875] I went to Salt Lake City. Conference convened on the 6th, ten thousand people were assembled. I listened with deep interest to the sound of familiar voices; some I [had] not heard for years. Their heads had whitened with age, time had stamped his impress on their features, and yet their spirits seemed buoyant and strong in the gospel of truth and salvation having lost none of the zeal and ardor they manifested in years past and gone. Many well remembered faces could I see as I looked over the vast congregation, and my heart was gladdened with the assurance they still remembered me. I spent two months in the City, in which time I renewed my acquaintance with many of my former associates; most of whom had remained firm and unshaken in the faith of the "Latter Day Work," in which many years ago we had suffered for, and together had rejoiced that we were counted worthy. Some I met who had grown cold in the cause in which once they were actively engaged. They could tell of errors committed by those of whom they had expected better things. Reminding me of the ancient apostle's words, "because iniquity shall abound the love of many will wax cold." Why could they not rememeber that every one must stand or fall for himself? Should I be unfaithful because another has betrayed the weakness of human nature? No; I should be admonished by such to be more closely on my guard, and watch, least I also fall into temptation.

I found myself in possession of a half Lot 10 rods square in the eight Ward of the City. I undertook the sale of it; which was attended with difficulties on account of hard times and scarcity of money. After several trials I at length found a brother by the name of Moroni Pratt, who with limited means undertook the purchase. I had great anxiety and perplexities to encounter, in securing to him the title, as he wished to transfer it to another party to whom he was indebted; and who required every thing done to an iota according to the technicalities of the law! Never did I feel so disgusted with law! I told the lawyer that good common sense was all the law I wanted any thing to do with. I had to get the consent of my children; and one was refractory and refused to sign the deed. This accasioned me great uneasiness, as it would involve the man who had made the purchase; and protract my stay in the city, which I did not desire as winter was drawing near.

Many a sleepless night did I pass; revolving in my mind the scenes of many years, wherein I had been compelled to do business for myself; often dealing with persons who were not reliable, and who would not in every instance make sacred their word. A principle which all my life I have been instructed to hold in the highest estimation!

During the seasons of suspense while waiting for the tide of fortune to ebb and flow, I availed myself of measures to divert my mind, and keep it from despondency. On first going to town and commencing to walk about to make calls on my friends I found it fatiguing to walk more than one block before stopping to rest. After practising a week or two, walking a little every day, I could walk four blocks with ease. There were social gatherings which sometimes required a long walk to attend; I would go with young people, and stand the walk as well as they; thus proving that a little excitement of the mind, pleasurable anticipations, congenial company, strengthens the nerves, invigorates the body, and proves the truth of Solomon's proverb. "A merry heart doeth good like a medicine."

The 10th of Nov. came again, my 73d birthday I was making my home with Dr. Linsey Sprague's. They were very kind and courteous, did what they could to make my stay agreable. On my birthday they made a dinner, to which some of my friends were invited. In the evening we went to the 7th Ward to Mr. J. A. Browning's, where we had a social party, were treated to cake, wine and fruit. Dr. Winslow, formerly Mr. Pratt's particular friend,[9] made one of the party, was very agreable, made a speech on the virtues, rights and superior qualities of women; contrasted with the opposite sex, he seemed by not disposed to give them the preference, either for strength of mind, fortitude or firmness. His speech was a flattering one to the ladies; was applauded by all present. As a birthday gift presented me a porcelain flower vase. The host while holding the glass gave an extravagant toast; he hoped I might live "73 years longer!" To which I replied, "that would be too long to be desirable, nevertheless you have my thanks." The gentleman who officiated as scribe the preceding year at my house in Beaver was present, and made a very appropriate speech. His wife also being a proficent in music, made the Piano reverberate its thrilling sounds: assisted by the two Miss Browning's; their father contributing an additional charm with his violin. Thus ended my 73d birthday, long to be remembered.

It was at length decided that the bargain for the land should be closed, a deed be given in my name, I should receive payment in part, and in process of time make the title secure to the party to whom the transfer was made. A great burden was off my mind when all was settled. I then had purchases to make amounting to $200 which were made at the Coop' M. Institution.[10] Five different departments I must visit, according to the nature of the goods I wished to purchase; a different clerk in each department. Mrs. Sprague kindly assisted me in making selections, but at the best the task was very annoying.

In one respect my frequent excursions to the store were rendered interesting. It was a place to meet old friends. Nearly all the settlements in the territory bought goods at wholesale at the parent store, as it is termed. Unexpectedly did I meet persons whom I had not seen for many years; young people who would in a moment recognize me; but they having changed from youth to manhood would look like strangers to me. In one instance I was joyfully surprised! A large portly man accosted me, saying, "How do you do Sister Pratt?" I stared him in the face and began to scan his features; they were familiar, but I could not call his name. I soon learned he was the son of father Parish; the good man who was always so mindful of my wants in Nauvoo. "So you are Joel Parish, the boy who was faithful at all times to help the widow and the fatherless, and I promised him he should be blessed! His reply to me was, "yes sister Pratt I have been blessed; I have two good wives and twelve children. Besides I have a competency, health and peace, for which I thank the Lord." The circumstance afforded me great pleasure and made me forget the perplexity I had had in selling land and buying goods.

When I first arrived in S. Lake Mrs Emeline B. Wells, invited me to her house, made me welcome to her accommodations, which were pleasant and convenient.[11] From her residence I could take the street cars to any portion of the city at stated periods. I was quite happy with her as she ever manifested the greatest interest in my peace and comfort, acting the part of a daughter in every particular. She was assistant editor in the *Exponent* office, a paper devoted to the interests of women and sustained by them; entitled, *Woman's Exponent.* When my spirits were worn and weary on account of perplexity in my business I felt no where so relieved and comforted as with sister W., in one of her private rooms where I could make my complaints and receive sympathy.

A sister Watmough of Scottish birth was often at the house, an inteligent lady whom I had not known before, but from the first seemed congenial company; she paid me polite attentions, invited me to her house in the 19th Ward, a pleasant home, on the bluffs: where she with her faithful companion lived in retirement with plenty around them. Their children all married and gone, only the two lonely beings to enjoy a good fruit orchard, a comfortable habitation and the blessings which come to old age through a well ordered life in the service of God. This lady of whom I write was acquainted with an old friend of mine whom I had not seen for 28 years. The lady had boarded with me when I lived in Nauvoo, had passed through reverses of fortune, at last made her home in S. L. City.

Mrs. Watmough escorted me on the street cars to the far end of 20th Ward South, where my friend lived alone, with a house full of cats, her favorite pets. I was introduced as sister Addison Pratt. The lady with whom she had resided in Nauvoo. No: she said, "it cannot be!" They assured her it was the same one, when she clasped me in her arms and exclaimed while tears were flowing fast, "Oh! when I knew you, you were a young woman; now you have grown so old!" Yes, I remarked, "time leaves its impress on us all, you too have changed." She had in early life been noted for beauty; she looked faded, her hair was turning gray. After a little time her appearance was familiar, and I could recognize in her the same "Catherine Philips." She had married a man on short acquaintance, he proved unfaithful, left her and went to parts unknown. So she was alone with the exception of ten beautiful cats! They would run to meet her like so many children, each one knowing its own name. I left her with a partial promise that I would go again, but did not see my way clear to go. And that was a visit long to be remembered. It was amongst the last I made.

On Thanksgiving day the 25th Nov. I was at the residence of Brigham Young Jun: his wife a dear good woman whom I had known in her childhood: likewise her two sisters who were with us on the occasion. Children they were of the much esteemed elder Orson Spencer, who were left orphans in Winter Quarters, their mother being dead, and their father gone on a foreign mission. I had in their lonely condition felt great sympathy for them; while they were daily associated with my daughters. To meet as we did under so widely different circumstances made the interview doubly interesting. They were all respectably married, and raising large families. We united our voices in prayer together, and rendered thanks that the Hand of the Lord had been over us for good in the years that had rolled over our heads.[12]

[Return Trip to Beaver]

About the 1st of Dec. I closed up my business and took the cars for home. I made my first stop in Pleasant Grove with a dear friend who was happy to see me. I spent two days with her, and came on to Payson, where I found the kindest people, who had been my neighbors in California. Time passed pleasantly for two days; I bade them farewell and came on to Salt Creek. I called to see a friend whom I had loved in the days of Nauvoo: and from that time at different periods we had known each other. I called at her place of residence and found to my surprise that she was not living! I met her daughter, and she urged me to go to her house; a pleasant comfortable place, but Oh, her heart was sad, for the loss of her dear mother! I offered all the condolence in my power; and in our lengthy conversations we dwelt on her many virtues, and the many sorrows that fell to her lot! She felt that if her mother could have seen a few good days before she had been called away, she could have borne it with more calmness; but when she thought of her mother's hard life she felt inconsolable!

From that point I came in the Stage Coach. The Agent was kind and reduced my fare; ordered a good carriage to be taken on my account. The weather was cold and I must ride two nights before I would reach home. A stranger from Nebraska took the coach at that point, a gentleman coming to do business at Camp Cameron. He was extremely kind to me; took the trouble to go himself and get hay to put in the coach that I might ride more comfortable. I found him very agreable company and all considered I had a pleasant journey home.

Ephraim Pratt, a.k.a. Frank Grouard

CHAPTER TWENTY-FOUR

Sunset Years at Home in Beaver

Memoirs, December 1875 to August 1880

[The character of Beaver as a community changed significantly during the 1870s, a result of the discovery in 1870 of rich mineral deposits in the west mountains. A great number of miners came into the area. Friction developed between them and the original settlers. Both parties asked for federal troops; four companies of soldiers came in 1872. Fort Cameron was garrisoned between 1874 and 1883. Minersville and Milford grew with the 1875 discovery of the Horn Silver Mine which became the richest silver producer in the territory, producing silver ore valued at $54,000,000 in ten years. Old Frisco, fifteen miles west of Milford was dubbed the wildest camp in Utah, with its twenty-one saloons. Life in Beaver was disrupted. The railroad did not reach Milford until 1880.]

[The Hunts Move to Sevier Valley]

I had been informed by letter that my soninlaw Mr. J H. [John Hunt] my third daughters husband had sold his house and Lot in Beaver and was preparing to move to the Sevier Valley some 40 miles away.[1] This had caused me great anxiety lest they should be gone before my arrival. But in that respect I was happily disappointed. At 4 oclock in the morning the stage coach rolled up the street to my eldest daughter's door. I knocked for admittance and was answered by the very voice of her of whom I had been in doubt. I heard the cry of a newly born infant and understood why she had been detained while the rest of the family had gone. I was joyfully surprised. The family were soon aroused and a table set for me which was refreshing indeed after riding all night in the cold. Cordial sentiments were exchanged, bundles of love delivered, the important news made known; and when the glorious sun had gilded the eastern horizon for a little time I repaired to my own house, which had been left solitary two

357

months. I found all safe and right, and my daughter with the new babe soon came to stay with me.

I had brought with me necessaries to make us all comfortable so we ate and drank and made merry. In about two weeks Lois followed her family to their new home. I felt grieved to part with her and have the children all taken away, but still it was not that poignant grief that wrung my heart when she left me and went to California. I knew she would be located near a branch of the church, and that I should often hear from them, and some of the family would frequently come and go.

[Town Quarrel and Shooting]

There was a great excitement in Beaver about that time. A quarrel ensued between . . . and . . . . the latter was shot and died instantly. The unfortunate young man was a brilliant fellow of some twenty years, his father had not been among the living for many years. . . . was arrested for murder and confined in jail. He had a respectable family and . . . an aged mother in the place.[2] Their grief knew no bounds and the sympathy of the [people] was awakened in their behalf. Likewise the mother of the deceased and his brother were nearly distracted and their immediate friends knew not which family had the greatest claim for pity. That of the accused criminal appealed most loudly as there was great uncertainty how the case would appear in court. All concerned in the affair were taken to S. L. prison for safe keeping untill the spring term of Court when they were to be returned to this district for trial. Great was the suspense! terrible the anxiety! Incessant were the prayers and tears! It was generally understood that the deed was done in self defence; yet there were some whose vengence was fearful! The afflicted soul of the mother poured forth continual supplication to the all Knowing, that her son might not be proven a willful murderer!

Spring [1876] came after a dreary winter had passed away, and the prisoners were returned to Beaver Co. for trial. The mother of the deceased was still borne down with the deepest anguish, mingled with agonizing resentment towards the unfortunate man who through fear mingled with anger fired the unlucky shot! Likewise the brother of the young man slain seemed determined on revenge; was heard to remark that he would not breathe the same atmosphere with the one who had sacrificed his noble and beloved brother! The trial was at last concluded, and the accused were acquitted; to the great joy of their anxious relatives, and to the extreme disappointment of the injured and bereaved party. Both families left the place; the bereaved to a far off territory the accused a short distance; as neither inclined to remain where every object that met their gaze would remind them of the fiery ordeal they had passed!

[Mountain Meadows Massacre: The Trials of John D. Lee]

After the disposal of the above named case another more exciting and soul stirring was brought before the publick.[3] The subject had been in agitation nineteen years, and never a thorough investigation had been brought to bear upon the case before. Although many were suspicioned of being allied with the Indians in committing the crime yet one man was only arrested, and imprisoned. Long and lingering was his confinement! At length the day of trial came. Witnesses were summoned from the extreme portions of the territory. Sought out and brought by detectives to the second district courts where the criminal was arraigned. It was a solemn sight to behold the unhappy man as he sat listening to the accusations by the prosecuting attorney. He strove to look calm and undisturbed, as though his soul was at rest, and he had nothing to fear. The last day of trial I attended. The Defense undertook to impeach the witnesses, accusing them of purjury! Men whom I knew, and believed to be as honest men, and truthful as ever broke the bread of life! I felt indignant, and exclaimed against such injustice! the reply was, "Oh, that is a Lawyers prerogative, to make truth appear a lie! As I sat looking at the poor man, I thought, "If I were in your place, I would rather be shot one dozen times, than sit one hour and hear those fearful things rehearsed!" I resolved never to attend another court, of my own free will. Sentence was delayed ten days by request, but it was uttered at last. A choice was granted in the mode of execution; the condemned chose to be shot. Then was uttered the solemn decree! "You are to be taken from the place of your confinement, to the place of execution and there be shot, untill you are dead! and may the Lord have mercy on your soul!" The condemned looked composed, not a muscle was seen to stir; every other one in the room seemed more affected, than the doomed man![4]

Three months previous or perhaps six, I had listened to a speech by Lawyer Baskin, greatly to my annoyance and disgust! He officiated then as prosecuting attorney. The main drift of his speech tended to abuse the people, and their religion: as also the prisoner. Such vilifying language I never heard fall from the lips of any man before. He even uttered invectives against our most holy ordinances; judging of matters as foreign to his comprehension as the knowledge of the fixed stars is above the capacity of an ignorant schoolboy. I marvelled that our bishop and elders would tamely submit to such insults! When afterwards I refered to it, the reply was, "Oh it was in a court room!" There was no evidence to substantiate the statements the lawyer made. The diabolical deed rested wholy with Indians and their allies, demonstrated beyond power of contradiction.

The year preceding the time of which I have spoken, a brother came to board with me. He was inteligent, extremely social; possessing a

high order of intellect; his habits were unexceptionable: withal a profound student. But with his admirable triats of character he possessed
one to be ignored. He was skeptical in matters pertaining to religious
faith. He contended that the great crime for which the "one man" was
condemned, was attributable to the entire church. The accusation was so
diametrically opposed to the views I entertained on the subject that it
often occasioned arguments by no means pleasant.

[Comments and Reflections]

I was often led to reflect, how frequently it occurs in our intimacy with
our fellow beings that among their lovable traits, and graces we discern
some feature sorely trying and hard to bear with! His should remind us
that we all have imperfections, with which our friends have to bear; and
we wish them to love us for the good we possess and throw a mantle of
charity over all our faults. A Phrenologist knows how to account for defi-
cencies and idiosyncrises in his fellow creatures; not he, who knows not
himself. "I have been young and now am old," and this one thing have I
learned: to be merciful and forbearing towards my erring brothers, and
sisters, who travel with me the weary road of life, all hoping to find the
goal of our aspirations, and enter a sphere where sin and sorrow will
have an end. More than half the years of my married life I have stood
alone. Created the means to sustain myself and children: and although I
had kind friends around me I had no one immediately interested to supply my daily wants. My cares often weighed heavily upon me, yet for the
most part I have been cheerful. My firm reliance on the Almighty arm
for protecting power kept me from desponding when dark clouds
seemed gathering, and ready to burst on my defenceless head. There has
been seasons in my life when had I not believed that the angels above
knew and pitied me, I should have sunk down in despair! These were
times when my grief was too great for utterance; I dared not breathe it to
mortal ears! Then was the time when the gospel in its fullness came to
my relief! The sound was heard, "A new dispensation is ushered in:
Christ has revealed himself again from the Heavens, and commanded
His kingdom to be set up on earth! No sound was ever so joyful in my
ears, and from thence to my heart, as that! I felt paid for all my sufferings; in that I had lived to see the day so long foretold by prophets and
apostles! It was like being born into a new world. Great and sore trials
fell to my lot, in consequence of my determination to gather with the
Saints; but the knowledge I had gained helped me to bear them cheerfully. And now in my advanced life I have peace in the reflection that I
have been obedient to the voice of conscience, have never wilfully trans-
gressed a law, either of God or man.

Another principle I have studied hard to learn. To weigh character, understand organizations, in order that I might be enabled to discern beauty where many would only see deformity. As in the man to whom I have above refered, as differing with me on many vital points; yet in him I saw redeeming qualities. To appreciate him one must throughly understand him. Many indulged a prejudice much to his disadvantage of them he would remark without any apparent ill will. "They do not understand me." Thus proving the benefit of a cultivated intellect which enabled him to reconcile injustice done him, without the least resentment. He went from the place; a few friendly hearts missed him, and would sometimes speak of his amiable qualities. Thus it is with human life; some are valued above their merits, others fall below. How desirable to understand human nature and judge righteously.

I am now bringing my history near its close.

[The Summer of 1876: Gardening]

The Spring of 1876 dawned upon me. I was alone and felt that I could not tend my own garden. I engaged a man to cultivate it on shares. When the bargain was made I felt relieved. The ground was plowed, and a few seeds planted for early use. The next thing was the man opened a law office, in the centre of town. I could find no one willing to carry forward the work; not even my sonsinlaw. There was no alternative I must let my lot go untilled, or do the work myself. I employed my neighbor's children to help and I went to work with a will, with a firm reliance on the strength the Lord would give me: thinking how pleasant it would look to see things growing; to have vegetables of my own, and some to give my neighbors who had none. My strength incrased daily. I was a marvel to myself. I would rise before the sun, take a cold water bath, then go out and work while the air was cool and delightful. Most remarkably did my strength hold out during the warm season. I had great pleasure in seeing the fruits of my toil coming forward for my own use and that of my neighbors, who had inclosures which might have been cultivated, but for love of ease and dread of exercising muscle and nerve. The summer wore away pleasantly, my health continued firm. My patch of lucerne and the weeds fed my cow, and I was constantly reminded of the reward of diligence and industry.

[Trip to Minersville, September 1876]

In September I was solicited to make a trip by Stage Coach to a mining town, some forty miles away, where I had acquaintance, who were pleased to see me, and cordially entertained and accompanied me to the mines; where I was again reminded of the wonderful effects of labor and perseverance. 205 feet underground twelve men were at work getting out ore, which was drawn out by means of a windlass and horse power. Men would come up and go down in the great basket; even women would venture down to explore the subterranean vault and contemplate the marvelous works of nature. The bullion as it ran from the smelter, excited great admiration in my mind. Oh, how laborious! What will not men undertake for money?

I rode home from the town of Minersville with Mr. H. R. owner in the "Cave Mines." He had in his carriage a silver brick which was valued at $1700. He sold it to the express Co. and took the money back with him. This gentleman informed me that every third day they could turn out that amount. Their expenses were $300 pr day. I came home with the conclusion that a mininig town had no attractions for me. Houses built of lumber on the side of a mountain; not an earthly thing growing but scrub cedars; not a fence, nor a garden for miles around: all their supplies obtained from settlements at a distance. I thought it was more desirable to own a spot of earth, sow seeds, and watch their growth, and have the pleasure of eating what my own hands had produced.

[Autumn 1876: Unwell]

Autumn with her frosty nights crept upon us earlier than usual. I made haste to gather in what I had raised. Making exertions too great for my strength. The first, change in the weather seriously affected me. I took a cold, which for one whole year had not been my misfortune. Weakness and loss of appetite succeeded; and I found myself in a poor condition. My daughters proposed bitters to strengthen me; reduced alcohol with wormwood. Not a particle of good did it do me. I continued bathing in cool water took one of Johnson's pills three mornings in succession my cold was entirely gone. I was still weak.

The 10th of Nov. was the aniversary of my 74th birthday. A surprize party was instituted by some of my friends. They came and found me in bed. Having had no intimation of the affair I was undecided what to do. It did not seem possible for me to sit up and entertain them. They began by saying "you must not be sick, we shall make you well." They prepared some refreshment; their earnest wishes acted like magic upon me, and I grew stronger every moment.

The birthday cake was presented by Mrs. Bettinson, an english lady of taste and inventive talent, and of Beaver Celebrity in its early history. The hearty and elegant construction of the cake so excited my admiration that I exclaimed, it must be sent to the Centennial!" The exercises grew more interesting when all were assembled and my strength and spirits kept pace with the varied turns in conversation, and the good wishes expressed in my behalf, till at length there were no signs of indisposition remaining. There were five gentlemen present who had known me twenty five years; others nearly as long. In their first acquaintance with me in the golden days of California, before time had set his impress so vividly upon me.

I was warmly congratulated in that my life had been protracted to such a length, and that my physical and mental powers continued measurably unimpaired. A picnic was spread upon the tables, a merry company surrounding them, many blessings were pronounced with hearty amens; my strength gradually increased, constantly reminding me of the truth of the proverb, "a merry heart doeth good like a medicine." Judge Cox being called on for the benediction moved that the party be adjourned to meet one year from that date at the residence of "Sister L. B. Pratt," and hoped the present company would "all be living and able to attend." Thus ended a pleasant evening's entertainment, with which all seemed highly satisfied.

[Prophetic Sermons: Wheat Storage]

I still continued to improve. The last day of Nov was a day of Thanksgiving throughout the Territory. I attended; listened with interest to the many admonitions from the speakers to the people to lay up grain for a famine. They said it was sure to come, and that before thoughtless careless people would be prepared to meet it. They prophesied that a season of plenty would precede the time of great scarcity.

The sisters of the church were encouraged to commence at once to collect grain, and store it up against a day of want; when perhaps our kindred might come to us from a far country to buy food; as Joseph's of old went to Egypt to buy corn of him whom they had illtreated and sold: little thinking how the Lord had overruled their wicked designs in selling their brother, thus making him their Savior. And who can tell but the very persons who were instrumental in driving us as a body of people from Nauvoo into the wilderness, may yet have to come to the Saints for protection and salvation; in a time when war will desolate their country, and famine and pestilence cause the proudest hearts to be humbled! Then will be another proof, that "God moves in a mysterious way."

[Ephraim Pratt: Frank Grouard, Scout]

In the ensueing autumn I had another proof, (added to the many I have recorded) that the Lord hears and answers prayer. My readers will recollect the many references I have made to a boy I brought from the Island of Tupuai in his very early childhood.[5] That he ran away from me when he was sixteen years old, went to Montanna in the capacity of a teamster.

Twice after he left me I heard from him: at length his employer wrote me that he had absconded and he knew not what had become of him. Ten years passed away and nothing did I hear. Many an anxious hour did I spend in conjecture. If alive, why did he not write, or return? I often prayed that I might some time know if he lived what had been his fate? if he had died, whether he had a decent burial.

In the month of Nov. 76 my mind was impressed to believe that it might be revealed to me by some means what had become of my lost boy! I prayed most earnestly for a dream or vision. Then came a letter from the boy's father written in Chicago, that the lost was found! Mr. Grouard the missionary companion of Mr. A. Pratt on the Pacific Isles, seeing the name of Frank Grouard ["]Kanaka Scout," General Crook's Division in the Black Hill war; thought it must be his eldest son, (of whom he had not heard for several years) wrote to him to learn for a certainty who he might be? He received for reply that he "was raised by a lady named Mrs. Pratt in California; ran away from her, went to Montana, and was captured by the Sioux; was with them six years." got away from them, changed his name from "Ephraim Pratt to Frank Grouard," which was his father's name. His father immediately sent the letter to me, with lengthy accounts in print of the bravery and intrepidity of the said Grouard; according to him great applause for his noble daring and untiring energy, in leading detachments through dangerous defiles and bringing them safely to their quarters; amid the shouts of comrades.

I immediately wrote to him, to the care of General Crook, then camped at Ft. Fetterman. An early reply came from the said Grouard, calling himelf by the familiar name of "Ephraim" in the letter so that I knew it was verily my own adopted son, whom I brought over the seas, when he was but two years old. His letter was couched in the most penitent affectionate terms; giving a thrilling account of his being captured by the Blackfeet Indians, while carrying the mail in Montana. Stript of all his clothing, and left 70 miles from any habitation. He made his way to Fort Hawley, and when recuperated was put on a still more dangerous route; and in the year 1871 was captured by the Sioux. He was with them five years; and in that time applied himself assiduously to the study of their character; their method of war, and the knowledge of their country; believing that in a future day he might be required to serve his country, in an Indian war. In 1875 he made his escape from them, and was soon employed by government, as guide and Scout under General Crook, in his campaign against the Sioux. Whether just or unjust his success has been unparalleled in evading the attacks of that powerful enemy.

My mind has been continually under excitement, hearing from him from time to time and learning from him that he contemplated making me a visit. At length his photograph was sent; a fine looking gentleman, with no appearance of an Indian, as I had expected, his having been with them so long. He has moreover made known a discovery he made among the Sioux: that of a white girl; evidently about sixteen years old, which we conclude at once to be the same stolen from Cache Valley when she was very young, not more than three years of age. She was the daughter of a Mr. Thurston: grand daughter of Pres't Erastus Snow, of St. George. Great rewards have been offered for her redemption. My adopted son writes, "I have twice attempted to capture her, but did not succeed. I believe I shall yet accomplish it, in some of our fights."

The whole affair seems a tragedy of great interest! The sympathies of all are enlisted, in regard to the lost girl grown to womanhood among the savages; and the circumstances of the boy I had brought from a distant Isle, in his early childhood and having been lost to me ten years, and that in finding him, should be brought about the discovery of the long lost girl! Nothing could be made to appear more romantic! And should he accomplish her rescue, it would indeed afford groundwork for a novel writer.

In the spring of 1877 a sad letter came from the young man, imploring sympathy from "Mother;" laboring as he was under a great disappointment. He had previously informed me that he was soon to be married; mentioning the lady's name to whom he was engaged. It seemed by what I could glean from the spirit of that letter that the matter was fully settled, and no obstacles in the way. I began to comtemplate meeting my long absent boy, and being introduced to his bride! Alas, for the poor confiding fellow! Three days later, there came to my address inteligence that a change of prospects was anticipated, to his great grief and anguish of heart; even bordering on dispair. I was moved with compassion, and immediately wrote a letter of condolence; assuring him of my deepest sympathy, and encouraging him to hold up his head and never to succumb to disappointment! that the world was full of failures of that kind, which should be bravely encountered. That if his lady love had proven false, he must remember he was not the first man who had been deceived by the blandishments of an artful woman! His next letter breathed a little more of manhood, and a resolution to be firm and overcome. He expressed his doubts concerning the white girl he had seen, being the same stolen from Cache Valley in 67. The one he knew was reported to have been stolen from an emigrant Company of the Platte river. "She is the pet of the Sioux tribe; they even keep her in a cage, but not as a prisoner." "Frank Grouard" still resolves to venture her rescue.

[The Hunt Family Answers the Call to Arizona]

On some of the last days of Feb. 1877 my daughter Lois B. Hunt came to me with her large family, six daughters and two sons, husband in the lead, who had volunteered to go on a mission to Arizona. They had for one year been located in the valley of the Sevier river: had been successful in raising crops, had built them a good house, and we their relatives felt flattered with their prospects. But in the order of nature disappointments come, often from an unsuspected source. Here they came, only to tarry two days, and then to go to an unknown quarter, from whence I could not expect them to return; and considering my advanced age I could scarcely expect ever to see them again. The eldest daughter [Ida Frances], a girl ever dear to me, had been staying with me for one month.[6] I had indulged a hope that she would be pursuaded to remain with me untill the family found a location suited to their minds. She had partially consented; but when the final test came, she could not part from her mother and the young children. For days the weeping was incessant: not only with the family and relatives, but the neighbors and old acquaintance were moved to tenderness and tears, at the parting scene!

A card was sent from Washington that a new route was proposed through an unsettled country.[7] it sounded in my ears like a funeral knell! Hostile Indians, of whom I had read so much in the history of Arizona seated on my brain! My mind was rocked with fearful apprehensions: I wrote to St. George informing them of my presentiments; they sent a reply that according to reliable information there was no danger to be feared from Indians. That however did not wholy relieve my mind. A month passed away, ere we heard anything more. Then a letter came from Ida Frances, dated Iron Springs, March 29th. "The train" 14 wagons were camped at that point, had been making a new road, emerging six miles per day.

The journey had been tedious, their animals had suffered for water. The weather had been excessively warm, they were still a long way from their destination. They were then 240 miles from Beaver. They fortunately met a man coming to St. George, by whom they sent the letter, and it was mailed there. Ida remarked, that her mother thought my forebodings were interpreted in the badness of the roads, and difficulties on the journey, instead of hostile Indians. A month and eight days have since passed away and not a word have we heard. My anxiety is very great.

[Dedication of St. George Temple, 6 April 1877]

The 6th of April [1877] the conference and dedication of the Temple took place in St. George. The highway was thronged with people coming from S. Lake and farther north, traveling to that City, to participate in the blessings attending the interesting occasion. The Twelve Apostles, and their families (a portion of them) were among the number. They held meetings in the different towns as they passed through. In Beaver they tarried two days, which afforded us an opportunity to greet our old dearly loved friends, whom we knew in our days of trial and tribulation; some we had not seen before for ten years. It was indeed "like water to a thirsty soul," to be permitted to look upon their faces, so familiar, though grown a little older, and remember the scenes through which we had passed together, when the Lord alone was our hope and trust. Thus bright spots spring up in our pathway as we travel on our weary pilgrimage, thus lightening the burdens of life, and cheering us on to the goal of our hopes. The voices of the Elders from the publick stand, familiar to my ears long long ago, caused joy to spring up in my heart, for clearly could I discern that they had increased in the wisdom and knowledge of God; they spake as men having authority, and with great assurance.

I had long anticipated going to the dedication, but my brotherinlaw and sister were not prepared to go at the time; it being necessary for us to go together to attend to ordinances pertaining to our departed kindred, my going was defered to an indefinite future. My eldest daughter and her husband made the journey and returned, delighted with all they saw and heard. My daughter describes the Temple as beautiful beyond description; a neighbor lady ardent in her appreciations of the sublime and marvelous, said to me in describing scenes in the Temple. "It seemed to me the gateway to heaven! I thought there would be a good time and place to resign my mortal life, and enter the portals of the spirtual spheres! which I felt I could do with no dread of uncertainty, and even with joy![8]

It is seldom that one in health and in the middle of life, feels it better to die than live. In the midst of all my sore trials, when sorrows seemed to roll with mountain weight upon me, I have ever felt a clinging to life! My desire has been to struggle on, combat bravely with the ills, and wait the next event.

[Reports from Her Scattered Family]

I see now a threatening trial, which I dare not speak of, only in secret to Him who holds the destinies of mortals in His sovereign power, and ask Him to avert the scene I see in the distance. Three weeks after receiving the letter from my granddaughter dated at Iron Springs, another message was received, more distressing than the first. It was dated at Sunset Crossing. Lott Smith's Camp, Arizona. They had come on to good roads, but the cattle were so drilled out, they could endure no longer. Three good oxen laid down and died! They could go no further without more team. Fortunately they were near the San francisco mountains, where a stockholder came to their assistance: bought their odd ox, two cows and a light wagon, in exchange for a fine span of horses and harness: so packing all their goods in two wagons, they went ahead with greater speed.

If the loss of the good old faithful cattle, and having to part with the two cows, (all they had taken with them) would be the fulfillment of my dismal forebodings, that mischief would befall them on the way, my mind would now be relieved. I will dare to hope. They have passed Arizona, and gone into N. Mexico, to the Zuni Villages. They seem a great way off. I have little hope of ever seeing them again.

A recent letter from my adopted son informs me he is camped at Ft. Robinson, Neb. The Indian war is ended for the present. He expects to be stationed at that Ft. for some indefinite time, contemplates a visit to Utah, his earliest convenience.

I feel a foreshadowing of some good that may come to me from a source once least expected. News reached me after waiting long in suspense that my daughter and family were safely moored in a pleasant isolated valley in N. Mexico, 22 miles from Ft. Wingate. A location selected by two missionaries sent there to preach to the Indians. Zunies and Navajos only one American family besides my daughter's have as yet settled there; more are expected soon. The Navajos are inclined to believe the "Fullness of the gospel" the Zunis are not; generally established in the Catholic faith. The Navajos rejoiced exceedingly when they learned the object for which the white people were coming to their country. One, by some means got the impression that the Lord of heaven and earth lived in S. Lake City! When he was informed of his mistake, he seemed greatly disappointed. A letter from my grandaughter, over whom I mourned at the parting scene, revives my drooping spirits; and awakens a hope that there will some good come to me yet in my old age. I quote her own words. "Be of good cheer, I will come to you the first good chance, when I see my folks comfortably settled here. I will then return and see after my grandmother."

My adopted son still writes that he will come whenever he obtains leave of absence. He is traveling from Ft. to Fort with Gen's Sheridan and Crook, in Wyo' and Neb. The white girl he has discovered does not answer the description of the one stolen from Cache Valley, grand daughter of E. Snow. The one Frank Grouard describes was captured from a company of emigrants crossing the plains; her family all massacred. She is now 21 years old. He has since informed that he is ordered out with a scouting party of Indians, to watch the movements of the Sioux, who are threatening to take the war path again.

[Birthday Anniversary Celebration]

Nov. 10th 1877 my 75th birthday aniversary was celebrated. A large party of brethren and sisters of the church assembled at my dwelling, according to adjournment from last year. The tables were set in fine style at 6:00 p.m. a variety of choice dishes were placed before the crowd who partook with wholesome appetites: but for myself there was nothing tempting.

Previous exertion in making things orderly, the excitement of receiving the guests so wrought on my nerves that I was completely exhausted. After making a slight attempt to partake of the bounties contributed by my friends, I retired to my room to rest for a short time; then returned and endeavored to perform my part as creditably as possible; in order to make the evening exercises pass off agreeably. I had prepared a short essay and poem for the occasion; likewise on being urged to sing, I made an attempt, and succeeded apparently to the pleasure of the company, as their mirthfulness seemed quite excited. The evening passed pleasantly; the party adjourned to meet one year from the date; all prophesying that I would continue another year, and promising their faith and prayers that I might witness a succession of celebrations, and have health and strength to enjoy them.

[Family News and Anniversaries]

My heart is often made glad by receiving communications from my far off daughters. The one in N. Mexico writes encouraging about her eldest daughter returning to me: the same loving one who has always twined herself about my heart. If she comes before the cold winter closes in I shall feel that I have great reason to be thankful to Him who gives me multiplied evidences that He hears and answers my prayers.

In California I have a grandson 18 years of age; whose amiable qualities commend him to the esteem of all who know him.[9] He even remembers his aged grandmother in Utah; is only waiting to get means to came and pay her a long visit. Ida remarks in her last letter to me, "who knows but you may yet have a "boy and girl" to live with you, and your last days prove to be your best?" "Hope springs eternal in the human breast."

My adopted son writes that after many trials and seasons of suspense, he is at length married! Still in government employ at Ft. Kenny Wyoming. He promises to send a description of his wife, and the particulars of his wedding. She is called by the name of Miss Richards; which I think indicates that she is a white girl either English or American.

Little do we know when toiling and laboring to raise children what their course will be when they draw near the age of maturity whether they return us gratitude for all our anxious hours over their well being, or whether they will turn from us with indifference, and launch into irregularities destructive to their own peace, and humiliating to us who reared them with fair prospects of their fidelity to us.

The death of our beloved President has spread a gloom over the whole territory; wherever a branch of the church is located. We know it is gain to him, and for his sake we can almost feel glad, in that his enemies are disappointed. They cannot serve writs upon him any more, he is beyond their power. Will there not be joy in the spirit world, when his freed spirit reaches the abode of those loved ones, who left us long ago!

In January 1878, news came from my daughter's family in N. Mexico, that the small pox had come among them. They did not seem at all alarmed, having learned from the citizens that in that climate the disease was easily disposed of. Five of the younger portion of the family passed through the ordeal with little or no injury; the older five were saved by vaccination in early life. One stout young man who went from Beaver Co. with the family who seemed by the nature of his constitution destined to live to old age, fell a victim to that fearful disease, after a sickness of twelve days. So little is youth health and strength a defence against the insidious attacks of that malignant enemy we feel a deep sympathy for his poor mourning mother! I know by my own experience that vaccination for the kine [cow] pox is a preventative of the other most dreaded malady; and how unfortunate that people should neglect their children in primeval childhood, and thus leave them exposed to that deadful epidemick! My hopes are revived by the cheering news that my grand daughter will be here this spring; whose going away we so much lamented! "Mixture of joy and sorrow we dayly do pass through."

While rejoicing over the return of the wandering one, came the news of my eldest brother's death. He had lived out his apppointed time, (81 years.) filled his life with usefulness, won the respect of all who knew him, left behind him the assurance of a joyful acceptance in that blissful sphere, where he would meet thousands of our beloved kindred, long gone from this world of sorrow and suffering. Although these reflections were comforting, I could not avoid feeling grieved in spirit, that I should see his face no more in this life!

July 24th 1878. The aniversary of another eventful day has again passed. The people assembled for a celebration. Not with the zeal & inspiration that was manifested on occasions of that kind in years gone by; proving how every thing grows old. We cannot always keep in vivid recollection our sufferings & privations in breaking up our homes & launching into the howling wilderness to begin anew, & how thankful we were to find this fertile valley, designated by our wise Heavenly Father, as a refuge and resting place from our oppressors. It is meet & right that we should remember the day with gratitude and thanksgiving; the day we first set our feet on this soil, which has been the peaceful home of the Saints for more than thirty years.

The summer passed quietly, though with excessive heat, and the toilsome exercise of tending my own garden. My spirits were enlivened with the hope that in September my grand daughter would be here: indeed, I had expected her in April, but having survived that disappointment another time was appointed to hope upon. The period arrived, but no Ida came. I then received inteligence that she would be here in November.

[Ida Frances Hunt, Granddaughter]

The 10th was to be the aniversary of my 76th birthday; A picnic party was appointment at my rsidence. I wrote to impress her mind with the importance of being present on that interesting occasion. The celebration took place, much to the satisfaction of all concerned, but the young relative did not appear. Towards the end of said month one day as the shades of evening were closing in upon me she came walking in as home like as though she had only been to a neighbor's house on a visit, and returned in due time.

In Oct. preceeding her arrival, I had heard the death of another brother; living in Sutton, Canada East, by the name of Cyprian Barnes; two years my senior. He died from the effects of a cancer, with which he had long been afflicted. He was a firm adherent to the Methodist faith, an active member of that church, a moral and upright man.

My granddaughter remained with me 'till after Christmas then went to the valley of the Sevier to visit her relatives.

Soon after she left I was taken sick, with a winter complaint, in the form of pneumonia. It seemed to be prevalent every where. In many instances with children it proved fatal.

My youngest daughter (Ann Louisa Willis) buried a beautiful child, 14 months old, her only daughter only one week's sickness. I was not able to go to the house except once, on the second day of her illness, not even to see her buried. She seemed an uncommonly attractive child, both in looks and in her disposition; cheerful and contented all the day long, like a sunbeam always shining before her mother's eyes. But she bore the bereavement with great fortitude. She seemed to consider that it was gain to the dear one to go, before she had sinned, or marred her soul with the unhallowed things of this hard world, of temptation and sorrow! Before I had recovered from my illness word came to me that my grand daugther was detained on account of sickness of herself and friends where she was staying. After a few days she returned, much to my rejoicing, and relief to my anxiety. It was several weeks before my usual strength returned to me. My cough I cured with coal oil and sugar. (The most effectual remedy I ever tried) stirred well together.

[William H. McGary]

I had neglected to mention an exciting circumstance which occurred in the fall of 1878. The return of W. H. McGary from Ogden on his route to N. Mexico; from whence he had come to visit his kindred in Weber Co. Utah. The reader will recollect this same man was the former husband of my eldest daughter, from whom she was separated in Ogden, many years

Louisa Barnes Pratt and her granddaughter Ida Frances Hunt

before this date; buried his second wife in N. Mexico. On his return to Beaver found his only child by his first wife married; a young girl of 17 years; whom he had comtemplated taking with him to his home, for the purpose of assisting in the care of an infant daughter, left by his deceased wife, promising to return with her and bring the child in due time. Meeting with disappointment in that case, and being greatly excited on the renewal of an acquaintance with the mother of his daughter, there was a general feeling of sympathy for the unfortunate man. There seemed no way of redemption for him, and he decided to go back to his lonely home, submit to his fate, and solace himself with the guardianship of his infant daughter. A few weeks passed, a letter to his daughter here announced the death of his child; which came to him as he neared his lonely home; causing him more fully to realize his bereavments, and to count himself a doomed man! But ah! we cannot be alone in sorrow, however great it may be.

The year 79 came in the most intensely cold weather ever felt in Beaver; more especially in the month of Dec. I was sick and alone but be it to the credit of my neighbors and friends I was not neglected. Wood was hauled and chopt, in many instances food ready cooked was brought to my table, and I felt to thank the Lord for a brotherhood.

[The Hunt Family Called to Snowflake, Arizona]

In the winter of 1879 news came to us that the parents of my grand daughter had moved from N. Mexico to Arizona, 130 miles nearer Utah, her father John Hunt, having been called to preside as bishop over a branch of the church in a new settlement, called Snow Flake.[10] It was pleasant news to us that they were nearer to us, for although I never expect to go there, it does not seem so impossible to go 400 miles, as it would to go 600. Now we can hear often & when I know they are all in good health, the settlement increasing in numbers, building new houses, opening farms, & prospering generally. I feel measurably reconciled to the separation; & I say with one of old, "when my father & mother forsake me then the Lord will take me up." So I say in regard to my children, going far away from me in my declining years; when I feel the infirmities of age creeping upon me, & I am compelled to walk cautiously about. Where duty bids me go; Not with light elastic step, But heavy dull and slow." When I contemplate my lonely condition without a husband or son, my sonsinlaw not in a condition to give me a home, or render me much assistance, So much the more do I depend on the Lord; & greater is my gratitude that my lot is cast among the Saints. I know of a surety that they will not be unmindful of my necessities; they will even anticipate my wants; they will be more to me than my kindred, who have not obeyed the gospel, reveled in this our day; & who would look suspiciously upon me should I attempt to teach them certain things, I know are true.

[Spring and Summer of 1879]

The spring of 1879 dawned upon me & I commenced to put in my own garden, and to plant over a half acre of ground. The brethren plowed the ground, and my little grandchildren helped to plant it. That was accomplished with tolerable ease. Then came the severe exercise of muscle and bone; the watering & hoeing up the weeds, which grew faster than the vegetables. The hot season came upon me, the heat was intolerable! The prostration it brought upon me prevented my doing any justice to the garden except to irrigate. The brethren came and plowed it out, I began to be encouraged a little; then as ill luck would have it I had a fall, which disabled me from doing any manner of work for three weeks. The hurt seated in my right side, and caused me great suffering. The sisters came, washed and annointed me, promised me I should recover my usual strength, likewise the elders prayed with and blessed me, & promised the same; all which is now being realized. I had assistance about the work in a poor way by little boys, but better than none.

In the winter previous my eldest daughter Ellen Coombs was attacked with inflammatory rheumatism, in a most alarming form! She became helpless as an infant. When it was possible to move her she was brought to my house. In the mean time her daughter, (married one year ago) did herself a serious injury by helping to lift a heavy sewing machine. Her husband being from home & mother not able to attend her, she was brought to my house; was confined to her bed for near two weeks, My house was like a hospital, but we had kind friends.

[Ellen's Illness; Ida Frances, Nurse]

My grand daughter who had come so far to visit us realized how fortunate it was that she was here, a help and comfort in time of need. It was not long till Nellie the daughter was able to wait on her mother, and in due time her husband returned, and she went to her own house. The injury she had received was overcome by faith, prayers, and good nursing and in due time she gave birth to a fine promising son; my first great grandchild. After three months my daughter could walk well with the help of crutches & was shortly able to walk about the house without them. There was great sympathy extended to her, and many prayers offered up in her behalf, and even fasting by the sisters, the effects of which she felt at the time; and though not made whole, she was relieved of pain, so far that it caused her to feel conscious that we were praying for her. From that time she gradually improved, untill her general health was excellent, and the swolen limb gave promise of performing its accustomed office; and while I am writing this she is able to walk abroad with the aid of one crutch, and a short distance without either, for which we all feel to thank the Lord. Had all parties concerned united their faith in the first instance she might have been healed but there was a lack where it should have been most potent; and the delay has by no means weakened my faith in the healing of the sick, by the administration of the elders; the annointing with oil, and laying on hands. The excessive heat of summer is fast passing away. I begin to enjoy the fruits of my hard labor; poorly as my garden has been tended it does me good.

[Contemporary Recordings]

The women of the Relief Society are storing up grain against a day of famine; which we are warned will surely come, sometime in the near future. We wish to follow the wise man, who fore seeth the evil and hideth himself, while "the simple pass on and are punished." Soon a suitable granary will be completed to receive the grain we already have on hand, and that which we propose to collect, by purchase, donation, and gleaning. A noble enterprise; who can deny the fact? The drouth has been very threatening but by the providence of our merciful Father, the harvest is more abundant than was anticipated. We believe He will be long suffering, and give us time to prepare for the trying events which are to come on those who reject his warnings, and will not come out of Babylon, before she falls to rise no more.

Nov. 10th The adjourned party again assembled to celebrate the aniversary of my 77th birthday. Six Elders were present, besides other gentlemen, twenty ladies were in attendance; all with warm hearts to congratulate me that I had attained to such an advanced age and so well retained my mental and physical powers. The company was duly organized; a chairman, chaplain, and secretary chosen, a picnic prepared, all conducted in parlimentary order. The social, and spiritual, enjoyment, seemed unrivalled. In the midst of the exercises a serenading party came to the door, were invited in, and entertained the company with beautiful music. The minutes of a former celebration were read, likewise the prospectus to my history. I was urged to sing a song composed on the first settlement of Southern Utah in which I succeeded quite well.

[Ida Frances, Granddaughter]

April 11th 1880 Five months have now passed away since I took my pen to record the event of my 77th aniversary. I have struggled through one of the coldest winters I ever experienced in my life. Cold succeeding cold, and fastening on my lungs kept me prostrated till at the present time I have but little strength left. At different times when urged to go out and visit my friends, I would summon all my resolution and acceded to their entreaties; being assured it would be better for me than keeping so close to my own fireside. Each time it proved the worse for me; an additional cold was sure to be the consequence. My grand daughter was steadily with me, engaged in teaching school; I had the pleasure of seeing her passing out and in every day, and when she was gone for a half day, I did not feel lonely, as I expected her to return, at the set time. But Oh, the scene has changed! Her friends in Arizona continued their importunities for her to "come home;" and she was constrained to yield to their entreaties; although we were equally as solicitous to have her remain. But father and mother have the first claim; a house full of sisters, & brothers, all filled with anticipation to witness her return, to hear her sweet strains of music on the guitar, and be cheered by hearing rehearsed the events of her protracted visit, and a thousand little incidents peculiar to long absence from home. "Ida Frances" passed two birthdays in Beaver, her 21st and 22d. She took her departure on the 6th of April, fifty years from the day this church was organized, with six members; an item to be remembered. It was my youngest daughter's birthday, and we were assembled at her house to dine; when the carriage drove to the door. With tears and incoherent good bys we wished her a pleasant and safe journey home.[11]

Nothing could exceed the loneliness in the house the first day where she had so long been an inmate. The gloom was like that we feel when a dearly loved one is borne from the family circle and laid in that silent place among the kindred dead, gone forever from our sight. Her Aunt Ellen was hopeful; she believed the dear girl would come again in the due time of the Lord. Since then we hear intimations that events may transpire to bring her back sooner than we had dared to expect.

Another grand daughter (younger than the first) stays with me, whose husband is from home. She has a beautiful babe ten months old; he cheers our hearts with his carrols and his bright smiling face, and I am led to acknowledge that blessings still remain to me. The mother of the little one is the same whose marriage I have mentioned in my record of events. I mourned over her marrying so young, but she seems very happy and contented, and her devotion to the child sometimes alarms me, through fear that it may be torn from her embraces, as hundreds have been the past year from their doting mothers, in this country, and throughout this territory, with that fatal disease, Diptheria! The spring is cold and backward, The wind is boisterous, which makes it impractical for me to do anything in my garden. Now the 20th of April, not a seed in my ground.

The dear old lady sister Jane Neyman, is lying very low, a parallytic stroke has prostrated her, when to all human appearance she bid fair to be active and enjoy life for several years longer, notwithstanding her great age. 87 years she has lived on the earth, a model of goodness. June 6th The blessed old sister & friend of humanity is gone! After three weeks illness she took, departure to the spirit land. She often seemed in communion with persons long gone behind the veil; mistaking some who called to see her for friends she had known and loved in life; and who knows but their spirits might have been hovering over her, waiting to convey her spirit away when the struggle for life was ended. Her trust in the mercy of God continued to the last, and she was heard to repeat audibly those comforting lines often on her tongue in health, "The soul that on Jesus has leaned for repose, I cannot I will not desert to his foes: That soul tho' all hell should endeavor to shake, I'll never, no never, no never forsake!" Thus ended a long and useful life, fraught with trials, intermingled with bright hopes of deliverance at every intervening turn in the weary path she had to pursue. The prophet Joseph, in Nauvoo was her unvarying friend; which often buoyed up her sinking spirit, in times when she was passing through some serious affliction! Long will she live in the memories of many whom she attended in sickness, & relieved by her faith and prayers.

[Ida's Return to Her Home in Snowflake]

I will now leave her in her quiet resting place and return to my grand daughter who left me on the 6th of April to go to her home in the wilds of Arizona. Long and tedious has been her journey! Instead of performing it as she had hoped in two weeks the company were detained by high water and sandy roads, scarcity of feed for their animals, till eight weeks labor would scarcely suffice to take them through. Returning travelers bring us news of their difficulties. An explorer brought us word that the company when they reached the Colorado found the river ten feet deep, the wagons had to be unloaded, taken to pieces, and by littles carried across the river in a canoe instead of a flat boat. Then the animals were made to swim the stream. What a labor to make repairs and load up again! The poor traveling Mormons! Exploring and settling new countries has been their destiny for fifty years! I am now waiting anxiously to hear, the dear girl is safely moored in the parental home, however homely it may be, the arrival will be a joyful event to her.

Since she left me there has been wind storms, and cold weather even to require winter fires. My wood pile was low, but in my needs some good samaritan came along and offered deliverance, proving to me who are my neighbors.

June 29th At this date no complaint of cold but quite the reverse. The sun beats down upon us with power and scorching heat as though to make amends for his delinquency in early spring. The seeds were planted in my garden in reasonable time but frost and cold north winds forbade their growth, and now the only hope for their maturing is protracted summer.

Letters from my granddaughter announce her safe arrival in Arizona in the home of her parents, after an absence of one year and six months. Great was the joy that she had returned in health and peace. The journey though tedious and fatiguing was rendered endurable and even agreable, by agreable congenial company, acts of kindness from her traveling companions, her anticipation of the cordial welcome she was sure to meet, even in the settlements she was to pass through where she met old acquaintance with warm hearts.

["Now the days pass heavily away"]

Now the days pass heavily away. I seem to dread loneliness more and more. When there are none sleeping in the house but myself and little grandson only eight years old, if I awake in the night a gloom seems hovering over me! I think of the children I struggled so hard to rear, in the absence of their father the many years he was called on his mission to the South Pacific Islands, before I was permitted to accompany him, or rather to join him there; not one to live with me in my advanced stage of life; and though two are living not far away they are not situated in a manner to make me comfortable at their homes, to take up my residence with them, neither have I room to accommodate them, that one family might dwell with me. "Hope springs eternal in the human breast." I trust in God and look for a brighter future. I can count a thousand blessings all the time. The burden of my prayer is, "strength of body and peace of mind." With these, what more do I want, with loving friends to administer in time of need? Then why am I often sad? Because I am not worthy to claim that blessing in full, for which I intercede every hour of my life. I need cheerful company in my house, daily; such is my organization, mirthfulness is what my spirit craves. My strength will not permit me to go much from home, to walk any considerable distance; how pleasant an occasional ride would be in an easy carriage, but that is not in the programe of my daily life. Once I had a carriage of my own, could even harness my horse myself, take my children and go where I pleased. That is among the scenes of the past. It was not destined always to last.

Aug 13th. July has come and gone; the intolerable heat was more than I felt able to endure; but I kept up, and attended to irrigating my garden; no rain, not even thunder, to cool the air as in former years. Since August came in we have been favored with a few sprinkles of rain to lay the dust, & a little thunder which molified the excessive heat, and brought some refreshing breezes from the mountain's top to cool our scorched flesh. Ah we need not complain, summer will soon be gone, too soon I fear, for late planted gardens like mine. It would grieve me to see my hard labor lost, to see a blighting frost wither the vegetation I have nourished with such anxiety. I can only hope and pray.

The first monday in this month was our election. There was a tolerable share of union, but not universal. However, our party won, on account of illegal votes on the opposite ticket, which were thrown out, leaving the Mormon votes the majority. There were some unpleasant things to be disposed of, even in our Relief S. such as rancor towards certain ones who had taken a stand against the woman's rights question; which, though we felt great injustice had been done us, we concluded to lay aside, and cling to the iron rod, & to the blessed Savior's example, and in every instance render good for evil; that we may prove ourselves children of our Father in heaven, who is kind to the unthankful, and to those who slight His counsels.

Now I am doubly alone! My granddaughter Nellie McGary Jones has moved to Frisco (a mining town 40 miles away.) and now her mother has gone to visit her, and I feel bereaved. Why I feel bereaved, my youngest daughter has moved with her family five blocks from me, too far for me to walk: and she not being strong, cannot come often to see me. A friend and family connexion has been staying near me for several weeks, has made it a point to sleep in my house, for the most part, helping me at night and morning in my household duties; affording comfort by her quiet spirit, and solicitude for my welfare for which I ask the Lord to bless her. Her life is lonely, having been compelled to leave her husband for intemperance.

A hope springs up in my heart that when the women of this great nation are allowed equal rights with men, and power is vested in them to bring about reforms, the liquor traffick will be abolished; and drunkenness will be considered a crime and punished accordingly. What a mockery to call this nation free when more than one half her legal loyal citizens are denied the right of the ballot, the foundation of a government. Ah! But the Lord rules! He can "cast down the mighty and exalt those of low degree." Let the faithful women trust in Him. He will ere long adjust their cause, & help them to fulfill their destiny the great reform; as Tulidge has spoken. (See women of Mormondom.) May I live to see that day, and be a coworker, aged as I am.

Sources

The biographer of Louisa Barnes Pratt is blessed with a wealth of original documents by primary witnesses. The central actors in this drama were intelligent and literate. They wrote letters and maintained personal records.

Provenance of the Louisa Barnes Pratt Writings

Louisa Barnes Pratt died in her cottage in Beaver, Utah, on 8 September 1880, and was buried in the Beaver Cemetery. Her daughter Ellen Pratt McGary lived nearby and was designated agent for her properties. Louisa had willed her journals to her granddaughter Ida Hunt Udall.[1] We do not know just when or how Ida received the writings, but she had them in 1887 when she wrote: "Dear Aunt Ellen this is your birthday but I cannot tell what age you are without taking time to look grandma's journal over and see what year you were born."[2] Upon Ida's death, 26 April 1915, her husband, David K. Udall, realizing that his daughter Pauline was unable to care for them properly, living in a small house on a ranch at Hunt with many little children around, took the journals to Nettie Hunt Rencher in Snowflake, Arizona, "for safe keeping."

In 1947, Nettie Hunt Rencher, Pauline Udall Smith, and Louise Willis Levine prepared a typescript from the journals for publication by the Daughters of Utah Pioneers.[3]

Years later, as work progressed on editing the Addison Pratt journals the need to look at the original manuscript of Louisa's journal became evident. Accordingly Nettie Hunt Rencher put them into Pauline Udall Smith's hands, and they were taken to the present editor in Logan, Utah, in October 1955.

In returning the journals to Pauline's family, Mrs. Rencher ("Aunt Nettie") did not request that they be turned over to her family. They were to be used in editing the Addison Pratt journals. There was, however, a sentiment that the journals were held as a stewardship, that upon completion of the work, the journals would be placed in the Latter-day Saints Church Historian's Office. On 2 April 1987 the original journals of Louisa Barnes Pratt and of Addison Pratt, holograph original manuscripts, were presented to the Archives Division of the Historical Department, the Church of Jesus Christ of Latter-day Saints, in Salt Lake City, Utah, in the name of Nettie Hunt Rencher. Typed copies are deposited in the S. George Ellsworth Collection, Special Collections, Merrill Library, Utah State University.

The Writings of Louisa Barnes Pratt (1802–1880)

Of the original diary and journal she wrote, two signatures have survived. They are the following:

Journal A, 26 July 1850 to September 1851. 17 leaves, 19.5 x 31.8 cm.; sewn.

Journal B, 15 April 1852 to 4 December 1852; 15 leaves, 21.6 x 27 cm. 4 leaves, 19.5 x 24.4 cm.; sewn; bound in tapa cloth.

Of her "history," or journal-memoir, all signatures have survived. The eleven signatures are described as follows:

Signature 1, to autumn 1825: 41 *l*, 19.7 x 24.5 cm., pages numbered 1–44; purple ink; sewn, loose.

Signature 2, to winter 1828: 12 *l*, 19.5 x 31.7 cm., pages numbered 45–56; purple ink; sewn.

Signature 3, to fall 1833: 22 *l*, 19.5 x 31.7 cm., pages numbered 57–78; purple ink; sewn, but threads missing.

Signature 4, September 1833 to June 1844: 36 *l*, 19.5 x 31.7 cm., pages numbered 79–114; purple and black ink; sewn, but threads missing.

Signature 5, June 1844 to September 1848: 40 *l*, 19.5 x 31.7 cm., pages numbered 115–153 (two pages numbered 132); purple and some black ink; sewn, but threads missing.

Signature 6, September 1848 to May 1851: 28 *l*, 19.5 x 31.7 cm., pages numbered 154–199; black ink; sewn, but threads missing.

Signature 7, June 1851 to January 1853: 45 *l*, 19.5 x 31.7 cm., pages numbered 200–297; black ink; sewn, but threads missing; pages 213–217 and 238–241 missing.

Signature 8, January 1853 to March 1859: 50 *l*, 19.5 x 31.7 cm., pages numbered 298–399; black ink; sewn, but threads missing.

Signature 9, April 1859 to January 1871: 28 *l*, 19.5 x 31.7 cm., pages numbered 400–455; black ink; sewn with string.

Signature 10, 1871 to 1872: 22 *l*, 19.5 x 31.7 cm., pages numbered 456–499; black ink; sewn, but threads missing.

Signature 11, 1873 to 1880: 26 *l*, 19.5 x 31.7 cm., pages numbered 500–550; black and purple ink; sewn, but threads missing.

It is this journal-memoir, her "history," or revised journal, that is published here, with the following exception. Journals A and B have been substituted for parallel portions of the journal-memoir and differing portions of the memoir inserted in brackets, affording the reader opportunity to sense the spirit of her original record, perhaps to compare two examples of her writing. As noted above, the holograph journals are in the Archives, Historical Department, the Church of Jesus Christ of Latter-day Saints, and typescript copies, with pages numbered, have been deposited at Utah State University's Special Collections.

The following articles were written by Louisa Barnes Pratt and printed in the *Woman's Exponent*, edited by Louisa L. Greene and Emmeline B. Wells, close friends of Louisa Pratt:

"Scenes on the Island of Tubuai, South Sea Ocean." 2 (1 November 1873): 87. Extract from the journal of Mrs. L. B. Pratt, kept Feb. 1851. Copied October 18th, 1873, Beaver.

"Scenes on Tupuai. South Pacific Ocean." 2 (15 December 1873): 110.

"Advantages of Being Old. Incidents of Travel." 2 (1 February 1874): 135. "Beaver, Jan. 13th."

"Address. To the Young Ladies' Retrenchment Association in Beaver." 3 (15 November 1874): 95. "H. S. Shepherd, Secretary, Beaver, Nov. 6th, 1874."

Blurb announcing Louisa's autobiography. 5 (15 August 1876): 44.

"A True Tale of the Past and Present." 5 (15 April 1877): 169. "Beaver, March 31st, 1877."

"Finding Fault With Old Folks." 8 (15 September 1879): 58.

"Filial Affection." 8 (15 October 1879): 79–80.

Obituary for Jane Neyman. 9 (1 June 1880): 5.

"A Few Incidents." 10 (1 September 1881): 49. Ellen J. Pratt McGary selection of quotations from LBP.

"A Woman Missionary: Mrs. Addison Pratt on the Society Islands, 1850." Sixteen installments, vols. 28–31 *passim.*

There are in the Addison Pratt Family Papers (APFP) about 375 items: letters sent, letters received, poems, essays, notes, and memorabilia. Holographs in the S. George Ellsworth Collection, Special Collections, Merrill Library, Utah State University.

The Salt Lake City newspapers failed to mention Addison's death, and Louisa wrote her own essay-tribute and sent it to an eastern publisher:

"Obituary of a Mormon Elder," *Phrenological Journal* 56 (March 1873): 203–4.

The Writings of Addison Pratt (1802–1872)

The Journals of Addison Pratt, ed. S. George Ellsworth (Salt Lake City: University of Utah Press, 1990) includes his memoirs and journal and a comprehensive list of the writings of his close associates under "Sources and Literature."

The Addison Pratt Family Papers, see APFP above.

Fifteen letters by Pratt have survived either as holographs or as printed in church periodicals. They are listed in *The Journals of Addison Pratt,* 567–68.

The Writings of Caroline Barnes Crosby (1807–1884)

Memoirs and journal in thirty-six signatures, begun at Tubuai, French Polynesia, January 1852. Holographs are in the custody of the Utah State Historical Society, along with a typewritten copy made under the direction of S. George Ellsworth and bound in four volumes; citations are to this typescript. Her memoirs extend to September 1846, the journal-memoir from 10 May 1848 to 7 February 1853, and journal from 10 February 1853 to 2 December 1882.

The Writings of Benjamin F. Grouard (1819–1894)

Journal, 1 vol., 175 pp. Holograph. Ms d 1388, Archives, Historical Department, the Church of Jesus Christ of Latter-day Saints, Salt Lake City, a mission diary, 1843 to 1846, taken by Addison Pratt to the LDS Church in America.

Letters published in the *Times and Seasons* and the *Latter-day Saints' Millennial Star.* See *Journals of Addison Pratt,* 569–70.

Family history furnished to the author by Mrs. Louise Grouard Mock, Santa Ana, California, October 17, 1955.

NOTES

Introduction

1. S. George Ellsworth, ed., *The Journals of Addison Pratt* (Salt Lake City: University of Utah Press, 1990).
2. Author's Preface, herein, xxvii.
3. Chapter 12, herein, 167-68.
4. Chapter 23, herein, 351.
5. Chapter 16, herein, 224.
6. Ellen Pratt McGary to Ellen Spencer Clawson, San Bernardino, Sunday, 12 April 1857. In S. George Ellsworth, ed., *Dear Ellen: Two Mormon Women and Their Letters* (Salt Lake City: University of Utah Library, 1974), 41–42.
7. Chapter 2, herein, 34.
8. *The Journals of Addison Pratt*, 5 March 1846, 273.
9. George William Beattie and Helen Pruitt Beattie, *Heritage of the Valley: San Bernardino's First Century* (Oakland: Biobooks, 1951), 230–32, 243. See also Edward Leo Lyman, *San Bernardino: The Rise and Fall of a California Community* (Salt Lake City: Signature Books, 1996).
10. Chapter 7, herein, 100.
11. Caroline Barnes Crosby (CBC), Journal, 614. Caroline heard on 4 May that Mormon ward visitors had found Brother Pratt "extremely skepticle and full of vain philosophy." CBC, Journal, 617.
12. CBC, Journal, 662 (13 September 1857).
13. CBC, Journal, 692 (27 December 1857).
14. CBC, Journal, 692 (29 December 1857). Louisa would be left to lead her family again without a head.
15. Addison Pratt to Ellen P. McGary, 10 July 1858. Addison Pratt Family Papers (APFP) 4, Letter 15.
16. Chapter 24, herein, 360.
17. Chapter 15, herein, 222.

Chapter 1

1. The family of Louisa consisted of Levina (married Stevens Baker), Horace (Susan Cane), Dolly (Walter Lockwood), Cyprian (Sarah Chadsey), Louisa (Addison Pratt), Lyman (Dolly Sikes), Caroline (Jonathan Crosby), Lois (died 12 April 1835), Catherine (died 3 August 1838), and Joseph Willard

(unmarried). Elvira Stevens Barney wrote *The Stevens Genealogy* (Salt Lake City: Skelton Publishing Co., 1907).

2. Horace's departure was "a source of great grief" to all, though it resulted from dissatisfaction arising between father and son. Later he and Addison Pratt farmed together at Ripley, New York.

Chapter 3

1. Jonathan and Caroline Crosby were married 26 October 1834. He had joined the Latter-day Saints on 2 December 1833, she a year later, 18 January 1835. They lived a year in Wendell, Massachusetts, before following other convert families of that area to the church center at Kirtland, Ohio. The Crosbys, en route to Kirtland, arrived at Ripley on 12 December and stayed until 5 January 1838.
2. Jonathan responded that he left Kirtland "on foot, with no money, the roads . . . muddy, and begged his way." CBC, Memoirs, 41–42.
3. Caroline "went about some with them; took them to see Martin Harris, who was all the witness there was in Kirtland at that time. And he was then at variance with Joseph, and had been disfellowshiped by the Church. Notwithstanding he bore his testimony to the Book of Mormon in the strongest terms, and that was sufficient to satisfy [Louisa]." CBC, Memoirs, 42–43.

Chapter 4

1. Horace was expected to go to Canada, but when he heard of the expulsion of the Mormons from Missouri, he became discouraged, remained behind, renewed his relationship with the Presbyterians, and married a young lady named Susan Cane. Caroline dates their exodus "Nov 20th 1838." CBC, Memoirs, 45.
2. The headstone is still in position, weather-worn but readable.
3. From Ripley their route took them by way of Kirtland southward through Ohio to Columbus, thence westward to Dayton and Richmond, "on the beautiful national road through delightful scenery," beyond Indianapolis toward Terre Haute, to a site named Pleasant Garden, where they paused, watchfully waiting resolution of the Mormon War in Missouri and the plight of the scattered Saints.
4. The financial means of the two families contrasted. Caroline lamented being in "a land of strangers, with little more than one dollar in money, very few clothes, one horse and an old one horse wagon." The Crosby cabinet-making business took time to bring in money, so Caroline took in washing to earn a little "for meat and butter." Apparently the Crosbys borrowed from the Pratts, but Addison purchased government land to his full extent and became quite needy. There were unpleasant words, but their difficulties were arbitrated and settled satisfactorily.

    The National Road, passing by Pleasant Garden, carried heavy traffic, including Mormons travelling between Kirtland, Ohio, and Independence, Missouri. The Pratts and Crosbys entertained so often that the name of "Mormon Tavern" was applied. A branch of the church, with from twenty-five to thirty members, was soon founded. Notable visitors included the Prophet Joseph Smith, Brigham Young, and Orson Hyde. Caroline wrote:

"We had some happy meetings, especially when br Joseph called and put up with us. He told me that he preferred stopping with us, that he felt more at home . . . ." CBC, Memoirs, 47–50.

5.   The Addison Pratt family reached Nauvoo in November 1841, two years after its founding, a refuge for the Saints expelled from Missouri and a home for those gathering to the church from the United States and England. By that time there were hundreds of log cabins, frame houses, and in time some red brick buildings. From a swampy flat the people were building a "city beautiful." Under construction on the eminence overlooking the city was the temple, symbol of spiritual aspirations.

6.   The history of Nauvoo is well treated by Robert B. Flanders, *Nauvoo: Kingdom on the Mississippi* (Urbana: University of Illinois Press, 1965), David E. Miller and Della S. Miller, *Nauvoo: The City of Joseph* (Salt Lake City: Peregrine Smith, 1974), and Dallin H. Oaks and Marvin S. Hill, *Carthage Conspiracy: The Trial of the Accused Assassins of Joseph Smith* (Urbana: University of Illinois Press, 1975).

Chapter 5

1.   The Crosby family arrived in August 1842. "On reaching the temple we found br Pratt at work raising the large stones, on the second story. He left his work and escorted us to his habitation, where we found them all rejoiced to see us, and welcome us with smiles and kisses. And then we found ourselves the second time gathered with the church and a temple building to the Lord." CBC, Memoirs, 53–54.

2.   On 11 May 1843 a few of the apostles met in Joseph Smith's office and voted these four to take a proselyting mission to the South Seas: Addison Pratt, Noah Rogers, Benjamin F. Grouard, and Knowlton Hanks. On 23 May the missionaries met with the Twelve and were given instructions. Addison was set apart and blessed by Brigham Young. Scott G. Kenney, ed., *Wilford Woodruff's Journal, 1833–1898*, 9 vols. (Midvale, Utah: Signature Books, 1983), 2:233–34, 23 May 1843.

    The mission was long but successful. Through great sacrifice the church was firmly established among the Polynesians on the island Tubuai, Tahiti, and on coral reef islands of the Tuamotu Archipelago. The missionaries followed their instructions to remain at their posts until replaced, but they did not hear from the church. An occasional letter from Addison Pratt found its way into the church periodicals the *Times and Seasons*, and the *Latter-day Saints' Millennial Star*. I tell the history of the mission in detail in *The Journals of Addison Pratt.*

3.   Caroline described the carpet. "Sister had a large quantity of wool to work into cloth, made her a nice carpet, coloured the yarn all at home, had 14 or 15 different colors and shades, and many other things too numerous to mention." CBC, Memoirs, 45.

4.   Addison Pratt, Letter, 4 November 1843, *Times and Seasons* 5 (1 August 1844): 602–5. APFP, Letter 2.

5.   Caroline's witness was held generally: "Sidney Rigdon came to stand and tried to show to the people that he was the rightful successor of Joseph. And his arguments were so powerful, that many were almost persuaded to believe him such. But as soon as the twelve apostles with bro Brigham Young at their head took the stand, it was shown conclusively where the

power rested. It was the first time, that I ever thought he resembled bro Joseph. But almost every one exclaimed that the mantle of Joseph had fallen on Brigham. For one I never had any doubts afterwards." CBC, Memoirs, 59–60.

The congregation voted to sustain the Quorum of the Twelve Apostles as leader of the church. Louisa was affected similarly.

6. Willard Richards was the only one of the four prisoners in the Carthage Jail at the martyrdom who escaped being shot.

7. The Saints did all they could to cooperate in establishing peace. The state government was slow to bring the accused men to trial. A grand jury was impaneled and indictments issued, but the case was postponed until the next term, when the trial was held from 19–30 May 1845. The court found the accused not guilty. The attitude of Louisa is true to the spirit of the time.

8. "Temple blessings" promised eternal rewards to endowed persons who covenanted to live by the teachings of the Bible and Latter-day Saint scriptures. Caroline described the time and event: "The upper part of the temple was finished this winter, and endowments were given to the majority of the brethren. We received our washings and anointings sometime in Jan. Afterwards were sealed by bro Kimball." CBC, Memoirs, 61.

Chapter 6

1. The letter, dated Tahiti, Jan 6, 1846, "My Dear Family," survives in a copy in the hand of May Hunt Larson. APFP, Letter 7. Pratt sent $60 by Captain Hall, "a Bostonian."

2. On the direction of Brigham Young, Jesse C. Little went to Washington, D.C. and solicited government aid for the Mormon westward migration. President Polk proposed the Mormons make up a special battalion of soldiers to fight in the Mexican War. Little accepted the offer and Captain James Allen was sent to the Iowa camps, where in June 1846 he recruited some 549 persons, officers, privates, and servants for the Mormon Battalion.

Chapter 7

1. The immigrants of 1848 saw signs of remarkable progress in Salt Lake Valley, made in so short a time. The Old Fort housed most of the people. Three sawmills, a grist mill, and a water-powered thrashing machine were in operation. Some 5,000 acres of farm land had been plowed and planted or sown. The wheat crop and gardens had produced well. Fencing the Big Field was progressing. All this and more had been accomplished by the first winter's population of 1,680. During 1848 immigration increased the population by 2,417. Excerpts from the Manuscript History of Brigham Young, 1847–67, supplied to H. H. Bancroft, deposited in the Bancroft Library, University of California, Berkeley; Bancroft Manuscripts P-F 22, P-F 26, and P-F 67.

2. The reunion scene was also described and recorded by the father:
    "My oldest daughter Ellen was down on her knees, scrubbing the floor. Br. Haight step'd in and said, 'Ellen, here is your Father.' She jumped up, as I stepped in after him, and caught hold of my hand, with an expression that

was as wild as a hawk, and exclaimed, 'Why, Pa Pratt!! Have you come?' The next two, Frances and Lois, were soon on hand, and look'd equally surprised. The youngest, Ann, was out to play. She was soon called, and when she came in, she stood and eyed me a while with a verry suspicious look, when one of her sisters tried to force her up to me, to shake hands, saying 'That is pa,' when she jerked her hand away and said, 'It is not,' and left the room.

"Their mother soon came in. She looked quite natural and quite as young as when I left home, being more fleshy now, than then. At Winter Quarters she, with the rest of the family, all but the youngest suffered under severe fits of sickness, and the scurvy deprived her of her upper front teeth, and when she spoke, her voice was unnatural. Except that, I could discover no change in her. But the children had all grown entirely out of my recollection, and none of them knew me. I left them June the 1st, 1843, and this was the 28th of September, 1848. Such a cruel separation causes emotions that none can know but those that experience it. It was more like the meeting of strangers than the meeting of a famly circle. I shall never forget it!!" *The Journals of Addison Pratt*, 358–59.

3.   No doubt their "discussions" of "certain principles" included polygamy, or plural marriage. The teaching and the practice were secret until August 1852 when the church formally announced the doctrine and practice. Addison didn't like it. In the islands he had defended the Prophet Joseph Smith against charges of immorality. He and his companion required of membership in the church strict observance to the Christian law of chastity, and the Saints' Word of Wisdom. In the valley he found a loose interpretation and observance of the Word of Wisdom. The issue of polygamy was a bone of contention the rest of their lives, for Addison never modified his contempt for the principle and practice.

4.   Two days after Pratt's arrival the October conference of the church convened. Addison reported his mission, and read the Pratt-Grouard letter of 6 October 1846, pointing out the urgent need for missionaries in that field. Conference was continued on 8 October when it was voted that Elder Pratt, his wife and daughters, and a dozen elders should go to the islands and preach. Manuscript History of Brigham Young, 1848.

5.   James S. Brown and Hiram H. Blackwell were also appointed to the mission with Addison. Excellent records of this trek were kept and have been published in *The Journals of Addison Pratt*, chapter 14; James S. Brown, *Life of a Pioneer* (Salt Lake City: George Q. Cannon & Sons, 1900); LeRoy R. Hafen and Ann W. Hafen, eds., *Journals of Forty-Niners* (Glendale: Arthur H. Clark, 1954).

Chapter 8

1.   The company of missionaries called and travelling together to the Society Islands Mission consisted of the following: named in charge, Thomas Tomkins, a wife, and two little girls; Louisa B. Pratt and four daughters; Jonathan Crosby, wife Caroline, and son Alma; Joseph Busby and wife; Samuel McMertry, wife and child; Sidney Alvarus Hanks; Simeon A. Dunn; Julian Moses; and Hiram E. W. Clark, a boy taken along as a favor to Louisa's friend, Emmeline B. Wells, a prominent woman in Salt Lake City. Altogether, there were twenty-one persons; seven of the company, the men, would preach.

The overland route taken by the company was well known. See George R. Stewart, *The California Trail, An Epic with Many Heroes* (New York: McGraw-Hill, 1962). Addison Pratt had taken the same route, but from west to east, Sacramento to Salt Lake City, in 1848, and left a good description of the route. *The Journals of Addison Pratt*, chapter 12.

2. Caroline wrote: "Sunday 16th [June] very cold and windy, we were surrounded by gold diggers who were almost entirely destitute of provision. They offered us almost anything they had for flour or meat. Several of the brethren bought boots and shoes of them in exchange for flour. . . ." CBC, Journal, 102.

3. Caroline noted the site on Monday, 8 July: "We passed Tragedy springs about noon or a little before where 3 of our brethren were killed by indians 2 years ago. I got out of the wagon and went to the tree read the inscription which was carved I understand by br Pratt. It was a melancholy sight. A large pile of stones covered their grave as they were all laid in one." CBC, Journal, 110.

Chapter 9

1. Samuel Brannan, president of the *Brooklyn* Saints' branch, became affluent during the founding days of San Francisco and the gold rush, mainly "by mining the miners." His wife Elizabeth's mother, Mrs. Fannie Corwin, lived with the Brannans. Northern California Mormon population at this time included men and families from among the *Brooklyn* Saints, the Mormon Battalion, gold missionaries, and proselyting missionaries.

2. Caroline's account is more specific: "We were expecting to have a lonesome day of it but in the afternoon Sister Pratt and girls came in with their supper which we put with ours and sister McMurtrey's and the whole formed quite a variety. We had baked pig, salt pork, fish and goat meat, stringbeans, radishes, lettuce, rice pudding, tarrow fayees, mummy apples baked, also pies made of mummy apples and bananas and finally the day closed with quite a merry Christmas. I spent the evening at sister P's had a very sociable time we called to mind our last Christmas anniversary, and the immence distance which time had born us from that place." CBC, Journal, 130–31.

Chapter 10

1. Grouard had built ships before his mission. In the islands he and Pratt had used the native outrigger *pahi paumotu*, and in Pratt's absence Grouard had built the *Anaura* (modeled after a whaleboat), the *Messenger* (sold to pay a debt), and now the *Ravaai*, a schooner of 80 tons burthen. The *Ravaai* would be used to transport missionaries from one island appointment to another and to engage in inter-island trade: animals, fruits, limes, and other island products.

2. She has been reading, no doubt, John Williams, *A Narrative of Missionary Enterprises in the South Sea Islands* (London, 1837). Williams was one of the ablest and most successful of Christian missionaries to Polynesia. Sponsored by the London Missionary Society, he went from island to island in central Polynesia, teaching in the native language, training native missionaries, and establishing commerce among the islanders. Louisa had a keen appreciation for the work of the London missionaries.

3. James Brown's contributions to the mission are told in his *Life of a Pioneer* and in *The Journals of Addison Pratt.*
4. The sister missionaries also had a male student for education and rearing, none other than Darius, age 6, son of the king, "heir apparent to the crown of Tubuai." One year on the island, Caroline measured their success: "Our young prince Darius begins to become a little civilized; speaks a few english words, can understand considerably but is still so wild that it requires one each side of him to keep him straight when we get him into the house, which is rather seldom." CBC, Journal, 147; *The Journals of Addison Pratt,* 251, 476.

    Both Caroline and Louisa shared racial attitudes which were common in Victorian America. Notice Louisa's pronouncements on Spanish-speaking residents of California later in this work.

Chapter 11

1. Caroline wrote of the meeting "Thursday 30th . . . I opened the meeting by singing a native hymn in company with 2 sisters, read a chapter in their bible and prayed in my own language. There were ten women of us with Louisa. The most of them spoke and prayed, and the good spirit of God was with us. We closed by singing a hymn and shaking hands all round, saying Iaorana 2 or 3 times apiece." CBC, Journal, 148–49.
2. Joseph Smith Jr. taught and the Saints in Nauvoo performed baptisms for and in behalf of their dead kindred who had not heard the gospel in this life. Such people were given the opportunity to receive it in the hereafter, together with confirmation and other ordinances. Addison Pratt performed baptisms for some of his near family just prior to his leaving on his first mission in 1843. Louisa likely did the same for her own before taking leave of the Nauvoo Temple. "Baptism for the Dead," in *Encyclopedia of Mormonism,* Daniel H. Ludlow, ed. (New York: Macmillan Publishing, 1992), 92–98. Pratt documents in APFP 4.
3. On Anaa, James S. Brown met opposition by two French Catholic priests who spied on Brown's teaching and caught him in indiscretions. He displayed the American flag, told of his military experiences, showed maps of western America, expressed his sympathy for the natives being under the French "yoke," and talked about the gathering of the Saints. On 28 October he was arrested on charges of sedition and sent in chains in a French man-of-war to Tahiti and there imprisoned until 15 November. On the 17th he was ordered expelled from the French Protectorate islands and to quit Tahiti on the first vessel leaving port. The *Ravaai* took him to Raivavai where he remained for ten months. James S. Brown, *Life of a Pioneer, The Journals of Addison Pratt,* and CBC, Journal, 150 ff.
4. Caroline described the New Year's Day celebration: ". . . we whitewashed the house inside and outside, got new grass for our floors, trimmed it with green bushes and ornamented it with pictures to the best of our ability. . . . There were some 40 persons who ate with us. We had not so great a variety as we might have had if we had given her longer notice. She had only one day to prepare the food. We had baked pig, fish, tarrow, popoi, tupinu, tairo, sweet potatoes, bananas, faii's, cabbage and tea, with cocoanut water to drink. . . . The day passed away very agreeably. Towards evening we resorted as usual to the church house to sing and pray." CBC, Journal, 152.

5. Monday, January 5, 1852 was Caroline's birthday. At age forty-five she began writing a brief history of her life.

Chapter 12

1. On Pratt's first mission he learned that William Dana had bought from the natives a tract of land on Tubuai. En route to his second mission, Pratt purchased from Dana that tract of land, having executed a quit claim deed. Pratt never acted upon the document. It is in APFP 3. *The Journals of Addison Pratt*, 421–23, 557–8.
2. The length of time required to learn the language varied from person to person and circumstances: Pratt was preaching in five months, Grouard in seven months, and Brown eight months.
3. Caroline: "April 1st [1852] . . . In the afternoon we attended our female prayer meeting as we now expect for the last time. I felt quite affected with the idea of its being the last of our assembling with them, some of them also seemed to regret our leaving them very much. After they had all ceased speaking and praying we (sister P, Ellen, and myself), went to each separately, laid our hands upon their heads and blessed them in the name of the Lord. The good spirit accompanied us, our meeting continued quite late." CBC, Journal, 169.
4. During the ten years after Pratt left on his first mission, he and Louisa were together for only two short periods: a year in Salt Lake Valley, and most of fourteen months on Tubuai.
5. Caroline: "Tuesday, 6th of April about 4 o'clock we sailed from Tupuai. . . . I knew not the day before whether we should have sufficient food brought to last us to Tahiti but when the day of our departure arrived the food was brought in so bountifully that Br. G. said we had plenty to go to California." CBC, Journal, 170.

Chapter 13

1. The "26th" is probably a slip since Sunday was on 25 April that year.
2. The two families numbered four adults and eight children. They were Addison and Louisa Pratt and their four daughters—Ellen, 20; Frances, 18; Lois, 15; and Ann Louise, 12—and Ephraim (Louisa's island boy, 2). Benjamin F. Grouard, wife Nahina (second Polynesian wife), Sophronia (Grouard's daughter by first wife), Nahina's sons Franklin and a baby boy. Benjamin F. Grouard family history was furnished to me by Mrs. Louise Grouard Mock, Santa Ana, California, October 17, 1955. On file is my notebook Benjamin F. Grouard Source Materials, containing copies of all materials found relating to him and his family.
3. Probably a slip, for the Sabbath was on 23 May that year.

Chapter 14

1. In the three communities of Saints in upper California—at San Francisco, San Jose, and San Bernardino—the members mingled in a loose organization. Whether as proselyting or gold missionaries, veterans of the Battalion march or *Brooklyn* passengers, membership was in flux, moving freely in northern California or southern. Of special importance to the

Pratts were Henry Christie and John M. Horner. George William Beattie and Helen Pruitt Beattie, *Heritage of the Valley: San Bernardino's First Century* (Oakland: Biobooks, 1951) had been the standard work but is now succeeded by Edward Leo Lyman's *San Bernardino: The Rise and Fall of a California Community* (Salt Lake City: Signature Books, 1996). Comprehensive in his coverage of the sources, Lyman uses them well throughout the book. His research has been thorough, his interpretation is sound. Good use has been made of personal, church, and contemporary records. See also Leonard J. Arrington, *Charles C. Rich: Mormon General and Western Frontiersman* (Provo, Utah: Brigham Young University Press, 1974), chapters 13 and 14. Lorin K. Hansen and Lila J. Bringhurst, *Let This Be Zion: Mormon Pioneers and Modern Saints in Southern Alameda California to "Stakes of Zion" in a World-wide Church* (Fremont California and Fremont California South Stakes of the Church of Jesus Christ of Latter-day Saints, 1996).

2. Louisa B. Pratt to Sister Hutchinson, San Francisco, 8 June 1855. APFP 6.
3. Among the Saints in San Jose was John M. Horner. His career was noteworthy. Born in 1821, he joined the church in 1840 and arrived in Nauvoo in 1843. After taking a mission campaigning for Joseph Smith for the presidency in 1844, he joined the *Brooklyn* journey to Yerba Buena (San Francisco) and reached port in July 1846. He served as branch president for some time, and by mining, agriculture, trade in farm produce, and land speculation, he amassed a fortune during the Gold Rush of 1849–54. He helped many of the Saints in northern California by giving them employment. However, he lost half a million dollars during the panic of 1854. John M. Horner, Autobiography, Archives, Historical Department, the Church of Jesus Christ of Latter-day Saints, Salt Lake City, Utah, and "Adventures of a Pioneer," *Improvement Era* 7 (May to December 1904): 510f, 580f, 665f, 767f, and 849f. See also Hansen and Bringhurst, *Let This Be Zion*, n. 48.
4. Louisa saw little reason to leave the Bay Area so long as there was plenty of work at high wages. Her real preference was to go to Salt Lake City, but Addison told the family they had no means to get there and had no guarantee of work when they got there.
5. Quartus S. Sparks, an attorney who came to California on the *Brooklyn*, presided over the San Francisco branch. In February 1853, however, he sold his house and lots and on 3 March moved to San Bernardino where he remained the rest of his life.
6. The Crosbys reached San Francisco 5 September 1852 aboard the *Agate*, having left Papeete, Tahiti, on 28 July. Jonathan and Caroline Crosby shared a cabin aboard ship which cost them $175, and Alma had a place in steerage. Also on board were Whitaker, Alexander, and Alfred Layton (son of Seth). CBC, Journal, 182 ff.

Chapter 15

1. These missionaries were likely among the 106 elders called at the 28 August 1852 conference in Salt Lake City. They were called to proselyte and to disabuse the public mind concerning the church's practice of plural marriage, which was publicly announced at the conference for the first time. Andrew Jenson, *Church Chronology* (Salt Lake City: Deseret News, 1899), 28–29, August 1852.

2.   Hiram Blackwell was called to the Society Islands Mission in October 1849 and was to accompany Addison Pratt on his return to the islands. He and Pratt travelled together to California, but Pratt refused to take him farther because Blackwell had failed to quit the use of tobacco. He eventually reached Hawaii. Louisa thought highly of Blackwell and defended him before her husband. He shows up at various times in her life.

3.   He had married Louisa Maria Hardy as a plural wife, the daughter of Jacob Hardy and Louisa Kimball, converts to the church. The record simply shows: "Pres. Young sealed a wife to Benj. F. Grouard." Grouard was in Salt Lake City from fall 1852 to spring 1853. Journal History, 9 and 25 January, 4 and 16 February, and 19 March, 1853; *Deseret News*, 3 January, 9 March, and 2 April 1853.

4.   Grouard's children included one daughter, Sophronia (born in early 1847), by his first Tahitian wife, Teara (who married him on 20 April 1846 and died in mid-1847) and three sons by Nahina (married in late 1847): Franklin (b. mid-1848), Ephraim (b. 20 September 1850), and the baby. The last returned to Tahiti with Nahina; Sophronia and Franklin stayed with BFG; and Ephraim was adopted by Louisa.

5.   Louisa uses kind words here, but she knows each picture has two sides. She describes the other side of the San Bernardino picture in a letter to Mrs. Hutchinson, San Bernardino, 8 June 1855, APFP 6.

6.   Philip B. Lewis maintained a close relation with the Society Islands Mission, and was related to Louisa by marriage. He put up the $300 to pay the passage of the missionaries on the *Timoleon* in 1843. He was named to accompany Pratt on the second mission, but his assignment was changed; he later went to Hawaii. He moved to St. George where he lived out his life. Andrew Jenson, *Latter-day Saints Biographical Encyclopedia*, 4 vols. (Salt Lake City: Andrew Jenson History Company, 1901–36), 3:672, 4:340. B. H. Roberts, ed., *History of the Church of Jesus Christ of Latter-day Saints: Period 1, History of Joseph Smith, the Prophet, by Himself,* 6 vols. (Salt Lake City: Deseret News Press, 1902–12), 6:10–30, especially, 14, 15, 27–28. Elvira Stevens Barney, *The Stevens Genealogy.*

7.   An obvious slip. He was born in 1802, and it was his fifty-fourth anniversary.

Chapter 16

1.   Louisa wrote in the Memory Book, APFP, under the heading "56, April 12th, San Bernardino":

Again you go far far from home
A foreign shore to greet,
And little do you know the ills
Of fortune we may meet.
No father brother husband friend
May faithful prove to me,
And yet I trust that to the end
God will remembered be
A friend in time, and in eternity.

2.   There were frequent fateful connections between Charles W. Wandell and the Addison Pratt family. He joined the church in 1837, undertook missions

in the States, and visited the Pratts in Indiana. After the martyrdom he took ship to San Francisco where he met with Samuel Brannan and Parley P. Pratt. In 1851 he and John Murdock took a mission to Australia; afterwards Wandell lived in San Bernardino. In 1857 he followed others to Beaver, Utah, where friendships were renewed. In time, he moved to northern Utah, where in 1873 he joined the Reorganized Church. That church called him and a companion to take a mission to Australia. En-route, he was stranded in Tahiti, where he used his friendship with the Pratt family to establish the RLDS church in the Society Islands. Wandell and companion reached Sydney in January 1874. Wandell died a year later, 14 March 1875. Andrew Jenson, *LDS Biographical Encyclopedia* 3:551.

3. John S. Eldredge was a close friend of the Pratt family in Nauvoo and the Salt Lake valley. He undertook a mission to Australia from 1852 to 1856. En route home he experienced the destruction and loss by storm of the bark *Julia Ann*. Many passengers were Latter-day Saints. He would have told how the *Julia Ann* was destroyed by strong winds, high waters, and coral reefs, and how fifty-six passengers suffered prolonged ordeals, cast upon uninhabited islands, living off shell fish, birds, fish, and turtles. It required eight to ten months for passengers to reach San Francisco, their destiny. The story is told in church annals. Andrew Jenson, "The Bark 'Julia Ann,'" *Historical Record* 6:161–63; Andrew Jenson, *LDS Biographical Encyclopedia* 4:700.

4. Judge W. W. Drummond, infamous in Utah history, had been sent to preside over one of the Utah territorial federal courts. He had left his post and was en route to Washington, D.C., with a list of charges against the Mormons. His charges figured in the decision of the president to send troops to Utah to put down an alleged uprising—the Utah War. B. H. Roberts, *Comprehensive History of the Church of Jesus Christ of Latter-day Saints* 6 vols. (Salt Lake City: Deseret News Press, 1930), 4:200–480 *passim.* Norman F. Furniss, *The Mormon Conflict, 1850–1859* (New Haven: Yale University Press, 1960).

5. The association of the Pratt and Pickett girls is of special interest and had Nauvoo antecedents. It began with Don Carlos Smith, the youngest brother of Joseph Smith. He married Agnes Coolbrith and had three children, Agnes, Sophronia, and Josephine, before his death 7 August 1841. His widow married William Pickett. The family moved overland in 1851, taking up residence in San Francisco and Los Angeles. The daughters assumed the surname of Pickett instead of Smith, except for Josephine, who took her mother's maiden name and became Ina Donna Coolbrith. As editor, poet, and librarian, she had a leading role in early California American literary circles and was named poet laureate of California. Josephine DeWitt Rhodehamel and Raymond Francis Wood, *Ina Coolbrith, Librarian and Laureate of California* (Provo, Utah: Brigham Young University Press, 1973).

6. There was a unique friendship between the Pratt girls, the Pickett family, and Frank Ball—young people who greatly enjoyed each other's company, dedicated, it seems, to wine, Mormons, and song—meaning poetry and poking fun. Frank Ball's letters from 1855–57 survive in APFP 16.

7. The Grouard family left San Bernardino about 1855 for San Francisco. The Pratts were without knowledge of them until 1873, after Addison's death. The final chapters herein record the latter contact between the Grouard family and Louisa.

Chapter 17

1. The Reformation was a church movement aimed at the supposed sinfulness of the people and was characterized by fiery sermons, calls for repentance, rededication to the Kingdom, and witnessing by rebaptism. It is quite likely that the excesses that occurred in Utah were not present in California. Gene A. Sessions, *Mormon Thunder: A Documentary History of Jedediah Morgan Grant* (Urbana, University of Illinois Press, 1982), chapters 13–21; "Jedediah M. Grant," Andrew Jenson, *LDS Biographical Encyclopedia*, 1: 56–62; Gustive O. Larson, "The Mormon Reformation," *Utah Historical Quarterly* 25 (January 1958): 45–64.

2. Parley P. Pratt, a favorite apostle, was murdered 16 May 1857 in Van Buren County, Arkansas, by Hector McLean. McLean's wife had converted to the church and became Pratt's plural wife. Conflicts over child custody led to New Orleans and Arkansas, where Pratt was arrested on a customs charge. The release of Pratt so angered McLean that he pursued Pratt and shot him. Parley was buried on the spot.

3. Quite likely the same C. E. Hutchinson who gave Ellen a leather-bound Bible inscribed to her 1 July 1854. See *Dear Ellen*, 21 n.2, 30, 33, 26.

4. The use of "fearful" here reminds us of Louisa's reflection on those times. In a letter dated Beaver, 25 May 1865, she wrote Ellen: "We were frightened away from San B. I do not believe I shall ever be excited any more. . . . When I set my hand again to deed away a homestead I shall be out of my right mind." APFP 6 (11).

5. The Mountain Meadows Massacre occurred at famous watering and recruiting grounds in southern Utah on 11 September 1857. About 120 men, women, and children were lured from their defenses, disarmed, and slain by men of the Utah militia and Indians of the area. Indians were blamed, though the involvement of whites was suspected. Only slowly, over the years, did the extent of non-Indian involvement come out. This tragic affair is best considered by Juanita Brooks in *The Mountain Meadows Massacre* (rev. ed., Norman: University of Oklahoma Press, 1991).

6. Louisa presumed her reader knew of the coming of the Utah War. She would remember that in Los Angeles, Judge W. W. Drummond of the Utah territorial judiciary spoke ill of the Mormons. She did not know that the judge went to Washington, D.C., where he submitted a statement of charges against the Mormons. President Buchanan appointed a new governor and sent a large military force to restore order. The people of northern Utah learned of the approaching army during late summer, 1857. Brigham Young took the approach of federal troops to Utah as a declaration of war against his people. Responding, he called foreign missionaries home and called settlers in distant settlements (including San Bernardino) to abandon their homes and head for the central valleys of Utah. The Utah War of 1857–58 precipitated crisis for Saints everywhere.

7. Addison Pratt's call to Utah was phrased in a letter from Charles C. Rich, dated Salt Lake City, 7 October 1857. Informing him of the situation, the letter added: "I wish you and yours was with us also all the good Saints." No compulsion. People were free to act as they wished. In San Bernardino, a debate ensued: to go or not to go. Louisa would never be satisfied until she lived in Salt Lake City, but she would not like to leave home and gardens, over which she had labored so long and hard. On the other hand, she

would enjoy associating with the leading figures in the church, to be in the circle of women friends from Nauvoo and Winter Quarters and be among those who shared the trials of crossing the plains. Her husband would take his rightful place among Mormon leaders because of his distinction as a missionary.

Chapter 18

1. Louisa's family and companions now consisted of the following: Ellen Pratt McGary, husband William McGary, and their baby, Emma Francelle; Lois Pratt Hunt and her husband, John Hunt (Lois was six months pregnant); Ann Louise Pratt (single but being courted by young McIntire); the seven-year-old island boy, Ephraim Pratt; Captain Jefferson Hunt and wife Harriett; and Louisa's sister Caroline B. Crosby, husband Jonathan Crosby, and son Alma. Captain Hunt knew the route, having served as a guide.
2. "Cajon Pass divides the San Gabriel and San Bernardino ranges and affords the best route between the Mojave Desert and southern California." *The Journals of Addison Pratt*, 406–08, 556.
3. These companies followed the well-established road traversed by Mexican traders during the 1820s and 1830s, by explorers in the 1840s, and by Mormon freighters, possibly annually since 1847. "While the route may have been fairly well defined, it was nonetheless a most difficult passage because it went through unexplored, life-threatening desert country, with little or no grass or water." *The Journals of Addison Pratt*, 370–71.
4. Las Vegas, Spanish for "the Meadows" "A constant flow of water produces a meadow year–round that affords an excellent recruiting place for stock before undertaking the next long haul across the desert. The traveler here is on the Old Spanish Trail. The Mormons had established missions here in the early 1850s to work with the Indians and to prospect for silver in the mountains nearby. It was described by Addison Pratt, *The Journals of Addison Pratt*, 395, 555.
5. Mormon travelers discovered rich deposits of lead at Cottonwood Springs, thirty miles southwest of Las Vegas. The discovery stimulated the establishment of a lead mission. In June 1855 a mission to the Indians at Las Vegas Springs was also founded. The undertaking was abandoned in January 1857. "Nevada" in Andrew Jenson, *Encyclopedic History of the Church* (Salt Lake City: The Church of Jesus Christ of Latter-day Saints, 1941), 571–73. "Pioneer Settlements in Nevada," *Encyclopedia of Mormonism*, 1006–7.
6. The Muddy (sometimes the Far Muddy) has its source in warm springs about eight miles northwest of present Glendale and passes through Moapa Valley to empty, then, into the Virgin River, but now into Lake Mead.
7. Santa Clara was the southernmost village in Utah at the time. The geography of the region changed significantly from the desert. When John C. Frémont reached this point, he exclaimed about the mountains wooded with cedar and pine and the clusters of trees that gave shelter to birds.
8. Virgin Hill is one of the most difficult obstacles to overcome on any western trail or road. Ascending or descending the distance from the plateau above and the Virgin River Valley below, travelers had to take it piecemeal, unloading, loading, doubling teams and chains. Described by Addison Pratt, *The Journals of Addison Pratt*, 392. See also my *Samuel Claridge: Pioneering the Outposts of Zion* (Logan, Utah: privately printed, 1987), 92–98.

9.   Ida Frances Hunt, daughter of John Hunt and Lois Pratt, was born near Hamilton's Fort. Maria S. Ellsworth, ed., *Mormon Odyssey: The Story of Ida Hunt Udall, Plural Wife* (Champaign: University of Illinois Press, 1992) publishes her diaries and personal records.

10. Cedar City was settled in November 1851 for the purpose of developing an iron industry. Philip Klingensmith was the first bishop.

The nearby pioneer settlement of Parowan dates from January 1851 when Apostle George A. Smith led his company of 118 men, some with families, and 101 wagons into Little Salt Lake Valley and chose a site for settlement. Merlo J. Pusey, *Builders of the Kingdom: George A. Smith, John Henry Smith, George Albert Smith* (Provo, Utah: Brigham Young University Press, 1981), "The Founding of Parowan," 80–85.

11. Isaac C. Haight had joined the church in 1839, served in the Mormon Battalion, and reached Salt Lake Valley in September 1847. At this time he was an explorer, mayor of Cedar City, and stake president.

12. Names of emigrants from San Bernardino show up now as residents of Beaver, illustrating the continuity of friendships—for example, Bryant, Button, Cox, Farnsworth, Gale, Lee, Lyman, Shepherd, and Wandell.

13. The Iron Mission produced some iron; but the amount was disappointing, and the project was given up.

14. John R. Young, a son of Lorenzo Dow Young, returning from a mission to Hawaii, passed through San Bernardino. He was later called to Dixie and lived out his life there. *Memoirs of John R. Young, Utah Pioneer, 1847, Written by Himself* (Salt Lake City: The Deseret News, 1920). Andrew Jenson, *LDS Biographical Encyclopedia* 2:274–76.

15. Philo T. Farnsworth, the first bishop of Beaver, was born 21 January 1827. He reached Utah in the fall of 1848 and settled Pleasant Grove and Fillmore before being called as bishop of Beaver. He served until 1864. Besides being a bishop, he was probate judge of Beaver county and a representative to the territorial legislature. "Philo Taylor Farnsworth," Andrew Jenson, *LDS Biographical Encyclopedia* 3:370.

16. Ross R. Rogers was Beaver County notary public.

17. Portions of a possible such letter are reproduced here in the introduction.

18. Louisa was devastated—as were hundreds of others still in the desert, wagons loaded with all one's earthly goods, moving to an unknown destination—when the war was over, before it began. Colonel Thomas L. Kane passed the Pratt and Crosby group near the Vegas, reached the camps of the federal troops in Wyoming, and induced Governor Cumming to enter Salt Lake Valley without the troops. Negotiations followed. The Peace Commissioners were satisfied and so reported. Issues resolved, Johnston's army passed through the city on 26 June 1858 and established headquarters at a site named Camp Floyd. The war was over, but not for the uprooted settlers. It would be months before Louisa and family could consider themselves settled. The historical literature on the Utah War is rather full. See works cited by Furniss, Roberts, Alexander, Poll, and Allen and Leonard.

19. Louisa chose to make Beaver her home though there was little to recommend it. Southern Utah historian James G. Bleak described it: "Situated at an altitude of 6500 feet, frosty and barren in appearance, part of its surface producing sage brush and very much of its soil impregnated with alkali; it was at first sight considered unfit for cultivation. Its chief attraction was the fine stream of water afforded by the Beaver River which runs

through the valley from east to west, its source being at an altitude of 12,000 feet."

In early 1856 Apostle George A. Smith, in charge of the southern settlements, selected a few families from Parowan and Cedar City to go to Beaver Valley. They arrived the first week in February and on 10 February organized a branch. In December 1857 Apostle Smith named Philo T. Farnsworth bishop of Beaver. Shortly thereafter San Bernardino exiles stopped in Beaver, augmenting the population.

Families obtained city lots as well as acreage in pasture. The meadow became a common herding ground for livestock. James G. Bleak, Annals of the Southern Utah Mission, Archives, Historical Department, the Church of Jesus Christ of Latter-day Saints, Salt Lake City, Utah, Ms d1301. See also *Monuments to Courage: A History of Beaver County* (Beaver County: Daughters of Utah Pioneers, 1948).

20.   The Crosby family reached Beaver on 19 November 1858. The two households obtained adjacent lots on which to build houses.

Chapter 19

1.   Amasa Lyman, a member of the Quorum of the Twelve Apostles, was the companion to Charles C. Rich in the management of San Bernardino. He may have had a responsibility over the Beaver Saints. At a later date he was charged with apostasy, teaching false doctrine on the nature of Christ. Andrew Jenson, *LDS Biographical Encyclopedia,* 1:96; 4:316, 322, and 712.

2.   The letter is preserved in APFP 11. Begun at Ogden City, 10 November 1859, the latter portion tells of the accident and death.

3.   Horace S. Eldredge was a foremost merchant and business man in Utah. He served as collector of taxes, brigadier general in the militia, general church immigration agent, a director of Zion's Cooperative Mercantile Institution and was one of the seven presidents of the Seventies. Andrew Jenson, *LDS Biographical Encyclopedia,* 1:196–7.

Chapter 23

1.   John Riggs Murdock was born 13 September 1826 to patriarch John Murdock and Julia Clapp in Orange, Ohio. His mother died in 1831 when he was but four and a half years old. He was taken into the home of Joseph Smith and during the years before the exodus worked for the prophet. He served in the Mormon Battalion and reached Salt Lake Valley 12 October 1847. He married Almira Lott and in 1851 was resident in Lehi, where he served as mayor. During his life he made eleven trips to St. Louis and back, shepherding church trains. He was ordained bishop of Beaver Ward in the spring of 1864 and served until 1877, when he was named president of the newly formed Beaver Stake. He was a member of the territorial legislature and the Constitutional Convention, was a colonel in the militia, and served as probate judge of Beaver County. Andrew Jenson, *LDS Biographical Encyclopedia,* 1:304.

2.   Marcus L. Shepherd's family was among the earliest converts of the church. They lived through the Missouri persecutions and settled near Carthage, Illinois, where the father prospered making wagons. Marcus served in the Mormon Battalion and reached Salt Lake Valley in the fall of 1848. He married and went to live in San Bernardino. After the break-up he settled

in Beaver, which became a permanent home. He was ordained a bishop in March 1869 and set apart to preside over the Beaver First Ward. In July 1877 he was chosen second counselor to President John R. Murdock in the Beaver Stake. Andrew Jenson, *LDS Biographical Encyclopedia*, 3:508–10.

3. The letter, dictated by Addison and in the handwriting of Frances, is in APFP, AP Letters sent, 16.

4. Louisa's Relief Society "Song," is preserved in APFP.

5. The Poland Act (1874) deprived local probate courts of "a general jurisdiction in civil and criminal cases and both in chancery and at common law." In effect it transferred jurisdiction of most cases from the people's courts to territorial courts presided over by the federal appointees. *Compiled Laws of Utah, 1888*, sec. 31, p. 104. B. H. Roberts, *Comprehensive History of the Church*, 5:439 ff.

6. *Woman's Exponent* 7 (1 February 1879): 189; *Woman's Exponent* 8 (1 February 1880): 133.

7. When Benjamin F. Grouard left San Bernardino, he went north to San Francisco before returning to Los Angeles. In 1867 his family sailed from San Pedro to Panama, then to New York. They visited relatives in Massachusetts before moving to Farmington, Fulton County, Illinois, where he continued brick manufacturing for nine years. In Illinois he became an advocate of women's rights. His wife trained and became a nurse, graduated from the Hospital Medical College of Chicago (which became Rush Medical), and practiced in Farmington. In 1876 the family returned to Santa Ana, California. All the while, Grouard studied and became a spiritualist. Contacts between the Grouards and the Pratt family were renewed after Pratt died in 1872. One letter survives. On 14 January 1873, Grouard wrote Louisa touching on his business and family and concluded by alluding to his adherence to spiritualism:

    "I lecture sometimes on spiritualism, & should if I was able, devote my whole time to proclaiming that glorious gospel. Not for one moment Sister Pratt, have I ever since I first became acquainted with the spiritual philosophy doubted its truth, And it is not a mear matter of faith, it is absolute knowledge from evidence of the senses. *Seeing hearing & feeling.* And all in perfect accord with the highest, holiest & grandest aspirations that the soul is capable of entertaining. I dont know whether you ever made yourself acquainted with the philosophy & facts of spiritualism but if you have not it would be worth your while to do so. If you would like I will send you some spiritual papers, & also write you relitive to it."

    He wrote a postscript for Ellen in Tahitian.

8. Samuel R. Wells (1820–1876), devoted his life to phrenology and physiognomy. He wrote many books and was editor of *The Phrenological Journal and Science of Health*. To this journal Louisa submitted "Obituary of a Mormon Elder," published in March 1873.

9. Dr. Charles F. Winslow, with wife and three children, were passengers with Addison and his companion missionaries on the 1843–44 voyage from New Bedford to Tahiti on the ship *Timoleon*. A strong friendship developed and letters were exchanged. While on a mining trip to Utah he suddenly died of a heart attack. His body was cremated on 31 July 1877, "having made provision for this disposition of his body, in his will." His was the first cremation in Utah. Louisa thought Addison and Dr. Winslow were much alike in religion, in faith and reason, and in their outlook on the world. She penned lines on the subject of the two men. The Charles F. Winslow papers are at

the California Historical Society in San Francisco. Andrew Jenson, *Church Chronology*, 100. Helen Oehler, "By Strangers Honored. The Story of Dr. Charles F. Winslow, of Nantucket," *Proceedings of the Nantucket Historical Association*, Forty-fourth Annual Meeting, 1948, pages 20–30.

10.   Zion's Cooperative Mercantile Institution was founded 1868. The parent store in Salt Lake City purchased goods in the east and shipped them to Salt Lake City for outlet in selected branches in various communities. Apparently Louisa made purchases to sell from her home in Beaver. Caroline benefitted: on December 27 Caroline purchased a pair of shoes and reported that Louisa and daughters were going to cooperate in selling them. "I thought they sold cheaper than the large store." CBC, Journal, 1096.

11.   Emmeline B. Wells was a close friend of Louisa from Nauvoo days. She was the wife of Daniel H. Wells, second counselor to Brigham Young from 1857. He had joined the church in 1846 and come to Utah in 1848. Wells was a commanding figure in early Utah, a leader in all political affairs. Emmeline was equally influential among the women of Utah. She had married Presiding Bishop Newel K. Whitney in 1845 and went to Utah with his family. She married Daniel H. Wells after Whitney's death in 1850. She was assistant to Eliza R. Snow in organizing the Relief Society in the church and in the wards and branches. She became the editor of the *Woman's Exponent* in 1874, the organ of the Relief Society. She stood at the head of the Relief Society throughout her days. Andrew Jenson, *LDS Biographical Encyclopedia*, 4:199; 2:731. *History of Relief Society, 1842–1966* (Salt Lake City: General Board of Relief Society, 1966).

          It will be remembered that as a favor to Emmeline, Louisa took the young man Hiram Clark, "a near relative" of Emmeline's, on the island mission. Addison's record only states: "a lad that has come from Salt Lake with my family to live with me." *The Journals of Addison Pratt*, 455, 466, 475.

12.   A look into the lives of some of these people is given in *Dear Ellen.*

Chapter 24

1.   Louisa's son-in-law John Hunt, sheriff of Beaver County, anticipated serious problems when his two younger brothers, Joseph and Hyrum, both drinkers and trouble-makers, moved to Beaver. To avoid entanglement, John resigned his office and moved part of his family a few miles south to Sevier, arriving there 11 October 1875.

2.   Less than three weeks later, on the night of 1 November, Joseph Hunt shot and killed instantly J. P. Hunter during a drunken brawl. Joseph was arrested, imprisoned, and tried. On 20 December he was released, the verdict being "not guilty." Apparently there were extenuating circumstances. Only Caroline supplies the names of the contestants. CBC, Journal, 1055, 1058, 1064, 1093, 1144.

3.   On Mountain Meadows Massacre see *supra*, and Juanita Brooks, *John Doyle Lee: Zealot, Pioneer Builder, Scapegoat* (Glendale, California: Arthur H. Clark, 1972; reprint, Logan, Utah State University Press, 1992).

4.   John D. Lee's first trial on the charge of murder for his part in the Mountain Meadows Massacre was held in Beaver from 22 July 1875 to August 1875. Imprisoned, his second trial lasted from 14 to 20 September 1876. He was convicted of murder in the first degree.

5.   Two holograph letters from Frank Grouard (her Ephraim) to Louisa survive in APFP 7: (a) Fort Laramie, Wyoming, 22 March 1871, and (b) Camp on Belle Fouche Cr. W. T. Powder River Expedition, 16 December 1876. Under

date of 31 March 1877 Louisa wrote "A True Tale of the Past and Present," in the *Woman's Exponent* 5 (15 April 1877): 169, telling Frank's story.

Benjamin F. Grouard in 1893 made his way to Sheridan, Wyoming, where father and son met for the first time in thirty-seven years. They spent a month together in Wyoming. En route home, Grouard went through Salt Lake City, as it happened, at the time of the dedication of the Salt Lake Temple. He greeted many friends. Back in Santa Ana, he died 18 March 1894.

Frank Grouard's exploits as scout for General Crook are treated fully in Joe DeBarthe, *The Life and Adventures of Frank Grouard* (St. Joseph, Missouri: Combe Printing Company, 1894). This book was condensed and edited by Edgar I. Stewart, and reprinted by the University of Oklahoma Press in 1958. See also John G. Bourke, *On the Border with Crook* (reprint, Glorieta, New Mexico: The Rio Grande Press, Inc., 1969); Margaret Brock Hanson, ed., *Frank Grouard Army Scout: True Adventures in the Early West* (Cheyenne: Frontier Printing, Inc., 1893); John S. Gray, *Centennial Campaign: The Sioux War of 1876* (Fort Collins, Colorado: The Old Army Press, 1976); Robert M. Utley, *The Lance and the Shield: The Life and Times of Sitting Bull* (New York: Ballantine Books, 1993).

6. The Hunt family lived in the Sevier River Valley a year and four months before moving again, much to Louisa's distress. Permission granted to settle in Arizona or New Mexico convinced Louisa she might never see them again. She did get to have granddaughter Ida with her a month before leaving. Maria S. Ellsworth, ed., *Mormon Odyssey*, 31–32.

7. The new route taken proceeded due south from St. George to Pearce's Ferry on the Colorado River, south to Hualapai Valley, thence eastward by way of Flagstaff, Winslow, and the established route to northeastern Arizona settlements. On this trip, granddaughter Ida witnessed stake president Jesse N. Smith's way with his plural wives, which convinced Ida she could live in polygamy. And so it turned out. Maria S. Ellsworth, ed., *Mormon Odyssey*, 32–34. *Journal of Jesse Nathaniel Smith* (Salt Lake City: Jesse N. Smith Family Association, 1953), 239, 241, 243.

8. The next summer Louisa accompanied Jonathan, Caroline, and their oldest granddaughter to the St. George Temple, where they performed rites for deceased loved ones. They left Beaver June 20 and left St. George for home on 1 July 1878. CBC, 1222, 1224.

9. Reference is made to Frances's son, Addison Pratt Dyer, born 11 May 1859 in San Lorenzo, California.

10. Snowflake dates as a Mormon settlement from July 1878, when the area was purchased from William J. Flake who had taken up the land in 1873. The townsite was surveyed, and people directed to the site. On 24 September Snowflake ward was organized with John Hunt as bishop.

11. Ellen is referring to the engagement of Ida to Johnny Murdock.

Sources

1. Nettie Hunt Rencher to S. George Ellsworth, 25 February 1958.
2. Ida Hunt Udall to Ellen Pratt McGary, 5 February 1887, APFP.
3. It appeared as "Journal of Louisa Barnes Pratt," in Kate B. Carter, comp., *Heart Throbs of the West* (Salt Lake City: Daughters of Utah Pioneers, 1947), 8:189–400. It was reprinted as *Mormondom's First Woman Missionary: Louisa Barnes Pratt: Life Story and Travels Told in Her Own Words*, published by Nettie Hunt Rencher.

LITERATURE CITED

Alexander, Thomas G. *Utah, The Right Place: The Official Centennial History*. Salt Lake City: Gibbs Smith, 1995.

Allen, James B., and Glen M. Leonard. *The Story of the Latter-day Saints*. Salt Lake City: Desert Book, 1976.

Arrington, Leonard J. *Charles C. Rich: Mormon General and Western Frontiersman*. Provo, Utah: Brigham Young University Press, 1974.

Barney, Elvira Stevens. *The Stevens Genealogy: Embracing Branches of the Family Descended from Puritan Ancestry, New England Families Not Traceable to Puritan Ancestry and Miscellaneous Branches Wherever Found*. Salt Lake City: Skelton Publishing Co., 1907.

Beattie, George William, and Helen Pruitt Beattie. *Heritage of the Valley: San Bernardino's First Century*. Oakland: Biobooks, 1951.

Beaver County Daughters of Utah Pioneers, *Monuments to Courage: A History of Beaver County*. Beaver County Daughters of Utah Pioneers, 1948.

Bleak, James G. Annals of the Southern Utah Mission. Archives, Historical Department, the Church of Jesus Christ of Latter-day Saints, Salt Lake City, Utah.

Bourke, John G. *On the Border with Crook*. Reprint, Glorieta, New Mexico: The Rio Grande Press, Inc., 1969.

Brooks, Juanita. *John Doyle Lee: Zealot, Pioneer Builder, Scapegoat*. Glendale, California: Arthur H. Clark, 1972, reprint, Logan: Utath State University Press, 1992.

———. *The Mountain Meadows Massacre*. Rev. ed., Norman: University of Oklahoma Press, 1991.

Brown, James S. *Life of a Pioneer, Being the Autobiography of James S. Brown*. Salt Lake City: George Q. Cannon & Sons, 1900. Reprinted with title *Giant of the Lord: Life of a Pioneer*. Salt Lake City: Bookcraft, 1960.

Carter, Kate B., comp. *Heart Throbs of the West*. Salt Lake City: Daughters of Utah Pioneers, 1947.

Compiled Laws of Utah, 1888.

DeBarthe, Joe. *The Life and Adventures of Frank Grouard*. St. Joseph, Missouri: Combe Printing Company, 1894; reprint Norman: University of Oklahoma Press, 1958, reduced and edited by Edgar I. Stewart.

Deseret News, 3 January, 9 March, and 2 April 1853.

Ellsworth, Maria S., ed. *Mormon Odyssey: The Story of Ida Hunt Udall, Plural Wife*. Champaign: University of Illinois Press, 1992.

Ellsworth, S. George. *Samuel Claridge: Pioneering the Outposts of Zion*. Logan, Utah: privately printed, 1987.

————, ed. *Dear Ellen: Two Mormon Women and Their Letters*. Salt Lake City: University of Utah Library, 1974.

————, ed. *The Journals of Addison Pratt: Being a Narrative of Yankee Whaling in the Eighteen Twenties, A Mormon Mission to the Society Islands, and of Early California and Utah in the Eighteen Forties and Fifties*. Salt Lake City: University of Utah Press, 1990.

———— and Kathleen C. Perrin. *Seasons of Faith and Courage: The Church of Jesus Christ of Latter-day Saints in French Polynesia, A Sesquicentennial History, 1843–1993*. Salt Lake City: Yves R. Perrin, 1994.

Flanders, Robert Bruce. *Nauvoo: Kingdom on the Mississippi*. Urbana: University of Illinois Press, 1965.

Furniss, Norman F. *The Mormon Conflict, 1850–1859*. New Haven: Yale University Press, 1960.

Gray, John S. *Centennial Campaign: The Sioux War of 1876*. Fort Collins, Colorado: The Old Army Press, 1976.

Hafen, LeRoy R., and Ann W. Hafen, eds. *Jounals of Forty-Niners: Salt Lake to Los Angeles . . . .* Glendale: Arthur H. Clark, 1954.

Hansen, Lorin K., and Lila J. Bringhurst. *Let This Be Zion: Mormon Pioneers and Modern Saints in Southern Alameda California to "Stakes of Zion" in a Worldwide Church*. Fremont California and Fremont California South Stakes of the Church of Jesus Christ of Latter-day Saints, 1996.

Hanson, Margaret Brock, ed. *Frank Grouard Army Scout: True Adventures in the Early West*. Cheyenne: Frontier Printing, Inc., 1893.

History of Relief Society, 1842–1966. Salt Lake City: General Board of Relief Society, 1966.

Horner John M., Autogiography. Archives, Historical Department, the Church of Jesus Christ of Latter-day Saints, Salt Lake City, Utah.

————. "Adventures of a Pioneer," *Improvement Era* 7 (May to December 1904).

Jenson, Andrew. "The Bark 'Julia Ann,'" *Historical Record* 6:161–63.

————. *Church Chronology: A Record of Important Events Pertaining to the History of the Church of Jesus Christ of Latter-day Saints*. Salt Lake City: Deseret News, 1899.

————. *Encyclopedic History of the Church*. Salt Lake City: The Church of Jesus Christ of Latter-day Saints, 1941.

————. *Latter-day Saints Biographical Encyclopedia*. 4 vols. Salt Lake City: Andrew Jenson History Company, 1901–36.

Journal History of the Church of Jesus Christ of Latter-day Saints, 1830–1972. Archives, Historical Department, the Church of Jesus Christ of Latter-day Saints, Salt Lake City, Utah.

Kenney, Scott G., ed. *Wilford Woodruff's Journal, 1833–1898*. 9 vols. Midvale, Utah: Signature Books, 1983.

Larson, Gustive O. "The Mormon Reformation," *Utah Historical Quarterly* 25 (January 1958): 45–64.

Ludlow, Daniel H., ed. *Encyclopedia of Mormonism*. New York: Macmillan Publishing, 1992.

Lyman, Edward Leo. *San Bernardino: The Rise and Fall of a California Community*. Salt Lake City: Signature Books, 1996.

Miller, David E., and Della S. Miller. *Nauvoo: The City of Joseph*. Salt Lake City: Peregrine Smith, 1974.

Monuments to Courage: A History of Beaver County. Beaver County: Daughters of
    Utah Pioneers, 1948.

Oaks, Dallin H., and Marvin S. Hill. *Carthage Conspiracy: The Trial of the Accused
    Assassins of Joseph Smith.* Urbana: University of Illinois Press, 1975.

Oehler, Helen. "By Strangers Honored. The Story of Dr. Charles F. Winslow, of
    Nantucket," Proceedings of the Nantucket Historical Association, Forty-
    fourth Annual Meeting, 1948.

Poll, Richard D., et al., eds. *Utah's History.* Provo, Utah: Brigham Young
    University Press, 1978.

Pusey, Merlo J. *Builders of the Kingdom: George A. Smith, John Henry Smith, George
    Albert Smith.* Provo, Utah: Brigham Young University Press, 1981.

Rhodehamel, Josephine DeWitt, and Raymond Francis Wood. *Ina Coolbrith,
    Librarian and Laureate of California.* Provo, Utah: Brigham Young University
    Press, 1973.

Roberts, B. H. *Comprehensive History of the Church of Jesus Christ of Latter-day Saints.*
    6 vols. Salt Lake City: Deseret News Press, 1930.

————. *The Mormon Battalion, Its History and Achievements.* Salt Lake City: Desert
    News Press, 1919.

————, ed. *History of the Church of Jesus Christ of Latter-day Saints: Period I, History of
    Joseph Smith, the Prophet, by Himself.* 6 vols. Salt Lake City: Deseret Book,
    1902–12; reprinted often.

Sessions, Gene A. *Mormon Thunder: A Documentary History of Jedediah Morgan
    Grant.* Urbana: University of Illinois Press, 1982.

Smith, Jesse Nathaniel. *Journal of Jesse Nathaniel Smith.* Salt Lake City: Jesse N.
    Smith Family Association, 1953.

Stewart, George R. *The California Trail, An Epic with Many Heroes.* New York:
    McGraw-Hill Book Company, 1962.

Tyler, Daniel. *A Concise History of the Mormon Battalion in the Mexican War,
    1846–1847.* Salt Lake City, 1881.

Utley, Robert M. *The Lance and the Shield: The Life and Times of Sitting Bull.* New
    York: Ballantine Books, 1993.

Williams, John. *A Narrative of Missionary Enterprises in the South Sea Islands.*
    London, 1837.

Woman's Exponent 7 (1 February 1879): 189, and 8 (1 February 1880): 133.

Young, Brigham. Manuscript History, 1847–67. Excerpted by the Church
    Historian's Office for H. H. Bancroft. 3 vols. Manuscripts P-F 22, P-F 26,
    and P-F 67, Bancroft Library, University of California, Berkeley

Young, John R. *Memoirs of John R. Young, Utah Pioneer, 1847, Written by Himself.* Salt
    Lake City: The Deseret News, 1920.

INDEX